MERCHANT
FLEETS ②
in profile

MERCHANT FLEETS in profile ②

Duncan Haws

With drawings to 1:1800 scale

Patrick Stephens, Cambridge

First published in 1979

British Library Cataloguing in Publication Data

Haws, Duncan
    Merchant fleets in profile.
    2: The ships of the Cunard, American, Red Star, Inman,
    Leyland, Dominion, Atlantic Transport and White Star lines.
    1. Merchant marine – History.
    I. Title
    387.2'09   HE735

    ISBN 0 85059 324 7

Text photoset in 9 on 10pt English 49
by Stevenage Printing Limited, Stevenage.
Printed in Great Britain (on 90 gsm Supreme Book Wove)
and bound by The Garden City Press, Letchworth,
for the publishers, Patrick Stephens Limited,
Bar Hill, Cambridge, CB3 8EL.

Contents

Introduction

This volume, the second in the series, deals with an important part of the North Atlantic saga and is the story of two great competitors, Cunard and the International Mercantile Marine Company up to the advent of the United States Line after the First World War.

Despite ups and downs the history of Cunard has been continuous since the company's formation and it has survived, and thrives, until this very day. The foundations of the International Mercantile Marine group were laid in 1872, when two local companies were formed with the intention of establishing a strong United States presence on the North Atlantic. From the early 1870s the Americans struggled to gain a firm grip on the ocean seaway, and although they never did assert themselves as a dominating force, for a brief period at the turn of the century the American Line vessels were a match for any on the route.

Pierpont Morgan intervened at this time to form the conglomerate into his famed IMMC group, proceeding to acquire the three great British names White Star, Dominion and Atlantic Transport. His creation sought, by the interchangeability of the component vessels, to maximise the opportunities and to dominate the North Atlantic. His adversaries, however, were immensely strong, skilful and determined. Above all they had the greater proportion of the market and in particular the emigrant trade.

The First World War cut across the development plans of all the North

Atlantic nations but ended with the temporary elimination of the German challenge, and the year 1920 saw Cunard poised to order a dozen replacement ships. The International Mercantile Marine group began to simplify their structure and the first name to disappear was the Dominion Line whose fleet was transferred in 1921 to the ownership of Frederick Leyland. Their passenger ships, however, continued to operate the 'White Star-Dominion' joint service, although surprisingly IMMC's White Star made little attempt to build new ships, contenting itself with group exchanges and ceded German liners. Instead the group's banner seemed to be shared largely between the Atlantic Transport and Red Star Lines, the latter reflecting recognition of the strength of the European market. But it is quite remarkable how IMCC failed to weld its fleet into one cohesive whole. They concentrated on routes rather than their seagoing reputation as a great world concern.

On January 1 1927 the shares of the White Star Line were acquired by the Royal Mail Line and the company returned to British ownership, reappearing by 1934 amongst the traditional North Atlantic owners with the formation of Cunard-White Star Ltd.

The depression of 1930, however, was particularly damaging. Cunard possessed a new and well balanced fleet and White Star had two magnificent new motor ships, but IMMC, with a mixture of old, new, large and small passenger ships, was forced to re-group. In 1933 the group disposed of the remnants of the Leyland Line, five ships. In 1934 the Atlantic Transport's major ships were broken up at the age of ten, and by 1936 this company too had faded from the scene. This process of elimination left IMMC with only the Red Star Line, and in 1935 this name and the two final ships – *Pennland* and *Westernland* – were sold to Arnold Bernstein of Hamburg, lasting until the Second World War.

But whilst this is the end of the IMMC story in this volume it is by no means the end of the saga. On October 31 1931 the United States Shipping Board sold a group of ships, including *Leviathan, Manhattan* and *Washington,* to the United States Lines Co which was controlled by IMMC, and in this guise IMMC continues to this day. The one historical reminder of the pre-1931 era is the white house flag with its blue American bald eagle, first flown by the American Line in 1893.

Duncan Haws
Cuckfield, Sussex

Explanatory notes

1 Company histories are arranged chronologically.

2 The ships owned are listed virtually chronologically except that sister ships are grouped together even when the period of their building covers more than one year.

3 Tonnage: the method of calculating tonnage has changed several times since 1830 and very few ships kept their initial tonnage. The gross and net tonnages shown are generally those recorded when the ship first entered service.

4 Dimensions: unless recorded as 'overall' the figures given are the registered dimensions between perpendiculars.

5 The speed given is service speed. This could vary according to route and ports of call.

6 Abbreviations: to assist all readers as few as possible have been used –

Apr	*April*
Aug	*August*
BHP	*Brake horse power*
Bt	*Built*
cabin	*Cabin class*
cm	*Centimetres*
cu m	*Cubic metres*
cu ft	*Cubic feet*
Cyl(s)	*Cylinder(s)*
dbl	*Double*
Dec	*December*
Dft	*Draught/draft*
diam	*Diameter*
Dim	*Dimensions*
disp	*Displacement*
dwt	*Dead weight*
E	*East*
Eng	*Engine*
exp	*Expansion*
fcsle	*Forecastle*
Feb	*February*
ft	*Feet*
fwd	*Forward*
g	*Gross*
GRT	*Gross registered tonnage*
H	*Hull*
HP	*Horse power/High pressure*
IHP	*Indicated horse power*
in	*Inch(es)*
Jan	*January*
kts	*Knots*
lb	*Pound(s)*
LP	*Low pressure*
m	*Metre*
Mar	*March*
mm	*Millimetres*
MP	*Medium pressure*
mph	*Miles per hour*
n	*Net*
N	*North*
NHP	*Nominal horse power*
Nov	*November*
oa	*Overall*
Oct	*October*
Pad	*Paddle*
Pass	*Passengers*
quad	*Quadruple/four*
refrig	*Refrigerated*
reg	*Registered*
RHP	*Registered horse power*
rpm	*Revolutions per minute*
S	*South*
scr	*Screw*
Sept	*September*
sgl	*Single*
Stm	*Steam*
Stm P	*Steam pressure*
T	*Tons*

tpl	*Triple/three*
tst	*Tourist*
tw	*Twin/two*
W	*West*

7 The technical data follows the same pattern throughout –
Bt (built); *T:* (tons), g (gross), n (net), dwt (dead weight). **Dim** (dimensions), oa (overall), length × breadth × depth; *Dft:* (draught). **Eng** (engine), Pad (paddle), **sgl** (single), dbl (double) scr (screw); Cyls: (cylinders); *Stroke;* IHP, NHP, SHP, BHP, RHP, HP; Boilers; *Stm P:* (steam pressure) lb (pounds); kts (knots); By (engine builder). **H** (hull details); *Coal; Cargo; Pass:* (passengers) 1st (first class), 2nd (second class), 3rd (third class), tst (tourist class); *Crew.*

Funnels

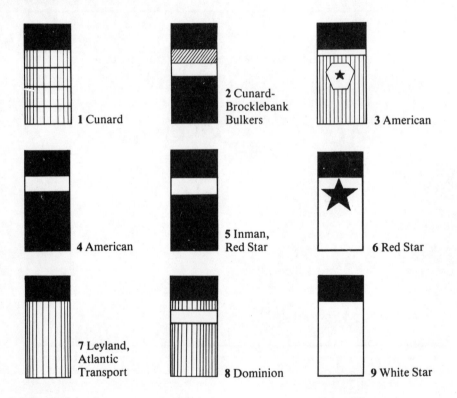

1 Cunard

2 Cunard-
Brocklebank
Bulkers

3 American

4 American

5 Inman,
Red Star

6 Red Star

7 Leyland,
Atlantic
Transport

8 Dominion

9 White Star

1 Bright red, black top, three black pin-
stripe bands.
2 Black, blue band over white.
3 Red, black top. White markings with
red star.
4 Black, white band.
5 Black, white band.
6 Buff, black top, red star.
7 Red, black top.
8 Red, black top, white band.
9 Buff, black top.

Cunard Line

History

1787 Nov 21: Samuel Cunard was born in Halifax, Nova Scotia, the second son of Abraham Cunard, a German emigrant Quaker. Originally resident in Philadelphia, Abraham Cunard crossed into Canada after the American declaration of Independence.
1813 July 2: Abraham Cunard & Son despatched the sailing ship *White Oak* across the Atlantic, their first venture to Europe.
1814 The contract for the carriage of mails between Halifax-Newfoundland-Boston-Bermuda was obtained.
1819 Abraham Cunard retired and the firm was then renamed Samuel Cunard & Co. The company also operated a whale fishery and an ironworks on Prince Edward Island, Nova Scotia.
1825 The agency in Halifax for the Honourable East India Company was secured.
1827 The company acquired the agency for the General Mining Association of London. Samuel Cunard was also the first Commissioner for Lighthouses, a director of Cogswell's Bank and was elected to the Council of Twelve who were the virtual rulers of the province.
1831 Cunard and his two brothers were leading stockholders in the pioneer Quebec-Halifax service inaugurated by the steamer *Royal William*.
1833 *Royal William* crossed the Atlantic entirely by steam but only in order that she might be sold.
1838 Some 40 sailing vessels were owned or operated under the Samuel Cunard flag, but in this year *Sirius, Great Western* and *Great Liverpool* each made

successful Atlantic steam crossings. The Admiralty, who were responsible for mails, at last recognised the need for a regular transatlantic mail service.
Nov: The Admiralty called for tenders for a North Atlantic mail service and a copy was sent to Samuel Cunard. Local support in Halifax was lacking so Cunard decided to go to London.
1839 Jan 24: Samuel Cunard sailed for Falmouth aboard the regular Government packet ship.
Feb 11: He submitted his tender for twice-monthly sailings to Halifax with 300 hp vessels coupled with two feeder services, one to Boston and the other from Pictou to Quebec, but only when the St Lawrence was unobstructed by ice. For this he asked £55,000 annually, payable quarterly in advance, and for a period of 10 years. If accepted the service would commence on May 1 1840. The Admiralty, after due consideration, awarded the contract to Cunard.

Next James C. Melvill, Secretary to the East India Company, for whom Cunard acted as agent in Halifax, introduced him to Robert Napier who had built the engines for their first steamer *Berenice*. Napier quoted £40 per ton or £32,000 per 800 ton vessel. Cunard's offer of £30,000 each for three identical ships was accepted.
Mar 18: The formal agreement was ratified, the vessels to be 960 tons, 1,375 hp and £32,000 each.
May 4: The formal contract for seven years was signed between the Lords of the Admiralty and Cunard, and was subject to 12 months notice by either

side. A Naval officer responsible for the mails was to be carried. A £15,000 fine was to be levied if a sailing did not take place and £500 per day where sailings were delayed by over 12 hours. Almost the day after the signing Robert Napier advised Cunard that his tests with the vessels he had built for the City of Glasgow Steam Packet Company had revealed that the proposed Cunarders were too small for the North Atlantic. He agreed to carry out the Mar 18 contract but advised against it, and though Samuel Cunard believed him he had no money for the 1,100-tonners proposed in their place. Napier offered all his resources, which only assisted partially. Cunard was introduced to James Donaldson, a Liverpool merchant connected with the City of Glasgow Steam Packet Company, who had recently merged his firm with G. & J. Burns.

May 10: Cunard met with Napier, Donaldson, George Burns and David McIver, the agent for the City of Glagow Steam Packet Company, to discuss the dilemma.

May 14: George Burns and David McIver paid £25,000 for a half interest in the mail contract and a half share of the three vessels. They had the right to take others into their share of the partnership. 18 other Glasgow businessmen joined, the shares being £100 each.

June: 'The Glasgow Proprietory in the British and North American Steam Packet Company' was formed. Napier was instructed to proceed and a fourth ship was added. The Government were advised and persuaded to allow the service to be extended from Halifax to Boston and, because of the larger ships, to increase the annual fee to £60,000.

July 4: The revised agreement was signed. On the maiden voyage of the steamer *British Queen* Cunard crossed to Halifax to establish his proposed terminal ports there and also at Boston.

1840 Feb 5: *Britannia* launched by Robert Napier's niece Isabella Napier with Samuel Cunard present. Cunard now had experience of winter North Atlantic conditions and realised that business would not warrant twice-monthly sailings; furthermore, damage to the vessels could result in missed sailings and £15,000 fines. The partners agreed that he should put the position to the Admiralty. They saw his point of view, although the Government was not pleased, and a penalty of £1,000 for each of four cancelled winter voyages from November to February was agreed.

Apr: Despite overtime and night and day working it became clear that the June 24 sailing date could not be met. Equally important the fortnightly sailings could not be introduced because *Acadia* was a month behind *Britannia*. A still forbearing Admiralty agreed to a month's grace for the opening of the service, and that *Caledonia* should inaugurate the fortnightly sailings when she entered service in Sept 1840.

In preparation for the branch service Pictou-Quebec (the mail travelling overland from Halifax to Pictou on the St Lawrence) the British & North American Royal Mail Steam Packet Co Ltd, the title under which the partners were to operate the mail contract, purchased G. & J. Burns' Liverpool-Glasgow coastal packet *Unicorn*. Her commander was to be Captain Walter Douglas who, in *Culinare,* had surveyed the St Lawrence for the Government of Canada.

May 15: *Unicorn* sailed with 27 passengers including the founder's son Samuel Cunard Jr.

June 1: *Unicorn* arrived in Halifax.

July 4: *Britannia* left Liverpool for Halifax to inaugurate the first transatlantic mail service to North America. She carried 63 passengers.

Aug 4: *Acadia* made her first voyage.

Sept 19: *Caledonia* joined the service.

1841 Jan 5: *Columbia* completed the foursome.

The winter experience was worse than expected and it became clear that further renegotiations would be necessary. The Admiralty was again approached and, with the encouragement of the Canadian Government, finally revised the terms.

Aug 28: The new agreement was concluded. The new remuneration became £81,000 per annum, but a fifth ship was to be built as reserve vessel.

Furthermore in future the ships were to be built stoutly enough to carry large calibre guns.

1843 Apr 19: The reserve ship *Hibernia* entered service.

July 2: *Columbia,* with 85 passengers aboard, grounded on a rock ledge en route Halifax-Boston. All aboard were saved but the vessel itself was lost.

1844 The replacement *Cambria* was built and entered service on Jan 4 1845.

1845 David MacIver died.

1846 The United States Government backed the establishment of the Ocean Steam Navigation Company on the route New York-Southampton-Bremen. To counteract this Cunard renegotiated the British contract to give weekly services for eight months of the year and fortnightly services in winter, New York to be the new terminal port. The annual contract fee became £156,000 in all. Because of the extra steaming involved an increase in the fleet became necessary.

1847 Dec 6: *Hibernia* inaugurated the New York service.

1848 Apr 15: *America,* the first of four new ships, made her maiden voyage.

May 20: *Niagara* followed.

July 15: *Europa* sailed.

Nov 25: *Canada,* the last of the four, took up station, the fleet of steamers now totalling eight. These four new vessels carried navigation lights, well ahead of the then general practice.

1850 The US Government subsidised the Collins Line who, on the strength of this backing, introduced four ships, *Atlantic, Arctic, Pacific* and *Baltic,* which were larger and superior to the four Cunarders. To match their competition on the New York run Cunard had to omit Halifax and operate a weekly service.

1852 Collins carried more passengers between Liverpool and New York than Cunard. Two new vessels, *Arabia* (I) and *Persia,* were ordered with accommodation more sumptuous than the Collins ships. *Arabia* was sold to Royal Mail prior to completion to replace the burnt out *Amazon,* and *Persia* (I) became *Arabia* (II). *Alps* and *Andes* joined the fleet.

1853 A Mediterranean cargo service was started. *Taurus, Melita, Jura* and *Balbec*

were ordered.

1854 Cunard's North Atlantic problems were made more severe by the outbreak of the Crimean War. Under the mail contract Cunard had to provide vessels for Government service and this prerogative was duly exercised. 11 vessels were taken over and operated to Admiralty orders.

1856 The Crimean War over, Cunard set about resurrecting their Atlantic trade, *Persia* (II) became Cunard's first iron-hulled ship. She had the finest accommodation afloat and in July took the Blue Riband with 9 days 4 hours 45 minutes and an average speed of 13½ kts.

1862 Robert Napier delivered *China,* the company's first transatlantic screw-propelled vessel, and from the same builder came *Scotia* (I), the largest and fastest paddle ship afloat, excepting the ever present *Great Eastern*.

1863 The American Civil War began and disrupted trade with North America.

1865 Apr 28: Sir Samuel Cunard died in London aged 78.

In just the same way that the Crimean War had denuded Cunard the American Civil War had caused the withdrawal of American shipping and virtually stopped the emigrant traffic. A trade in war supplies, for both sides, had tided Cunard over the worst of the depression and now, in 1865, the war was over. The surge of emigrants restarted and in 1864-65 25 new transatlantic liners entered service. Cunard's contribution was *Java*.

1867 *Russia* and *Siberia* were commissioned.

1868 *Samaria* (I) followed.

1870 *Abyssinia* and *Algeria* entered service.

1871-72 Cunard's supremacy was challenged by the advent of Thomas Ismay's White Star Line ships *Oceanic* (I), *Atlantic, Baltic* (I) and *Republic* (I). These outshone all existing North Atlantic ships. Cunard was faced with the need to answer this new challenge.

1874 But Cunard's two newest ships commissioned in this year, the *Bothnia* (I) and *Scythia* (I), were still behind the standards of White Star's new ships.

1881 *Servia* (I) entered service. Steel-hulled and engined for 17 kts she was the first express passenger ship built to rely solely on passenger revenues derived from fast passages. She represented Cunard's leap ahead.

1882 *Aurania* (I) joined *Servia*. She consolidated the new practice of having suites of accommodation; to her fell the role of catering for the wealthy and the aristocracy. However neither ship took the Blue Riband.

1884 Guion Line ran into difficulties in making payments for their new liner *Oregon,* built to outpace all competition. Therefore Cunard took her over, and she duly regained for them the coveted speed trophy.

If Cunard had initially been slow to react to the White Star challenge the company nevertheless had not been idle in embarking on a course of new building aimed at reasserting their traditional role. First came *Etruria* and *Umbria,* outclassing all their rivals in size and capacity.

1888-89 These two ships were sharply challenged by Inman's beautiful *City of New York* (III) and *City of Paris* (II) and White Star's magnificent *Teutonic* and *Majestic (I)*. Cunard, aware of the increase in size and speed, ordered what were to be the largest, fastest and finest-equipped ships in the world.

1893 Thus on Apr 22 *Campania* was commissioned and in September *Lucania.* They were record breakers from the start. Indeed their first challenger did not come until 1897 when Norddeutscher Lloyd introduced *Kaiser Wilhelm der Grosse.*

1898 Satisfied with their New York quartet Cunard strengthened their Boston service. Here speed was of less importance than the need to move the cargo displaced by the ocean greyhound policy dictated by the New York run's fast turn around. *Ultonia* entered service in early 1898, having been purchased on the stocks.

1900 For the Boston run Cunard had two vessels purpose-built; *Ivernia* (I) came first, in April, and *Saxonia* (I) in May. Both carried over 2,300 passengers and 14,000 tons of cargo. Their particular claim to fame lies in the 106 ft tall funnels, which dominated their appearance and made them somewhat ungainly in profile.

The Boer War led to the requisitioning of six Cunard mail-ships including *Servia* (I), *Aurania* (I) and *Umbria.* Unfortunately *Carinthia* (I) was wrecked during her war service; she was carrying mules from New Orleans to Capetown at the time.

1902 J. Pierpont Morgan finalised the purchase of several transatlantic companies, forming the International Mercantile Marine Co. British firms acquired included the White Star, Dominion and Leyland Lines, Cunard fortuitously managing to stay outside of the combine. Nevertheless the situation gave rise to national concern.

1903 The Government concluded a 20 year agreement with Cunard. The company was to remain British owned. Two new record breakers, of troopship capability, were to be built and £2,600,000 at 2¾% was to be loaned to finance them, repayable over the period of the agreement. A 20 year subsidy of £150,000 per annum was also to be paid to cover the Admiralty specification built into the construction of the new ships. Thus were born the plans for *Lusitania* and *Mauretania* (I).

Nov: *Aurania* (I) opened a new service Fiume-Trieste-Venice-Palermo-New York.

1905 In February *Caronia* (I) was commissioned followed in December by her sister, *Carmania* (I). The vessels were known as the 'pretty sisters'. They had the distinction of being powered differently, *Carmania* having turbines and *Caronia* quadruple expansion. As expected *Carmania* was nearly 1½ kts faster and steam turbines became the norm in all Cunard's subsequent large ships.

1907 July 28: *Lusitania* commissioned. On her second voyage she took the Blue Riband at an average speed of 24 kts. Nov 16: *Mauretania* (I) left Liverpool on her maiden voyage. On her homeward run she beat *Lusitania's* record by 21 minutes in 4 days 22 hours and 29 minutes.

1911-12 *Franconia* (I) and *Laconia* (I) were completed. These two ships were designed to strengthen the Liverpool-Boston service. However, they had the capability to undertake cruises during the winter months.

Hamburg-America Line and White Star began introducing giant liners of over 40,000 tons, *Bismarck, Imperator, Vaderland, Olympic* and *Titanic.* Cunard replied by laying down one of the most beautiful ships of them all, *Aquitania.*

1912 Cunard purchased all the shares in the Anchor Line.

1913 Apr 23: *Aquitania* was launched by the Countess of Derby.

1914 May 31: The maiden voyage of *Aquitania* took place, distressingly overshadowed by the loss, by collision in the St Lawrence, of Canadian Pacific's *Empress of Ireland* in which 1,023 died. Aug 4: First World War started. *Aquitania, Caronia* (I) and *Carmania* (I) were called up. Although *Lusitania* was requisitioned she was returned to Cunard in order to maintain a passenger service with New York.

Sept 9: *Carmania* (I) fought and sank the German armed merchant cruiser *Cap Trafalgar* (Hamburg-Sud Amerika Line) off the Atlantic coast of South America.

1915 May 7: Off the Old Head of Kinsale *U-20* torpedoed and sank *Lusitania.* She went down in under 20 minutes with the loss of 1,198 lives.

1917 Cunard Building, the new headquarters at Liverpool Pier Head, was completed.

1918 Nov: End of war. Cunard had lost *Ultonia, Veria, Ivernia* (I), *Carpathia, Lusitania, Thracia, Lycia* (I), *Franconia* (I), *Caria, Vandalia* (I), *Valeria* (burnt out), *Laconia* (I), *Ascania* (I) (wrecked), *Ausonia* (I), *Alaunia* (I), *Andania* (I), *Volodia, Vinovia, Aurania* (II), *Flavia, Feltria* and *Folia,* in all 22 ships. To replace these losses Cunard ordered 13 ships for building as soon as conditions permitted. This was then the largest tonnage order ever placed by a single company.

1921 *Albania* (II) was Cunard's first post-war ship. She was followed by five 20,000-tonners, six 'A's of 14,000 tons, and one vessel of 16,000 tons. *Scythia* (II), and *Samaria* (II) were commissioned.

1922 *Laconia* (I), *Lancastria, Andania*
(II), *Antonia* (II) and *Ausonia* (II) entered service.

With the allocation of Hapag's *Imperator,* renamed *Berengaria,* the decision was taken to use the refurbished and oil fuel burning *Mauretania* (I) and *Aquitania* to open up a threesome service from Southampton to New York in place of the traditional Liverpool route.

1923 *Franconia* (II) arrived.

1924 *Aurania* (III), fourth of the 'A' class, was delivered.

1925 *Ascania* (II), *Alaunia* (II) and *Carinthia* (II) concluded the post-war rebuilding. Cunard settled down with this fleet and route coverage.

1929 Norddeutscher Lloyd's *Bremen* entered service and took both Atlantic records from *Mauretania* (I), which had held the record since 1907. However, Cunard were designing two giant liners to replace their ageing Southampton trio.

1930 Dec: The keel of 534 *(Queen Mary)* was laid down at the yard of John Brown on the Clydebank.

1931 The economic depression caused work on 534 to be stopped.

1933 The Government advanced £3 million to complete 534, with £1½ million as working capital. The assistance was also conditional on the merging of Cunard with White Star, which then took place.

1934 Feb: Formal agreement was reached to amalgamate the two companies. The new name became Cunard-White Star Ltd and work on 534 restarted. White Star contributed *Majestic* (II), *Olympic* (II), *Homeric, Britannic* (III), *Georgic* (II), *Laurentic* (II), *Doric* (II), and the old *Adriatic* (II) which was scheduled for breaking up; she was sold in November. Sept 26: 534 was launched as *Queen Mary* by HM Queen Mary.

1935 May 29: French Line's *Normandie* entered service, taking the transatlantic records from Norddeutscher Lloyd.

1936 May 27: *Queen Mary*'s maiden voyage Southampton-Cherbourg-New York.

Dec: The keel of consort *Queen Elizabeth* was laid, also at John Brown's yard.

1938 July: *Mauretania* (II) was launched, followed in September by *Queen Elizabeth,* named by the Queen in the

presence of her husband King George VI.
1939 Sept 3: Second World War began.
Initially *Queen Mary* was laid up in New
York, and *Queen Elizabeth* was hurriedly
completed and joined her sister in
America.
1940 Both the Queens became
outstanding troopships. Additionally
Georgic, Britannic, Franconia (II),
Scythia (II), *Samaria* (II), *Laconia* (II)
and *Lancastria* all served as troopships,
whilst *Carinthia* (II), *Laurentic* (II) and
all six 'A' class vessels were requisitioned
and converted into armed merchant
cruisers.
1942 Oct: *Queen Mary* collided with and
cut in two her escorting cruiser
HMS *Curacao* which sank with the loss
of over 300 of her crew. After the war the
courts exonerated the *Queen Mary*.
1945 The Second World War ended.
Cunard had lost *Laconia* (II), *Lancastria,
Laurentic* (II), *Carinthia* (II), *Bosnia* and
Andania (II). In addition *Antonia* had
become HMS *Wayland, Aurania* (III)
was HMS *Artifex* and *Alaunia* (II) ended
up as HMS *Alaunia,* so the company's
fleet had been reduced by nine ships
in all.
1946-48 Saw the reintroduction of
Cunard vessels on the North Atlantic.
Queen Mary, Queen Elizabeth and
Mauretania (II) were overhauled and
refurnished. *Ascania* (II) was internally
rebuilt, initially on austere lines. New
cargo vessels to replace lost wartime
tonnage came into service starting with
Asia (II) and *Arabia* (III), and two new
intermediate-type liners – with first class
only accommodation – became the first
post-war passenger ships. They were
named *Media* (I) and *Parthia* (II).
1949 Jan: *Caronia* (II) sailed on her
maiden voyage. In size and speed a
consort for *Mauretania* (II) she had been
built nevertheless as a dual purpose
vessel – to sail on the North Atlantic
during the summer season but to
undertake dollar-earning world cruises at
other times of year. Because of her all-
green livery with Cunard funnel she was
known as the Green Goddess.
Nov: *Aquitania,* after 35 years service
and 580 Atlantic crossings, with 1½
million passengers safely carried, made

her final voyage for Cunard and was
disposed of early in 1950.
Dec: Cunard Line took over the Cunard-
White Star assets and liabilities for the
purpose of streamlining the organisation.
White Star thus disappeared, except that
Georgic (II) and *Britannic* (III) still bore
their black-topped buff funnels.
1953-54 Replacement vessels for the
ageing *Franconia* (II), *Scythia* (II),
Samaria (II) and *Ascania* (II) were
planned and launched. These vessels were
designed for the Canadian service.
1955-57 *Saxonia* (II), *Ivernia* (II),
Carinthia (III) and *Sylvania* (II) were all
commissioned, the largest Cunarders ever
built for the Canadian service.
1960 Cunard now had ten splendid
passenger ships. The two Queens,
Mauretania (II), *Caronia* (II), *Media* (I)
and *Parthia* (II) plus the four new
Canadian vessels. But jet passenger
aircraft began to bite severely into sea
traffic, operating costs began to rise
dangerously, and even with winter
cruising the ships were rapidly becoming
uneconomic. A policy of passenger
retrenchment began. *Media* and *Parthia*
were sold for further trading.
1963 *Saxonia* (II) was rebuilt for cruising
and renamed *Carmania* (II). *Ivernia* (II)
was similarly treated and renamed
Franconia (III). The effect was to reduce
the North Atlantic passenger fleet to six
ships, and they too took turns to cruise
whenever the opportunity arose,
particularly in the winter months.
1965 The decline in passenger ship
profitability continued and *Mauretania*
(II) was sold for breaking up at the end
of the Atlantic season.
1966 Nov 24: *Sylvania* (II) took the last
Cunard passenger sailing from Liverpool,
the port where it all started, to New
York, leaving Southampton as Cunard's
only passenger base.
1967 In November, at the end of a
thousand voyages, *Queen Mary* was sold
to the City of Long Beach in California
to become a floating convention and
entertainment centre.
1968 Before the commencement of the
summer season *Queen Elizabeth* was also
sold. She went to Fort Lauderdale to
begin a chequered final career that ended

with her conversion into a floating university and a funeral pyre of flames at Hong Kong. *Caronia* (II), a ship that never really caught on as a transatlantic liner and yet was a popular cruise ship, was also sold for further cruising at the end of only 19 years' service. At the same time the two remaining Canadian ships, *Sylvania* (II) and *Carinthia* (III), were sold to the Sitmar Line who intended to use them on the Australian emigrant service. These two ships languished for two years in Southampton before being taken to Italy for rebuilding.

Despite these sales Cunard still believed in the concept of the giant passenger liner built with cruising capabilities. They faced the demise of *Queen Mary* and the ageing *Queen Elizabeth* by building a single replacement.

1969 *Queen Elizabeth 2* entered service, joining the two white-hulled cruising ships *Carmania* (II) and *Franconia* (III) to make up Cunard's passenger fleet. The new ship achieved notoriety by experiencing a considerable period of turbine trouble during the first year of her career.

1971 The passenger fleet was temporarily reduced by the sale to Russia of *Carmania* and *Franconia,* but two new custom-built cruise ships, *Cunard Adventurer* and *Cunard Ambassador* (1972) took up station for cruising in the Caribbean.

1972 Cunard went to Spain for a bulk carrier fleet of eight ships. These were placed under the management of a new company, Cunard-Brocklebank Bulkers Ltd, and wore Brocklebank funnel colours.

1974 Saw the arrival of two new cruise liners, *Cunard Countess* and *Cunard Conquest,* but the year was marred by a fire which gutted *Cunard Ambassador.* Although not destroyed the company decided against rebuilding her and after being sold she was rebuilt as a sheep-carrier.

1976 The company acquired a substantial part of the fleet of Maritimecor, the Maritime Fruit Carriers Co, and pleased the shipping world by giving them traditional Cunard names. The new additions became *Alaunia* (IV), *Alsatia* (III), *Andania* (IV), *Andria* (II), *Carinthia* (IV), *Carmania* (III), *Samaria* (IV), *Scythia* (IV) and *Servia* (III).

1977 Mar: *Cunard Adventurer* sold.

1978 The process of grouping continued and ships of the Port and Brocklebank Lines were progressively transferred to Cunard operating companies, as were the product tankers of H. E. Moss & Co. But the traditional names and funnel markings used by their respective groups have been retained, and for that reason they do not appear in this section on Cunard.

Routes

1840 Liverpool-Halifax-Boston, with feeder service Quebec-Pictou-rail-Halifax.

1847 Liverpool-Boston-New York.

1851-1966 Liverpool-New York.

1853-1978 Liverpool-Gibraltar-Malta-Mediterranean ports.

1858-70 Connecting service New York-Nassau-Havana-West Indies.

1859 Queenstown (Cobh) calls commenced.

1872-74 Glasgow-West Indies.

1911-66 Southampton-Quebec-Montreal.

1913-66 Liverpool-Quebec-Montreal.

1919-78 Southampton-Cherbourg-New York.

1922-40 London-Southampton-New York.

These routes were subject to several variations and Hamburg, Rotterdam, Antwerp, Bristol, Fishguard, Glasgow and Belfast have all been ports of call during the career of the company. Deep sea cargo carrying has also ranged world wide.

Livery

Funnel Bright red with a tinge of orange in it, black top, three pin-stripe black bands evenly spaced. When the funnel is short only two bands are used.

Hull Black. Red waterline divided from the black by a white stripe.

Uppers White.

Masts Biscuit brown.

Lifeboats White.

Fleet index

Ivernia (III)	183	Parthia (II)	166	Skirmisher	96
		Parthia (III)	181	Slavonia	98
Jackal	35	Pavia (I)	87	Stromboli	31
Java	50	Pavia (II)	171	Sumatra	57
Jura	29	Pavonia	76	Sylvania (I)	86
		Persia (I)	19	Sylvania (II)	177
Karnak	24	Persia (II)	32		
Kedar	44	Phrygia (I)	103	Tarifa	53
		Phrygia (II)	173	Taurus	22
Laconia (I)	107			Teneriffe	23
Laconia (II)	139	Queen Elizabeth	157	Thracia	104
Lancastria	144	Queen Elizabeth 2	187	Trinidad	63
Lebanon	28	Queen Mary	155	Tripoli	54
Lotharingia	147			Tyria	88
Lucania	84	Royal George	120	Tyrrhenia	144
Lusitania	101	Russia	56		
Lycia (I)	105			Ultonia	90
Lycia (II)	172	Samaria (I)	58	Umbria	81
		Samaria (II)	138	Unicorn	1
Malta	52	Samaria (III)	185		
Marathon	41	Samaria (IV)	206		
Margaret	8	Saragossa	68	Valacia (I)	122
Mauretania (I)	102	Satellite (I)	15	Valacia (II)	158
Mauretania (II)	156	Satellite (II)	134	Valeria	118
Media (I)	165	Saxonia (I)	94	Vandalia (I)	116
Media (II)	180	Saxonia (II)	174	Vandalia (II)	161
Melita	26	Saxonia (III)	182	Vardulia (I)	128
Morocco	45	Saxonia (IV)	207	Vardulia (II)	160
		Scotia (I)	39	Vasconia (I)	129
Nantes	66	Scotia (II)	186	Vasconia (II)	159
Niagara	10	Scythia (I)	70	Vellavia	126
		Scythia (II)	137	Vennonia	130
Olympus	38	Scythia (III)	184	Venusia	131
Oregon	78	Scythia (IV)	208	Verbania	133
Otter	74	Servia (I)	79	Verentia	132
		Servia (II)	146	Veria	91
Palestine	37	Servia (III)	209	Vinovia	117
Palmyra	55	Shamrock	20	Virgilia	125
Pannonia	97	Siberia	57	Vitellia	127
Parthia (I)	62	Sidon	43	Volodia	119

Illustrated fleet list

1 UNICORN

Bt 1838 Robert Steele & Son, Greenock; *T:* 648 g, 390 n. **Dim** 185 ft (56.39 m) oa, 162 ft (49.38 m) × 23 ft 6 in (7.16 m) × 17 ft 4 in (5.28 m), width over pad sponsons 45 ft 2 in (13.77 m). **Eng** Pad, side lever; 2 cyls: 60 in (152.4 cm); *Stroke:* 69 in (175.26 cm); 570 IHP; *Stm P:* 5 lb; 9 rpm; 9½ kts; By Caird & Co, Greenock. **H** Wood, 2 decks; *Coal:* 453 tons at 18 tons per day; *Pass:* 40.

Two sisters, Eagle *and* City of Glasgow *(II), remained in the G. & J. Burns fleet.*

1836 May: Launched for G. &. J. Burns for their Glasgow-Liverpool service.
1840 The first ship to be operated by Samuel Cunard. The new mail contract called for a feeder service between Quebec-Pictou-Halifax and *Unicorn* was chartered for six years to perform this duty.
May 16: First voyage Liverpool-Halifax-Boston under Captain Walter Douglas with 27 passengers. She reached Halifax on May 30 and Boston on June 2.
1843 Nov: Rescued the passengers of the sailing ship *Premier* wrecked at the mouth of the St Lawrence.
1846 Used as a corvette in the Portuguese Navy.
1848 Reboilered. Sent to the Pacific coast of North America for the Panama-San Francisco trade.
1853 Served in Australian waters and then on the China coast.

2 BRITANNIA

Bt 1840 Robert Duncan & Co, Greenock; *T:* 1,156 g, 619 n. **Dim** 230 ft (70.1 m) oa figurehead to taffrail, 207 ft (63.09 m) × 34 ft 6 in (10.51 m) × 22 ft 6 in (6.86 m), width over pad boxes 56 ft (17.06 m). **Eng** Pad, side lever; 2 cyls: 72 in (182.88 cm); *Stroke:* 82 in (208.28 cm); 440 NHP; 4 boilers; *Stm P:* 9 lb; 8½ kts; Pad diam 28 ft (8.53 m) × 8.8 ft (2.64 m) wide; 16 rpm; By Robert Napier & Sons, Vulcan Foundry, Glasgow. **H** Wood, 2 decks; *Coal:* 640 tons at 37 tons per day; *Cargo:* 225 tons; *Pass:* 115 cabin; *Crew:* 89.

1840 Feb: Launched by Miss Isabella Napier. The first ship to be built for Cunard's British & North American Royal Mail Steam Packet Company. The ship was an enlargement on vessels of the Glasgow Steam Packet Company.
July 4: Maiden voyage, with the mails, Liverpool-Halifax-Boston under the command of Captain Henry Woodruff RN.
Britannia's maiden voyage, as the first regular mail service across the Atlantic, caused no excitement in Liverpool. Her arrival from the Clyde on June 12, docking at Coburg Dock, had attracted no more than two lines in the press and the only announcements were by Cunard. The reason for this was that in size *Britannia* represented nothing special; the *Great Western* of 1838 was larger and more powerful, and *Liverpool*, also of 1838, had better accommodation.
On Friday July 3 *Britannia* had anchored in the Mersey off Laird's yard,

 2,4-7

 3

Birkenhead, at what was to become Cunard's buoy. At noon on Saturday July 4, the date chosen because it was American Independence Day, a full complement of 63 embarked by tender from Liverpool Pier Head at the Egremont slip (she was too large to berth alongside). Samuel Cunard and his daughter were passengers. It was a cold bleak day with nor'westerly winds. By 2 pm she was away. 11 days 4 hours later she was off Halifax, docking in the early hours of Thursday July 17 to a gun salute from HMS *Winchester,* staying eight hours to disembark passengers and mail.

At 10 pm Saturday July 19 she arrived at Boston, Mass, in 14 days 8 hours having averaged 8¼ kts, her best distance covered in 24 hours being 280 miles. There was a tremendous reception. The USN cutter *Hamilton* escorted her in and shore batteries saluted her. The following monday, July 21, 2,000 people marched in procession to Cunard Wharf where an enormous banquet was served.

1844 Boston Harbour froze over and to free the ship the City of Boston cut a seven mile channel through the ice to the sea.

1849 After completing 40 crossings she was sold to the North German Confederate Navy for conversion into a frigate and renamed *Barbarossa.*

1852 Transferred to the Prussian Navy. She was later hulked at Kiel and used as a target ship.

1880 Broken up at Kiel (though some records say she was sunk by gunfire).

3 ACADIA

Details as *Britannia (2)* except: **Bt** John Wood & Co, Port Glasgow; *T:* 1,154 g, 616 n.

1840 Aug 4: Maiden voyage Liverpool-Halifax-Boston, her owners being recorded as the North American Ocean Steam Navigation Company. Captain E. C. Miller RN.

1849 Mar 9: Sold. Became *Erzherzog Johann* of the North German Confederate Navy and was commanded by Admiral Brommy.

Mar 12: Grounded at Terschelling, Holland, during the delivery voyage Liverpool-Bremen.

1853 North German Confederate Navy disbanded and ship sold.

Aug 3: Became *Germania* of Karl Lehmkuhl and opened a New York-Bremen service.

1855 Chartered by the British Government for use as a Crimean War transport. Returned to her German owners.

1858 Broken up River Thames.

4 CALEDONIA

Details as *Britannia (2)* except: **Bt** 1840 Robert Duncan & Co, Greenock; *T:* 1,156 g, 619 n.

1840 Sept 19: Maiden voyage Liverpool-Halifax-Boston under Captain Richard Cleland.

1850 Sold to the Spanish Navy and converted into a frigate. With her went *Hibernia (6).* The price for the two was £35,000.

1851 Wrecked at Havana, Cuba, by running on to a shelf of rocks at the harbour mouth. The damage was so great that the ship had to be abandoned.

5 COLUMBIA

Details as *Britannia (2)* except: **Bt** 1841 Robert Steele & Son, Greenock; *T:* 1,175 g, 625 n.

1841 Jan 5: Maiden voyage Liverpool-Halifax-Boston under Captain Ewing.

1843 July 2: Wrecked in dense fog on rock ledge near Seal Island, Halifax, en route Halifax-Boston with 85 passengers.

No lives were lost and both mails and cargo were saved, but the ship was finally abandoned.

6 HIBERNIA

Bt 1843 Robert Steele & Son, Greenock; *T:* 1,422 g, 791 n. **Dim** 240 ft (73.15 m) oa figurehead to taffrail, 217 ft 4 in (66.24 m) × 37 ft 8 in (11.48 m) × 24 ft (7.31 m), width over pad sponsons 58 ft (17.68 m). **Eng** Pad, side lever jet condensing; 2 cyls: 77½ in (196.85 cm); *Stroke:* 90 in (228.6 cm); 450 NHP; 4 boilers, 16 furnaces; *Stm P:* 8 lb; 10 kts; By Robert Napier & Sons, Glasgow. **H** Wood, 2 decks; *Coal:* 740 tons at 44 tons per day; *Cargo:* 300 tons; *Pass:* 215 cabin; *Crew:* 90.

1843 Apr 19: Maiden voyage Liverpool-Halifax-Boston. Captain Ryrie.
1847 Dec: Inaugurated the Liverpool-New York service.
1849 Aug 31: Grounded and salvaged near Halifax.
1850 Sold with *Caledonia (4)*. Became *Habanois* of the Spanish Navy.

7 CAMBRIA

Details as *Hibernia (6)* except: *T:* 1,423 g, 792 n, 2,580 disp.

1845 Jan 4: Maiden voyage Liverpool-Halifax-Boston. Nicknamed the 'Flying Cambria'. Commissioned barque-rigged.
1852 Mizzen mast removed. Brig rigged.
1854 Chartered as a Crimean War transport.
1856 Placed on the Marseilles-Malta service of the European & Australian Royal Mail Company, which had been subcontracted to Cunard together with the Southampton-Alexandria route.
1860 Sold to Italian owners. Later used for towing barges.

8

8 MARGARET

Bt 1839 Caird & Co, Greenock; *T:* 700 g. **Dim** 185 ft (56.39 m) × 26 ft 2 in (7.98 m) × 17 ft (5.18 m). **Eng** Pad, side lever; 2 cyls; 200 IHP; *Stm P:* 8 lb; 9 kts.

H Wood; *Cargo:* 1,200 tons.
Sister of British Queen (73).

1839 Owned by G. & J. Burns.
1840 Used on Cunard service.
1856 Sold and converted into a coal hulk.

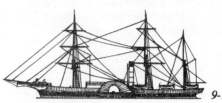

9-12

9 AMERICA

Bt 1848 Robert Steele & Son, Greenock; *T:* 1,826 g, 984 n, 3,400 disp. **Dim** 249 ft 5 in (79.1 m) × 35 ft 2 in (10.72 m) × 25 ft (7.62 m). **Eng** Pad, side lever jet condensing; 2 cyls: 90 in (228.6 cm); *Stroke:* 96 in (243.84 cm); 670 NHP; 4 flue boilers, 16 furnaces; *Stm P:* 18 lb; 10 kts; By Robert Napier & Sons, Glasgow. **H** Wood, 2 decks; *Coal:* 840 tons at 60 tons per day; *Cargo:* 450 tons; *Pass:* 140 cabin.

This class carried night navigation lights, a new innovation. Port: red; Starboard: green; Foremast-head: white.

1848 Apr 15: Maiden voyage Liverpool-Halifax-New York alternating with Boston. The average New York passage time was 12 days 22 hours.
1863 Chartered to Allan Line for four round voyages Liverpool-Quebec-Montreal.
1866 Sold. Became the sailing ship *Coalgaconder*.

10 NIAGARA

Details as *America (9)* except: *T:* 1,824 g, 984 n. **Dim** Length 251 ft (76.5 m).

1848 May 20: Maiden voyage Liverpool-Halifax-Boston alternating with New York.
1854 Used as a Crimean War transport.
1866 Nov: Sold to J. & G. Thompson the shipbuilders, who converted the ship to sail only. Then sold to Duncan Dunbar. Same name.
1875 Wrecked near South Stack, Anglesey, N Wales.

11 EUROPA

Details as *America (9)* except: **Bt** John

Wood & Co, Port Glasgow; *T:* 1,834 g, 992 n. **Dim** Length 251 ft (76.5 m).

1849 June 15: Maiden voyage, with 113 passengers, Liverpool-Halifax-Boston. June 27: Collided with and sank the barque *Charles Bartlett* in fog. 135 lost.
1854 Crimean War transport.
1858 Collided off Cape Race with *Arabia (19)* in dense fog.
1865 Apr 1: Final voyage Liverpool-Halifax-Boston.
1867 Sold and converted into a sailing ship after being lengthened.

12 CANADA

Details as *America (9)* except: *T:* 1,831 g, 990 n.

1848 Nov 25: Maiden voyage Liverpool-Halifax-New York.
1859 Nov 6: Made Cunard's first call at Queenstown (Cobh), Ireland.
1866 Feb 3: Last Cunard sailing.
1867 Sold. Renamed *Mississippi*. Converted to sailing ship under the Portuguese flag.
1883 Broken up, though it is reported that after this date she was seen at Bombay trading to Mauritius.

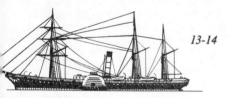

13-14

13 ASIA (I)

Bt 1850 Robert Steele & Son, Greenock; *T:* 2,226 g, 1,214 n. **Dim** 280 ft (85.34 m) oa forerake to taffrail, 226 ft (68.88 m) × 40 ft 6 in (12.34 m) × 27 ft 7 in (8.41 m), width over pads 58 ft (17.68 m). **Eng** Pad, side lever jet condensing; 2 cyls: 96 in (243.84 cm); *Stroke:* 108 in (274.32 m); 814 NHP, 2,400 IHP; 4 flue boilers, 20 furnaces; *Stm P:* 18 lb; 12 kts; Pad diam 37 ft 7 in (11.46 m), 28 blades; By Robert Napier & Sons, Glasgow. **H** Wood, double oak planked inside and outside of the frames with the space between filled with rot-preventing rock salt, 2 decks, fitted to carry guns; *Coal:* 900 tons at 76 tons per day; *Cargo:* 600 tons; *Pass:* 160 cabin; *Crew:* 112 of which the engine

room staff comprised 6 engineers and 32 stokers on four six-hour shifts working two men per boiler. A shift moved 18 tons of coal.

The longest steamer afloat.

The Admiralty rules for the carriage of the mails stipulated that the vessels used should be wood-hulled and paddle driven. They also required that a Naval officer should travel in charge of the consignment. It was not until the Royal Mail Line's wooden-hulled Amazon *was lost by fire on Jan 3 1852 that iron-hulled mail liners were permitted. But for this edict Cunard would have introduced screw propulsion and metal hulls much earlier. They were left with Asia and Africa (14)* in service and *Arabia (I) (18)* then Arabia *(II) (19) ordered.*

1850 May 18: Maiden voyage Liverpool-Halifax-Boston under Captain C. H. Judkins, the Mails Officer being Lt Ellis RN. In service *Asia* and her sister *Africa (14)* were not up to the standard of Collins Line competition.
1852 Mizzen mast removed. *Pass:* 140 1st, 30 2nd.
1867 May 11: Final Cunard voyage to Boston. Sold and converted to sail only by Robb & Co, Port Glasgow.
1877 Burnt out at Bombay whilst loading cotton.

14 AFRICA

Details as *Asia (13)*.

1850 Oct 26: Maiden voyage Liverpool-New York direct.
1867 Dec 7: Final voyage Liverpool-Halifax-Boston. Then used as a depot ship during the Fenian Riots.
1868 Sold.

15

15 SATELLITE (I)

Bt 1848 Robert Napier & Sons, Glasgow; *T:* 157 g, 82 n. **Dim** 108 ft 6 in (32.46 m) × 18 ft 8 in (5.69 m) × 9 ft 7 in (2.92 m). **Eng** Pad; 2 cyls: 50 in (127 cm); *Stroke:* 42 in (106.68 cm); 80 NHP; 1 boiler, 4 furnaces; *Stm P:* 11¾ lb; 8 kts; By

builder. **H** Iron, 1 deck; *Pass:* 600 and
their baggage.

1848 Passenger tender at Liverpool.
Captain Parry.
1902 Sept: Sold for £410 to Alexander
Gordon of Annalong, County Down,
N Ireland. Broken up.

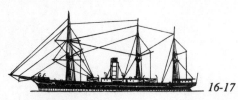

16-17

16 ANDES

Bt 1852 Wm Denny & Co, Dumbarton;
T: 1,852 reg, 1,440 g. **Dim** 236 ft
(71.93 m) oa × 34 ft (10.36 m) × 24 ft
(7.31 m). **Eng** Sgl scr, beam geared; 1 cyl:
66 in (167.64 cm); *Stroke:* 54 in
(137.16 cm); 300 NHP; 2 boilers, 12
furnaces; 9 kts; By Tulloch & Denny,
Dumbarton. **H** Iron, 2 decks; *Cargo:*
1,000 tons; *Pass:* 62 cabin, 122 2nd.

The company's first iron-hulled ship.

1852 Dec 8: Maiden departure for
Liverpool-New York but due to
abnormally low tides she had to put back
into dock. The voyage resumed on
Dec 25.
1853 Jan: Inaugurated the experimental
service New York-Chagres, Isthmus of
Panama. Remained on this route until
the abandonment of the service in 1858
except for Crimean War service.
1854 Chartered to the British
Government for £505 per month for use
as a Crimean War hospital ship.
1859 Sold to J. & G. Thomson. Resold to
Spanish owners.

17 ALPS

Details as *Andes (16).*

1853 Jan 2: Maiden voyage Liverpool-
New York.
1854 Joined *Andes* as Crimean War
hospital ship.
1859 Sold to J. & G. Thomson with
Andes. Lengthened by 30 ft (9.14 m) at
Harland & Wolff, Belfast. Then sold to
West Indies & Pacific SN Co (Leech,
Harrison & Forwood).

18-19

18 ARABIA (I)

*In 1850 the US Collins Line began
operating their Liverpool-New York
direct service. To counteract this
competition* Asia (13), Africa (14), Andes
(16) *and* Alps (17) *omitted Boston and
from 1852 onwards second class berths
were added. During 1852 Collins actually
carried more passengers than Cunard.*
Andes *and* Alps *were of only moderate
speed, at 9 kts, but despite their low
running costs were too small to stand up
to the size and opulence of the
competition. Despite their iron hulls they
were retained for only seven years.*

*Cunard found it necessary to take steps
to counter the competition. They ordered
two vessels from Robert Steele & Son.
They were* Arabia *(I) and* Arabia *(II)
(19), originally to have been named*
Persia. *Both were designed with slightly
more passenger accommodation than
previous vessels but on a larger hull. The
machinery was more powerful and both
were to be fitted out to exceed their rivals
in comfort and splendour.*

1852 Laid down by Robert Steele & Son,
Greenock. Purchased from Cunard on
the stocks, with construction well
advanced, by the Royal Mail line for
£125,000 to replace their burnt out
Amazon. Arabia was renamed *La Plata.*

19 ARABIA (II)

Bt 1852 Robert Steele & Son, Greenock;
T: 2,402 g, 1,474 n. **Dim** 309 ft (94.18 m)
oa, 284 ft (86.56 m) × 41 ft 1 in (12.53 m),
× 27 ft 5 in (8.36 m), width over pads
66 ft 6 in (20.27 m); *Dft:* 19 ft (5.79 m);
length:breadth ratio 7:1. **Eng** Pad, side
lever; 2 × 1 cyl: 103 in (259.08 cm);
Stroke: 108 in (274.32 cm); 938 NHP,
3,250 IHP; 4 tubular boilers, 24 furnaces;
Stm P: 18 lb; 15 rpm; 13 kts; By Robert
Napier & Sons, Glasgow. **H** Wood, 2
decks; *Coal:* 1,400 tons at 120 tons per
day; *Cargo:* 750 tons; *Pass:* 180 cabin.
Originally to have been named Persia *(I).*

Because *Arabia* (II) was the last great wooden paddler a few notes need adding:
Hull The hull was flat bottomed with round bilges. The oak frames were closely spaced and diagonally tied with crossed iron braces. All fastenings below the water line were copper. The outer planking was sheathed with hair felt followed by rock elm planking and finally an overall copper sheath. Her figurehead was, incidentally, of an Arab chieftain. Contrary to previous Cunard practice she had two funnels and was rigged as a brig, with no mizzen mast.

Accommodation Nominally for 180 all in one class although at rush times a further 20 could be accommodated on settees or in cot-beds in the cabins. The main saloon was abaft the main mast and had a stained glass dome. The ship carried a library, smoking room and childrens' nursery. One new innovation was that she was steam-heated throughout and this put her ahead of her Collins' contemporaries.

Performance Because of her fine lines forward (she was 20 ft (6.1 m) longer than *Asia (13)* on virtually the same beam) there was insufficient buoyancy to lift the bow in rough weather, consequently *Arabia* was a very wet ship. Worse, she lost headway easily and her average voyage speed was nearly always lower than design speed. Moreover her powerful engines shook the hull.

Engines They were, at the time, the largest in a British ship, so large that they were installed as the hull was built. Normally an engine consisted of one cylinder, its piston, the connecting rods and the crank which turned the paddles. *Arabia* had two such engines bolted to the bed plate, and at full speed the 9 ft (2.74 m) stroke took two seconds to traverse, so that one piston cycle of four seconds equalled one paddle revolution.

Boilers *Arabia* had two pairs of box bodies fitted with tubes. Because of their size they, too, were assembled and rivetted into position as the construction continued. There were six furnaces to each boiler. Because the boilers faced each other the stokers found them hard to work as they got in each others' way. The boilers were paired to each funnel with two forward of the engine and two aft.

Paddles The diameter was 35 ft 6 in (10.82 m) with 28 blades each of 10 ft 6 in (3.2 m) wide × 3 ft 2½ in (0.98 m) deep. The paddles revolved 15 times per minute but in a calm sea, at full speed, 17 rpm was achieved.

Fuel The consumption was far too high, 120 tons per day compared with *Asia's* 76 tons for only one knot of extra speed (and 20 more passengers!). The bunkers held 1,400 tons. At the commencement of a voyage the paddle axles were only two feet above the water line, but by the end of the journey *Arabia* stood a further five feet out of the water. Old illustrations drawn in America, of Cunard ships arriving in Boston or New York, all illustrate the way they stood out of the water.

1852 Dec 29: Maiden voyage Liverpool-New York. Captain C. H. Judkins. Some records give Jan 1 1853. Because of adverse winds the ship refuelled at Halifax.
1854 Crimean War transport at 50 shillings per ton per month. During her Crimean service *Arabia* carried 289 officers, 5,074 men and 803 horses.
1858 Collided with *Europa (11)*.
1864 Sold and converted to sail. She had not proved to be a successful ship in service.

20 SHAMROCK

Bt 1847 Caird & Co, Greenock; *T:* 714 g. **Dim** 195 ft (59.43 m) oa, 186 ft (56.69 m) × 25 ft (7.62 m) × 18 ft (5.49 m). **Eng** Sgl scr, vertical direct acting; 1 cyl: 48 in (121.92 cm); *Stroke:* 33 in (83.82 cm); 140 NHP; 1 boiler; *Stm P:* 18 lb; 9 kts; By builder. **H** Iron, 1 deck; *Pass:* 25 cabin, 100 3rd.

1847 Operated by Charles MacIver & Co on the Liverpool-Levant-Constantinople trade. MacIver's first iron hull.
1856 Cunard services to the Mediterranean.

21 BALBEC

Bt 1853 Wm Denny & Co, Dumbarton; *T:* 774 g. **Dim** 209 ft 2 in (63.75 m) oa, 201 ft (61.26 m) × 30 ft (9.19 m) × 17 ft

21

25

(5.18 m). **Eng** Sgl scr, beam geared; 1 cyl: 48 in (121.92 cm); *Stroke:* 33 in (83.82 cm); 137 NHP; 9 kts; By Tulloch & Denny, Dumbarton. **H** Iron; *Pass:* 29 cabin, 157 3rd.

1853 Mediterranean services to Constantinople.
1859 Sept 10: Liverpool-New York service.
1863 Liverpool-Havre route.
1884 Mar 28: Lost off Land's End

22 TAURUS

Bt 1853 Wm Denny & Co, Dumbarton; *T:* 1,126 g. **Dim** 210 ft (64 m) oa, 202 ft (61.56 m) × 30 ft 4 in (9.24 m) × 18 ft (5.49 m). **Eng** Sgl scr, beam geared; 2 cyls: 42 in (106.68 cm); *Stroke:* 33 in (83.82 cm); 220 NHP; 2 boilers; 9 kts; By Tulloch & Denny, Dumbarton. **H** Iron, 1 deck.

1853 Built for the Mediterranean trade. July 6: Liverpool-New York. Made two round voyages.
1859 Sold to the Spanish Government.

23 TENERIFFE

Details as *Taurus (22)*.

1853 Built for the Levant trade. The cost of a passage Liverpool-Constantinople was £40.
1859 Sold to the Spanish Government.

24 KARNAK

Details as *Taurus (22)* except: *T:* 1,116 g.

1853 Built for Mediterranean service. Transferred to the New York-Nassau-Havana mail service which connected over New York with Liverpool.
1862 Wrecked off Bermuda.

25 DELTA

Bt 1853 Barclay Curle & Co, Glasgow; *T:* 645 g. **Dim** 205 ft (62.48 m) × 29 ft 2 in (8.89 m) × 15 ft 9 in (4.8 m). **Eng** Sgl scr, beam geared; 2 cyls: 42 in (106.68 cm); *Stroke:* 38 in (96.52 cm); 120 NHP;

2 boilers, 6 furnaces; 9 kts; By builder. **H** Iron, carried 18 lb pivot guns.

1853 Used on Halifax-New York-Bermuda route. Operated by Samuel Cunard, not the British & North America RMSP Co.

26 MELITA

Bt 1853 Wm Denny & Co, Dumbarton; *T:* 1,254 g. **Dim** 233 ft (71.02 m) × 29 ft 4 in (8.94 m) × 18 ft 2 in (5.54 m). **Eng** Sgl scr, beam geared; 2 cyls; By Tulloch & Denny, Dumbarton. **H** 1 deck; *Pass:* Steerage only.

1853 Built for Mediterranean services.
1861 Sold to P. Denny & Co.
Same name.
1866 Sold to Warren Line.
June 6: First voyage Liverpool-Queenstown (Cobh)-Boston-Philadelphia.
1868 Sept 5: Burnt at sea. No lives lost.

27

27 EMEU

Bt 1854 Robert Napier & Sons, Glasgow; *T:* 1,538 g. **Dim** 268 ft 9 in (81.91 m) × 34 ft 5 in (10.49 m) × 27 ft 6 in (8.38 m). **Eng** Sgl scr, beam geared; 2 cyls: 64 in (162.56 cm); *Stroke:* 48 in (121.92 cm); 276 NHP; *Stm P:* 20 lb; 10 kts. **H** 2 decks.

1854 Built for Australian Pacific Mail Steam Packet Co. Her sisters were *Kangaroo, Dinornis, Black Swan* and *Minura*.
1855 Purchased by Cunard for the Mediterranean service.
1856 Placed on Liverpool-New York route.
1859 Feb: Sold to P&O, delivered in Sydney.
1873 Sold. Became the sailing ship

Winchester, owned by W. MacArthur. British.
1898 Became a hulk. Some records give her as wrecked in 1880 on the coast of Borneo.

28 LEBANON

Bt 1855 J. & G. Thomson & Co, Glasgow; *T:* 1,383 g. **Dim** 252 ft 6 in (76.96 m) × 30 ft 5 in (9.27 m) × 25 ft 3 in (7.7 m). **Eng** Sgl scr, oscillating, geared; 2 cyls: 54 in (137.16 cm); *Stroke:* 60 in (152.4 cm); 220 NHP; 2 boilers, 8 furnaces; *Stm P:* 30 lb; 10 kts. **H** Iron, 2 decks. *Pass:* Cabin class only.

1855 Built for Mediterranean services. Acted as a relief or extra vessel on Liverpool-New York route as required.
1859 Sold to the Spanish Government.

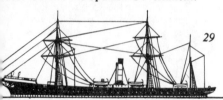

29

29 JURA

Bt J. & G. Thomson & Co, Glasgow; *T:* 2,241 g. **Dim** 316 ft (96.32 m) × 36 ft (10.97 m) × 22 ft (6.7 m). **Eng** Sgl scr, beam geared; 2 cyls: 76 in (193.04 cm); *Stroke:* 65½ in (166.37 cm); 440 NHP; 2 boilers, 8 furnaces; 11 kts; By builder. **H** Iron, 2 decks.

1854 Sept 24: On arrival at Liverpool taken over as a Crimean War transport.
1856 Entered Cunard service to the Mediterranean.
1857 Sept 16: Placed on Liverpool-New York service.
1861 Sold to the Allan Line for their Liverpool-Quebec-Montreal route after being chartered by Allan for two round voyages.
1864 Jan 3: Ran aground at Crosby, River Mersey, and broke her back to become a total loss. No lives lost.

30 ETNA

Bt 1855 Caird & Co, Greenock; *T:* 2,215 g. **Dim** 305 ft (92.96 m) × 36 ft 3 in (11.05 m) × 27 ft (8.23 m). **Eng** Sgl scr, beam geared; 2 cyls: 76¾ in (194.94

cm); *Stroke:* 63 in (160.02 cm); 434 NHP; 4 boilers, 14 furnaces; 11 kts; By builder. **H** Iron, 2 decks; *Pass:* 120 1st, 400 3rd.

1855 Jan 21: Arrived at Liverpool, taken over as a Crimean War transport.
1856 Feb 5: First voyage Havre-New York, then Liverpool-New York. Served on the New York-Chagres route with *Andes (16).*
1857 Ran for the European and Australian RMSP Co on the Southampton-Malta-Alexandria route.
1860 Oct: Sold to Inman Line as *Etna.*
1871 Rebuilt: Lengthened to 349 ft (106.38 m). *T:* 2,655 g. Engine compounded by Laird Bros, Birkenhead; 2 cyls: 48½ in (123.19 cm) and 84½ in (214.63 cm); *Stroke:* 42 in (106.68 cm); *Stm P:* 60 lb; 12 kts. Renamed *City of Bristol.*
May 30: First voyage Liverpool-New York.
1880 Sold for breaking up.

31 STROMBOLI

Bt 1856 J. & G. Thomson & Co, Glasgow; *T:* 734 g. **Dim** 198 ft 4 in (60.45 m) × 28 ft 9 in (8.76 m) × 17 ft 6 in (5.33 m). **Eng** Sgl scr, vertical, direct acting; 1 cyl: 42½ in (107.95 cm); *Stroke:* 31 in (78.74 cm); 2 boilers, 4 furnaces; 105 NHP; 9 kts; By builder. **H** Iron, 1 deck.

1856 Built for Liverpool-Mediterranean service. Also served on Liverpool-Havre route.
1866 Reboilered.
1877 Re-engined. Compound inverted; Cyls: 29 in (73.66 cm) and 54 in (137.16 cm); *Stroke:* 36 in (91.44 cm).
1878 Lost off the Lizard, Cornwall.

32,39

32 PERSIA (II)

Bt 1856 Robert Napier & Sons, Glasgow; *T:* 3,300 g. **Dim** 390 ft (118.87 m) oa bowsprit to taffrail, 376 ft (114.6 m) × 45 ft (13.72 m) × 31 ft 6 in (9.6 m). **Eng**

Pad, side lever jet condensing; 2 cyls: 100 in (254 cm); *Stroke:* 144 in (365.76 cm); 974 NHP, 4,570 IHP; Pad diam 41 ft (12.5 m), 38 blades; By builder. **H** Iron, 2 decks; *Cargo:* 1,050 tons; *Pass:* 200 cabin, 50 2nd; *Crew:* 440.

1855 July 3: Launched. Cost £130,000.
1856 Jan 8: Trials. The longest vessel afloat and the first iron-hulled transatlantic liner. *Persia* was commanded for most of her career by Captain Lott, who did over 300 crossings in her. *Andes (16)* although iron-hulled was not intended for regular Atlantic service.
Dec 26: Maiden voyage Liverpool-New York but commanded by Captain Judkins. During the voyage she scraped the side of an iceberg but arrived safely at her destination. Tragically Collins' *Pacific* left Liverpool the previous day and was never heard of again. It was the record holding *Pacific* that *Persia* had been designed to beat.
1868 Sold for £10,000. Engines removed.
1872 Broken up on the Thames.

33

33a

33 AUSTRALASIAN

Bt 1857 J. & G. Thomson & Co, Glasgow; *T:* 2,760 g. **Dim** 360 ft (109.73 m) oa, 338 ft (103.02 m) × 42 ft 1 in (12.83 m) × 20 ft 9 in (6.32 m). **Eng** Sgl scr, vertical, direct acting; 2 cyls: 90 in (228.6 cm); *Stroke:* 42 in (106.68 cm); 600 NHP; 6 boilers, 30 furnaces; 14 kts; By builder. **H** Iron, 2 decks and spar deck, equipped with Cunningham patent reefing sails and Clifford patent lifeboat launchers; *Coal;* 1,180 tons; *Cargo:* 1,100 tons and 400

tons in a deep tank; *Pass:* 200 saloon, 60 2nd.

1857 Sept 21: Trials. Built for European & Australian Royal Mail Co at a cost of £110,000 for Suez-Australian service. Her consorts were *Oneida, European, Columbian, Tasmanian, Asian, African,* and *Simla,* with Cunard's *Cambria (7), Jura (29)* and *Etna (30)* to carry the mails to Alexandria. Burns & MacIver were advertised as agents.
Oct 12: Maiden voyage Suez-Sydney under Captain Geoffrey Scales.
1859 Sold for £50,000 to Cunard after being arrested at Sydney because £3,000 crew wages failed to arrive on time.
1860 Feb 25: First voyage Liverpool-New York.
1869 Re-engined with vertical direct acting type with surface condensers; 2 cyls: 72 in (182.88 cm); *Stroke:* 48 in (121.92 cm); 450 NHP; 4 tubular boilers, 24 furnaces; 12½ kts. *Coal:* 86 tons per day. Fore funnel removed. *T:* 2,901 g. Renamed *Calabria (33a)*.
1870 Jan 8: First voyage as *Calabria*.
1876 Sold to Telegraph Construction & Maintenance Co.
1879 Re-engined. Compound; 2 cyls: 37½ in (95.25 cm) and 67½ in (171.45 cm); *Stroke:* 48 in (121.92 cm); 220 NHP; New boilers.
1897 Broken up at Bolnes, Holland.

34 ITALIAN

Bt 1855 J. & G. Thomson & Co, Glasgow; *T:* 784 g, 533 n. **Eng** Sgl scr, 1 cyl. **H** Iron, 1 deck.

1855 Built for Lamont & McLarty & Co, Liverpool.
1856-57 Chartered by Cunard for their Mediterranean service.
1864 Sold.

35

35 JACKAL

Bt 1853; *T:* 185 g. **Dim** 125 ft 4 in (38.2 m) × 19 ft 5 in (5.92 m) × 9 ft 8 in (2.95 m). **Eng** Pad, oscillating; 2 cyls: 36 in (91.44 cm); *Stroke:* 36 in (91.44 cm); 80 NHP; 8 kts. **H** Iron, 1 deck.

1853 Cunard tug based at Glasgow.

_36_

_37a_

36 DAMASCUS

Bt 1856 Wm Denny & Co, Dumbarton;
_T:_ 1,214 g. **Dim** 253 ft 6 in (77.27 m)
× 31 ft 2 in (9.5 m) × 22 ft 2 in (6.76 m).
Eng Sgl scr, vertical, direct acting; 2 cyls:
52 in (132.08 cm); _Stroke:_ 36 in
(91.44 cm); 2 boilers, 5 furnaces; 10 kts;
By Tulloch & Denny, Dumbarton.
H Iron, 1 deck; _Pass:_ 40 1st, 300 3rd.

1856 Built as _G. Lanza,_ Italy. Acquired
by Cunard for Mediterranean service.
Renamed _Damascus._
1860 May: Sold to the patriot Guiseppe
Garibaldi and renamed _Guiseppe
Garibaldi_ for the invasion of Sicily. The
ship was not delivered and reverted to
Damascus. Transferred to Liverpool-New
York route.
1862 Chartered to Allan Line.
April 30: First voyage Glasgow-Quebec-
Montreal.
1865 Sold to Allan Line.
1870 Rebuilt. _T:_ 1,517 g. Length 280 ft
(85.34 m). Engine compounded by
Greenock Foundries Co; 218 NHP;
10 kts. Renamed _Corinthian._
Sept 13: Resumed Glasgow-Quebec-
Montreal service.
1881 Sold to Italian owners. Renamed
Genoa.
18?? Sold to Turkish owners. Renamed
Foulazi Osmani.
1901 Became _Sakariah,_ Idarei
Massousieh, Constantinople.
1912 Broken up.

_37_

37 PALESTINE

Bt 1858 Robert Steele & Son, Greenock;
_T:_ 1,800 g. **Dim** 276 ft (84.12 m) oa,
255 ft 2 in (77.77 m) × 34 ft 3 in
(10.44 m) × 24 ft 3 in (7.39 m). **Eng** Sgl

scr, oscillating, geared; 2 cyls: 57 in
(144.78 cm); _Stroke:_ 57 in (144.78 cm);
232 NHP; 2 boilers, 12 furnaces; 10 kts;
By McNab & Clark. **H** Iron, 2 decks;
Pass: 32 1st, 280 steerage.

1858 Placed on the Boston-
Mediterranean service.
1860 London-Boston-New York route.
May 16: Chartered to Allan Line for
Liverpool-Montreal service.
1870 Sold to Langlands & Co, Glasgow.
Modernised. _T:_ 2,867 g. Length 352 ft
(107.29 m). Engine compounded by J. &
G. Thomson, Glasgow; inverted; 2 cyls:
43 in (109.22 cm) and 76 in (193.04 cm);
Stroke: 42 in (106.68 cm); 300 NHP;
Stm P: 60 lb; 12 kts. _(37a)._
1872 Chartered to the Dominion Line.
Mar 26: First voyage Liverpool-Portland.
1876 Chartered to the Warren Line.
Liverpool-Boston run.
1896 Broken up.

_38_

38 OLYMPUS

Bt 1860 J. & G. Thomson & Co,
Glasgow; _T:_ 1,794 g. **Dim** 328 ft
(99.97 m) × 36 ft 3 in (11.05 m) × 25 ft
8 in (7.82 m). **Eng** Sgl scr, oscillating; 2
cyls; 10 kts. **H** Iron; _Pass:_ 70 cabin,
900 3rd.

1860 Built for Mediterranean service.
1863 Liverpool-New York service.
1872 Modernised. _T:_ 2,415 g. Length
340 ft (103.63 m). Engine compounded;
2 cyls: 44 in (111.76 cm) and 78 in
(198.12 cm); _Stroke:_ 42 in (106.68 cm);
270 NHP; _Stm P:_ 64 lb; 10 kts; By J. &
G. Thomson. Two masts.
1879 Used as transport for the Zulu War.
1881 July 13: Sold to J. & G. Thomson &
Co for £2,700 in part payment for
Pavonia (76).

1891 Broken up at Manchester.

39 SCOTIA (I)

Bt 1862 Robert Napier & Sons, Glasgow; *T:* 3,871 g, 2,125 n. **Dim** 397 ft (121 m) oa bowsprit to taffrail, 379 ft 4 in (115.62 m) × 47 ft 8 in (14.53 m) × 30 ft 6 in (9.3 m). **Eng** Pad, side lever jet condensing; 2 cyls; 100 in (254 cm); *Stroke:* 144 in (365.76 cm); 1,200 NHP; 8 tubular boilers, 40 furnaces; *Stm P:* 20 lb; 13½ kts; By builder. **H** Iron, 2 decks; *Coal:* 150 tons per day; *Cargo:* 1,050 tons; *Pass:* 275 cabin, 300 2nd; *Crew:* 440.

Scotia *was completed with three masts but these were reduced to two before her first sailing. Except for* Great Eastern *she was the largest ship afloat. For drawing see* Persia (32).

1862 May 10: Maiden voyage Liverpool-New York. Captain C. H. Judkins.
1863-69 During her career she held the eastbound Blue Riband for five years with a time of 8 days 3 hours and an average speed of 14.02 kts.
1878 Sold to Telegraph Construction & Maintenance Co. Converted to cable layer by Laird Bros, Birkenhead. She was fitted with twin screws and re-engined. Three cable tanks were fitted.
1903 Sold to Commercial Pacific Cable Company.
1904 Wrecked on Spanish Rock, Guam.

40-42

40 ATLAS

Bt 1860 J. & G. Thomson & Co, Glasgow; *T:* 1,794 g. **Dim** 276 ft (84.12 m) × 36 ft 4 in (11.07 m) × 25 ft 8 in (7.82 m). **Eng** Sgl scr, oscillating, geared; 2 cyls: 59¼ in (150.5 cm); *Stroke:* 60 in (152.4 cm); 650 NHP; 2 boilers, 12 furnaces; *Stm P:* 22 lb; 25 rpm; By builder. **H** Iron, 2 decks; *Coal:* 30 tons per day; *Pass:* 69 cabin, 833 3rd.

1860 Built for Mediterranean services.
1873 Modernised. *T:* 2,393 g. Length

339 ft (103.33 m). Engine compounded; direct acting; 2 cyls; 44 in (111.76 cm) and 78 in (198.12 cm); *Stroke:* 42 in (106.68 cm); 300 NHP; 2 boilers, 12 furnaces; 10½ kts; By builder. 2 masts.
May 1: First voyage Liverpool-Boston.
1884 May 14: Last transatlantic voyage. Mediterranean services thereafter.
1896 Broken up.

41 MARATHON

Bt 1860 Robert Napier & Sons, Glasgow; *T:* 1,784 g. **Dim** 274 ft (83.52 m) × 36 ft 4 in (11.07 m) × 25 ft 8 in (7.82 m). **Eng** Sgl scr, oscillating, geared; 2 cyls: 59¼ in (150.5 cm); *Stroke:* 60 in (152.4 cm); 650 NHP; 2 boilers, 12 furnaces; *Stm P:* 22 lb; 25 rpm; By builder. **H** Iron, 2 decks; *Coal:* 30 tons per day; *Pass:* 69 cabin, 850 3rd.

1860 Built for Mediterranean service.
1866 Transferred to Liverpool-Boston route.
1873 Modernised as *Atlas (40)* but length 336 ft (102.41 m).
1882 Chartered to the Government for 30 shillings per ton per month for use in the Egyptian Campaign.
1892 Sept 8: Last transatlantic voyage.
1898 Sold to Workman, Clark & Co, Belfast, for £2,615. Broken up in Italy as *Cypria.*

42 HECLA

Details as *Marathon (41)* except: *T:* 1,790 g. *Pass:* 70 cabin, 800 3rd.

1860 Entered Mediterranean service and extra vessel on the North Atlantic.
1863 June 16: Transferred to North Atlantic routes.
1871 Modernised. *T:* 2,421 g. Length 339 ft (103.33 m). Engine compounded.
1881 Taken over by Laird Bros, Birkenhead, in part payment for *Cephalonia (77).* Overhauled and sold to Conde de Vilana, Spain. Renamed *Conde de Vilana.*
1882 Sold to Gartland y Cia, Buenos Aires. Renamed *P. A. Gartland.*
1892 Renamed *Pedro Tercero.*
1895 Traded as *Tiempo.*
1897 Transferred to Ministry of Marine, Argentina. Served initially as *Tiempo,* then renamed *Rio Negro* and operated

Buenos Aires-Volmaia with passengers and convicts.
1954 Broken up after serving for some years as a pontoon.

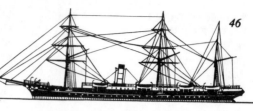

46

43-45

43 SIDON

Bt 1861 Wm Denny & Co, Dumbarton; *T:* 1,872 g, 799 n. **Dim** 275 ft 6 in (83.97 m) × 36 ft 2 in (11.02 m) × 25 ft 8 in (7.82 m). **Eng** Sgl scr, oscillating, geared; 2 cyls; 10 kts. **H** Iron, 2 decks; *Pass:* 69 cabin, 550 3rd.

1861 Built for Mediterranean service.
1865 May 19: Commenced to operate on North Atlantic.
1873 Engine compounded; 2 cyls: 39 in (99.06 cm) and 68 in (172.72 cm); *Stroke:* 45 in (114.3 cm); 212 NHP; *Stm P:* 60 lb; 12 kts; By J. Jack, Rollo & Co, Liverpool.
1885 Wrecked on the coast of Spain.

44 KEDAR

Details as *Sidon (43)* except: *T:* 1,763 g, 1,215 n.

1860 Nov 27: Maiden voyage Liverpool-New York.
1865 Placed on Mediterranean routes.
1873 Engine compounded; 2 cyls: 39 in (99.06 cm) and 68 in (172.72 cm); *Stroke:* 45 in (114.3 cm); 212 NHP; *Stm P:* 60 lb; 12 kts; By J. Jack, Rollo & Co, Liverpool. Masts reduced to two.
1897 Sold to Workman Clark & Co, Belfast, for £2,105. Broken up at Genoa.

45 MOROCCO

Details as *Sidon (43)* except: *T:* 1,855 g, 1,193 n.

1861 Placed on Mediterranean services.
1874 Engine compounded; 2 cyls: 39 in (99.06 cm) and 68 in (172.72 cm); *Stroke:* 45 in (114.3 cm); 212 NHP; *Stm P:* 50 lb; 12 kts; By J. Jack, Rollo & Co, Liverpool. Masts reduced to two.
1896 Sold to Workman Clark & Co, Belfast, for £2,150. Broken up Mersey.

46 CHINA

Bt 1862 Robert Napier & Sons, Glasgow; *T:* 2,638 g. **Dim** 326 ft 2 in (99.42 m) × 40 ft 6 in (12.34 m) × 27 ft 6 in (8.38 m). **Eng** Sgl scr, oscillating, geared; 2 cyls: 80 in (203.2 cm); *Stroke:* 66 in (167.64 cm); 480 NHP; 4 boilers, 24 furnaces; 12 kts; By builder. **H** Iron, 2 decks; *Coal:* 1,200 tons at 82 tons per day; *Cargo:* 1,050 tons; *Pass:* 150 1st, 753 3rd.

1862 Mar 15: Maiden voyage Liverpool-New York. The sailing connected with that of *British Queen (73)* for Nassau.
1874 Engine compounded by Barclay Curle & Co, Glasgow; 2 cyls: 51 in (129.54 cm) and 86 in (218.44 cm); *Stroke:* 48 in (121.92 cm); 420 NHP; *Stm P:* 63 lb.
1879 Zulu War transport.
1880 Sold to Spain. Renamed *Magallanes.*
18?? Sold to Norway. Renamed *Theodore.* Converted into a four-masted barque.
1907 Missing on voyage Tampa-Japan.

47 ALPHA

Bt 1863 Barclay Curle & Co, Glasgow; *T:* 653 g. **Dim** 216 ft (65.84 m) × 27 ft (8.23 m) × 18 ft 4 in (5.59 m). **Eng** Sgl scr, oscillating; 2 cyls. **H** Iron, 1 deck.

1863 Registered as owned by W. Cunard, 68 Cromwell Road, London.
Used on Halifax-New York-Bermuda service.
1869 Sold.
1900 Wrecked.

48 CORSICA

Bt 1863 J. & G. Thomson & Co, Glasgow; *T:* 1,134 g, 681 n. **Dim** 224 ft (68.28 m) × 32 ft 2 in (9.8 m) × 24 ft (7.32 m). **Eng** Sgl scr, oscillating, geared; 2 cyls: 51 in (129.54 cm); *Stroke:* 45 in (114.3 cm); 182 NHP; 2 boilers,

8 furnaces; 10 kts; By builder. **H** Iron, 1 deck; *Pass:* Berthed aft.

1863 Placed on Mediterranean service.
1868 Sold to the Royal Mail Steam Packet Co for West Indies services.
1877 Sold for further trading to R. Foll Jr.
1879 Re-engined by Wallsend Shipping Co, Wallsend.
1888 Out of register.

49-50

49 CUBA

Bt 1864 Tod & McGregor, Glasgow; *T:* 2,832 g, 1,534 n. **Dim** 338 ft 2 in (103.07 m) oa, 327 ft (99.67 m) × 42 ft 4 in (12.9 m) × 27 ft 6 in (8.38 m). **Eng** Sgl scr, oscillating, geared with surface condensers; 2 cyls: 82 in (208.28 cm); *Stroke:* 72 in (182.88 cm); 650 NHP; 4 boilers, 24 furnaces; 12½ kts. **H** Iron, 2 decks, 9 compartments, saloon seating 300, fcsle 60 ft (18.29 m), Cunningham patent top-sails; *Coal:* 1,100 tons; *Cargo:* 1,230 tons; *Pass:* 300 1st, 1,500 troops.

1864 July: Launched. Cost £110,000.
1865 Jan 14: Maiden voyage Liverpool-New York. Captain J. Stone.
1876 Sold to D. Brown & Sons, London. Became the four-masted sailing vessel *Earl of Beaconsfield.*
1887 Nov: Wrecked near Withernsea en route Calcutta-Hull.

50 JAVA

Bt 1865 Tod & McGregor, Glasgow; *T:* 2,696 g, 1,761 n. **Dim** 337 ft 1 in (102.75 m) oa, 327 ft (99.67 m) × 42 ft 4 in (12.9 m) × 27 ft 6 in (8.38 m). **Eng** Sgl scr, inverted direct action, surface condensing; 2 cyls: 86 in (218.44 cm); *Stroke:* 45 in (114.3 cm); 540 NHP; 4 boilers, 24 furnaces; 12½ kts. **H** Details as *Cuba (49).*

1865 Oct 21: Maiden voyage Liverpool-New York. Acquired the nickname 'Jumping Java'. She was also J. & G.

Thomson's first designed transatlantic liner.

1877 Engine compounded by Fawcett, Preston & Co, Liverpool; Inverted type; Cyls: 48 in (121.92 cm) and 86 in (218.44 cm); *Stroke:* 45 in (114.3 cm); 350 HP; Reboilered. Chartered to Warren Line for the North Atlantic.
1878 Sold through Richardson, Spence & Co to the Red Star Line. Renamed *Zeeland.* Antwerp-New York service.
1889 Sold. Converted to sailing barque. Renamed *Electrique,* French owner.
1892 Became *Lord Spencer,* still as a sailing vessel.
1895 Disappeared at sea.

51-53

51 ALEPPO

Bt 1865 J. & G. Thomson & Co, Glasgow; *T:* 2,057 g, 1,399 n. **Dim** 292 ft 6 in (89.15 m) × 38 ft 2 in (11.63 m) × 26 ft 2 in (7.98 m). **Eng** Sgl scr, oscillating; 2 cyls: 61 in (154.94 cm); *Stroke:* 54 in (137.16 cm); 280 HP; *Stm P:* 25 lb; 10 kts; By builder. **H** Iron, 1 deck; *Pass:* 46 cabin, 593 3rd.

1865 Mediterranean service.
1879 Re-engined and rebuilt by J. Jack & Co, Liverpool. Compound direct acting, surface condensers; 2 cyls: 38 in (96.52 cm) and 68 in (172.72 cm); *Stroke:* 48 in (121.92 cm); 212 NHP; *Stm P:* 60 lb; 10 kts. *Coal:* 35 tons per day.
1890 Re-engined. Tpl exp; Cyls: 22¼ in (56.51 cm), 35¾ in (90.8 cm) and 58½ in (148.59 cm); 220 NHP; 2 boilers, 4 furnaces on 18 tons coal per day with Howden's forced draught; *Stm P:* 160 lb.
1909 Sold to Thos Ward for £4,000. Broken up.

52 MALTA

Bt 1865 J. & G. Thomson & Co, Glasgow; *T:* 2,132 g, 1,450 n. **Dim** 303 ft 1 in (92.38 m) × 39 ft 3 in (11.96 m) × 25 ft (11.96 m). **Eng** Sgl scr, oscillating; 2 cyls: 60½ in (153.67 cm); *Stroke:* 66 in (167.64 cm); By builder. **H** Iron, 1 deck; *Pass:* 46 cabin, 593 3rd.

1865-73 Liverpool-New York or Boston service.
1874-81 Mediterranean routes out of Liverpool.
1882 Reverted to the North Atlantic.
1883-89 Mediterranean service.
1889 Qct 15: Wrecked off Cape Cornwall, near Land's End. All saved.

53 TARIFA

Bt 1865 J. & G. Thomson & Co, Glasgow; *T:* 2,058 g, 1,400 n. **Dim** 292 ft 6 in (8.92 m) × 38 ft 2 in (11.63m) × 26 ft 2 in (7.98 m). **Eng** Sgl scr, oscillating, geared; 2 cyls: 61 in (154.94 cm); *Stroke:* 60 in (152.4 cm); 280 HP; 2 boilers, 12 furnaces; *Stm P:* 25 lb; 10 kts; By builder. **H** Iron, 1 deck; *Coal:* 40 tons per day; *Pass:* 50 cabin, 600 3rd.

1865-71 Liverpool-New York or Boston service.
1872-98 Mediterranean service.
1879 Engine compounded by J. Jack & Co, Liverpool; Cyls: 38 in (96.52 cm) and 68 in (172.72 cm); *Stroke:* 48 in (121.92 cm); 212 HP; 10 kts.
1898 Sold and broken up in Italy.

54 TRIPOLI

Details as *Tarifa (53)* except: *T:* 2,146 g, 1,271 n.

Identification note: First lifeboat omitted, square-rigged mainmast, rails along deck well, funnel three widths forward.

1865 Mediterranean routes.
1866-72 Liverpool-New York or Boston service.
1892 May 9: Wrecked during her fiftieth voyage at Tuskar Rock, Southern Ireland.

55 PALMYRA

Bt 1866 Caird & Co, Greenock; *T:* 2,044 g, 1,390 n. **Dim** 290 ft 8 in (88.6 m) × 38 ft (11.58 m) × 26 ft 1 in (7.96 m). **Eng** Sgl scr, oscillating; 2 cyls:

61 in (154.94 cm); *Stroke:* 60 in (152.4 cm); 260 NHP; *Stm P:* 23 lb; 10 kts; By builder. **H** Iron, 1 deck; *Pass:* 46 1st, 656 3rd.

1866 Placed on the Liverpool-New York or Boston route.
1879 Re-engined and reboilered by J. Jack, Rollo & Co, Liverpool; Compound inverted; 2 cyls: 38 in (96.52 cm) and 68 in (172.72 cm); *Stroke:* 48 in (121.92 cm); 212 HP; 10 kts.
1880-81 Zulu War transport.
1882 Chartered for 22s 6d per ton per month for the Egyptian campaign.
1896 Sold for £2,600 and broken up.

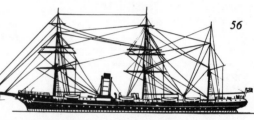

56 RUSSIA

Bt 1867 J. & G. Thomson & Co, Glasgow; *T:* 2,960 g, 1,710 n. **Dim** 358 ft (109.12 m) × 43 ft (13.11 m) × 27 ft 8 in (8.43 m). **Eng** Sgl scr, inverted; 2 cyls: 86 in (218.44 cm); *Stroke:* 45 in (114.3 cm); 600 HP; 4 boilers, 28 furnaces; *Stm P:* 25 lb; 13 kts; By builder. **H** Iron, 2 decks; *Coal:* 1,180 tons at 90 tons per day; *Cargo:* 1,260 tons; *Pass:* 430 saloon.

Russia was the last Cunarder built with a clipper stem. Her nickname was 'Rolling Russia'.

1867 June 15: Maiden voyage Liverpool-New York.
1878 Nov 2: Last Cunard voyage to New York.
1881 Sold to Red Star Line. Became *Waesland*. Lengthened to 435 ft (132.59 m). *T:* 4,752 g, 3,736 n.
1889 Tpl exp engine fitted by J. & G. Thomson; 3 cyls: 32 in (81.28 cm), 48 in

59-60,62

(121.92 cm) and 86 in (218.44 cm); *Stroke:* 54 in (137.16 cm); 582 NHP; *Stm P:* 160 lb; 15 kts.
1902 Mar 7: Sunk in collision with Houston's *Harmonides* off Holyhead. Two lives lost.

57-58

57 SIBERIA

Bt 1867 J. &. G. Thomson & Co, Glasgow; *T:* 2,498 g, 1,698 n. **Dim** 320 ft (97.54 m) × 39 ft 2 in (11.94 m) × 26 ft 3 in (7.09 m). **Eng** Sgl scr, inverted, direct action; 2 cyls: 81 in (205.74 cm); *Stroke:* 42 in (106.68 cm); 280 NHP; 2 rectangular tubular boilers, 14 furnaces; *Stm P:* 25 lb; 13 kts; By builder. **H** Iron, 2 decks; *Pass:* 124 1st, 800 3rd.

1866 Laid down as *Sumatra* but renamed to avoid confusion with the P&O ship of the same name.
1867 Sept 24: Maiden voyage Liverpool-New York.
1879 Mar 26: Last voyage Liverpool-Boston.
1880 Sold for £15,000. Renamed *Manila,* Marquis de Campo, Spain.
1881 Wrecked.

58 SAMARIA (I)

Details as *Siberia (57)* except: **Bt** 1868; *T:* 2,500 g, 1,695 n. **Dim** Length 320 ft 6 in (97.69 m).

1868 Sept 29: Maiden voyage Liverpool-New York.
1878 Compound engine installed.
1896 Jan 30: Final voyage Liverpool-Boston.
1902 Sold for £5,600 and broken up in Italy.

59 ABYSSINIA

Bt 1870 J. & G. Thomson & Co, Glasgow; *T:* 3,376 g, 2,159 n. **Dim** 367 ft 6 in (112.01 m) × 42 ft 2 in (12.85 m) × 34 ft 6 in (10.52 m). **Eng** Sgl scr, inverted; 2 cyls: 72 in (182.88 cm); *Stroke:*

48 in (121.92 cm); 500 NHP; 4 boilers, 24 furnaces; *Stm P:* 60 lb; 12½ kts; By builder. **H** Iron, 2 decks and spar deck; *Coal:* 1,180 tons at 90 tons per day; *Cargo:* 1,600 tons; *Pass:* 200 1st, 1,050 3rd.

The first Cunarders with bathrooms, one port side and one starboard side.

1870 Liverpool-New York service.
1871 Outmoded by the introduction of White Star's *Oceanic* class.
1880-81 Sold back to builder in part payment for *Catalonia (75)* and *Servia (79).* Resold to Guion Line.
1887 Operated the Canadian Pacific Railway Co's Vancouver-Hong Kong-Japan route.
1891 Dec 18: Abandoned on fire five days outward bound from New York. The passengers were saved by Norddeutscher Lloyd's *Spree.*

60 ALGERIA

Details as *Abyssinia (59)* except: *T:* 3,428 g, 2,193 n.

1870 Sept 27: Maiden voyage Liverpool-New York.
1881 Oct 22: Last voyage to New York. Sold to Red Star Line. Renamed *Pennland.*
1882 compound engine fitted by J. Jack & Co, Liverpool; 2 cyls: 48½ in (123.19 cm) and 84 in (213.36 cm); *Stroke:* 54 in (137.16 cm); 432 NHP; *Stm P:* 80 lb; 12 kts.
1903 Dec: Sold and broken up in Italy.

61

61 BATAVIA

Bt 1870 Wm Denny & Co, Dumbarton; *T:* 2,593 g, 1,828 n. **Dim** 327 ft 4 in

(99.77 m) × 39 ft 3 in (11.96 m) × 28 ft 5 in (8.66 m). **Eng** Sgl scr, compound inverted, direct acting surface condensers: 2 cyls: 51 in (129.54 cm) and 86 in (218.44 cm); *Stroke:* 48 in (121.92 cm); 450 NHP; 2 boilers, 12 furnaces; *Stm P:* 60 lb; 12 kts; By builder. **H** Iron, 4 decks; *Coal;* 655 tons at 40 tons per day; *Cargo:* 2,650 tons; *Pass:* 150 saloon, 800 steerage.

1870 Feb 1: North Atlantic service.
1880 Feb 12: Made one trial voyage Liverpool-Bombay.
1882 Chartered for the Egyptian campaign.
1883 Sept: Last Cunard voyage. Sold to John Elder in part exchange for *Etruria (82)* and re-engined with new boilers. Tpl exp; 4 cyls: 2 × 23 in (58.42 cm), 26 in (66.04 cm) and 58 in (147.32 cm); *Stroke:* 42 in (106.68 cm); 218 NHP.
1887 Operated Canadian Pacific Railway Co's Vancouver-Hong Kong-Japan route.
1893 Sold to Guion Line. Renamed *Tacoma.*
1898 Sold to North American Mail SS Co, later North Western SS Co.
1905 Sailed Tacoma-Vladivostock during Russo-Japanese War with food for Russians.
Feb 4: Captured by Japanese in an ice field off Hokkaido. Became *Shikotan Maru.*
1924 Oct 23: As a Chinese collier became stranded 60 miles from Shanghai. Salved but condemned and broken up.

62 PARTHIA (I)

Bt 1870 Wm Denny & Co, Dumbarton; *T:* 3,167 g, 2,035 n. **Dim** 360 ft 6 in (109.89 m) × 40 ft 4 in (12.29 m) × 34 ft 3 in (10.44 m). **Eng** Sgl scr, compound inverted, direct action surface condensing; 2 cyls: 58 in (147.32 cm) and 97 in (246.38 cm); *Stroke:* 48 in (121.92 cm); 480 NHP; 2 boilers, 12 furnaces; *Stm P:* 60 lb; 12 kts; By builder. **H** Iron, 4 decks; *Coal:* 881 tons at 40 tons per day; *Cargo:* 3,139 tons; *Pass:* 150 1st, 1,030 steerage.

Identification note: No steam pipe abaft funnel, which was thinner and slightly taller.

1870 Dec 17: Maiden voyage Liverpool-New York.
1884 Acquired by John Elder & Co in part payment for *Umbria (81)* and *Etruria (82).* Tpl exp engine fitted; 3 cyls: 31 in (78.74 cm), 50 in (127 cm) and 76 in (1933.04 cm); *Stroke:* 54 in (137.16 cm); 424 NHP.
1887 Operated for Canadian Pacific Rly Co's transpacific routes.
1891 Guion Line ownership. Renamed *Victoria.*
1892 Ran for Northern Pacific SS Co.
1898 Still as *Victoria* operated by North American Mail SS Co.
1904 Sold to North Western SS Co.
1908 Sold to Alaska SS Co. San Francisco-Seattle-Alaska.
1940 Cargo only.
1952 Laid up at Houghton, Lake Washington.
1954 Purchased by Straits Towing & Salvage Co. Converted into a log barge. Renamed *Straits No 27.*
1956 Oct 16: As *Straits Maru* arrived Osaka in tow of tug *Sudburg* for scrapping.

63-64

63 TRINIDAD

Bt 1872 J. & G. Thomson & Co, Glasgow; *T:* 1,900 g, 1,230 n. **Dim** 307 ft 6 in (93.73 m) × 34 ft 1 in (10.39 m) × 24 ft 6 in (7.47 m). **Eng** Sgl scr, compound inverted; 2 cyls: 39 in (99.06 cm) and 69¾ in (177.16 cm); *Stroke:* 45 in (114.3 cm); 300 NHP; 2 boilers, 8 furnaces; *Stm P:* 70 lb; 10½ kts; By builder. **H** Iron; *Coal:* 400 tons at 22 tons per day; *Cargo:* 2,150 tons; *Pass:* 46 1st.

1872 Built for Glasgow-West Indies service but spent first year on Mediterranean routes.
1898 Sold for £3,925 to German owners.
Sept: Foundered in the China Sea.

64 DEMERARA

Details as *Trinidad (63)* except: *T:* 1,904 g, 1,230 n.

35

A third sister, Barbados, *was never delivered.*

1872 Built for Glasgow-West Indies route.
1887 Dec 25: Left Liverpool for Gibraltar and disappeared.

65 BETA

Bt 1873 Aitken & Mansel, Glasgow; *T:* 1,070 g, 677 n. **Dim** 235 ft 1 in (71.66 m) × 28 ft 6 in (8.69 m) × 14 ft 7 in (4.44 m). **Eng** Sgl scr, compound inverted; 2 cyls: 33½ in (85.09 cm) and 58½ in (148.59 cm); *Stroke:* 36 in (91.44 cm); 160 HP; By J. & G. Thomson, Glasgow. **H** Steel, 2 decks and spar deck, 3 masts.

1873 Built for Halifax-Boston or New York-Bermuda routes. Registered as owned by W. Cunard, 48 Cromwell Road, London.
1889 Sold to Halifax & West India SS Co (Pickford & Black).

66 NANTES

Bt 1874 Blackwood & Gordon, Port Glasgow; *T:* 1,473 g, 949 n. **Dim** 238 ft 3 in (72.62 m) × 32 ft 2 in (9.8 m) × 26 ft 6 in (8.08 m). **Eng** Sgl scr, compound inverted, direct action surface condensing; 2 cyls: 33½ in (85.09 cm) and 58½ in (148.59 cm); *Stroke:* 42 in (106.68 cm); 160 NHP; 2 boilers, 6 furnaces; *Stm P:* 65 lb; 10 kts; By builder. **H** Iron, 1 deck; *Coal:* 240 tons at 15 tons per day; *Cargo:* 2,000 tons; *Pass:* 8 1st, 386 3rd.

1874 French Channel port services from Liverpool.
1888 Nov 6: Lost 36 miles south-east of the Lizard, Cornwall, after colliding with the *Theodor Ruger,* which also sank. *Nantes* stayed afloat until 10 am next day when she suddenly capsized, drowning all her crew except for one man found clinging to wreckage.

67 BREST

Details as *Nantes (66)* except: *T:* 1,472 g, 949 n. *Pass:* 127 3rd.

1874 Liverpool-French ports.
1879 Sept: Wrecked off Hot Point, Cornwall.

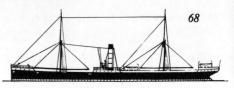

68

68 SARAGOSSA

Bt 1874 J. & G. Thomson & Co, Glasgow; *T:* 2,263 g, 1,430 n. **Dim** 316 ft 3 in (96.39 m) × 35 ft 3 in (10.74 m) × 17 ft 7 in (5.36 m). **Eng** Sgl scr, compound, direct acting; 2 cyls: 40 in (101.6 cm) and 71 in (180.34 cm); *Stroke:* 45 in (114.3 cm); 300 NHP; 2 cylindrical boilers, 12 furnaces; *Stm P:* 70 lb; 11 kts; By builder. **H** Iron; *Coal:* 572 tons at 26 tons per day; *Cargo:* 2,500 tons; *Pass:* 74 1st, 548 3rd; *Crew:* 34.

1874 Built for Mediterranean service. Apr 22: Maiden voyage Liverpool-Boston. Remained on the Atlantic for three months then went onto her station.
1909 Sold for £400 to Thos Ward for breaking up.

69-71

69 BOTHNIA (I)

Bt 1874 J. & G. Thomson & Co, Glasgow; *T:* 4,535 g, 2,923 n. **Dim** 422 ft 3 in (128.7 m) × 42 ft 2 in (12.85 m) × 34 ft 6 in (10.52 m). **Eng** Sgl scr, compound, vertical, direct acting with surface condensers; 2 cyls: 60 in (152.4 cm) and 104 in (264.16 cm); *Stroke:* 45 in (114.3 cm); 600 NHP; 8 boilers, 24 furnaces; *Stm P:* 65 lb; 12½ kts; By builder. **H** Iron, 2 decks and spar deck; *Coal:* 1,016 tons at 75 tons per day @ 50½ rpm; *Cargo:* 1,692 tons; *Pass:* 200 1st, 1,100 3rd; *Crew:* 150.

The mizzen mast was wood to avoid distorting the compass.

1874 Aug 8: Maiden voyage Liverpool-New York.
1885 Transferred to Liverpool-Boston service.

1898 Sold to Italy.
1899 Broken up.

70 SCYTHIA (I)

Details as *Bothnia (69)* except:
T: 4,557 g, 2,907 n. **Dim** Length 420 ft
8 in (128.22 m).

1875 May 1: Maiden voyage Liverpool-
New York.
1884 July 9: First sailing on the
Liverpool-Boston service.
1898 Sept 20: First voyage Liverpool-New
York.
1899 Broken up in Italy.

71 GALLIA

Details as *Bothnia (69)* except: **Bt** 1879;
T: 4,809 g, 3,801 n. **Dim** Length 430 ft
1 in (131.09 m), width 44 ft 6 in
(13.56 m). **Eng** Inverted; Cyls: 64 in
(162.56 cm) and 2 × 80 in (203.2 cm);
Stroke: 60 in (152.4 cm). *Coal:* 110 tons
per day; *Pass:* 300 1st, 1,200 3rd.

1879 Apr 5: Maiden voyage Liverpool-
New York.
1896 Chartered to Cia Trasatlantica.
Renamed *Don Alvado de Bazan*.
1897 Sold for £21,250 to D. & C.
MacIver. Operated for Beaver Line.
Transferred with Beaver Line to Elder
Dempster ownership.
1900 Sold to Allan Line. Wrecked near
Sorel Point, Quebec, on her first voyage
for them. Salved and broken up at
Cherbourg.

72 CHERBOURG

Bt 1875 J. & G. Thomson & Co,
Glasgow; *T:* 1,614 g, 1,038 n. **Dim** 251 ft
2 in (76.56 m) × 32 ft 4 in (9.86 m) × 26 ft
5 in (8.08 m). **Eng** Sgl scr, compound,
vertical, direct acting; 2 cyls: 33½ in
(85.09 cm) and 58½ in (148.59 cm);
Stroke: 42 in (106.68 cm); 155 NHP;
2 boilers, 6 furnaces; *Stm P:* 60 lb;
10 kts; By builder. **H** Iron, 1 deck; *Coal:*
215 tons at 16 tons per day; *Cargo:* 2,121
tons; *Pass:* 4 1st.

1875 Built for Mediterranean service.
Cost £30,886.
1900 Jigger mast removed.
1909 Sold for £3,000 to Thos Ward and
broken up.

73 BRITISH QUEEN

Bt 1849 Wm Denny & Co, Dumbarton
(Yard No 18); *T:* 773 g. **Dim** 195 ft
(59.43 m) × 29 ft 2 in (8.89 m) × 18 ft
(5.49 m). **Eng** Sgl scr, vertical, direct
acting; 1 cyl: 48 in (121.92 cm); *Stroke:*
33 in (83.82 cm); 140 NHP; 1 boiler,
6 furnaces; *Stm P:* 18 lb; 10 kts. **H** Iron,
2 decks; *Pass:* 71 saloon, 166 steerage.

Sister of Margaret (8).

1849 Built for Charles MacIver.
Employed in the Mediterranean trade.
1850 Operated by Charles MacIver & Co,
later Burns & MacIver.
1856 Burns & MacIver became the British
& Foreign Steam Navigation Co.
1878 Cunard SS Co became the owners.
Liverpool-Havre. Re-engined by James
Jack & Co, Liverpool; Compound,
inverted; Cyls: 29 in (73.66 cm) and 54 in
(137.16 cm); *Stroke:* 36 in (91.44 cm);
125 NHP; 10 kts. *Coal:* 13 tons per day.
1898 Sold for breaking up after 49 years
of service.

74 OTTER

Bt 1880 Blackwood & Gordon, Port
Glasgow; *T:* 287 g, 270 n. **Dim** 142 ft
2 in (43.33 m) × 23 ft 2 in (7.06 m) × 10 ft
2 in (3.1 m). **Eng** Sgl scr, compound;
2 cyls: 14 in (35.56 cm) and 25 in
(63.5 cm); *Stroke:* 21 in (53.34 cm);
40 RHP; 10 kts; By builder. **H** Iron,
1 deck.

Water and stores ship at Liverpool.

75 CATALONIA

Bt 1881 J. & G. Thomson & Co,
Glasgow; *T:* 4,638 g, 3,093 n. **Dim** 429 ft

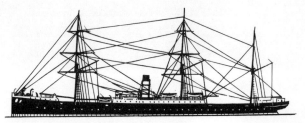

75

6 in (130.91 m) × 43 ft (13.11 m) × 33 ft
8 in (10.26 m). **Eng** Sgl scr, compound,
inverted, direct acting surface
condensing; 2 cyls: 51 in (129.54 cm) and
88 in (223.52 cm); *Stroke:* 60 in
(152.4 cm); 500 NHP; 2 boilers,
12 furnaces; *Stm P:* 78 lb; 12 kts; By
builder. **H** Iron, 2 decks; *Coal:* 975 tons
at 70 tons per day; *Pass:* 308 1st in 85
staterooms, 680 3rd; *Crew:* 118.

1881 Aug 6: Maiden voyage Liverpool-
New York.
1883 Apr 18: Transferred to Boston
service.
1899-1900 Boer War transport. Chartered
at 15 shillings per ton per month.
1901 Sold for £10,305 to Thos Ward and
broken up.

76 PAVONIA

Bt 1882 J. & G. Thomson & Co,
Glasgow; *T:* 5,588 g, 3,490 n. **Dim** 430 ft
6 in (131.22 m) × 46 ft 4 in (14.12 m) ×
34 ft 10 in (10.62 m). **Eng** Sgl scr,
compound, vertical, direct acting surface
condensers; 2 cyls: 52 in (132.08 cm) and
93 in (236.22 cm); *Stroke:* 66 in
(167.64 cm); 700 NHP; 6 boilers,
18 furnaces; *Stm P:* 90 lb; 12 kts; By
builder. **H** Iron, 4 decks and promenade
deck; *Coal:* 924 tons; *Cargo:* 4,000 tons;
Pass: 100 1st, 1,060 3rd.

*Entered service square rigged on fore and
main masts. Yards later removed. Steered
by steam from the bridge. Cost £137,123.*

1882 Sept 13: Maiden voyage Liverpool-
New York.

1884 Apr 23: Transferred to Liverpool-
Boston service.
1899 Feb 18: Arrived at the Azores with
engine trouble. Towed to Liverpool.
Made one final voyage.
1900 Sold to Thos Ward for £13,250 and
broken up.

77 CEPHALONIA

Details as *Pavonia (76)* except: **Bt** Laird
Bros, Birkenhead; *T:* 5,606 g, 3,515 n.
Pass: 200 1st, 1,500 3rd.

*Built in dry dock, the largest ship yet
built on Merseyside. Cost £141,671.*

1881 May 21: Keel laid.
1882 Aug 12: Trials.
Aug 23: Maiden voyage Liverpool-
Boston.
1899 Sept 12: Final Cunard voyage. Boer
War transport.
1900 Sold to the Chinese Eastern Railway
Co. Renamed *Hai Lor.*
1904 Sunk as a blockship at Port Arthur.

78 OREGON

Bt 1883 John Elder & Co, Fairfield,
Glasgow; *T:* 7,017 g, 3,529 n. **Dim** 520 ft
(158.5 m) oa, 501 ft (152.7 m) × 54 ft 2 in
(16.51 m) × 36 ft (10.97 m). **Eng** Sgl scr,
compound, inverted; 3 cyls: 70 in
(177.8 cm) and 2 × 104 in (264.16 cm);
Stroke: 72 in (182.88 cm); 3,000 NHP;
9 dbl ended boilers, 72 furnaces with
surface area 31,790 sq ft (2,967.06 sq m);
Stm P: 110 lb; 18½ kts; By builder.
H Iron, 4 decks, 1 ladies' and 4
gentlemen's bathrooms, 10 watertight
compartments, water ballast 237 tons

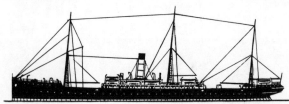

76-77

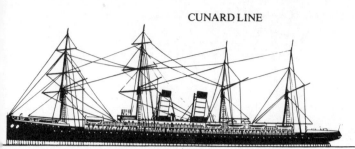

78

fore and 78 tons aft; *Coal:* 2,357 tons at 268 tons per day @ 64 rpm; *Cargo:* 2,427 tons; *Pass:* 472 1st in 155 staterooms, 1,000 3rd; *Crew:* 255.

Designed by Bryce Douglas.

1883 June: Launched.
Sept: Trials. Built for Guion Line.
Oct 7: Maiden voyage Liverpool-New York.
1884 June: Guion Line were unable to keep up their payments to John Elder & Co and *Oregon* was taken over by Cunard. Same name.
June 7: First Cunard voyage Liverpool-New York.
1885 During the Russian scare *Oregon* was taken over for use as an armed scouting cruiser.
Nov: Resumed Cunard service.
1886 Mar 14: 4.00 pm. While approaching New York *Oregon* was hit below the bridge by an unknown wooden schooner. She was 26 miles south-east of Fire Island, New York Bay. The watertight doors were clogged with coal dust and would not close properly. The ship flooded and sank. All 641 passengers and 255 crew together with 600 bags of mail were rescued by Norddeutscher Lloyd's *Fulda.* The unknown schooner is thought to have been the *Charles Morse,* which disappeared with all hands at about the same date.

79 SERVIA (I)

Bt 1881 J. & G. Thomson, Glasgow;

T: 7,391 g, 3,971 n. **Dim** 515 ft (156.97 m) × 52 ft 1 in (15.88 m) × 37 ft (11.28 m). **Eng** Sgl scr, compound; 3 cyls: 72 in (182.88 cm) and 2 × 100 in (254 cm); *Stroke:* 78 in (198.12 cm); 1,000 NHP; 6 dbl and 1 sgl ended boilers, 38 Fox type furnaces; By builder. **H** Siemen's Martin mild steel, 4 decks, double bottom (Cunard's first), 741 tons ballast, 10 gun mountings for service as an armed merchant cruiser, electric light (also Cunard's first); *Coal:* 1,800 tons at 190 tons per day; *Cargo:* 4,000 tons; *Pass:* 480 1st in 202 staterooms, 500 3rd; *Crew:* 252, of which 105 were stewards.

Cost £256,903. The mild steel hull saved 620 tons of metal.

1881 Nov 26: Maiden voyage Liverpool-New York. *Servia,* was, with the exception of *Great Eastern,* the largest ship afloat.
1893 Passenger accommodation refitted. 400 1st, 200 2nd, 500 3rd.
1899 Boer War transport at 21 shillings per ton per month.
1901 Sept 17: Final voyage to New York.
1902 Sold for £15,265 to Thos Ward and broken up at Preston, Lancashire.

80 AURANIA (I)

Bt 1883 J. & G. Thomson & Co, Glasgow; *T:* 7,269 g, 4,030 n. **Dim** 470 ft (143.26 m) × 57 ft 2 in (17.42 m) × 37 ft 2 in (11.33 m). **Eng** Sgl scr, compound, vertical, direct acting, surface condensing; 3 cyls: 68 in (172.72 cm) and

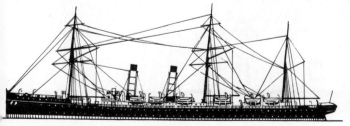

79

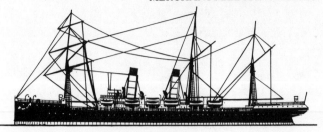

80

2 × 91 in (231.14 cm); *Stroke:* 72 in (182.88 cm); 1,500 NHP, 9,500 IHP; 6 dbl and 1 sgl ended boilers, 42 furnaces; *Stm P:* 90 lb; 16 kts; By builder. **H** Steel, 2 decks; *Coal:* 2,282 tons at 205 tons per day; *Cargo:* 2,755 tons; *Pass:* 500 1st in 213 staterooms, 700 3rd; *Crew:* 275.

Aurania's *narrow beam made her roll badly. Never a very popular ship.*

1883 June 23: Maiden voyage Liverpool-New York. During the voyage the engines failed due to overheating and the journey was completed under sail.
1899 Oct: Boer War transport No 20. Chartered at 16s 6d per ton per month.
1903 Nov: Inaugurated the Fiume-Trieste-Venice-Palermo-New York route.
1905 Sold for £14,850 and broken up in Italy.

81 UMBRIA

Bt 1884 John Elder & Co, Fairfield, Glasgow; *T:* 8,128 g, 3,699 n. **Dim** 519 ft (158.19 m) oa, 501 ft 6 in (152.86 m) × 57 ft 2 in (17.42 m) × 38 ft 2 in (11.63 m). **Eng** Sgl scr, compound; 3 cyls: 71 in (180.34 cm) and 2 × 105 in (266.7 cm); *Stroke:* 72 in (182.88 cm); 14,500 IHP; 9 dbl ended boilers, 36 furnaces; *Stm P:* 110 lb; 19 kts; By builder. **H** Steel, 4 decks, fcsle 112 ft (34.14 m), cellular double bottom; *Coal:* 300 tons per day @ 68 rpm; *Pass:* 550 1st, 800 3rd.

Umbria *and* Etruria (82) *were the last Cunarders to be built with auxiliary sail.*

The company went to John Elder for these two ships because of their satisfaction with the performance of Oregon (78).

1884 Nov 1: Maiden voyage Liverpool-New York.
1890 Apr 16: Rescued the crew of the barque *Magdalena* in mid-Atlantic.
1893 Passenger accommodation altered to 500 1st, 160 2nd, 800 3rd.
Dec 23: The propeller shaft fractured and the German *Bohemia,* of Hamburg America Line, took her in tow but the hawser snapped. *Umbria* drifted for three days before temporary repairs enabled her to reach New York.
1900-1 Boer War transport.
1903 An attempt was made to blow her up in New York. A case of dynamite was used.
1910 Sold for £20,000 to the Forth Shipbreaking Co and scrapped.

82 ETRURIA

Details as *Umbria (81)* except: **Bt** 1885; *T:* 8,120 g, 3,690 n. 19 kts, but slightly the faster of the pair.

1884 Sept: Launched.
1885 Apr 25: Maiden voyage Liverpool-New York. Prior to this she was hurriedly prepared as an armed merchant cruiser during the Russian scare.
1893 Accommodation altered as *Umbria (81).*
1901 Fitted with wireless.

81-82

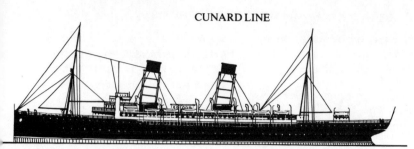

83-84

1902 When she lost her propeller sail was set for the Azores. But she was towed there by Frederick Leyland's *William Cliff*. Salvage of £11,000 was awarded. Cunard chartered Royal Mail's *Ebro* to bring home the passengers, and *Etruria* was towed to Liverpool.
1909 Sold for £16,750 and broken up at Preston, Lancashire.

83 CAMPANIA

Bt 1893 Fairfield Shipbuilding Co, Glasgow; *T:* 12,950 g, 4,974 n. **Dim** 620 ft (188.98 m) oa, 601 ft (183.18 m) × 65 ft 2 in (19.86 m) × 37 ft 8 in (11.48 m). **Eng** Tw scr, tpl exp; 2 × 5 cyls: 2 × 37 in (93.98 cm), 79 in (200.66 cm) and 2 × 98 in (248.92 cm); *Stroke:* 69 in (175.26 cm); 319 NHP; 12 boilers, 96 furnaces; *Stm P:* 165 lb; 21 kts; By builder. **H** Steel, 4 decks and promenade deck, fcsle 120 ft (36.58 m), the fcsle and poop later being extended to give a continuous upper deck; *Coal:* 12 tons per hour; *Pass:* 600 1st, 400 2nd, 1,000 3rd; *Crew:* 400.
1893 Apr 22: Maiden voyage Liverpool-New York. The largest and fastest ship afloat. Blue Riband holder on her second voyage.
1894 Aug: Made her fastest crossing in 5 days 9 hours and 21 minutes at an average speed of 21.59 knots.
1901 Fitted with wireless.
1914 Apr: Completed 250 round voyages. Chartered to Anchor Line for five voyages.
Oct 15: Sold for breaking up but purchased by the Admiralty and

converted into a seaplane carrier.
1918 Nov 5: Broke from her moorings, collided with the battle cruiser *Glorious* in the Firth of Forth and sank. All crew saved.

84 LUCANIA

Details as *Campania (83)* except: *T:* 12,952 g, 4,975 n.
1893 Sept 2: Maiden voyage Liverpool-New York.
Oct: Took Blue Riband.
1894 In August, September and October broke the record with average speeds of 21.49 kts, 21.66 kts and 21.75 kts respectively.
1901 Marconi wireless fitted.
1903 Oct 10: Became the first liner to publish the Cunard bulletin, made up from radio news.
1909 Aug 14: Burnt out at Huskisson Dock, Liverpool, and condemned. Sold to Thos Ward and broken up at Swansea. *Lucania* steamed there under her own power and made 17 kts.

85 CARINTHIA (I)

Bt 1895 London & Glasgow Shipbuilding & Engineering Co, Glasgow; *T:* 5,598 g, 3,623 n. **Dim** 445 ft (135.63 m) × 49 ft (14.93 m) × 31 ft 10 in (9.7 m). **Eng** Tw scr, tpl exp; 2 × 3 cyls: 22½ in (57.15 cm), 36½ in (92.71 cm) and 60 in (152.4 cm); *Stroke:* 48 in (121.92 cm); 766 NHP; 2 dbl and 1 sgl ended boilers, 14 furnaces; *Stm P:* 180 lb; 13½ kts; By builder. **H** Steel, 3 decks, fcsle 84 ft (25.6 m), bridge 163 ft (49.68 m), poop

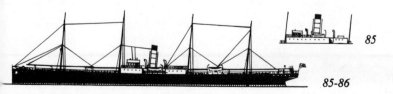

85

85-86

88 ft (26.82 m); *Coal:* 768 tons; *Cargo:* 6,232 tons.

1895 Built for North Atlantic cargo service.
1900 Boer War. Carried mules New Orleans-Capetown.
July 30: Stranded off Cape Gravoes, coast of Haiti. No lives lost.

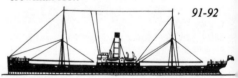

87-89

86 SYLVANIA (I)

Details as *Carinthia (85)* except: *T:* 5,598 g, 3,623 n. **H** Poop 98 ft (29.87 m).

1895 North Atlantic cargo services.
1910 Broken up in Italy.

87 PAVIA (I)

Bt 1897 Workman, Clark & Co, Belfast; *T:* 2,945 g, 1,885 n. **Dim** 332 ft 1 in (101.22 m) × 45 ft 7 in (13.89 m) × 15 ft (4.57 m). **Eng** Sgl scr, tpl exp; 3 cyls: 24 in (60.96 cm), 40 in (101.6 cm) and 66 in (167.64 cm); *Stroke:* 45 in (114.3 cm); 354 NHP; 2 sgl ended boilers, 6 furnaces; *Stm P:* 200 lb; 10½ kts; By Barclay Curle & Co, Glasgow. **H** Steel, 1 deck and spar deck, fcsle 33 ft (10.06 m), bridge 76 ft (23.16 m), poop 25 ft (7.62 m); *Coal:* 480 tons at 10 tons per day.

Identification note: No poop deckhouse.

1897 Mediterranean services.
1928 Sold. Broken up.

88 TYRIA

Details as *Pavia (87)* except: *T:* 2,936 g, 1,884 n.

1897 Mediterranean services.
1928 Broken up.

89 CYPRIA

Details as *Pavia (87)* except: **Bt** 1898; *T:* 2,950 g, 1,884 n. **Eng** By builder.

1898 Mediterranean services.
1928 Sold for breaking up.

90 ULTONIA

Bt 1898 C. S. Swan & Hunter, Newcastle; *T:* 8,845 g, 5,748 n. **Dim** 500 ft (152.4 m) × 57 ft 5 in (17.5 m) × 33 ft 10 in (10.31 m). **Eng** Tw scr, tpl exp; 2 × 3 cyls: 23½ in (59.69 cm), 38½ in (97.79 cm) and 68 in (172.72 cm); *Stroke:* 48 in (121.92 cm); 863 NHP; 5 sgl ended boilers, 15 furnaces; *Stm P:* 200 lb; 12½ kts; By Sir Christopher Furness, Westgarth & Co, Middlesbrough. **H** Steel, 2 decks, bridge 140 ft (42.67 m).

1898 Built for Sir Christopher Furness and purchased on the stocks. Employed on the cargo and cattle trade.
1899 Feb 28: Maiden voyage Liverpool-Boston.
1903 Cunard obtained a ten year Hungarian Government emigrant contract. *Ultonia,* together with *Carpathia (95), Pannonia (97)* and *Slavonia (98)* were placed on the Fiume-Gibraltar-New York route.
1917 June 27: Torpedoed 350 miles west of Land's End. One passenger and one crewman lost.

91-92

91 VERIA

Bt 1899 Armstrong Whitworth & Co, Newcastle; *T:* 3,229 g, 2,064 n. **Dim** 330 ft 6 in (100.74 m) × 45 ft 2 in (13.77 m) × 16 ft 9 in (5.11 m). **Eng** Sgl scr, tpl exp; 3 cyls: 24 in (60.96 cm), 40 in (101.6 cm) and 66 in (167.64 cm); *Stroke:* 45 in (114.3 cm); 361 NHP;

90

93-94

Stm P: 200 lb; 10½ kts. **H** Steel, fcsle 42 ft (12.8 m), bridge 78 ft (23.77 m), poop 41 ft (12.5 m).

1899 Mediterranean service.
1915 Dec 8: Torpedoed 24 miles from Alexandria. No lives lost.

92 BRESCIA (I)

Details as *Veria (91)* except: **Bt** 1903 J. L. Thompson & Co, Sunderland; *T:* 3,255 g, 2,058 n. **Dim** Length 330 ft (100.58 m). **Eng** By Wallsend Slipway Co, Newcastle. **H** Fcsle 39 ft (11.89 m), bridge 80 ft (24.38 m), poop 39 ft (11.89 m).

93 IVERNIA (I)

Bt 1900 C. S. Swan & Hunter, Newcastle; *T:* 14,067 g, 9,058 n. **Dim** 582 ft (177.39 m) × 64 ft 10 in (19.76 m) × 37 ft 8 in (11.48 m). **Eng** Tw scr, quad exp; 2 × 4 cyls: 28½ in (72.39 cm), 41 in (104.14 cm), 58½ in (148.59 cm) and 84 in (213.36 cm); *Stroke:* 54 in (137.16 cm); 1,668 NHP; 9 sgl ended boilers, 27 furnaces; *Stm P:* 210 lb; 16 kts; By Wallsend Slipway Co, Newcastle. **H** Steel, 3 decks, bridge 275 ft (83.82 m); *Coal:* 152 tons per day; *Cargo:* 14,000 tons; *Pass:* 164 1st, 200 2nd, 1,600 3rd.

Cost £400,000. The funnel on Ivernia, *and* Saxonia (94), *was 106 ft (32.31 m) tall from boat deck to rim cowl.*

1900 Apr 14: Maiden voyage Liverpool-New York. Normal service was Liverpool-Queenstown (Cobh)-Boston.
1911 May 24: Hit Daunt's Rock, Queenstown. Out of service for five months.
Nov: New York-Mediterranean service. *Pass:* 485 cabin, 978 3rd.
1912 Mar: Fiume-Trieste-Messina-Palermo-Naples-Funchal-New York

service.
1914 Sept: Requisitioned as a troop transport.
1917 Jan 1: Torpedoed by *UB-47* 58 miles off Cape Matapan, Italy, with 2,800 troops on board en route for Alexandria. 87 troops and 36 crew lost. *UB-47* had been sent overland to Pola and reassembled there. Her commander, Lt Cdr Steinbauer, had sunk the French battleship *Gaulois* on Dec 27 1916.

94 SAXONIA (I)

Details as *Ivernia (93)* except: **Bt** John Brown & Co, Glasgow; *T:* 14,281 g, 9,100 n. **Eng** Cyls: 29 in (73.66 cm), 41½ in (105.41 cm), 59 in (149.86 cm) and 84 in (213.36 cm); 1,700 NHP; By builder.

1900 May 22: Maiden voyage Liverpool-Queenstown (Cobh)-Boston.
1909 Used during the winter on New York-Mediterranean services.
1912 Placed on Fiume-New York service with *Ivernia*.
1914 Troopship. Then used as German prisoner of war accommodation ship.
1915 May 1: Returned to Liverpool-New York service. Later withdrawn.
1919 Jan 25: Resumed New York service. May 14: Placed on London-New York route after reconditioning. Funnel shortened by 16 ft (4.88 m).
1920 Apr 12: Placed on Hamburg-New York route.
1925 Mar: Broken up in Holland.

95 CARPATHIA

Bt 1902 C. S. Swan & Hunter, Newcastle; *T:* 13,603 g, 8,660 n. **Dim** 540 ft (164.59 m) × 64 ft 6 in (19.66 m) × 37 ft 4 in (11.38 m). **Eng** Tw scr, quad exp; 2 × 4 cyls: 26 in (66.04 cm), 37 in

95

(93.98 cm), 53 in (134.62 cm) and 76 in (193.04 cm); *Stroke:* 54 in (137.16 cm); 1,341 NHP; 7 sgl ended boilers, 21 furnaces, forced draught; *Stm P:* 210 lb; 17 kts; By Wallsend Slipway Co, Newcastle. **H** Steel, 3 decks, bridge 290 ft (88.39 m); *Pass:* 204 2nd, 1,500 3rd (486 in rooms, remainder in dormitories).

1903 May 5: Maiden voyage Liverpool-Queenstown (Cobh)-Boston.
1904 Mar 5: New York-Mediterranean services.
1905 Sept: New York-Funchal-Gibraltar-Naples-Palermo-Messina-Trieste-Fiume service with occasional calls at the Azores or Lisbon.
1912 Apr 14: En route to Fiume Captain A. H. Rostron brought *Carpathia* to the rescue of the 705 survivors from *Titanic,* arriving at the scene around 4 am.
1918 July 17: Sunk by three torpedoes 170 miles west of Bishop's Rock. Five lost in the boiler room. 215 saved by HMS *Snowdrop.*

96

96 SKIRMISHER

Bt 1884 J. & G. Thomson & Co, Glasgow; *T:* 612 g, 194 n. **Dim** 165 ft (50.29 m) × 32 ft 2 in (9.8 m) × 15 ft (4.57 m). **Eng** Twr scr, compound; 2 × 2 cyls: 21 in (53.34 cm) and 42 in (106.68 cm); *Stroke:* 32½ in (81.28 cm); 168 NHP; 10 kts; By builder. **H** Steel, 1 deck; *Pass:* 1,200 and their baggage.

Cunard tender at Liverpool.

97 PANNONIA

Bt 1903 John Brown & Co, Glasgow; *T:* 9,851 g, 6,210 n. **Dim** 486 ft 6 in (148.28 m) × 59 ft 3 in (18.06 m) × 33 ft (10.06 m). **Eng** Tw scr, tpl exp; 2 × 3 cyls: 25½ in (64.77 cm), 42 in (106.68 cm) and 70 in (117.8 cm); *Stroke:* 48 in (121.92 cm); *Stm P:* 190 lb; 12 kts. **H** Steel, 2 decks; *Pass:* 91 1st, 71 2nd, 2,066 emigrants in dormitories.

1903 Laid down for Sir Christopher Furness. Purchased on the stocks.
1904-14 Fiume-New York service.
1915-19 London-New York route.
1919-21 Trieste-New York route.
1922 Oct: Sold for breaking up at Hamburg.

98 SLAVONIA

Bt 1903 James Laing & Co, Sunderland; *T:* 10,606 g, 6,725 n. **Dim** 510 ft (155.45 m) × 59 ft 6 in (18.14 m) × 34 ft 7 in (10.54 m). **Eng** Tw scr, tpl exp; 2 × 3 cyls: 24 in (60.96 cm), 40 in (101.6 cm) and 70 in (177.8 cm); *Stroke:* 48 in (121.92 cm); 929 NHP; 6 sgl ended boilers, 18 furnaces; *Stm P:* 200 lb; 12½ kts; By Wallsend Slipway Co, Newcastle. **H** Steel, 3 decks, bridge 184 ft (56.08 m); *Pass:* 71 1st, 74 2nd, 1,954 emigrants in dormitories.

1903 Laid down as *Yamuna,* British India SN Co. Purchased on the stocks for Fiume service.
June 20: Completed.
1904 Fiume-Trieste-Messina-Palermo-Naples-Gibraltar-New York service.
Mar 17: Maiden voyage to Trieste.

97

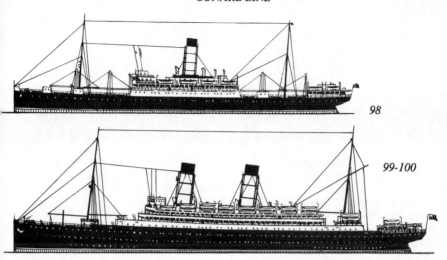

98

99-100

1909 June 10: Wrecked on Flores, Azores, en route to Trieste. No lives lost.

99 CARONIA (I)

Bt 1905 John Brown & Co, Glasgow; *T:* 19,687 g, 10,306 n. **Dim** 675 ft (205.74 m) oa, 650 ft (198.12 m) × 72 ft 2 in (22 m) × 40 ft 2 in (12.24 m). **Eng** Tw scr, quad exp; 2 × 4 cyls: 39 in (99.06 cm), 54½ in (138.43 cm), 77 in (195.58 cm) and 110 in (279.4 cm); *Stroke:* 66 in (167.64 cm); 3,353 NHP; 8 dbl and 5 sgl ended boilers, 63 furnaces; *Stm P:* 210 lb; 18 kts; By builder. **H** Steel, 3 decks and shelter deck, bridge 400 ft (121.92 m); *Pass:* 300 1st, 350 2nd, 1,100 3rd.

The first Cunarder to be fitted with Stone-Lloyd bridge controlled watertight door closing system.

1905 Feb 25: Maiden voyage Liverpool-New York.
1914 Armed merchant cruiser.
1919 Jan 11: Resumed Liverpool-New York service.
1920 Converted to oil fuel.
1922 Placed on Hamburg-Southampton-New York run.
1923 Reverted to Liverpool sailings. Placed on Quebec-Montreal route.
1924 Passenger accommodation remodelled; 425 cabin, 365 tst, 650 3rd.
1926 Placed on London-Southampton-Havre-New York route.
1931 Laid up. Sold for £20,000 to Hughes Bolckow for scrapping.

1932 Resold for £39,000 to Japanese breakers. Renamed *Taiseiyo Maru* for the journey.

100 CARMANIA (I)

Details as *Caronia (99)* except:
T: 19,524 g, 9,982 n. **Dim** Length 650 ft 4 in (198.22 m). **Eng** 3 steam direct action turbines; 20 kts.

Cunard wished to test in twin ships the relative effectiveness of turbines against a piston driven ship. In service Carmania *was a good ½ kt faster.*

1905 Dec 2: Maiden voyage Liverpool-New York.
1912 June 4: Caught fire at Liverpool but not seriously damaged.
1913 Oct 9: Rescued the survivors from the Canadian Northern SS Co's *Volturno,* which had caught fire. But for the intervention of the oil tanker *Narragansett,* which poured oil on the wild seas, it is likely that more than 133 out of the 654 aboard would have been lost.
1914 Aug 15: Requisitioned to be an armed merchant cruiser.
Sept 14: Fought with and sank the German armed merchant cruiser *Cap Trafalgar,* Hamburg Sud Amerika Line, off Trinidad. *Carmania* herself was hit 79 times.
1918 Dec 21: Resumed Liverpool-Queenstown (Cobh)-New York service.
1923 Converted to oil burning.
1924 Passenger accommodation altered;

425 cabin, 365 tst, 650 3rd. Inaugurated Liverpool-Belfast-Quebec-Montreal sailings.
1925 Liverpool-Boston-New York route.
1926 London-Southampton-Plymouth-Havre-New York service.
1931 Aug: Final Cunard voyage then laid up at Tilbury.
1932 Broken up at Blyth.

101 LUSITANIA

Bt 1907 John Brown & Co, Glasgow; *T:* 31,550 g, 9,145 n. **Dim** 790 ft (240.79 m) oa, 762 ft 2 in (232.31 m) × 87 ft 9 in (26.75 m) × 56 ft 5 in (17.2 m). **Eng** Quad scr, 4 direct acting Parsons steam turbines by builder, 2 HP and 2 LP; *Stm P:* 195 lb; 25 kts. **H** Steel, 5 decks and shelter deck, fcsle 305 ft (92.96 m); *Coal:* 850 tons per day; *Pass:* 563 1st, 464 2nd, 1,138 3rd.

To accommodate Lusitania *and* Mauretania (102) *the Mersey Docks and Harbour Board had to remove 200,000 tons of sand from abreast the Liverpool floating landing stage. Special buoys were also installed at the Sloyne in mid river. The landing stage had to have elevated platforms built from which the gangways could reach the upper decks.*

1907 June 7: Launched by Lady Inverclyde. The world's largest ship.
Sept 7: Maiden voyage Liverpool-Queenstown (Cobh)-New York.
Oct: On her second voyage *Lusitania* took the transatlantic record from Norddeutscher Lloyd's *Kaiser Wilhelm II* with an average speed of 23.99 kts from Queenstown to Sandy Hook, the passage time being 4 days 19 hours 52 minutes. The Blue Riband of the Atlantic was held by Britain for the next 22 years.
1915 May 7: Torpedoed by *U-20* off the Old Head of Kinsale whilst approaching Queenstown. One or two torpedoes hit between the first and second funnels. The ship heeled over to starboard and sank within 18 minutes. 1,198 lives were lost.

102 MAURETANIA (I)

Details as *Lusitania (101)* except;
Bt Swan, Hunter & Wigham Richardson, Newcastle; *T:* 31,938 g, 8,948 n.**Eng** By Wallsend Slipway Co, Newcastle.

1907 Nov 16: Maiden voyage Liverpool-Queenstown (Cobh)-New York. On return leg she took the record from *Lusitania* with a run of 23.69 kts average between Ambrose Lightship and Queenstown and a passage time of 4 days 22 hours and 29 minutes.
1908 *Lusitania* retook the Blue Riband.
1909 July: *Mauretania* crossed in 4 days 17 hours and 20 minutes at 25.89 kts, and held the record until 1929 when Norddeutscher Lloyd's *Bremen* took it from her.
1914 Aug: Commissioned as a transport. Later used as a hospital ship.
1916-17 Laid up at Greenock.
1917 US troop transport.
1919 June 27: Resumed Cunard service Southampton-New York.
1921 July 25: Damaged by fire at Southampton. Repaired and converted to oil fuel. *Pass:* 589 1st, 400 2nd, 767 3rd.
1922 Mar 25: Back in service Southampton-Cherbourg-New York.
1929 Aug: Improved her own Atlantic record with an average speed of 27.65 kts, crossing in 4 days 17 hours and 50 minutes.
1931 Hull painted white for cruising. Known as the 'Grand Old Lady'.
1934 Sept 26: Final voyage New York-Plymouth-Cherbourg-Southampton. Coincidentally this was the date of the launching, at John Brown's, of *Queen*

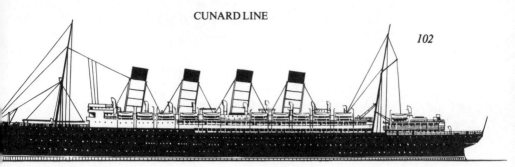

102

Mary (155). Withdrawn from service.
1935 Apr 2: Sold to Metal Industries for scrap.
July 1: Left Southampton for Rosyth, Firth of Forth. To pass under the Forth Bridge her masts had to be cut off at funnel height.

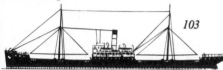

103

103 PHRYGIA (I)

Bt 1900 Sir Raylton Dixon & Co, Middlesbrough; *T:* 3,352 g. **Dim** 340 ft (103.63 m) × 47 ft 1 in (14.36 m) × 15 ft 5 in (4.7 m). **Eng** Sgl scr, tpl exp; 3 cyls: 25 in (63.5 cm), 40 in (101.6 cm) and 66 in (167.64 cm); *Stroke:* 45 in (114.3 cm); 337 NHP; 2 sgl ended boilers; *Stm P:* 180 lb; 10 kts; By Sir Christopher Furness & Westgarth & Co. H Steel, 1 deck and spar deck, fcsle 36 ft (10.97 m), bridge 78 ft (23.77 m), poop 30 ft (9.14 m).

1900 Built as *Oro* for Plate SS Co (Gellatly, Hankey & Co).
1909 Purchased by Cunard. Renamed *Phrygia.*
1915 Sank a German U-boat.
1928 Sold.
1933 Broken up.

104 THRACIA

Bt 1895 Sir Raylton Dixon & Co, Middlesbrough; *T:* 2,891 g, 1,850 n. **Dim** 310 ft (94.49 m) × 44 ft 1 in (13.44 m) × 15 ft 7 in (4.75 m). **Eng** Sgl scr, tpl exp; 3 cyls: 24 in (60.96 cm), 36 in (91.44 m) and 59 in (149.86 cm); *Stroke:* 42 in (106.68 cm); 258 NHP; 2 sgl ended boilers; *Stm P:* 180 lb; 10 kts; By T. Richardson & Sons, Hartlepool. H Steel, 1 deck, fcsle 34 ft (10.36 m), bridge 74 ft (22.56 m), poop 30 ft (9.14 m).

1895 Built as *Orono* for Plate SS Co (Gellatly, Hankey & Co).
1909 Purchased and renamed *Thracia.*
1917 Mar 27: Torpedoed off Belle Isle, France, carrying iron ore from Bilbao. Two survivors.

105 LYCIA (I)

Details as *Thracia (104)* except: **Bt** 1896; *T:* 2,715 g, 1,739 n. **Dim** 308 ft (93.88 m) × 43 ft 4 in (13.21 m) × 14 ft 8 in (4.47 m). **Eng** HP cyls: 23 in (58.42 cm); By NE Marine, Newcastle.

1896 Built as *Oceano* for Plate SS Co (Gellatly, Hankey & Co).
1909 Purchased and renamed *Lycia.*
1917 Feb 11: Torpedoed off the South Bishop Light.

106 FRANCONIA (I)

Bt 1911 Swan, Hunter & Wigham Richardson, Newcastle; *T:* 18,150 g, 11,247 n. **Dim** 600 ft 3 in (182.96 m) × 71 ft 3 in (21.72 m) × 40 ft 5 in (12.32 m). **Eng** Tw scr, quad exp; 2 × 4 cyls: 33 in (83.82 cm), 47 in (119.38 cm), 67 in (170.18 cm) and 95 in (241.3 cm); *Stroke:* 60 in (152.4 cm); 2,170 NHP; 6 dbl ended boilers, 48 furnaces; *Stm P:* 210 lb; 17 kts; By Wallsend Slipway Co, Newcastle. H Steel, 3 decks and shelter deck, fcsle and bridge 491 ft (149.66 m); *Pass:* 300 1st, 350 2nd, 2,200 3rd.

1911 Feb 25: Maiden voyage Liverpool-Queenstown (Cobh)-Boston. New York-Mediterranean route in winter.
1915 Feb 15: Requisitioned. Became a troopship.
1916 Oct 4: Torpedoed and sunk by *UB-47* 200 miles north-east of Malta. 12 lost.

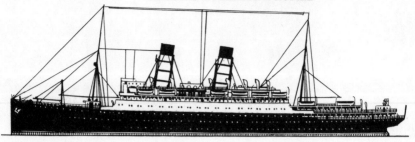

106-107

107 LACONIA (I)

Details as *Franconia (106)* except:
T: 18,099 g, 11,226 n.

1912 Jan 20: Maiden voyage Liverpool-Queenstown (Cobh)-New York, then placed on the Boston service.
1914 Requisitioned and converted into an armed merchant cruiser. Used as the HQ ship in Tanganyika during operations against the German cruiser *Konigsberg.*
1916 Sept 9: Returned to commercial service.
1917 Feb 25: Sunk by *U-50* 160 miles from Fastnet, Ireland. The first torpedo failed to sink her but a second exploded in the engine room. Of 292 aboard only six passengers and six crew were lost.

108 CARIA

Bt 1900 Tyne Iron SB Co, Newcastle; *T:* 3,032 g, 1,928 n. **Dim** 318 ft (96.93 m) × 43 ft (13.1 m) × 25 ft 2 in (7.67 m). **Eng** Sgl scr, tpl exp; 3 cyls: 24 in (60.96 cm), 39 in (99.06 cm) and 64 in (162.56 cm); *Stroke:* 42 in (106.68 cm); 265 NHP; 10 kts; By Wallsend Slipway Co, Newcastle. **H** Steel, 1 deck, fcsle 35 ft (10.67 m), bridge 30 ft (9.14 m), poop 29 ft (8.84 m).

1900 Built as *Clematis* for Stag Line (J. Robinson & Sons).
1911 Purchased and renamed *Caria.*
1915 Nov 6: Torpedoed by U-boat in the Mediterranean.

109 ASCANIA (I)

Bt 1911 Swan, Hunter & Wigham Richardson, Newcastle; *T:* 9,111 g, 5,699 n. **Dim** 466 ft 6 in (142.19 m) × 56 ft 1 in (17.1 m) × 29 ft 5 in (8.97 m). **Eng** Tw scr, tpl exp; 3 cyls: 25½ in (64.77 cm), 41 in (104.14 cm) and 68 in (172.72 cm); *Stroke:* 48 in (121.92 cm); 4 sgl ended boilers; *Stm P:* 180 lb; 13 kts; By Palmers Co, Newcastle. **H** Steel, 2 decks and shelter deck, fcsle 52 ft (15.85 m), bridge 187 ft (57 m), poop 60 ft (18.29 m); *Pass:* 200 1st, 1,500 3rd.

1911 Laid down as *Gerona* for Thomson Line. Taken over before completion and renamed *Ascania.*
May 23: Maiden voyage Southampton-Quebec-Montreal.
1918 June 13: Wrecked 20 miles east of Cape Ray, Newfoundland, en route Liverpool-Montreal in ballast. No lives lost.

110 AUSONIA (I)

Bt 1909 Swan, Hunter & Wigham Richardson, Newcastle; *T:* 7,907 g, 4,955 n. **Dim** 450 ft 6 in (137.31 m) × 54 ft 2 in (16.51 m) × 29 ft 2 in (8.89 m). **Eng** Tw scr, tpl exp; 3 cyls: 25½ in (64.77 cm), 41 in (104.14 cm) and 68 in (172.72 cm); *Stroke:* 48 in (121.92 cm); 888 NHP; 4 sgl ended boilers; *Stm P:* 180 lb; 12 kts; By Palmers Co, Newcastle. **H** Steel, 2 decks and shelter deck, bridge 117 ft (35.66 m); *Pass:* 50 2nd, 1,000 3rd.

109

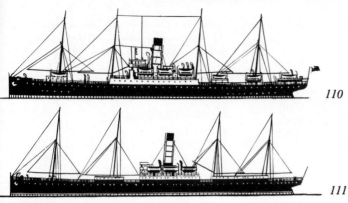

110

111

1909 Built as *Tortona* for Thomson Line.
1911 Acquired and renamed *Ausonia*.
May 16: First voyage for Cunard
London-Southampton-Quebec-Montreal.
1917 June: Torpedoed but reached port.
1918 May 30: Torpedoed and sunk off
Fastnet Rock, Ireland. 44 lost. The
survivors were in their lifeboats for eight
days before being rescued by HMS
Zennia.

111 ALBANIA (I)

Bt 1900 C. S. Swan & Hunter, Newcastle;
T: 7,682 g, 5,012 n. **Dim** 461 ft 6 in
(140.67 m) × 52 ft 1 in (15.88 m) × 38 ft
8 in (11.79 m). **Eng** Tw scr, tpl exp; 2 × 3
cyls: 22 in (55.88 cm), 37 in (93.98 cm)
and 64 in (162.56 cm); *Stroke:* 42 in
(106.68 cm); 783 NHP; *Stm P:* 200 lb;
11 kts. **H** Steel, 2 decks and shelter deck;
Pass: 50 1st, 800 3rd.

1900 Built as *Consuelo* for the Wilson
Line. Hull-New York service.
1909 Sold to Thomson Line. Renamed
Cairnrona for their Newcastle-London-
Canada route.
1911 Purchased by Cunard and renamed
Albania.
May 2: First Cunard sailing London-
Southampton-Quebec-Montreal.
1912 Sold to Andrew Weir & Co.
Renamed *Poleric*.

112 ALAUNIA (I)

Bt 1913 Scotts SB Co, Greenock;
T: 13,405 g, 8,464 n. **Dim** 520 ft 5 in
(158.62 m) × 64 ft 8 in (19.71 m) × 42 ft
6 in (12.95 m). **Eng** Tw scr, quad exp;
4 dbl ended boilers, 32 furnaces; By
builder. **H** Steel, 3 decks, bridge 243 ft
(74.07 m); *Pass:* 520 2nd, 1,540 3rd.

Built for Canadian trade.

1913 Dec 3: Maiden voyage Liverpool-
Portland.
1914 Aug 27: Sailed for Canada for
trooping for six months.
1916 May 11: Commenced sailings
London-Falmouth-Plymouth-New York.
Oct 19: Mined two miles from the Royal
Sovereign lightship. Two lost.

113 ANDANIA (I)

Details as *Alaunia (112)* except: **Eng** Tpl
exp.

1913 July 17: Maiden voyage London-
Southampton-Quebec-Montreal.
1916 Joined *Alaunia* on the London-New
York route.
1918 Jan 27: Torpedoed near Rathlin
Island Lighthouse. Seven lost.

114 AURANIA (II)

Details as *Alaunia (112)* except: **Bt** 1917

112-114

Swan, Hunter & Wigham Richardson, Newcastle; *T:* 13,936 g, 8,499 n. **Eng** 4 geared turbines; By Wallsend Slipway Co, Newcastle.

1917 Mar: Entered service.
1918 Feb 4: Torpedoed 15 miles northwest of Inishtrahull, Donegal. Eight killed. Taken in tow but the hawser parted and *Aurania* went ashore near Tobermory and was lost.

115 AQUITANIA

Bt 1914 John Brown, Clydebank, Glasgow; *T:* 45,647 g, 21,998 n. **Dim** 901 ft (274.62 m) oa, 868 ft 7 in (264.74 m) × 97 ft (29.57 m) × 49 ft 8 in (15.14 m). **Eng** Quad scr, 4 direct acting steam turbines, 3 HP and 1 LP; 56,000 SHP; *Stm P:* 195 lb; 23 kts; By builder. **H** Steel, 4 decks and shelter deck, indoor swimming pool; *Fuel:* 8,638 tons oil at 680 tons per day; *Cargo:* 141,000 cu ft (3,993 cu m); *Pass:* 597 1st, 614 2nd, 2,052 3rd; *Crew:* 972.

The last liner built with four funnels.

1914 May 30: Maiden voyage Liverpool-Queenstown-New York. Completed three round voyages before First World War. Aug: Taken over as an armed merchant cruiser but did not enter service as such, being classed as too large.
1915 Dazzle painted. Used as a troopship to Dardanelles.
1916-17 Hospital ship.
1917-18 Brought 60,000 US troops to Europe in nine voyages.
1919 May: Cunard Commodore Sir James Charles took her out of Southampton without tugs.
June 14: Resumed North Atlantic service Southampton-Cherbourg-New York.
1919-20 Converted to oil burning. Fitted with Gyro compass.
1920-39 Southampton-Cherbourg-New York route.
1939 Nov 21: Requisitioned as a troopship.
1948 Used to repatriate US troops.
May: Commenced 12 austerity class Canadian Government voyages Southampton-Halifax.
1949 Nov: Final Cunard sailing Halifax-Southampton, arriving Dec 1.

1950 Feb: Sold to British Iron & Steel Corporation. Broken up at Gareloch, Scotland. During her career *Aquitania* steamed over three million miles and carried almost 1,200,000 passengers. She crossed the Atlantic 475 times.

116 VANDALIA (I)

Bt 1912 Short Bros, Sunderland; *T:* 7,333 g, 4,618 n. **Dim** 425 ft (129.54 m) × 56 ft 3 in (17.15 m) × 36 ft 4 in (11.07 m). **Eng** Sgl scr, quad exp; 4 cyls: 25½ in (66.77 cm), 36½ in (92.71 cm), 52½ in (133.35 cm) and 76 in (193.04 cm); *Stroke:* 54 in (137.16 cm); 601 NHP; 3 sgl ended boilers, 9 furnaces; *Stm P:* 220 lb; 12 kts; By NE Marine Engine Co, Newcastle. **H** Steel, 2 decks and shelter deck.

1912 Built as *Anglo-Californian* for Lawther & Latta.
1915 Purchased and renamed *Vandalia*.
1918 June 9: Torpedoed and sunk.

117 VINOVIA

Bt 1906 Short Bros, Sunderland; *T:* 7,046 g, 4,545 n. **Dim** 418 ft 2 in (127.46 m) × 54 ft 5 in (16.59 m) × 37 ft 2 in (11.33 m). **Eng** Sgl scr, quad exp; 4 cyls: 24½ in (62.23 cm), 35 in (88.9 cm), 51 in (129.54 cm) and 74 in (187.96 cm); *Stroke:* 54 in (137.16 cm); 539 NHP; 3 sgl ended boilers, 9 furnaces; *Stm P:* 220 lb; 12 kts; By NE Marine Engine Co, Newcastle. **H** Steel, 2 decks.

1906 Built as *Anglo-Bolivian* for Lawther & Latta.
1915 Purchased and renamed *Vinovia*.
1917 Dec 19: Torpedoed and sunk in English Channel.

118 VALERIA

Bt 1913 Russell & Co, Port Glasgow; *T:* 5,865 g, 3,055 n. **Dim** 423 ft 2 in (129.98 m) × 56 ft 2 in (17.12 m) × 34 ft 6 in (10.52 m). **Eng** Sgl scr, tpl exp; 3 cyls: 25 in (63.5 cm), 36 in (91.44 cm) and 51 in (129.54 cm); *Stroke:* 42 in (106.68 cm); 540 NHP; *Stm P:* 200 lb; 12 kts; By Rankin & Blackmore, Greenock. **H** Steel, 2 decks.

1913 Built as *Den of Airlie* for Charles Barrie, Dundee.

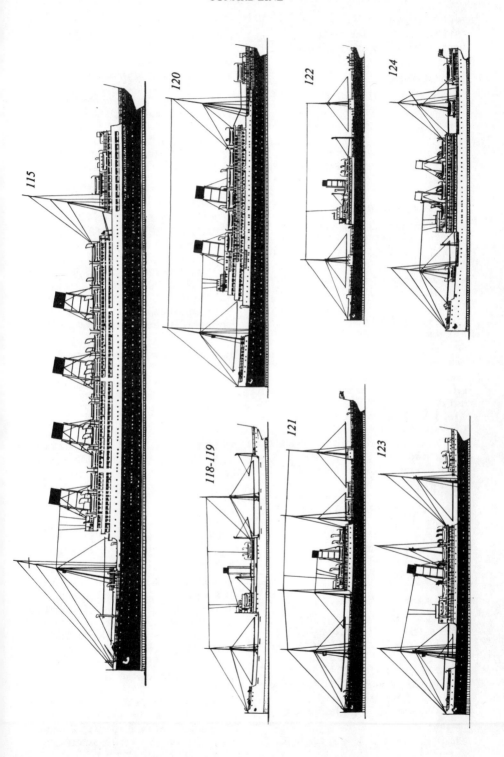

1915 Purchased and renamed *Valeria*.
1918 Mar 21: Burnt out on Taylor's
Bank, River Mersey. A total loss.

119 VOLODIA

Details as *Valeria (118)* except:
T: 5,689 g, 3,010 n.

1913 Built as *Den of Ogil* for Charles
Barrie, Dundee.
1915 Purchased and renamed *Volodia*.
1917 Aug 21: Torpedoed 285 miles west
of Ushant. Ten killed.

120 ROYAL GEORGE

Bt 1907 Fairfield Co, Glasgow;
T: 11,146 g, 5,685 n. **Dim** 525 ft 8 in
(160.22 m) × 60 ft 2 in (18.34 m) × 27 ft
(8.23 m). **Eng** Tpl scr, 3 steam turbines;
4 dbl and 4 sgl ended boilers, 48
furnaces; *Stm P:* 180 lb; 14 kts; By
builder. **H** Steel, 3 decks, fcsle 70 ft
(21.33 m), bridge 308 ft (93.88 m); *Coal:*
170 tons per day; *Pass:* 344 1st, 210 2nd,
560 3rd.

1907 Built as *Heliopolis* for the Egyptian
Mail SS Co. Marseilles-Alexandria
service. (Her sister *Royal Edward,* built
as *Cairo,* was lost at Gallipoli.)
1914 Sold to Canadian Northern Railway
Co for Bristol-Quebec route.
1916 Cunard took over the five steamers
of Canadian Northern Railway Co,
*Royal George, Uranium, Principello,
Campanello* and *Ekaterina*.
1919 Feb 8: First post-war voyage
Liverpool-New York. Nicknamed
'Rolling George'.
1920 Became a depot ship at Cherbourg.
Later laid up at Falmouth.
1922 July: Sold and broken up a
Wilhelmshaven, Germany.

121 FLAVIA

Bt 1902 Palmers Co, Jarrow; *T:* 9,285 g,
4,693 n. **Dim** 470 ft (143.26 m) × 56 ft
9 in (17.3 m) × 32 ft 1 in (9.78 m). **Eng**
Tw scr, tpl exp; 2 × 3 cyls: 26 in
(66.04 cm), 43 in (109.22 cm) and 71 in
(180.34 cm); *Stroke:* 48 in (121.92 cm);
795 NHP; *Stm P:* 190 lb; 13 kts. **H** Steel,
2 decks and shelter deck, bridge 110 ft
(33.53 cm).

1902 Built as *British Empire* for British

Shipowners Ltd.
1907 Sold to Navegazione Generale
Italiana. Renamed *Campania*.
Genoa-Naples-New York service.
1910 Acquired by Uranium SS Co,
British. Rotterdam-New York.
1911 Renamed *Campanello* by Uranium.
1914 The company's services ceased with
the outbreak of war.
1916 Acquired and renamed *Flavia*.
1918 Aug 24: Struck two mines off Tory
Island, Ireland. One life lost.

122 VALACIA (I)

Bt 1910 Russell & Co, Port Glasgow;
T: 6,526 g, 4,100 n. **Dim** 460 ft
(140.2 m) × 57 ft (17.37 m) × 28 ft 10 in
(8.79 m). **Eng** Sgl scr, tpl exp; 3 cyls:
28½ in (72.39 cm), 47 in (119.38 cm) and
78 in (198.12 cm); *Stroke:* 54 in
(137.16 cm); 690 NHP; *Stm P:* 180 lb;
13 kts; By Rankin & Blackmore,
Greenock. **H** Steel, 2 decks and shelter
deck.

1910 Built as *Luceric* for Andrew Weir,
Glasgow.
1916 Acquired and renamed *Valacia*.
1931 Sold to Italian shipbreakers.

123 FELTRIA

Bt 1891 Wm Denny & Co, Dumbarton;
T: 5,254 g, 3,287 n. **Dim** 420 ft
(128.02 m) × 48 ft 2 in (14.68 m) × 30 ft
(9.14 m). **Eng** Sgl scr, quad exp; 4 cyls:
31 in (78.74 cm), 41½ in (105.41 cm),
64½ in (163.83 cm) and 92 in
(233.68 cm); *Stroke:* 60 in (152.4 cm);
666 NHP; 3 dbl ended boilers,
8 furnaces; *Stm P:* 180 lb; 13 kts; By
builder. **H** Steel, 2 decks. *Pass:* 400 3rd.

1891 Built as *Avoca* for British India.
1896 Chartered to Cia Trasatlantica,
Spain. Renamed *San Fernando*. Reverted
to British India as *Avoca*.
1907 June: Chartered to Danish East
Asiatic Co for use as the Royal Yacht for
the visit of the King and Queen of
Denmark to Greenland. Renamed
Atlanta.
1908 Became *Avoca* of the New York and
Continental Line, but in the same year
the company was wound up and she was
sold to the North West Transport Line

and renamed *Uranium.*
1910 Sold to new owners, who retained the name *Uranium* and gave the company the name Uranium SS Co.
1916 May: Acquired and renamed *Feltria.*
1917 May 5: Torpedoed eight miles off the south-east coast of Ireland near Mine Head, Waterford. 45 lost.

124 FOLIA

Bt 1907 James Laing & Co, Sunderland; *T:* 6,704 g, 4,211 n. **Dim** 430 ft (131.06 m) × 52 ft 7 in (16.03 m) × 25 ft (7.62 m). **Eng** Tw scr, tpl exp; 2 × 3 cyls: 24 in (60.96 cm), 39 in (99.06 cm) and 69 in (175.26 cm); *Stroke:* 45 in (114.3 cm); 807 NHP; 5 sgl ended boilers, 12 furnaces; *Stm P:* 180 lb; 14 kts; By George Clarke & Co, Sunderland. **H** Steel, 2 decks.

1907 Built as *Principe di Piemonte* for Lloyd Sabaudo, Italy.
1913 Following the loss of their *Volturno* the Uranium SS Co purchased this ship and renamed her *Principello.* Rotterdam-New York run.
1916 Acquired by Cunard and renamed *Folia.* Used for cargo only Liverpool-New York.
1917 Mar 11: Torpedoed off Waterford. 11 lost.

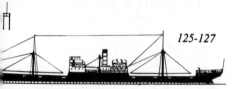

125-127

125 VIRGILIA

Bt 1918 Russell & Co, Port Glasgow; *T:* 5,697 g, 3,619 n. **Dim** 423 ft 3 in (129.01 m) × 56 ft (17.07 m) × 28 ft 7 in (8.71 m). **Eng** Sgl scr, tpl exp; 3 cyls: 27 in (68.58 cm), 44 in (111.76 cm) and 73 in (185.42 cm); *Stroke:* 48 in (121.92 cm); 550 NHP; 3 sgl ended boilers; *Stm P:* 180 lb; 12 kts; By J. G. Kincaid & Co, Greenock. **H** Steel, 2 decks, fcsle 43 ft (13.11 m), bridge 123 ft (37.49 m), poop 38 ft (11.58 m).

Identification note: Pole masts, slight rake to stem, forward bridge house stanchioned.

1918 Wartime standard design. Cargo only.
1925 Sold to James Chambers & Co, Liverpool. Renamed *Corby Castle.*
1927 Sold to Japan. Renamed *Tatsuha Maru,* Tatsuuma Kisen. Lost during Second World War.

126 VELLAVIA

Bt 1918 Armstrong Whitworth & Co, Newcastle; *T:* 5,272 g, 3,195 n. **Dim** 400 ft 2 in (121.97 m) × 52 ft 4 in (15.95 m) × 28 ft 5 in (8.66 m). **Eng** Sgl scr, tpl exp; 3 cyls: 27 in (68.58 cm), 44 in (111.76 cm) and 73 in (185.42 cm); *Stroke:* 48 in (121.92 cm); 517 NHP; 3 sgl ended boilers; *Stm P:* 180 lb; 12 kts; By George Clarke & Co, Sunderland. **H** Steel, 2 decks, fcsle 39 ft (11.89 m), bridge 112 ft (34.14 m), poop 49 ft (14.94 m).

Identification note: Goal post masts.

1918 Built as *War Setter.* 'A' type standard ship.
1919 Renamed *Vellavia* by Cunard.
1931 May: Renamed *Ines Corrado,* Soc Anon di Nav Corrado, Italy.
1941 Dec: Seized by Argentina. Renamed *Rio Diamante.*
1946 Returned to Italy. Renamed *Ines Corrado.*
1951 July 26: Scuttled in Porto Vecchio Bay when cargo of coal took fire. Refloated and repaired.
1959 Apr: Broken up at Tokyo.

127 VITELLIA

Bt 1918 Earles Co, Hull. **Dim** 375 ft 6 in (114.45 m) × 51 ft 7 in (15.9 m) × 26 ft 6 in (8.08 m). **Eng** Sgl scr, tpl exp; 3 cyls: 27 in (68.58 cm), 44 in (111.76 cm) and 73 in (185.42 cm); *Stroke:* 48 in (121.92 cm); By builder. **H** Steel, 2 decks, fcsle 39 ft (11.89 m), bridge 113 ft (34.44 m), poop 41 ft (12.5 m).

1918 Built as *War Pintail.* Acquired by Anchor Line and renamed *Vitellia.*
1923 Acquired by Cunard as.*Vitellia.*
19?? Sold to Scindia SN Co. Renamed *Jalarashmi.*
1953 Sold to Jhajharia Trading Co, Bombay. Renamed *Asha.*

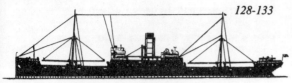

128-133

128 VARDULIA (I)

Bt 1917 Russell & Co, Port Glasgow; *T:* 5,691 g, 3,613 n. **Dim** 423 ft 3 in (129 m) × 56 ft (17.07 m) × 28 ft 8 in (8.74 m). **Eng** Sgl scr, tpl exp; 3 cyls: 27 in (68.58 cm), 45 in (114.3 cm) and 74 in (187.96 cm); *Stroke:* 51 in (129.54 cm); 564 NHP; 3 sgl ended boilers; *Stm P:* 180 lb; 12 kts; By Rankin & Blackmore, Greenock. **H** Steel, 2 decks, fcsle 43 ft (13.11 m), bridge 123 ft (37.49 m), poop 38 ft (11.58 m).

1917 Built as *Verdun* for Gow, Harrison & Co, British.
1918 Acquired by Cunard. Renamed *Vardulia*.
1929 Sold to Donaldson & Co.
1935 Oct: Lost with all hands en route West Hartlepool to Saint John with a cargo of anthracite coal. Two messages were picked up, 'dangerous list' and 'abandoning ship'.

129 VASCONIA (I)

Details as *Vardulia (128)* except: *T:* 5,680 g, 3,613 n.

1918 Built as *Valverda* for Gow, Harrison & Co, British. Acquired by Cunard. Renamed *Vasconia*.
1927 Sold to Japan.

130 VENNONIA

Details as *Vellavia (126)* except: **Bt** Caledon SB & E Co, Dundee; *T:* 5,225 g, 3,193 n. **Dim** Length 400 ft 6 in (122.07 m).

1918 Built as *War Carp*. 'B' type standard ship.
1924 Sold to American Levant Line. Renamed *River Hudson*.
1931 Renamed *Zeffiro,* Soc Anon di Nav Corrado, Italy.
1941 May 20: Sunk by HM submarine *Urge* near Cape Bon.

131 VENUSIA

Details as *Vellavia (126)* except: **Bt**

Harland & Wolff, Belfast; *T:* 5,222 g, 3,172 n. **Eng** By builder.

1918 Built as *War Snake*. 'B' type standard ship.
1923 Sold to American Levant Line. Renamed *River Delaware*.
1931 Sold to Soc Anon di Nav Corrado, Italy. Renamed *Rina Corrado*.
1941 Nov 11: Sunk by Naval gunfire east of Syracuse.

132 VERENTIA

Details as *Vellavia (126)* except:
Bt Harland & Wolff, Belfast; *T:* 5,185 g, 3,152 n. **Eng** By builder.

1918 Built as *War Lemur*. 'B' type standard ship.
1927 Sold to Andrew Weir & Co (Bank Line). Renamed *Foreric*. Resold and named *Galvan,* Buenos Aires and Great Southern Railway Co, British. Collier service to Buenos Aires.
1937 Sold. Renamed *Hokutai Maru,* Kitagawa Sangyo Kaiun, Japan.
1944 Mar 30: Sunk by US air attack off the Pelew Islands, Pacific.

133 VERBANIA

Details as *Vellavia (126)* except: **Bt** R. Duncan & Co, Port Glasgow; *T:* 5,021 g, 3,180 n. **Dim** 405 ft 4 in (123.55 m) × 53 ft (16.15 m) × 27 ft 4 in (8.33 m). **Eng** By J. G. Kincaid & Co, Greenock.

1918 Built as *Trafalgar* for Lawrence Glen & Co. Acquired by Cunard and renamed *Verbania*.
1926 Sold to Lyle Shipping Co, Glasgow, for £25,000. Renamed *Cape Cornwall*.
1934 Broken up in Shanghai.

134

134 SATELLITE (II)

Bt 1896 J. Scott & Co, Kinghorn; *T:* 333 g, 132 n. **Dim** 160 ft (48.77 m) × 27 ft 1 in (8.26 m) × 9 ft 10 in (2.3 m). **Eng** Pad, compound; 2 cyls: 30 in (76.2 cm) and 51 in (129.54 cm); *Stroke:* 57 in (144.78 cm); 164 NHP; 10 kts; By builder. **H** Steel, 1 deck; *Pass:* 1,200 with baggage.

1896 Built as the Mersey ferry *John Herron* for Wallasey Corporation.
1920 Acquired for use as a tender at Cherbourg. Registered as owned by Societé Maritime de Transbordment, their only vessel.
1924 Replaced by *Lotharingia (147)* and broken up.

135 BERENGARIA

Bt 1913 Vulkan Werke, Hamburg; *T:* 52,226 g, 21,506 n. **Dim** 899 ft (274.01 m) oa, 883 ft 6 in (269.29 m) × 98 ft 4 in (29.97 m) × 57 ft 1 in (17.4 m). **Eng** Quad scr, Curtis-AEG Vulkan steam turbines; 46 water tube boilers; *Stm P:* 228 lb; 23½ kts. **H** Steel, 4 decks, shelter deck and shade deck; *Pass:* 970 1st, 830 2nd, 1,000 3rd.

1913 Built as *Imperator* for Hamburg America Line.
1920 Ceded to Britain by the Treaty of Versailles. Acquired by Cunard and reconditioned.
Feb 21: First Cunard voyage, still as *Imperator,* from Liverpool to New York.
1921 Apr 16: Renamed *Berengaria* sailed Southampton-Cherbourg-New York.
Sept: Converted to oil fuel. 750 tons per day.
1922 May: Back in service.
1936 Passenger accommodation revised to cabin, tourist and third.
1938 Mar: Final voyage New York-Cherbourg-Southampton. Then sold for breaking up. However, the war intervened and it was not until 1946 that the hull was finally dismantled.

136 ALBANIA (II)

Bt 1921 Scotts SB & E Co, Greenock; *T:* 12,767 g, 7,519 n. **Dim** 523 ft 1 in (159.44 m) × 64 ft (19.51 m) × 43 ft 10 in (13.36 m). **Eng** Tw scr, 4 turbines, dbl reduction geared; 1,340 NHP; 3 dbl ended boilers, 18 furnaces; *Stm P:* 200 lb; By builder. **H** Steel, 2 decks and shelter deck, fcsle 86 ft (26.22 m); *Pass:* 500 cabin.

1921 Jan 18: Maiden voyage Liverpool-New York.
1922 Transferred to Liverpool-Quebec-Montreal route.
1925 Laid up. Built with a large cargo

capacity she was not successful as an Atlantic liner.
1930 Sold to Liberia Triestina, Italy, and renamed *California*.
1937 With the reorganisation of Italian shipping companies *California* was transferred to Lloyd Triestino.
1938 Served as a hospital ship during the Italo-Abyssinian war.
1941 Aug 11: Sunk in Italian port by air attack.

137 SCYTHIA (II)

Bt 1921 Vickers Armstrong, Port Glasgow; *T:* 19,930 g, 11,927 n. **Dim** 625 ft (190.5 m) oa, 600 ft 8 in (183.08 m) × 73 ft 9 in (22.48 m) × 40 ft 8 in (12.4 m). **Eng** Tw scr, turbines dbl reduction geared; 2,528 NHP; 3 dbl and 3 sgl ended boilers, 36 furnaces; *Stm P:* 220 lb; 16 kts; By builder. **H** Steel, 2 decks and shelter deck, bridge 284 ft (86.56 m); *Pass:* 350 1st, 350 2nd, 1,500 3rd; *Crew:* 434.

1921 Aug 20: Maiden voyage Liverpool-New York.
1939 Taken over for trooping.
1942 Nov: After being seriously damaged by bombing in Algiers during the North African campaign *Scythia* went via Gibraltar to New York for repairs.
1948 Sept: Carried displaced persons from Germany to Canada. Ten voyages.
1949 Passenger accommodation 248 1st, 630 tst.
1950 Aug 17: Re-entered service after extensive reconditioning. Liverpool-Quebec.
1951 Apr 10: Southampton-Havre-Quebec service.
1952 June 5: Collided with the Canadian steamer *Wabana* in the St Lawrence.
1958 Broken up at Inverkeithing, Firth of Forth.

138 SAMARIA (II)

Details as *Scythia (137)* except: **Bt** 1921 Cammell Laird & Co, Birkenhead; *T:* 19,597 g, 11,834 n. **Dim** Length 601 ft 6 in (183.34 m). **Eng** By builder.

1922 Apr 19: Maiden voyage Liverpool-Boston.
1926 Liverpool-Queenstown (Cobh)-Halifax-Boston service.

1934 Summer cruises out of London.
1939-48 Served as troopship. In 1946
carried the Cunard funnel and all-grey
livery.
1948 Carried Canadian troops and their
families back from Europe.
1950 Passenger accommodation 250 1st,
650 tst.
1951 Refitted and placed on
Southampton-Havre-Quebec service.
1952 Grounded near Quebec.
1953 June 15: Represented Cunard at the
Coronation Naval Review at Spithead.
1956 Jan: Sold for breaking up at
Inverkeithing, Firth of Forth.

139 LACONIA (II)

Details as *Scythia (137)* except: **Bt** 1922
Swan Hunter & Wigham Richardson,
Newcastle; *T:* 19,695 g, 11,804 n. **Dim**
Length 601 ft 4 in (183.29 m).

1922 May 25: Maiden voyage
Southampton-New York, alternatively to
Boston with some voyages from
Hamburg.
1930-39 Used frequently for periods of
cruising.
1942 Sept 12: Torpedoed twice 700 miles
off Freetown by *U-156*. It was then
found that the ship was carrying 1,800
Italian prisoners. Commander Werner
Hartenstein, with the agreement of
Admiral Dönitz, stayed with the
survivors. The French in Casablanca were
informed and the cruiser *Gloire,* together
with the sloops *Dumont d'Urville* and
Annamite, was ordered to the scene.
Hartenstein broadcast a message to all
ships in the area requesting them to assist
and promised not to attack any that
responded.
Sept 16: An American type aircraft
bombed the red cross marked submarine
and forced Hartenstein to jettison over
200 survivors. Admiral Dönitz then
issued his 'Laconia' order, that U-boats
should not in future attempt to assist
survivors. He was rightly acquitted at the
Nuremburg trials of issuing an order that
was a war crime (but found guilty on
other counts). There is, in fact, only one
recorded case of a submarine killing
survivors and her Commander, Eck, was
executed.

140 ANDANIA (II)

Bt 1922 Hawthorn Leslie & Co,
Newcastle; *T:* 13,950 g, 8,391 n.
Dim 520 ft 2 in (158.55 m)×65 ft 4 in
(19.91 m)×39 ft 2 in (11.94 m). **Eng** Tw
scr, turbine dbl reduction geared; 1,660
NHP; 2 dbl and 2 sgl ended boilers, 24
furnaces; *Stm P:* 220 lb; 15 kts; By
builder. **H** Steel, 2 decks and shelter
deck, 7 hatches, 20 derricks, fcsle and
bridge 426 ft (129.84 m); *Pass:* 500 1st,
1,200 3rd; *Crew:* 270.

1922 June 1: Maiden voyage London-
Southampton-Quebec-Montreal.
1925-26 Hamburg-Southampton-New
York route.
1927 Liverpool-Glasgow-Belfast-
Quebec-Montreal service in conjunction
with Anchor-Donaldson Line sailings.
1939 Taken over for use as an armed
merchant cruiser.
1940 June 16: Torpedoed by U-boat *UA*
off Iceland, 70 miles from Reykjavik.
She sank next day.

141 ANTONIA

Details as *Andania (140)* except: **Bt**
Vickers Armstrong, Barrow-in-Furness;
T: 13,867 g, 8,445 n.

1922 June 15: Maiden voyage
Southampton-Quebec-Montreal service.
1928-39 Liverpool-Glasgow-Belfast-
Montreal route.
1940 Requisitioned for service as an
armed merchant cruiser.
1942 Mar 24: Acquired by the Admiralty
for conversion into a Naval repair ship.
Renamed HMS *Wayland.*
1948 Broken up.

142 AUSONIA (II)

Details as *Andania (140)* except: **Bt**
Armstrong Whitworth & Co, Newcastle;
T: 13,912 g, 8,527 n. **Eng** By builder.

1922 June 22: Maiden voyage Liverpool-
Quebec-Montreal.
1923-39 Transferred to the London-
Southampton-Quebec-Montreal run.
1939 Sept 2: Requisitioned by the
Admiralty and converted into an armed
merchant cruiser.
1944 Sept 16: Purchased and converted to
a heavy repair ship. Same name.

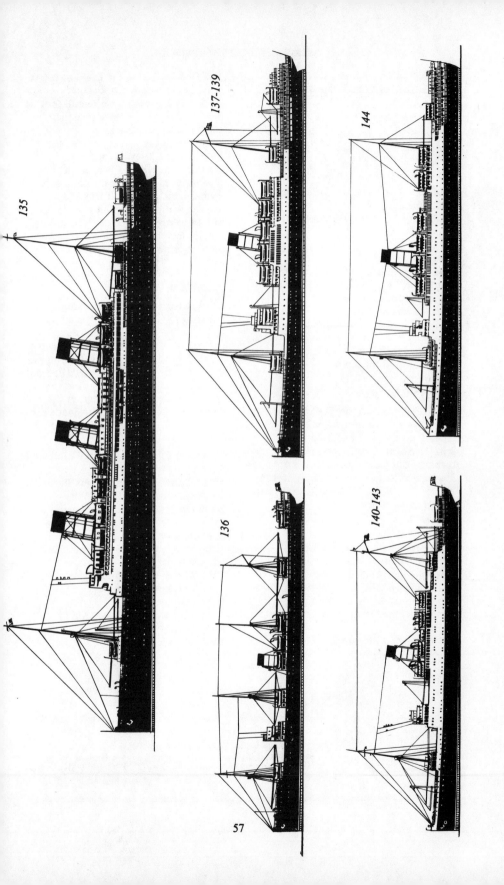

135

137-139

144

136

140-143

57

1964 Sept: De-commissioned.
1965 Aug: Broken up in Spain.

143 AURANIA (III)

Details as *Andania (140)* except: **Bt** 1924
Swan Hunter & Wigham Richardson,
Newcastle; *T:* 13,984 g, 8,473 n. **Eng** By
Wallsend Slipway Co, Newcastle.

1924 Sept 9: Maiden voyage Liverpool-
New York.
1925 Transferred to Liverpool-Quebec-
Montreal route.
1939 Aug 24: Equipped as an armed
merchant cruiser.
1941 July: Collided with an iceberg in
convoy between Iceland and Halifax but
without serious damage.
Oct: Torpedoed but reached Rothesay.
1942 Purchased by the Admiralty and
converted into a heavy repair ship.
Renamed HMS *Artifex*.
1961 Jan: Sold for scrap.

144 LANCASTRIA

Bt 1922 Wm Beardmore & Co, Glasgow;
T: 16,243 g, 9,645 n. **Dim** 552 ft 8 in
(168.45 m) × 70 ft 5 in (21.46 m) × 38 ft
9 in (11.81 m). **Eng** Tw scr, 6 stm
turbines, dbl reduction geared; 3 dbl and
3 sgl ended boilers, 36 furnaces; *Stm P:*
220 lb; By builder. **H** Steel, 2 decks and
shelter deck, fcsle and bridge 455 ft
(138.68 m). *Pass:* 235 1st, 355 2nd, 1,256
3rd; *Crew:* 300.

1922 Entered service as *Tyrrhenia*.
June 13: Maiden voyage Glasgow-
Quebec-Montreal. Thereafter she served
on the Liverpool-Quebec-Montreal route.
Her name proved to be unpopular and
she carried the nickname of the 'Soup
Tureen'.
1924 Renamed *Lancastria*.

1926 Transferred to the London-Havre-
Southampton-New York route.
1936 Cruising. Had a white hull for this
period, giving her an elegance that
enhanced her popularity.
1939 Trooping.
1940 June 17: Bombed and sunk by
German aircraft in St Nazaire Roads.
Lancastria had been sent to evacuate
civilians and troops. All day she was
loading with evacuees but at 4 pm a salvo
of bombs ripped open her hull and she
sank in less than 20 minutes. Of some
5,000 persons aboard over 3,000 were
lost. 2,477 were saved.

145 FRANCONIA (II)

Bt 1923 John Brown, Clydebank,
Glasgow; *T:* 20,175 g, 12,162 n. **Dim**
625 ft (190.5 m) oa, 601 ft 3 in
(183.26 m) × 73 ft 8 in (22.45 m) × 40 ft
6 in (12.34 m). **Eng** Tw scr, 6 turbines,
dbl reduction geared; 2,562 NHP; 3 dbl
and 3 sgl ended boilers, 36 furnaces; *Stm
P:* 220 lb; 16 kts; By builder. **H** Steel, 2
decks and shelter deck, promenade deck
419 ft (127.71 m); *Pass:* 350 1st, 350 2nd,
1,500 3rd.

1923 June 23: Maiden voyage Liverpool-
New York. Winter cruising.
1931 Chartered to the Furness-Bermuda
Line for five months. New York-
Bermuda.
1934 Transferred to London-Havre-
Southampton-New York route.
1935 Reverted to 1923 routings. Hull
painted white.
1938 Carried out a world cruise of 41,727
miles with calls at 37 ports.
1939 Trooping duties.
Oct 5: Collided with Royal Mail Line's
Alcantara.
1940 June 16: Bombed off Brittany. All

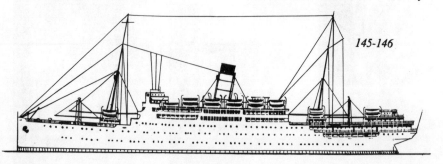

145-146

close misses but they unseated the engines.
1945 HQ ship for the Yalta, Crimea, conference between Churchill, Roosevelt and Stalin.
1949 June 2: Returned to Liverpool-Quebec-Montreal route. *Pass:* 250 1st, 600 tst.
1950 Ran aground on Orleans Island near Quebec.
1956 Dec: Sold for breaking up at Rosyth, Firth of Forth.

146 CARINTHIA (II)

Details as *Franconia (145)* except: **Bt** 1925 Vickers Armstrong & Co, Barrow-in-Furness. *T:* 20,277 g, 12,086 n. **Dim** Length 600 ft 7 in (183.06 m). **Eng** By builder.

1924 Laid down as *Servia* (II). Renamed before launching.
1925 Aug 22: Maiden voyage Liverpool-New York. Remained on this route with winter cruising.
1933 A world cruise calling at 40 ports.
1934 Transferred to London-Havre-Southampton-New York route.
1935-39 Reverted to New York and winter cruising. White hull.
1939 Converted into an armed merchant cruiser.
1940 June 6: Torpedoed off Northern Ireland by *U-46*. *Carinthia* stayed afloat for 36 hours before sinking.

147-148

147 LOTHARINGIA

Bt 1923 Wm Hamilton & Co, Port Glasgow; *T:* 1,256 g, 598 n. **Dim** 199 ft 10 in (60.91 m) × 38 ft 1 in (11.61 m) × 15 ft 6 in (4.72 m). **Eng** Tw scr, tpl exp;

Cyls: 13¼ in (33.65 cm), 21¼ in (54.11 cm) and 34 in (86.36 cm); *Stroke:* 21 in (53.34 cm); 170 NHP; 2 sgl ended boilers, 6 furnaces; *Stm P:* 180 lb; 12 kts; By D. Rowan & Co, Glasgow. **H** Steel, 1 deck, bridge 95 ft (28.95 m); *Pass:* 1,200 plus baggage.

1923 Replaced *Satellite (134)* as tender at Cherbourg. Registered as owned by Compagnie Nord Atlantique.
1933 Sold to Soc Cherbourgeoise de Remorquage et de Sauvetage. Renamed *Alexis de Tocqueville.*
1940 Taken over by the Germans. Became a war loss.

148 ALSATIA (I)

Details as *Lotharingia (147)* except: **Bt** Coaster Construction Co, Montrose; *T:* 1,310 g, 632 n.

1923 Tender at Cherbourg. Ownership as *Lotharingia.*
1933 Sold Soc Cherbourgeoise de Remorquage et de Sauvetage. Renamed *Ingenieur Cachin.*
1942-46 Renamed *Voluntaire.*
1947 Reverted to *Ingenieur Cachin.*

149 ALAUNIA (II)

Bt 1925 John Brown & Co, Clydebank, Glasgow; *T:* 14,030 g, 8,448 n. **Dim** 519 ft 6 in (158.34 m) × 65 ft 2 in (19.86 m) × 39 ft 2 in (11.94 m). **Eng** Tw scr, 2 turbines, dbl reduction geared; 1,640 HP; 2 dbl and 2 sgl ended boilers, 24 furnaces; *Stm P:* 220 lb; 15 kts; By builder. **H** Steel, 2 decks and shelter deck, fcsle and bridge 425 ft (129.54 m); *Pass:* 500 cabin, 1,200 3rd.

1925 July 24: Maiden voyage Liverpool-Quebec-Montreal route.
1926-39 London-Southampton-Quebec-Montreal service.
1939 Aug 24: Converted into an armed

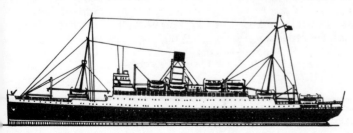
149-150

merchant cruiser.
1944 Dec 8: Purchased by the Admiralty and converted into a heavy repair ship. Renamed HMS *Alaunia*. Stationed at Devonport.
1957 Sept 10: Broken up at Blyth.

150 ASCANIA (II)

Details as *Alaunia (149)* except: **Bt** Armstrong Whitworth & Co, Newcastle; *T:* 14,013 g, 8,437 n. **Dim** Length 520 ft (158.49 m). **Eng** By builder.
1925 May 22: Maiden voyage London-Southampton-Quebec-Montreal.
1934 Dec: Rescued the crew of the sinking steamer *Unsworth* in mid-Atlantic.
1939 Requisitioned as an armed merchant cruiser.
1942 Trooping duties.
1943 Refitted as an Infantry Landing Ship.
1944 Reverted to trooping.
1947 Dec 20: Reopened the Liverpool-Halifax service with austerity accommodation.
1949 Refitted and reconditioned. *Pass:* 200 1st, 500 tst.
Apr 21: Resumed service Liverpool-Quebec-Montreal.
1956 Dec: Sold for scrap and broken up at Newport, South Wales.

151-154

151 BACTRIA

Bt 1928 J. L. Thompson & Co, Sunderland; *T:* 2,407 g, 1,209 n. **Dim** 292 ft 4 in (89.1 m) × 45 ft (13.72 m) × 20 ft 3 in (6.17 m). **Eng** Sgl scr, tpl exp; 3 cyls: 24 in (60.96 cm), 40 in (101.6 cm) and 66 in (167.64 cm); *Stroke:* 45 in (114.3 cm); 403 NHP; 2 sgl ended boilers, 8 furnaces; *Stm P:* 180 lb; 12 kts; By J. Dickinson & Sons, Sunderland. **H** Steel, 2 decks, fcsle 28 ft (8.53 m), bridge 129 ft (39.32 m); *Coal:* 114 tons; *Cargo:* 200,000 cu ft grain (5,663 cu m); *Crew:* 30.

1928 Built for Mediterranean service.
1954 Sold to Compania Isla Bella, Costa

Rica, and renamed *Theo*.
1958 Sold. Renamed *Catalina S* by Bahamas Pearl Co, British.

152 BANTRIA

Details as *Bactria (151)* except: *T:* 2,402 g, 1,209 n.

1928 Built for Mediterranean service.
1954 Sold to Costa Line and renamed *Giorgina Celli*.
1955 Sold. Renamed *Sacrum Cor,* Lauro & Montello, Naples.

153 BOTHNIA (II)

Details as *Bactria (151)* except: *T:* 2,402 g, 1,209 n.

1928 Built for Mediterranean service.
1950 Sold to Vivalet Shipping and Trading Co SA, Panama, and renamed *Emil*.

154 BOSNIA

Details as *Bactria (151)* except: *T:* 2,402 g, 1,209 n.

1928 Built for Mediterranean service.
1939 Sept 5: Torpedoed and sunk by a U-boat in the Bay of Biscay. The date was only two days after the outbreak of war and *Bosnia* was still wearing her peacetime livery.

155 QUEEN MARY

Bt 1936 John Brown & Co, Clydebank, Glasgow; *T:* 81,235 g, 34,120 n. **Dim** 1,019 ft (310.59 m) oa, 975 ft 2 in (297.23 m) × 112 ft 6 in (34.29 m) × 68 ft 6 in (20.88 m), keel to base of funnels 125 ft (38.1 m), keel to top of fore funnel 184 ft (56.08 m), keel to top of foremast 236 ft (71.93 m), fore funnel height 59 ft (17.98 m). **Eng** Quad scr, 16 turbines, sgl reduction geared; 160,000 SHP, 33,653 NHP; 24 watertube boilers; *Stm P:* 446 lb; 29 kts; By builder. **H** Steel, 12 decks, fcsle 93 ft (28.35 m), bridge 715 ft (217.93 m), upper bridge 540 ft (164.59 m); *Pass:* 711 1st, 707 cabin, 577 tst; *Crew:* 1,285.

1930 Dec 27: Laid down. Construction work ceased the following December.
1934 Apr: Work recommenced.
Sept 26: Launched by HM Queen Mary.

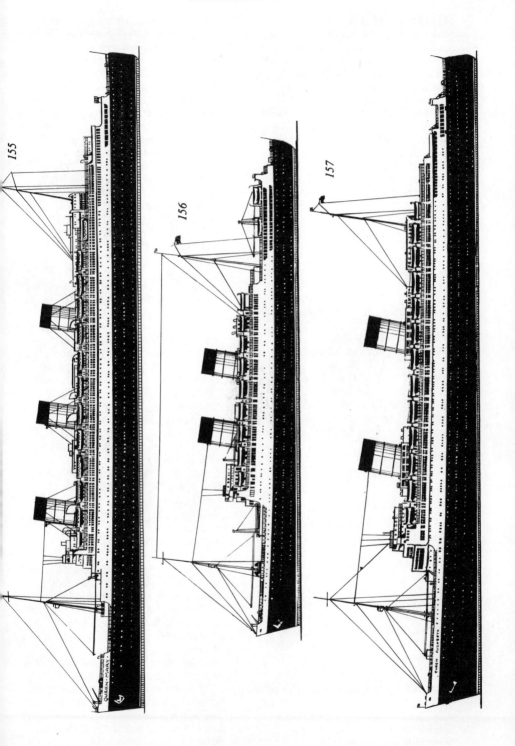

155

156

157

1936 May 27: Maiden voyage
Southampton-Cherbourg-New York.
Aug: Took the Blue Riband from
Normandie, sailing westbound in 4 days
and 27 minutes at 30.14 kts and
eastbound in 3 days 23 hours and 57
minutes at 30.63 kts.
1939 Sept: After the outbreak of the war
Queen Mary was laid up at New York.
1940 Mar 1: Commissioned as a
troopship and sailed to Sydney,
Australia, for conversion.
1942 Oct 2: While zig-zagging at speed
Queen Mary sliced the stern off her
escorting cruiser HMS *Curacao* with the
loss of 338 lives. At a later court hearing
Queen Mary was exonerated.
1946 Sept 24: Final trooping voyage
Halifax-Southampton. Sent to John
Brown's for conversion back to passenger
liner.
1947 July 31: First post-war voyage
Southampton-Cherbourg-Plymouth-New
York.
1958 Fitted with stabilizers.
1967 Sept 27: Arrived at Southampton at
the end of her 1,000th, and final, voyage.
Nov: Sold to the City of Long Beach,
California, for $3,450,000.
1971 May 10: Conversion completed and
opened as a maritime museum, hotel and
convention centre. Her machinery was
removed.
1978 Apr: Put up for sale due to losses
said to be $2 million a year.

156 MAURETANIA (II)

Bt 1939 Cammell Laird & Co,
Birkenhead; *T:* 35,739 g, 20,170 n **Dim**
771 ft 9 in (23.23 m) oa, 739 ft 4 in
(225.35 m) × 89 ft 4 in (27.23 m) × 57 ft
8 in (17.58 m). **Eng** Tw scr, 6 turbines,
sgl reduction geared; 8,373 NHP;
6 watertube boilers; *Stm P:* 465 lb;
23 kts; By builder. **H** Steel, 5 decks, fcsle
and bridge 614 ft (187.17 m), upper
bridge 381 ft (116.13 m); *Pass:* 475 1st,
390 cabin, 304 tst; *Crew:* 593.

1938 July 28: Launched.
1939 June 17: Maiden voyage Liverpool-
New York.
Aug: Transferred to London-Havre-
Southampton-New York route.
Sept: Laid up in New York.

1940 Mar: Taken over as a troopship.
Mar 20: New York-Bilbao-Honolulu-
Sydney for trooping conversion.
1945 Made 48 trooping voyages and
carried over 350,000 personnel.
Overhauled at Birkenhead by her builder.
1947 Apr 26: Resumed service Liverpool-
New York then transferred to the
Southampton berth. Cruised out of New
York during the winter.
1958 Fitted with air conditioning
throughout. Used for world cruises.
1962 Green hull. Used on New York-
Mediterranean service plus cruising.
Became increasingly unprofitable.
1965 Nov 23: Sold to Thos Ward and
broken up at Inverkeithing, Firth of
Forth, during 1966.

157 QUEEN ELIZABETH

Bt 1940 John Brown & Co, Clydebank,
Glasgow; *T:* 83,673 g, 42,011 n. **Dim**
1,030 ft (313.94 m) oa, 987 ft (300.84 m) ×
118 ft 6 in (36.12 m) × 68 ft 4 in
(20.83 m), keel to base of funnel 131 ft
(39.93 m), keel to top of fore funnel
187 ft (57 m), keel to top of foremast
233 ft (71.02 m), height of funnels 71 ft
(21.64 m). **Eng** Quad scr, 16 turbines, sgl
reduction geared; 160,000 SHP;
12 watertube boilers; *Stm P:* 450 lb;
29 kts; By builder. **H** Steel, 12 decks,
fcsle and bridge 875 ft (266.7 m), upper
bridge 567 ft (178.82 m); *Pass:* 823 1st,
662 cabin, 798 tst; *Crew:* 1,296.

1936 Dec: Laid down.
1938 Sept 27: Launched by HM Queen
Elizabeth.
1940 Mar 2: Completed after the
outbreak of war and sailed in secret from
the Clyde to New York, where she was
laid up. En route, whilst maintaining
radio silence, she met the battleship
HMS *Queen Elizabeth.* As they passed a
signal lamp flashed from the bridge of
the battleship. All it said was one word:
'Snap'.
1941-46: With all her furnishings stored
in San Francisco *Queen Elizabeth* was
used as a troopship with a capacity for
20,000 troops. She carried 811,324 during
her wartime career and steamed 492,635
miles. She returned to her builder for
refitting.

1946 Oct 16: Made her first true commercial voyage from Southampton to New York.
1955 Fitted with two sets of stabilizers.
1968 Apr 5: Sold, after 907 crossings, to The Queen Ltd of Fort Lauderdale and sailed on Nov 28 to Port Everglades as a tourist attraction. Her new owners went into liquidation after a few months.
1970 Purchased by C. Y. Tung of the Orient Overseas Line for £1,333,000. She was converted, at Hong Kong, into a floating university at a cost of £5 million and renamed *Seawise University.*
1972 Jan: The conversion was completed. Jan 9-10: Caught fire in Hong Kong harbour and finally capsized onto her side. No lives were lost but the wreck had to be dismantled as it lay.

158 VALACIA (II)

Bt 1943 Short Bros, Sunderland; *T:* 7,052 g, 4,760 n. **Dim** 446 ft 6 in (136.09 m) oa, 431 ft (131.37 m) × 56 ft 4 in (17.17 m) × 35 ft 2 in (10.71 m). **Eng** Sgl scr, tpl exp; 3 cyls: 24½ in (62.23 cm), 39 in (99.06 cm) and 70 in (177.8 cm); *Stroke:* 48 in (121.92 cm); 542 NHP; 2 sgl ended boilers, 9 furnaces; *Stm P:* 220 lb; 9½ kts; By NE Marine Eng Co (1938), Newcastle. **H** Steel, 1 deck, 5 hatches, fcsle 40 ft (12.19 m).

1943 Built for the Ministry of War Transport as *Empire Camp.*
1946 Acquired by Cunard and renamed *Valacia.*
1950 Sold to Charles Hill & Co, Bristol. Renamed *New York City.*

159 VASCONIA (II)

Details as *Valacia (158)* except: **Bt** 1944; *T:* 7,058 g, 4,757 n.

1944 Built for the Ministry of War Transport as *Empire Pendennis.*
1946 Acquired by Cunard and renamed *Vasconia.*
1950 Sold to the Blue Star Line. Renamed *Fresno Star.*
1957 Became *Millais,* Lamport & Holt.
1960 Sold to Grosvenor Shipping Co. Renamed *Grosvenor Navigator.*
1966 Sept 9: Arrived for breaking up at Kaohsiung.

160 VARDULIA (II)

Bt 1944 J. A. Jones Construction Co, Brunswick, Georgia; *T:* 7,276 g, 4,483 n. **Dim** 422 ft 8 in (128.83 m) × 57 ft (17.37 m) × 34 ft 8 in (10.57 m). **Eng** Sgl scr, tpl exp; 3 cyls; 24½ in (62.23 cm), 37 in (93.98 cm) and 70 in (177.8 cm); *Stroke:* 48 in (121.92 cm); *Stm P:* 270 lb; 10 kts; By Filer & Stowell Co, Milwaukee, Wisconsin. **H** Steel, 1 deck.

1944 Built as Liberty ship *Samfoyle.* Cost $1,992,000. Managed by Cunard.
1947 Purchased and renamed *Vardulia.*
1954 Sold to Nueva Valencia Cia Nav, Panama. Renamed *Valencia.*
1957 Renamed *Seacob.*
1968 Dec: Broken up at Hong Kong.

161 VANDALIA (II)

Details as *Vardulia (160)* except: **Bt** 1945 California Shipbuilding Corp, Los Angeles; *T:* 7,276 g, 4,493 n.

1945 Built as Liberty ship *Granville Stuart.* Transferred to British registry and renamed *Samaritan* by the Ministry of War Transport. Assigned to Cunard management.
1947 Purchased by Cunard and renamed *Vandalia.*
1954 Sold and renamed *Sideris.*

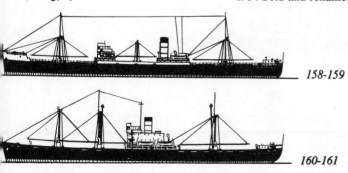

158-159

160-161

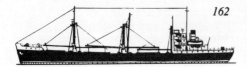

162

162 BRESCIA (II)

Bt 1945 Consolidated Steel Corp, Wilmington, California; *T:* 3,834 g, 2,124 n. **Dim** 323 ft 10 in (98.7 m) × 51 ft 1 in (15.58 m) × 26 ft 6 in (8.08 m). **Eng** Sgl scr, oil engine; 6 cyls: 21½ in (54.61 cm); *Stroke:* 29 in (73.66 cm); 12 kts; By Nordberg Manufacturing Co, Milwaukee, Wisconsin. **H** Steel, 1 deck, fcsle 38 ft (11.58 m), poop 90 ft (27.43 m).

1945 Built as C1-MAV type standard ship *Hickory Isle.* Bare boat chartered by Ministry of War Transport. Managed by Common Bros.
1947 Acquired by Cunard and renamed *Brescia.*
1966 Sold to Timbir Shipping Co SA, Panama, and renamed *Timbir I.*

163 ASIA (II)

Bt 1947 Sir James Laing & Sons, Sunderland; *T:* 8,723 g, 5,077 n. **Dim** 508 ft 8 in (155.04 m) oa, 488 ft 6 in (14.83 m) × 64 ft 1 in (19.54 m) × 32 ft 3 in (9.83 m). **Eng** Sgl scr, 2 turbines, sgl reduction geared; 2 watertube boilers; *Stm P:* 475 lb; 15½ kts; By Richardsons, Westgarth & Co, Hartlepool. **H** Steel, 2 decks, fcsle 54 ft (16.46 m), bridge 168 ft (51.2 m), poop 44 ft (13.41 m); *Pass:* 12 1st.

1946 Sept 12: Launched. The first post-war construction for Cunard.

1947 Placed on North Atlantic cargo service.
1963 May 17: Sold to the Eddie Steamship Co, Taipeh, and renamed *Shiru.*

164 ARABIA (III)

Details as *Asia (163)* except: **Bt** 1948; *T:* 8,632 g, 4,949 n.

1947 July 18: Launched.
1948 Jan 8: Maiden voyage Liverpool-New York.
1963 Mar: Sold to the International Marine Corp, Panama (Neptune Marine Corp managers). Renamed *Onshun.*
1966 Sold to Cosmos Marine Development.

165 MEDIA (I)

Bt 1947 John Brown & Co, Clydebank, Glasgow; *T:* 13,345 g, 7,480 n. **Dim** 531 ft (161.85 m) oa, 500 ft (152.4 m) × 70 ft 4 in (21.44 m) × 46 ft (14.02 m). **Eng** Tw scr, turbine, dbl reduction geared; 15,000 SHP; 2 watertube boilers; *Stm P:* 450 lb; 17 kts; By builder. **H** Steel, 3 full decks, fcsle 46 ft (14.02 m), bridge 202 ft (61.57 m); *Cargo:* 458,895 cu ft (12,994 cu m); *Pass:* 250 1st.

1946 Dec 12: Launched.
1947 Aug 20: Maiden voyage Liverpool-New York.
1952 Fitted with stabilizers.
1961 Oct: Sold to Compagnia Genovese di Armamento, Genoa, for £740,000. Completely rebuilt and renamed *Flavia* with accommodation for 1,200 passengers.
1962 Sept: Placed on Genoa-Suez-

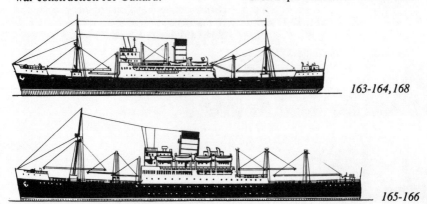

163-164,168

165-166

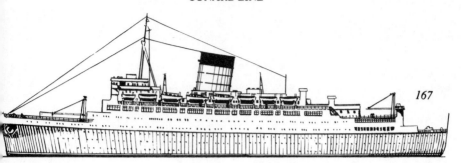

167

Australia service.
Dec: Bremerhaven-Southampton-
Australia route.

166 PARTHIA (I)

Details as *Media (165)* except: **Bt** 1948
Harland & Wolff, Belfast; *T:* 13,362 g,
7,393 n.

1947 Feb 25: Launched.
1948 Apr 10: Maiden voyage Liverpool-
New York.
1961 Nov 1: Sold to the New Zealand
Shipping Co and rebuilt aft by Alexander
Stephen at Glasgow to provide additional
passenger accommodation. Renamed
Remuera.
1962 June 1: First voyage London-
Panama Canal-Auckland-Wellington.
1965 Jan 12: Transferred to the Eastern
and Australian SS Co. Renamed *Aramac.*
Placed on the New Zealand-Australia-
Hong Kong-Japan route.

167 CARONIA (II)

Bt 1949 John Brown & Co, Clydebank,
Glasgow; *T:* 34,274 g, 7,921 n. **Dim**
715 ft (217.93 m) oa, 666 ft (203 m) × 91 ft
6 in (27.89 m) × 65 ft 3 in (16.23 m). **Eng**
Tw scr, 1 sgl and 1 dbl reduction geared
turbine; 35,000 SHP; 6 watertube boilers;
Stm P: 725 lb; 22 kts; By builder.
H Steel, 5 decks, fcsle and bridge 594 ft
(181.05 m), promenade 495 ft
(150.88 m); *Cargo:* 69,450 cu ft g
(1,967 cu m); *Pass:* 580 1st, 350 cabin;
Crew: 600.

*A dual purpose design for the North
Atlantic and world cruising. Carried six
45 ft (13.72 m) launches for shore
excursion passengers. Green hull and
cream green upperworks.*

1947 Oct 30: Launched by Princess

Elizabeth.
1949 Jan 4: Maiden voyage
Southampton-New York. Seasonal world
cruises.
1967 Nov 18: Final Cunard voyage. Sold
to Universal Lines Inc and renamed
Columbia.
1968 Sold to the Star Shipping Co,
Panama, and renamed *Caribia.* The
operating company was Universal Cruise
Lines. Whilst at New York she was
damaged by fire and laid up in an
unseaworthy condition.
1969 Mar 11: An engine room explosion
whilst cruising off St Thomas killed one
person. The ship drifted for 20 hours.
Mar 20: Docked at New York.
1970 Laid up at New York with debts
totalling $5 million.
1974 Apr 27: Left New York in tow by
the German tug *Hamburg* for breaking
up at Taiwan. Wrecked en route at Apra,
Guam. Broke into three pieces.

168 ASSYRIA

Bt 1950 Swan, Hunter & Wigham
Richardson, Newcastle; *T:* 8,530 g,
4,856 n. **Dim** 508 ft 10 in (155.09 m) oa,
480 ft 8 in (146.51 m) × 64 ft 1 in
(19.54 m) × 34 ft 10 in (10.62 m). **Eng** Sgl
scr, 2 turbines, dbl reduction geared;
8,000 SHP; 2 watertube boilers; *Stm
P:* 490 lb; 15½ kts; By Richardsons,
Westgarth. **H** Steel, 2 decks, fcsle 57 ft
(17.37 m), bridge 168 ft (51.21 m), poop
46 ft (14.02 m); *Cargo:* 588,762 cu ft g
(16,672 cu m); *Pass:* 12.

1950 Jan 19: Launched.
Aug 24: Maiden voyage Liverpool-
Boston-New York.
1963 Sept: Sold to N. J. Vlassopulos and
renamed *Laertis.* Operated by Stala Cia
Nav SA.

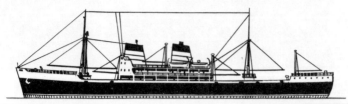

169-170

169 ALSATIA (II)

Bt 1948 J. L. Thompson & Sons, Sunderland; *T:* 7,226 g, 5,080 n. **Dim** 503 ft 4 in (153.42 m) oa, 468 ft 9 in (142.88 m) × 64 ft 11 in (19.79 m) × 31 ft 11 in (9.73 m). **Eng** Sgl scr, 3 turbines, dbl reduction geared; 8,800 SHP; 2 watertube boilers; *Stm P:* 590 lb; 16 kts; By Parsons Marine Steam Turbine Co, Newcastle. **H** Steel, fcsle 97 ft (29.56 m), poop 41 ft (12.5 m); *Cargo:* 762,880 cu ft g (21,602 cu m); *Pass:* 12.

Forward funnel a dummy.

1948 Built as *Silverplane* for Silver Line, S. J. Thompson & Co.
1951 Sept: Purchased by Cunard and renamed *Alsatia*. Converted to motorship.
Oct 6: First voyage on Cunard's North Atlantic cargo service.
1963 Jan 28: Sold to China Union Lines, Taiwan. Renamed *Union Freedom*.
1977 Broken up at Kaohsiung.

170 ANDRIA (I)

Details as *Alsatia (169)* except: *T:* 7,301 g, 4,002 n.

1948 Built as *Silverbriar* for Silver Line, S. J. Thompson & Co.
1951 Acquired by Cunard and renamed *Andria*. Converted to motorship.
1963 Feb 4: Sold to China Union Lines, Taipeh, and renamed *Union Faith*.
19?? Lost at sea by fire.

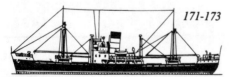

171-173

171 PAVIA (II)

Bt 1953 Wm Hamilton & Co, Port Glasgow; *T:* 3,411 g, 1,828 n. **Dim** 348 ft 4 in (106.17 m) oa, 320 ft (97.54 m) × 49 ft 10 in (15.19 m) × 28 ft 6 in (8.69 m). **Eng** Sgl scr, diesel; 4 cyls sgl acting; 3,600 BHP; dbl and sgl ended boilers; 13 kts; Doxford type by David Rowan & Co, Glasgow. **H** Steel, 4 holds, 13 derricks, fcsle 32 ft (9.75 m), poop 29 ft (8.84 m); *Cargo:* 8,000 cu ft refrig (226 cu m).

1953 Mar 19: Launched.
June 1: Maiden voyage. The first motorship actually built for Cunard. Mediterranean services.
1965 Aug 25: Sold to Seaswift Maritime Co, Piraeus, and renamed *Toula N*.

172 LYCIA (II)

Details as *Pavia (171)* except: **Bt** 1954; *T:* 3,543 g, 1,731 n.

1954 Sept 24: Maiden voyage to Greece and Turkey with general cargo. Built for Mediterranean services.
1963 Sept 23: Sold to Diapora SA, Piraeus. Renamed *Flora N*.

173 PHRYGIA (II)

Details as *Pavia (171)* except: *T:* 3,534 g, 1,730 n.

1955 Apr 10: Maiden voyage to Mediterranean ports. Continued in Mediterranean service.
1965 Sept 7: Sold to Firgounes SA, Panama, and renamed *Dimitris N*.

174 SAXONIA (II)

Bt 1954 John Brown & Co, Clydebank, Glasgow; *T:* 22,592 g, 11,721 n. **Dim** 608 ft 4 in (185.4 m) oa, 570 ft (173.74 m) × 80 ft 4 in (24.49 m) × 46 ft 3 in (14.1 m). **Eng** Tw scr, 4 turbines, dbl reduction geared; 24,500 SHP; 4 watertube boilers; *Stm P:* 550 lb; 19½ kts; By builder. **H** Steel, 9 decks, 5 holds; *Cargo:* 30,000 cu ft (849 cu m); *Pass:* 125 1st, 800 tst (one class when cruising); *Crew:* 457.

First of the four largest Cunarders built for the Canadian run.

66

174-177

174a-175a

1954 Feb 17: Launched by Lady Churchill.
Sept 2: Maiden voyage Liverpool-Quebec-Montreal, cutting two days off the previous voyage times.
1961 Placed on New York service. Winter cruising out of Port Everglades.
1962 Extensively rebuilt aft for a dual Atlantic and cruising role; given lido decks and 'Caronia' green livery *(174a)*.
1963 Jan 1: Renamed *Carmania* (II).
1964-70 Used on Mediterranean fly-cruise operations.
1969 Jan 14: Ran aground on San Salvador Island during a cruise.
1971 Laid up for sale. Sold to Russia and renamed *Leonid Sobinov*.

175 IVERNIA (II)

Details as *Saxonia (174)* except:
T: 22,637 g, 11,721 n.

1954 Dec 14: Launched.
1955 July 1: Her maiden voyage, because of a dock strike, was Greenock-Quebec-Montreal. Thereafter sailings were from Liverpool.
1957 Apr 17: Commenced Southampton-Havre-Quebec-Montreal sailings. Denny-Brown stabilizers fitted.
1962 Rebuilt by John Brown & Co similarly to *Saxonia (174)* and used for cruising out of New York in the summer and Port Everglades in the winter *(175a)*.
1963 Jan 1: Renamed *Franconia* (III).
June 4: First voyage Rotterdam-Quebec-Montreal.
1971 Put up for sale because of high costs

and unprofitability. Sold to Russia and renamed *Fedor Shalyapin*.

176 CARINTHIA (III)

Details as *Saxonia (174)* except: **Bt** 1956;
T: 21,947 g, 11,630 n.

1954 Dec 14: Launched by Princess Margaret.
1956 June 27: Maiden voyage Liverpool-Quebec-Montreal.
1967 Given a white hull.
1968 Jan: Sold to the Sitmar Line, Genoa. Renamed *Fairland*. Remained at Southampton for over two years with Sitmar funnel colouring. Then renamed *Fairsea*.
1971 Taken to Italy for rebuilding and conversion for the Australian route.

177 SYLVANIA (II)

Details as *Saxonia (174)* except: **Bt** 1956;
T: 22,017 g, 11,679 n.

1957 June 5: Maiden voyage Greenock-Quebec-Montreal. Subsequently from Liverpool.
1967 Given a white hull.
1968 Jan: Sold to Sitmar Line, Genoa, and renamed *Fairwind*. Remained with her sister at Southampton for over two years.
1971 Taken to Italy for rebuilding and conversion for the Australian route. The resultant ship was unrecognisable in her new form.

178 ANDANIA (III)

Bt 1959 Wm Hamilton & Co, Port

178-179

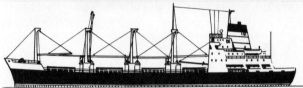

180-186

Glasgow; *T:* 7,004 g, 3,501 n. **Dim** 490 ft 5 in (149.48 m) × 63 ft 3 in (19.28 m) × 26 ft 7½ in (8.12 m). **Eng** Sgl scr, 2 turbines, dbl reduction geared; 2 watertube boilers; *Stm P:* 690 lb; 17½ kts; By D. Rowan & Co, Glasgow. **H** Steel, 1 deck and shelter deck.

1960 May 3: Maiden voyage North Atlantic cargo service.
1969 Transferred to Thos Brocklebank. Renamed *Macharda*.
1971 Sold. Renamed *Humi Mahis*.
1973 Sold. Renamed *Yungjian*.
1975 Sold. Renamed *Hong Qi No 107*, People's Republic of China.

179 ALAUNIA (III)

Details as *Andania (179)* except: **Bt** 1960.

1960 Oct 9: Maiden voyage North Atlantic cargo service.
1969 Transferred to Thos Brocklebank. Renamed *Malancha*.
1971 Sold. Renamed *Humi Nasita*.
1973 Sold. Renamed *Yungming*.
1975 Sold. Renamed *Hong Qi No 108*, People's Republic of China.

180 MEDIA (II)

Bt 1963 John Readhead & Co, South Shields; *T:* 5,586 g, 2,658 n. **Dim** 436 ft 9 in (133.12 m) oa, 400 ft (121.92 m) × 60 ft 3 in (18.36 m) × 37 ft 6 in (11.43 m). **Eng** Sgl scr, Sulzer diesel type 7RD68, 2 stroke; 7 cyls: 680 mm (26.77 in); *Stroke:* 1,250 mm (49.21 in); 17 kts; By Hawthorn Leslie (Eng) Co, Newcastle. **H** Steel, 1 deck and shelter deck, fcsle 52 ft (15.85 m); *Cargo:* 385,795 cu ft (10,924 cu m); *Crew:* 45.

Strengthened for navigation in ice.

1963 Oct 18: Maiden voyage on North Atlantic cargo service.
1971 Sold to Western Australia Coastal Shipping Commission and renamed *Beroona*.

181 PARTHIA (III)

Details as *Media (181)* except: **Bt** 1963 Caledon SB & E Co, Dundee. **Dim** Length 437 ft (133.2 m). **Eng** By John Brown & Co, Clydebank.

1963 July 18: Launched.
Nov 29: Maiden voyage North Atlantic cargo service.
1971 Sold to Western Australian Coastal Shipping Commission and renamed *Wambiri*. During 1971 *Parthia* also bore the name *Staship 1*.

182 SAXONIA (III)

Details as *Media (181)* except: **Bt** 1964 J. Readhead & Sons, South Shields.

1963 Oct 17: Launched.
Feb: Maiden voyage North Atlantic cargo service.
1970 Transferred to Cunard-Brocklebank Ltd and renamed *Maharonda*.
1972 Chartered to Christian Haaland and renamed *Concordia Foss*. Returned to Cunard-Brocklebank Ltd and again named *Maharonda*.

183 IVERNIA (III)

Details as *Media (180)* except: **Bt** 1964 Caledon SB & E Co, Dundee. **Eng** By John Brown & Co, Clydebank, Glasgow.

1964 Entered North Atlantic cargo service.

1970 Transferred to Cunard-Brocklebank Ltd and renamed *Manipur*.
1971 Chartered to Christian Haaland and renamed *Concordia Manipur*. Reverted to Cunard-Brocklebank as *Manipur*. Present fleet.

184 SCYTHIA (III)

Bt 1964 Cammell Laird & Co, Birkenhead; *T:* 5,837 g, 2,829 n. **Dim** 456 ft 10 in (139.24 m) oa, 420 ft (128.01 m) × 60 ft 2 in (18.34 m) × 37 ft 6 in (11.43 m). **Eng** Sgl scr, Sulzer diesel, turbocharged; 6 cyls; 8,640 BHP; 17½ kts; By Sulzer Bros, Winterthur. **H** Steel, 1 deck and shelter deck, fcsle 52 ft (15.85 m); *Cargo:* 24,015 cu m (848,077 cu ft) insulated; *Crew:* 45.

Strengthened for navigation in ice. A slightly enlarged version of the Media *(180) class.*

1964 Dec 4: Maiden voyage Liverpool-New York. Registered as owned by the North Western Line (Mersey) Ltd.
1972 Sold to T. & J. Harrison, Liverpool, and renamed *Merchant*.

185 SAMARIA (III)

Details as *Scythia (184)* except: **Bt** 1965; *T:* 5,837 g, 2,844 n.

1965 Feb 11: Maiden voyage Liverpool-New York. Registered as owned by North Western Line (Mersey) Ltd.
1972 Sold to T. & J. Harrison, Liverpool, and renamed *Scholar*.

186 SCOTIA (II)

Details as *Scythia (184)* except: **Bt** 1965; *T:* 5,825 g, 2,822 n.

Scotia *was the first Cunarder with the engine room controlled from the bridge. She was also equipped with special winches and deck handling gear for low temperature work.*

1966 Jan: Maiden voyage Liverpool-St Lawrence Seaway-Montreal through the frozen river. Registered as owned by United Dominions Leasing Ltd.
1970 Sold to Neptune Orient Lines, Singapore, and renamed *Neptune Amber*.

187 QUEEN ELIZABETH 2

Bt 1967 John Brown & Co, Clydebank, Glasgow; *T:* 66,852 g, 36,930 n. **Dim** 963 ft (293.53 m) oa, 887 ft (270.39 m) × 105 ft 3 in (32.09 m) × 56 ft (17.07 m), keel to base of funnel 134 ft (40.84 m), keel to top of mast 202 ft 4 in (61.57 m), height of funnel 67 ft 4 in (20.52 m). **Eng** Tw scr, turbines, dbl reduction geared; 110,000 SHP; 3 watertube boilers; 28½ kts; By builder; 2 Kamewa bow thrusters. **H** Steel, 13 decks, 10 lounges, 11 bars, fully air-conditioned, Denny-Brown stabilizers, promenade 750 ft (229 m); *Pass:* 564 1st, 1,979 tst (total 1,400 when cruising); *Crew:* 906.

1969 Apr 22: Preview cruise.
May 2: Maiden voyage Southampton-New York. Turbine trouble was encountered and the ship was out of service for four months. North Atlantic service during the summer and world cruising during the winter. Present fleet.

188 CUNARD ADVENTURER

Bt 1971 Rotterdam Dockyard Co, Rotterdam; *T:* 14,151 g, 8,135 n. **Dim** 483 ft 9 in (147.52 m) oa, 412 ft 9 in (125.9 m) × 70 ft 6 in (21.5 m). **Eng** Tw scr, 4 Werkspoor diesels, geared; 12 cyls: 410 mm (16.14 in); *Stroke:* 470 mm (18.5 in); 7,000 BHP; 21½ kts; By Stork-Werkspoor, Amsterdam; Pleuger bow thrust propeller. **H** Steel, 10 decks, ram bow, air conditioned throughout, fcsle and bridge 434 ft 9 in (132.6 m); *Pass:* 740 one class in 320 cabins plus 86 pullman berths; *Crew:* 300.

1971 Dec: Entered service.
1977 Mar: Sold to Lauritz Kloster, Norway. Renamed *Sunward II*.

189 CUNARD AMBASSADOR

Details as *Cunard Adventurer (188)* except: **Bt** 1972 P. Smit & Co, Rotterdam.

1974 Sept 13: Caught fire and abandoned en route to pick up passengers at New Orleans for a cruise. The crew were taken off by the US tanker *Tallulah*.
1975 Sold and rebuilt into a livestock carrier. Renamed *Linda Clausen,* C. Clausen, Denmark.

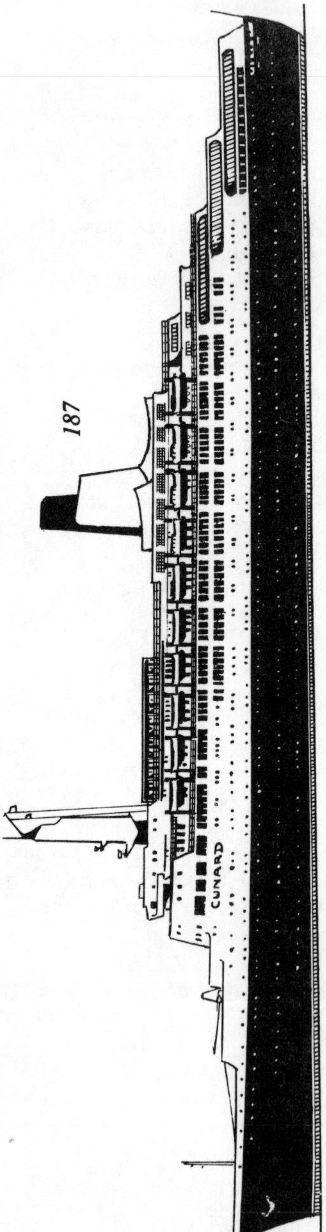

187

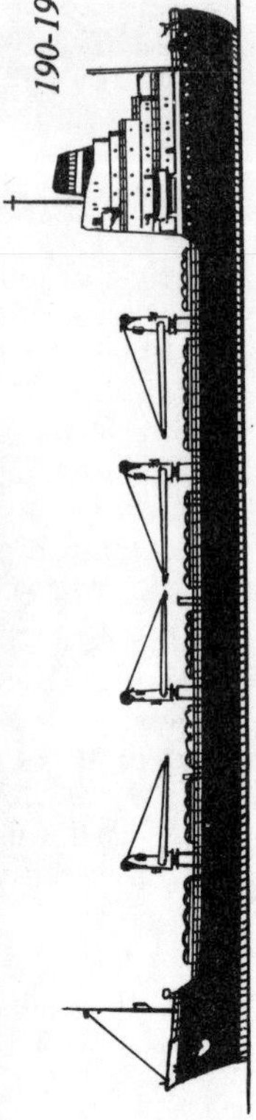

190-197

188-189

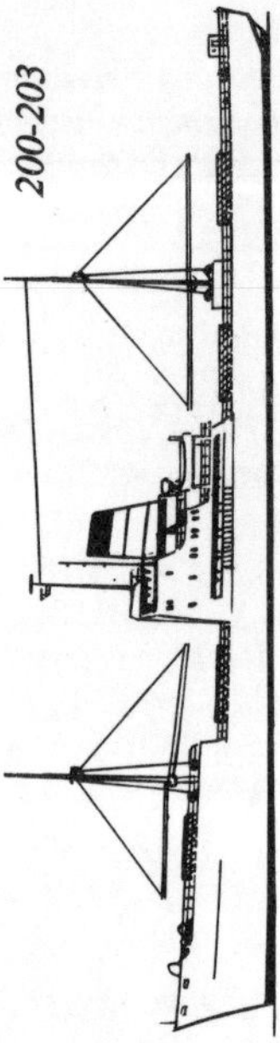

200-203

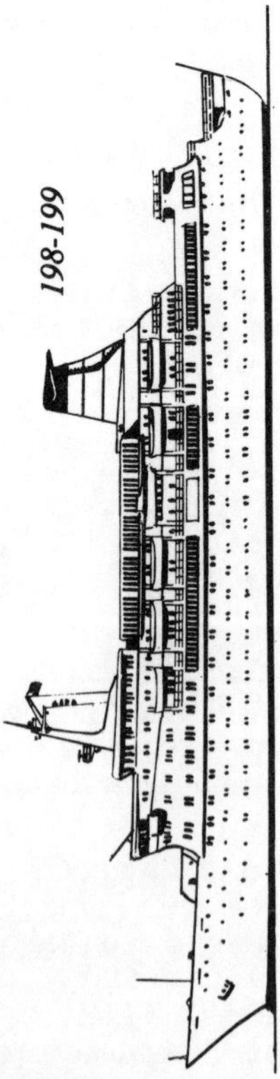

198-199

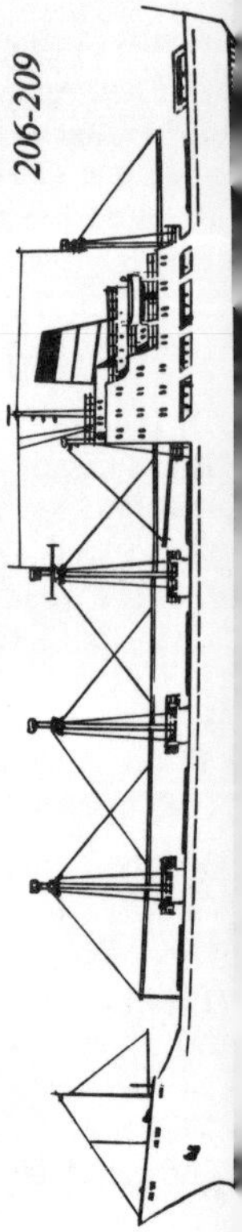

206-209

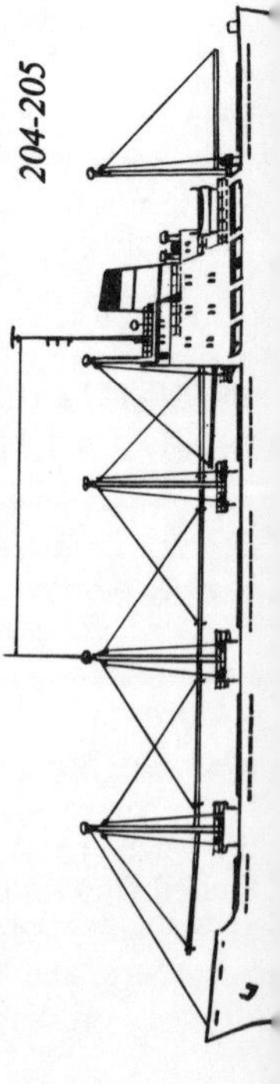

204-205

190 CUNARD CAMPAIGNER

Bt 1972 Astilleros Espanoles SA, Seville; *T:* 15,498 g, 11,227 n. **Dim** 598 ft 9 in (182.6 m) oa, 563 ft 11 in (171.68 m) × 73 ft 6 in (22.4 m) × 46 ft 6 in (14.2 m). **Eng** Sgl scr, Sulzer diesel RND68 type; 6 cyls: 680 mm (26.77 in); *Stroke:* 1,250 mm (49.21 in); 9,900 BHP; 15½ kts; By builder. **H** Steel, 4 × 15 ton Hagglund electro-hydraulic deck cranes, fcsle 52 ft (15.9 m), poop 100 ft (30.5 m); *Cargo:* 1,270,551 cu ft (35,978 cu m).

Eskalduna Type 27 design. The first of eight bulk carriers ordered by Cunard and to be operated by Cunard-Brocklebank Bulkers Ltd. The ships wear Brocklebank funnels.

1972 Oct: Launched by Mrs Nigel Broakes.
1974 Sold. Renamed *Jag Shanti* by Great Eastern Shipping Co, Bombay.

191 CUNARD CARAVEL

Details as *Cunard Campaigner (190)* except: *T:* 15,498 g, 11,227 n.

1972 Sept 19: Delivered.
1974 Sold. Renamed *Jag Shakti* by Great Eastern Shipping Co, Bombay.

192 CUNARD CARRONADE

Details as *Cunard Campaigner (190)* except: *T:* 15,498 g, 11,227 n.
1972 Nov 9: Delivered. Present fleet.

193 CUNARD CALAMANDA

Details as *Cunard Campaigner (190)* except: *T:* 15,498 g, 11,237 n.
1973 Feb: Completed. Present fleet.

194 CUNARD CAVALIER

Details as *Cunard Campaigner (190)* except: *T:* 15,498 g, 11,227 n.
1973 Sept: Completed. Present fleet.

195 CUNARD CARRIER

Details as *Cunard Campaigner (190)* except: *T:* 15,498 g, 11,227 n.
1973 Dec: Completed. Present fleet.

196 CUNARD CHAMPION

Details as *Cunard Campaigner (190)*
except: *T:* 15,448 g, 11,221 n.
1973 Aug: Completed. Present fleet.

197 CUNARD CHIEFTAIN

Details as *Cunard Campaigner (190)* except: *T:* 15,448 g, 11,221 n.
1973 Nov: Completed. Present fleet.

198 CUNARD COUNTESS

Bt 1974 Burmeister & Wain Skibs, Copenhagen; *T:* 17,495 g, 10,096 n. **Dim** 534 ft 6 in (163 m) oa, 459 ft 1 in (139.99 m) × 74 ft 8 in (22.81 m) × 49 ft 6 in (15.14 m). **Eng** Tw scr, 4 diesels, geared sgl acting, type 7S5OHU; 7 cyls; 500 mm (19.69 in); *Stroke:* 540 mm (21.26 in); 21,000 BHP; 21½ kts; By Hitachi Zosen; Controllable pitch propellers. **H** Steel, 6 decks; *Pass:* 950 one class; *Crew:* 400.

The hull and machinery were built in Denmark but the ship was completed by Industrie Navali Meccaniche Affini SpA, Spezia.

1974 Cruise liner. Entered service with a white funnel but Cunard livery was introduced later. Caribbean based. Present fleet.

199 CUNARD PRINCESS

Details as *Cunard Countess (198)* except: *T:* 17,586 g, 12,387 n.

1974 Completed as *Cunard Conquest.*
1977 Renamed *Cunard Princess* by Princess Grace of Monaco in New York harbour. Used for cruising out of her home port of San Juan, Puerto Rico.

200 ALAUNIA (IV)

Bt 1973 Smith's Dock Co, Middlesbrough; *T:* 4,938 g, 2,636 n, 7,689 dwt. **Dim** 461 ft 6 in (140.7 m) oa, 426 ft 3 in (130 m) × 60 ft 3 in (18.04 m) × 38 ft 1 in (11.64 m). **Eng** Sgl scr, Sulzer diesel, 2 stroke, sgl acting; 9 cyls: 680 mm (26.77 in); *Stroke:* 1,250 mm (49.21 in); 14,850 BHP; 23 kts; By G. Clark & NEM, Wallsend. **H** Steel, 4 decks, fcsle 132 ft (40.3 m), bridge 85 ft (26 m); *Cargo:* 10,342 cu m g (365,222 cu ft).

1973 Built as *Cardiff Clipper* for
Maritime Fruit Carriers Co
(Maritimecor SA). Chartered to Salen
Rederi, Stockholm.
1976 Acquired with Maritimecor fleet
and renamed *Alaunia*. Present fleet.

201 ALSATIA (III)

Details as *Alaunia (200)* except: **Bt** 1972;
T: 7,722 dwt.

1972 Built as *Edinburgh Clipper* for
Maritime Fruit Carriers Co. Chartered
to Salen Rederi, Stockholm.
1976 Acquired by Cunard and renamed
Alsatia. Present fleet.

202 ANDANIA (IV)

Details as *Alaunia (200)* except: **Bt** 1972;
T: 7,742 dwt.

1972 Built as *Glasgow Clipper* for
Maritime Fruit Carriers Co. Chartered
to Salen Rederi, Stockholm.
1976 Acquired by Cunard and renamed
Andania. Present fleet.

203 ANDRIA (II)

Details as *Alaunia (200)* except: **Bt** 1972;
T: 7,689 dwt.

1972 Built as *Teeside Clipper* for
Maritime Fruit Carriers Co. Chartered
to Salen Rederi, Stockholm.
1976 Acquired by Cunard and renamed
Andria. Present fleet.

204 CARINTHIA (IV)

Bt 1973 Nylands & Verkstad, Oslo; *T:*
7,330 g, 3,542 n, 9,551 dwt. **Dim** 511 ft
2 in (155.8 m) oa, 471 ft 5 in (143.69
m) × 70 ft 1 in (21.37 m) × 41 ft 7 in
(12.7 m). **Eng** Sgl scr, oil, 2 stroke; 9
cyls: 740 mm (29.13 in); *Stroke:* 1,600
mm (62.99 in); 17,400 BHP; 22 kts; By
builder. **H** Steel, 3 decks, fcsle 50 ft
(15.24 m); *Cargo:* 13,634 cu m (481,477
cu ft).

1973 Built as *Cantaloup* for Maritime
Fruit Carriers Co.
1976 Acquired with the fleet and
renamed *Carinthia*. Present fleet.

205 CARMANIA (III)

Details as *Carinthia (204)* except: *T:*
7,323 g, 3,546 n, 9,561 dwt.

1972 Built as *Orange* for Maritime Fruit
Carriers Co.
1976 Acquired by Cunard and renamed
Carmania. Present fleet.

206 SAMARIA (IV)

Bt 1973 Aalborg Vaerft A/S, Aalborg;
T: 8,577 g, 4,722 n, 12,180 dwt. **Dim**
575 ft 3 in (175.34 m) oa, 533 ft 6in
(162.62 m) × 75 ft (22.86 m) × 44 ft 4 in
(13.52 m). **Eng** Sgl scr, oil, 2 stroke sgl
acting; 9 cyls: 840 mm (33.07 in);
Stroke: 1,800 mm (70.87 in); 23,200
SHP; 23½ kts; By Burmeister & Wain,
Copenhagen. **H** Steel, 3 decks, fcsle 46
ft (14.1 m); *Cargo:* 16,356 cu m
(577,603 cu ft).

1973 Built as *Chrysantema* for Maritime
Fruit Carriers Co.
1976 Acquired by Cunard and renamed
Samaria. Present fleet.

207 SAXONIA (IV)

Details as *Samaria (206)* except: **Bt**
1972; *T:* 8,547 g, 4,706 n, 12,182 dwt.

1972 Built as *Gladiola* for Maritime
Fruit Carriers Co.
1976 Acquired by Cunard and renamed
Saxonia. Present fleet.

208 SCYTHIA (IV)

Details as *Samaria (206)* except: **Bt**
1072; *T:* 8,557 g, 4,772 n, 12,182 dwt.

1972 Nov: Built as *Iris Queen* for
Maritime Fruit Carriers Co.
1976 Acquired by Cunard and renamed
Scythia. Present fleet.

209 SERVIA (III)

Details as *Samaria (206)*

1972 July: Built as *Orchidea* for
Maritime Fruit Carriers Co.
1976 Acquired by Cunard and renamed
Servia. Present fleet.

American Line

History

American Steamship Company 1872-1884

1872 Clement A. Griscom, a partner in the shipbroking firm of Peter Wright & Sons, put up a scheme to establish a premier American-owned transatlantic shipping company. He finally succeeded in forming the American Steamship Company with a capital of $2½ million. The principal shareholder was the Pennsylvania Railroad Company, whose Atlantic railhead terminated at Philadelphia. They had a strong commercial interest in the development of Philadelphia in place of New York. The Board of the new company was drawn from local personalities and they decided that the first ships for the American Line, as it was named, should be built at the Philadelphia yard of W. Cramp & Sons. Four vessels were ordered for delivery in 1873.

1873 May: *Pennsylvania,* the first of the quartet, inaugurated the new service from Philadelphia to Liverpool via Queenstown (now Cobh). The enterprise was one which was welcomed in the United States. The nation's lack of prestige on the North Atlantic was sorely felt in commercial and maritime circles.

To the alarm of the shareholders the reaction from fellow Philadelphians was swift. The Red Star Line, or more correctly the International Navigation Co, a Philadelphian company, chartered two steamers, *Abbotsford* and *Kenilworth,* and placed them on a parallel service from Liverpool. The American Line's embarrassment was that they had only one ship, *Ohio* not being due for delivery until August. Urgent negotiations followed and the charter of the two ships was assigned to the American Line.

1874-75 *Kenilworth* continued to serve the Philadelphia-Liverpool route but in 1875 *Abbotsford* had the misfortune to be wrecked on the coast of Anglesey. To replace her Inman's *City of Bristol* was chartered.

1875-76 With the growth of the business two more Inman vessels were chartered for the summer seasons. They were *City of Limerick* and *City of New York.*

1875 Dec: *Kenilworth* was replaced by *Lord Clive,* owned by G. M. Papayanni, which had been operating for the Dominion Line on the Liverpool-Boston route.

1877 During the short period since its inception the American Steamship Company had seen that the economics of operating ships under the British flag were considerably better than under the Stars and Stripes. In Liverpool there existed a company which owned high quality steamships; these were operated solely on a charter basis to meet the needs of ship owners who were short of tonnage. The Bristol Shipowners Company, Liverpool, therefore contracted to supply a number of vessels for the Philadelphia route.

1878 The first of the British Shipowners Company's ships to be chartered was *British Empire.*

1879 *Lord Gough,* sister of *Lord Clive,*

joined the route.

1880 The four company-owned ships, *Pennsylvania, Ohio, Indiana* and *Illinois,* with six chartered vessels, maintained a twice-weekly service between Philadelphia and Liverpool.

British Crown, British Queen, British King, British Prince and *British Princess* were all variously employed by the company, but no new building for the US flag owners was ordered.

1884 Passenger traffic on the North Atlantic had fallen by almost half between 1880 and 1884. The American Line had been even more seriously affected because Philadelphia was less popular and convenient then New York.

The outcome was that the International Navigation Company of Philadelphia (the Red Star Line) acquired the company. But the acquisition was not the end of the American Line, an emotive name in the United States where the operation of major US-controlled ships under the British flag was still cause for concern in shipping circles. But the Line's subsequent history belongs to the story of its new owners.

American Line 1892-1923

1892 By the formation in 1886 of the Inman and International Steamship Company (which resulted from the purchase of the Inman Line by American Line's owners, the International Navigation Company) Inman Line's four major vessels remained under the British flag, these being the *City of Berlin, City of Chester, City of New York* and *City of Paris.* The agitation which followed resulted in an Act of Congress being passed on May 10 1892 which ensured that the two larger vessels, *City of New York* and *City of Paris,* would transfer to the United States register with the International Navigation Company of New Jersey as owners, and that they would carry the mails.

In the autumn it was announced that from Feb 1893 the US Mail Contract

would be awarded to the American Line. The two ships to be transferred were renamed *New York* and *Paris* respectively. The operating company of the two British ships, the International Navigation Company of Liverpool, followed suit and their two vessels emerged as *Berlin* and *Chester.* They too traded under the name of the American Line. One of the mail contract conditions was that two similarly sized consorts should be constructed in the USA for the route, and two new ships were ordered accordingly from Cramp's Philadelphia yard.

1893 Feb: *New York* took the first sailing as the US mail ship and berthed at her new terminal at Southampton in place of Liverpool. She was followed at weekly intervals by *Chester, Paris* and *Berlin.*

1895 The two consorts to *New York* and *Paris* were delivered, named *St Louis* and *St Paul.* In service the two ships were disappointingly slow.

1896 *St Louis* and *St Paul* were each withdrawn from service for machinery and boiler modifications which included the heightening of the funnels of *St Paul.* The changes had the desired effect. Although not as fast as their contemporary Cunard competitors *Campania* and *Lucania,* they made their crossings at an average speed of over 20 kts, which gave them a six day passage time.

1898 The outbreak of the Spanish-American War led to the US Government taking over all four ships. *New York* became *Yale* and *Paris* became *Harvard. St Louis* and *St Paul* retained their peacetime names. To bolster the New York-Southampton route *Berlin* and *Chester* were transferred from the Antwerp service. But in July these two ships were purchased outright by the US Government. This resulted in the suspension of the American Line service between New York and Southampton until it was resumed in October.

1899 May 21: *Paris* stranded on the Manacles for almost two months. When refloated on July 11 she was taken to

Belfast for repairs and modernisation.
Nov: Marconi set up a wireless
receiver aboard *St Paul* and contacted
the station on the Isle of Wight. He
published the world's first news bulletin
aboard ship in the 'Transatlantic
Times'.
1900 Red Star's *Vaderland* (II) and
Zeeland (II) both made voyages for the
American Line during the continued
absence of *Paris*.
1901 *Haverford* entered service
Liverpool-Philadelphia.
1902 The parent company of the
American Line, the International
Navigation Company of New Jersey,
changed its name to the International
Mercantile Marine Company. The
subsequent history of the American Line
in this context is covered as part of the
Red Star Line's history in the next
section.

Routes

1873-84 Philadelphia-Liverpool.
1892-1933 Philadelphia-Liverpool.
1902-33 Occasional IMMC voyages to
other US east coast ports and Europe.

Livery

Funnel 1873-84 Red funnel, narrow
white dividing band below the black
top; on the red a keystone (coffin
shaped!) device with a red star in the
centre. 1892-1933 Black with white
band.
Hull Black with red waterline.
Uppers 1873-84 Rust brown, deck vents
black. 1892-1933 White.
Masts Rust brown.
Lifeboats White.

Fleet index

Illustrated fleet list

1 PENNSYLVANIA

Bt 1873 W. Cramp and Sons, Philadelphia; *T:* 3,343 g, 2,567 n. **Dim** 343 ft (119.36 m) × 43 ft (13.11 m) × 24 ft 10 in (7.57 m). **Eng** Sgl scr, compound; 2 cyls; *Stroke:* 36 in (91.44 cm); 12 kts; By builder. **H** Iron, 2 decks and spar deck; *Pass:* 76 cabin, 854 3rd.

As built the four sister ships Pennsylvania, Ohio (2), Indiana (3) *and* Illinois (4) *all resembled drawing 3-4, but early on in their careers both* Pennsylvania *and* Ohio *had fcsle and bridge decks added.*

1873 May 22: Maiden voyage Philadelphia-Liverpool.
1891 Tpl exp engine fitted by builder; 3 cyls; 23 in (58.42 cm), 36 in (91.44 cm) and 60 in (152.4 cm); *Stroke:* 36 in (91.44 cm); 216 NHP.
1892 Operated for Red Star Line from Antwerp. Cabin class renamed intermediate.
1897 Operated by the Empire Transportation Co.
1898 Sold to Alaska SS Co. Same name.
1910 Sold to Pacific Mail SS Co, New York.
1918 Destroyed by fire.

2 OHIO

Details as *Pennsylvania (1)* except: *T:* 3,488 g, 2,072 n.

1873 Aug: Maiden voyage Philadelphia-Liverpool.
1887 Tpl exp engine fitted by James Howden & Co, Glasgow. Operated by Inman Line. Liverpool-New York.

1-2

1889 Returned to American Line.
1897 Operated by the Empire Transportation Co.
1898 Sold to Alaska SS Co. Same name.
1909 Nov 20: Wrecked on the coast of British Columbia. Out of 213 persons aboard only two were lost.

3-4

3 INDIANA

Details as *Pennsylvania (1)* except: *T:* 3,386 g, 2,206 n.

1874 Jan: Maiden voyage Philadelphia-Liverpool.
1891 Tpl exp engine fitted by James Howden & Co, Glasgow.
1892 Third class only.
1897 Sold to Empire Transportation Co for the gold-rush trade.
1898 Sold for service on the Pacific.
1918 Destroyed by fire in Iquique Bay, Chile.

4 ILLINOIS

Details as *Pennsylvania (1)* except: *T:*

3,386 g, 2,206 n.
1874 Jan: Maiden voyage Philadelphia-
Liverpool.
1891 Tpl exp engine fitted by builder.
1892 Transferred to Antwerp-
Philadelphia route under the Red Star
flag.
1898 Sold with *Indiana* for service on
the Pacific but acquired by US
Government and used as a supply ship.
Renamed *Supply*. Stationed at Guam
for 30 years.
1928 Broken up.

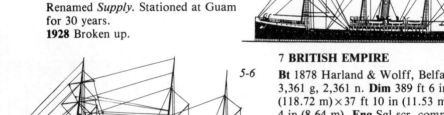

5 LORD CLIVE

Bt 1871 R. & J. Evans & Co, Liverpool;
T: 3,386 g, 2,206 n. **Dim** 381 ft (116.13
m) × 40 ft 1 in (12.22 m) × 30 ft (9.14
m). **Eng** Sgl scr, compound; 2 cyls: 32
in (81.28 cm) and 68 in (172.72 cm);
Stroke: 42 in (106.68 cm); 450 HP; 12
kts; By G. Forrester & Co, Liverpool. **H**
Iron, 2 decks; *Pass:* Cabin and 3rd.

1871 Built for George M. Papayanni for
charter work.
1872 Operated by Dominion Line.
1875 Dec 15: First voyage for American
Line. Liverpool-Philadelphia. Later
purchased by them without any change
of name.
1893 Sept 27: Final American Line
sailing.
1896 Broken up.

6 LORD GOUGH

Details as *Lord Clive (5)* except: **Bt** 1879
Laird Bros, Birkenhead; *T:* 3,656 g,
2,370 n. **Dim** Length 382 ft 9 in (116.66
m), width 40 ft 2 in (12.24 m). **Eng** LP
cyl: 64 in (162.56 cm); *Stroke:* 48 in
(121.92 cm); By builder.

1879 Built for George M. Papayanni.
Chartered to American Line. Maiden
voyage Liverpool-Philadelphia.
1885 Purchased by American Line.

1894 Out of American Line service at
end of season.
1896 Purchased by Aberdeen Atlantic
Line.
1898 Broken up. Out of Register.

7 BRITISH EMPIRE

Bt 1878 Harland & Wolff, Belfast; *T:*
3,361 g, 2,361 n. **Dim** 389 ft 6 in
(118.72 m) × 37 ft 10 in (11.53 m) × 28 ft
4 in (8.64 m). **Eng** Sgl scr, compound; 4
cyls: 2 × 28 in (71.12 cm) and 2 × 60 in
(152.4 cm); *Stroke:* 54 in (137.16 cm);
300 HP; *Stm P:* 80 lb; 12 kts; By
builder. **H** Iron, 3 decks, fcsle 78 ft
(23.77 m); *Pass:* Cabin class only.

1878 Constructed for British Shipowners
Co. Chartered to American Line.
Liverpool-Philadelphia.
1880 Returned to owners.
1886 Sold to Holland America Line.
Renamed *Rotterdam*.
1899 Sold to Italy.

8 BRITISH CROWN

Details as *British Empire (7)* except: **Bt**
1880; *T:* 3,629 g, 2,602 n. **Dim** 410 ft 4
in (125.07 m) × 39 ft (11.88 m) × 28 ft 10
in (8.79 m). **Eng** 375 HP; 12 kts; By G.
Forrester & Co, Liverpool. **H** Poop 48
ft (14.63 m).

1880 Built for British Shipowners Co
for charter to the American Line.
1887 Returned to owners and sold to
Holland America Line. Renamed
Amsterdam. Pass: 94 1st, 638 3rd.
Pass: 94 1st, 638 3rd.
1893 Tpl exp engines fitted; 4 cyls: 30 in

(76.2 cm), 47 in (119.38 cm) and 2 × 60 in (152.4 cm); *Stroke:* 54 in (137.16 cm); 502 NHP; 2 dbl ended boilers; *Stm P:* 150 lb; By Ned Industrie SM, Rotterdam.
1905 Sold for scrap. Final voyage to breakers as *Amsterda.*

9 BRITISH QUEEN

Details as *British Crown (8)* except: **Bt** 1881; *T:* 3,558 g, 2,277 n. **Eng** by J. Jack & Co, Liverpool. **H** Steel, fcsle 86 ft (26.21 m), poop 50 ft (15.24 m).
1881 Built for British Shipowners Co. Chartered to American Line.
1883 Chartered to New Zealand S Co and Shaw Savill & Albion.
Mar 22: London-Capetown-Wellington-Lyttleton. Four round voyages.
1889 Sold to Holland America Line. Renamed *Obdam.*
1890 Tpl exp engine fitted as in *Amsterdam (8).*
1898 Sold to US Government as Spanish-American War transport. Renamed *McPherson.*
1906 Became *Brooklyn,* Zotti Line, New York.
1908 Sold to Luckenbach Transport and Wrecking Co. Renamed *S.V. Luckenbach.*
1914 Renamed *Onega,* Barber SS Co, New York.
1918 Aug 30: Torpedoed in the English Channel.

10 BRITISH KING

Details as *British Queen (9)* except: *T:* 3,559 g, 2,289 n.
1881 Built for British Shipowners Co. Chartered to American Line.
1883 Operated by New Zealand S Co and Shaw Savill & Albion.
Jan 20: London-Capetown-Wellington-

Lyttleton run. Four round voyages.
1886 Returned to American Line service.
1889 Sold to Holland America Line. Renamed *Werkendam.*
1900 Became *Harbin,* Chinese Eastern Railway Co.
1904 Mar: Scuttled by the Russians at Port Arthur during the Russo-Japanese war.

11 BRITISH PRINCE

Details as *British Queen (9)* except: **Bt** 1882; *T:* 3,974 g, 2,548 n. **Dim** 420 ft 1 in (128.05 m) × 42 ft 2 in (12.85 m) × 29 ft (8.84 m). **Eng** Cyls: 43 in (109.22 cm) and 86 in (218.44 cm); *Stroke:* 60 in (152.4 cm); 450 HP; By builder. **H** fcsle 88 ft (26.82 m).
1882 Built for British Shipowners Co. Chartered to American Line.
1894 Mar 28: Final sailing for American Line. Liverpool-Philadelphia.
1895 Sold and renamed *Les Andes* by Societé Général de Transports Maritimes à Vapeur.
1910 Broken up.

12 BRITISH PRINCESS

Details as *British Prince (11)* except: *T:* 3,995 g, 2,558 n.
1882 Built for British Shipowners Co. Chartered to American Line.
1895 Sold with her sister to the same owners and renamed *Les Alpes.*
1910 Sold for scrap.

13 NEW YORK

Formerly Inman's *City of New York.* For details of this vessel see Inman section, entry 32.

The illustration is as she was rebuilt in 1903 with two funnels. Later

13-14

photographs depict a white fcsle and poop.

14 PARIS

Formerly Inman's *City of Paris.* For details of this vessel see Inman section, entry *33.*

15 CHESTER

Formerly Inman's *City of Chester.* For details of this vessel see Inman section, entry *27.*

16 BERLIN

Formerly Inman's *City of Berlin.* For details of this vessel see Inman section, entry *29.*

17 SOUTHWARK

Bt 1893 William Denny & Bros, Dumbarton; *T:* 8,607 g, 5,642 n. **Dim** 480 ft (146.3 m) × 57 ft 2 in (17.42 m) × 37 ft (11.28 m). **Eng** Tw scr, quad exp; 2 × 4 cyls: 25½ in (64.77 cm), 37½ in (95.25 cm), 52½ in (133.35 cm) and 74 in (187.96 cm); *Stroke:* 54 in (137.16 cm); 1,237 NHP; 2 dbl and 1 sgl ended boilers; *Stm P:* 200 lb; 14 kts; By builder. **H** Steel, 3 decks; *Pass:* 60 1st, 1,000 3rd.

Name pronounced 'South-wark'.
For drawing see Dominion Line 39-40.

1893 Dec 27: Maiden voyage Liverpool-Philadelphia.
1895 In Red Star service Antwerp-New York.
1903 Transferred by International Mercantile Marine to Dominion Line. Liverpool-Quebec-Montreal.
1911 Broken up.

18 KENSINGTON

Details as *Southwark (17)* except: **Bt** 1894 J. & G. Thomson, Glasgow; *T:* 8,671 g, 5,556 n. **Eng** By builder.

1894 June 27: Maiden voyage Liverpool-Philadelphia.
1895 Red Star Line's Antwerp-New York service.
1903 Apr 29: Liverpool-Quebec-Montreal for Dominion Line, an International Mercantile Marine transfer.
1910 Broken up in Italy.

19 ST LOUIS

Bt 1895 W. Cramp & Sons S & EB Co, Philadelphia; *T:* 11,629 g, 5,894 n. **Dim** 535 ft 6 in (163.22 m) × 63 ft (19.2 m) × 26 ft 9 in (8.15 m). **Eng** Tw scr, quad exp; 2 × 6 cyls; 2 × 28½ in (72.39 cm), 55 in (139.7 cm) and 3 × 77 in (195.58 cm); *Stroke:* 60 in (152.4 cm); 1,837 NHP; *Stm P:* 200 lb; 19 kts; By builder. **H** Steel, 4 decks and promenade deck, fcsle 150 ft (45.72 m), poop 104 ft (31.7 m); *Pass:* 350 1st, 220 2nd, 800 3rd.

1895 June 5: Maiden voyage New York-Southampton.
1898 During the Spanish-American War *St Louis* was taken over as an armed merchant cruiser.
1900 Resumed American Line service.
1914-17 Transferred to New York-Liverpool route.
1917 Became the USS *Nashville.* Used as a troopship.
1920 Caught fire during refitting. Damaged beyond commercial repair. Converted into an exhibition ship.
1923 Towed to Italy and broken up.

20 ST PAUL

Details as *St Louis (19)* except: *T:* 5,874 n.

1895 Oct 9: Maiden voyage New York-Southampton.
1898 Armed merchant cruiser during Spanish-American War.
1908 Apr 25: During a sudden

19-20

21-22

snowstorm collided with and sank the British cruiser HMS *Gladiator* with the loss of 27 lives.
1914-18 Renamed USS *Knoxville*. Used as a troopship.
1918 Apr 24: Capsized at her berth in New York. *St Paul* was being edged into the dock when she began to list. Her masts were snapped off by a warehouse and the ship slithered sideways on the mud until she came to rest with her funnels touching the quayside. Though safely raised the reason for her suddenly keeling over was never explained. Superstitious seamen noted that it was ten years after the sinking of *Gladiator*.
1920 Mar: Resumed New York-Cherbourg-Southampton service.
Oct 9: Final voyage to Southampton.
1921 New York-Hamburg route.
1923 Broken up in Germany.

21 HAVERFORD

Bt 1901 John Brown & Co, Clydebank; *T:* 11,635 g, 7,493 n. **Dim** 531 ft (161.85 m) × 59 ft 2 in (18.03 m) × 27 ft 2 in (8.28 m). **Eng** Tw scr, tpl exp; 2 × 3 cyls: 29 in (73.66 cm), 46½ in (118.1 cm) and 75 in (190.5 cm); *Stroke:* 51 in (129.54 cm); 893 NHP; 2 dbl and 2 sgl ended boilers, 24 furnaces; *Stm P:* 160 lb; 14 kts; By builder. **H** Steel, 3 decks and shelter deck, bridge 150 ft (45.72 m); *Pass:* 150 2nd, 1,700 3rd.

1901 Liverpool-Philadelphia service. Sept 4: Southampton-Cherbourg-New York.
1902 Returned to Liverpool station.
1914-18 Trooping duties.
1919 Resumed Liverpool-Philadelphia service.
1921 Transferred to White Star.
1922 Returned to American Line. Hamburg-New York.
1925 Broken up in Italy.

22 MERION

Details as *Haverford (21)* except: **Bt** 1902; *T:* 11,621 g, 7,459 n.

1902 Operated by Dominion Line.
1903 Apr: Transferred to Liverpool-Philadelphia berth.
1914 Acquired by British Admiralty and rebuilt to resemble the battleship HMS *Tiger*.
1915 May 30: Torpedoed in the Aegean.

23 PITTSBURGH

Laid down for the American Line but commissioned by White Star. For details of this vessel see White Star section, entry *82*.

Note

Various other IMMC vessels took spells on the Philadelphia service from either Liverpool or Southampton. None, however, had their ownership transferred to American Line. The vessels were:

Belgenland (I)	Red Star *7*
Celtic (II)	White Star *44*
City of Bristol	Inman *11*
City of Limerick	Inman *14*
Finland	Red Star *17*
Friesland	Red Star *13*
Germanic	White Star *15*
Kroonland	Red Star *16*
Manchuria	Atlantic Transport *43*
Minnekahda (I)	Atlantic Transport *48*
Noordland	Red Star *11*
Pennland (I)	Red Star *10*
Rhynland	Red Star *8*
Vaderland (II)	Red Star *14*
Waesland	Red Star *9*
Westernland (I)	Red Star *12*
Zeeland (II)	Red Star *15*

81

Red Star Line

History

1872 Philadelphian business interests had just founded the American Line supported by the Pennsylvanian Railroad Company. In parallel with this another group of financiers set up and backed a Belgian registered organisation to cater for the surging emigrant traffic coming from Central Europe. They called the company the Société Anonymé de Navigation Belge-Americaine, with control being vested in the Philadelphia Steam Navigation Company, a name which was almost immediately changed to the International Navigation Company. The new concern ordered three steamers from British yards. American Line had already launched their pioneer ship, the *Pennsylvania*.

1873 Jan 19: *Vaderland* (I) inaugurated the Antwerp-Philadelphia service and flew the Belgian flag. The funnel was buff with a five-pointed red star and black top. The house flag was white with a red star. The company was at once labelled the Red Star Line, a sobriquet which lasted the whole of its career even when Arnold Bernstein and, later, when the Holland America Line became owners.

May: The American Line introduced their sailings between Liverpool and Philadelphia with *Pennsylvania*. In a bold move to counteract this competition Red Star (as it will be called throughout this section) chartered two vessels, *Abbotsford* and *Kenilworth,* and placed them on the same route. Urgent negotiations ensued and the result was an agreement by which Red

Star would stick to Antwerp and American Line to Liverpool. The charter contracts for *Abbotsford* and *Kenilworth* were thereupon assigned. Aug: *Nederland* joined her sister.

In Belgium Steinmann's White Cross Line reacted by ordering or purchasing three steamers (*Steinmann, C.F. Funch* and *Auguste André*) for the North Atlantic.

1874 Third of the curious engines-aft trio, *Switzerland* came into service.

1875 Another Belgian competitor, the Engels Line (Theodore C. Engels & Co), came onto the North Atlantic with an Antwerp-New York service by their steamer *De Ruyter*.

1876 Red Star's expanding trade obliged them to purchase another passenger vessel, and this they named *Russland*. She was placed on the Antwerp-New York service.

1877 Mar: *Russland* was wrecked on Long Island. Two new ships were immediately ordered, but to replace *Russland* Cunard's *Java* became *Zeeland* (I) and *Nemesis,* once P&O, came across from Inman, who had her on charter, and was renamed *Perusia*.

1879 The new ships *Belgenland* (I) and *Rhynland* were both placed on Red Star's expanding Antwerp-New York route. Philadelphia obstinately refused to match New York in popularity and Red Star's emphasis had, perforce, to shift north to this swiftly growing metropolis.

1880 *Perusia* was sold after *Rhynland* had established herself.

1881 Cunard's *Russia* was acquired and

thoroughly rebuilt to emerge as *Waesland* for the New York service.

1882 Another Cunarder, *Algeria,* was merely compounded and renamed *Pennland* (I) for her role on the New York route.

1883 Red Star's vigorous expansion continued and the New York berth saw the addition of *Noordland* and *Westernland* (I).

1884 The White Cross Line ceased as passenger carrying rivals when they lost *Daniel Steinmann* off Halifax. Red Star, in the guise of its owners the International Navigation Co, purchased the shares and assets of the American Line.

1886 The International Navigation Co were again in the headlines by the purchase of the Inman Line. Such was the prestige of the acquisition that the Philadelphia concern now changed its name to the Inman and International Steamship Co.

1888 The Engels Line discontinued passenger services to North America. *Vaderland* (I) was sold to French owners.

1889 *Friesland* entered service Antwerp-New York.

1892 Two new company moves were introduced. The Inman and International SS Co was split into two new companies, the International Navigation Co of New Jersey and the International Navigation Co of Liverpool (for which see the history of the Inman Line). The whole Red Star group now adopted Inman's black funnel and white band. American Line's *Pennsylvania* and *Illinois* were switched to the Antwerp-Philadelphia route, joining *Nederland* and *Switzerland.*

1895 *Kensington* and *Southwark* came across from the American Line and *Berlin* (ex-*City of Berlin*) from Inman on to the Antwerp-New York run. They were replaced by the transfer of *Belgenland* (I), *Pennland* (I), *Rhynland* and *Waesland* to the Liverpool berth. Inman's *Chester* (ex-*City of Chester*) took up station on Philadelphia.

1898 The Spanish-American War broke out. *Illinois, Ohio* and *Pennsylvania* were eventually sold to Alaska SS Co

for service on the Pacific coast during the gold-rush days. To replace them *Berlin* and *Chester* returned to Philadelphia from the New York route.

1900 *Vaderland* (II) entered the New York route. She and her sister *Zeeland* (II) were allocated to the International Navigation Co of Liverpool and therefore flew the British flag.

1901 At 11,905 grt *Zeeland* (II) became the company's largest ship when she joined her sister on the New York route, but two larger ships were already well advanced. *Noordland* and *Westernland* (I) went to the American Line's Philadelphia service.

1902 *Kroonland* and *Finland,* built by Cramp, joined their consorts. They were the group's largest ships and were therefore operated by the American company, the International Navigation Co of New Jersey.

Feb: The International Navigation Co of New Jersey changed its name to the International Mercantile Marine Co. The financier Pierpont Morgan increased the company's capital from £3 million to an astonishing £24 million. By May the group owned or had negotiated and acquired the shareholdings in the following companies:

Red Star Line (The International Navigation Co of New Jersey and Société Anonymé de Navigation Belge-Americaine).

American Line (already owned by Red Star and used as the trading name for the International Navigation Co of Liverpool, ex-Inman Line).

Atlantic Transport Line (who since 1896 had also owned the National Line).

Dominion Line (British & North Atlantic Steam Navigation Co).

Frederick Leyland (1900) Ltd.

White Star Line (Oceanic Steam Navigation Co).

This vast group had the makings of becoming the most powerful shipping combine on the North Atlantic and possibly even in the world. But it is a fact of history that nations which comprise very large land-masses are obliged to devote their moneys and efforts to the land. The seagoing races are islanders or seaport peoples, like the British, the Greeks, the north Germans and the Norwegians. Thus too many IMMC decisions were made by bankers and not enough by seamen imbued with the talent to beat the vagaries of the sea and to compete ship for ship with men they respected and admired.

Following the founding of IMMC wholesale ship transfers took place between the constituent companies and these are detailed in the appropriate chapters. From Red Star *Kensington* and *Southwark* were transferred to the Dominion Line's Canadian routes and *Noordland* and *Westernland* (I) moved across to American Line's Philadelphia berth. Red Star gave up Philadelphia as a base port and became a New York concern.

1904 *Switzerland* was sold to Italian owners.

1906 *Samland* (formerly ATL's *Mississippi*) was transferred to the Philadelphia route to replace *Nederland,* which went to Italian breakers.

1907 White Star's *Gothic* became *Gothland* when she was moved to the Philadelphia station.

1908 *Noordland,* always a Belgian flag carrier, was broken up.

1909 Apr: The handsome *Lapland* became Red Star's largest ship to date when she left Antwerp on her maiden voyage flying the Belgian flag.

1912 *Westernland* (I) and *Friesland* scrapped.

1914 Red Star ordered a 27,000-tonner, *Belgenland* (II). Because of the war she only entered their service in 1923 after a spell as White Star's *Belgic.*

Aug 4: The First World War began and Red Star's European home port fell into German hands. Red Star ships were then, in grey livery, freely interchanged on to other IMMC routes.

1915 Because of their Germanic names *Vaderland* (II) was renamed *Southland* and *Zeeland* (II) became *Northland.* They operated on the 'White Star-Dominion Line Joint Service.'

1916 *Kroonland* and *Finland* operated the American Line's Liverpool-New York service.

1917 June 4: *Southland,* ex-*Vaderland*

(II), torpedoed off Ireland.

1920 Aug: *Northland* reverted to *Zeeland* (II) and joined *Kroonland* in reopening the Antwerp-Southampton-New York route.

1923 *Kroonland* and *Finland* were transferred to the American Line for a Hamburg-New York service, but in October both were sold to the Panama Pacific SS Co.

1925 *Pennland* (II) came from White Star on to the Antwerp-New York berth. White Star also supplied, without change of name or colours, *Arabic.*

1926 Arnold Bernstein Reederei founded the Bernstein Line which in 1935 acquired the last two Red Star ships. *Gothland* broken up. IMMC sold White Star to the Royal Mail group; the effect was to leave the process of ship reshuffling to ATL, Leyland and Dominion although the latter concern had disappeared into Leyland back in 1921.

1927 *Zeeland* (II) was transferred to the Atlantic Transport Line and renamed *Minnesota.* From Leyland, for a year, came *Devonian* (II) and *Winifredian.* Red Star now followed earlier practice and transferred their three remaining owned vessels, *Belgenland* (II), *Lapland* and *Pennland* (II), to Frederick Leyland & Co who already had *Regina, Pennland*'s sister.

1930 The great depression hit the IMMC fleet. ATL went out of the passenger trade and Red Star operated their two remaining ships *Minnewaska* and *Minnetonka.* Dominion's *Regina* was renamed *Westernland* (II) and was placed on the Antwerp-Southampton-New York route.

1931 *Samland,* after being laid up out of service for the better part of two years, was broken up.

1932 *Belgenland* (II) was laid up at Antwerp. *Lapland* took Mediterranean cruises.

1934 *Lapland* was broken up in Japan but *Belgenland* was transferred to the Atlantic Transport Line of West Virginia and opened their New York-Panama-California route in 1935.

1935 *Pennland* (II) and *Westernland* (II) were sold to Arnold Bernstein of

Hamburg together with the name Red Star Line. He added a red star to the white band on the funnel. Both continued on the Antwerp-Southampton-New York route. With their departure IMMC's Red Star involvement ceased, and the International Navigation Co came to an end.

Routes

1872-1902 Antwerp-Philadelphia.
1876-1904 Antwerp-New York.
1902-4 Antwerp-Southampton-New York.

1904-14 Antwerp-Dover-New York.
1920 (one season) Hamburg-New York.

Livery

Funnel 1872 Buff, red five-pointed star and black top. 1893-1935 Black, white band. The band was one-tenth of the funnel height.
Hull Black with bright red waterline, deck vents black and small ones white, deck fittings black.
Uppers White. The earliest vessels had brown deckhouses.
Masts Biscuit brown.
Lifeboats White.

Fleet index

Illustrated fleet list

1-3

1 VADERLAND (I)

Bt 1873 Palmers & Co, Jarrow; *T:*
2,748 g, 2,001 n. **Dim** 320 ft 6 in (97.68
m) × 38 ft 6 in (11.73 m) × 23 ft 9 in
(7.23 m). **Eng** Sgl scr, compound
inverted; 2 cyls: 40 in (101.6 cm) and 80
in (203.2 cm); *Stroke:* 42 in (106.68 cm);
290 HP; *Stm P:* 75 lb; 12 kts; By
builder. **H** Iron, 2 decks and spar deck;
Pass: 70 1st, 500 3rd.

*Belgian registry. Intended to carry
petrol in bulk on the basis of carrying
passengers to the USA and petrol back.
Stringent restrictions led to the
discontinuation of this scheme.*

1872 Aug 21: Launched.
1873 Jan 19: Maiden voyage Antwerp-
Philadelphia.
1888 Sold. Became *Geographique.*
French.

2 NEDERLAND

Details as *Vaderland (1)* except: *T:*
2,839 g, 1,819 n. **Dim** Length 329 ft 2 in
(100.33 m). **H** 3 decks.

1873 June 23: Launched.
Dec: Maiden voyage Antwerp-
Philadelphia.
1906 May: Sold for breaking up in
Italy.

3 SWITZERLAND

Details as *Vaderland (1)* except:
Bt 1874; *T:* 2,816 g, 2,104 n. **Dim**
Length 329 ft 5 in (100.41 m). **H** 3
decks.

1874 Jan 17: Launched. Belgian
registry. Placed on Antwerp-
Philadelphia service.
1907 Sold. Became *Sansone.* Italian.
1908 Broken up.

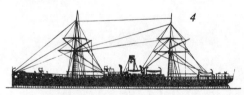

4

4 RUSSLAND

Bt 1872 Gourlay & Co, Dundee; *T:*
2,595 g, 1,912 n. **Dim** 345 ft (105.16
m) × 37 ft 8 in (11.48 m) × 23 ft 6 in
(7.16 m). **Eng** Sgl scr, compound; 2
cyls; 12 kts. **H** Iron, 2 decks; *Pass:* 20
1st.

1872 Built as *Kenilworth.* Chartered to
Red Star.
1876 Acquired to meet expanding
business needs for the Antwerp-New
York service.
1877 Mar 17: Wrecked on Long Island,
New York. No lives lost.

5 ZEELAND (I)

Bt 1865 J. & G. Thomson, Glasgow; *T:*
2,866 g, 1,850 n. **Dim** 337 ft 1 in
(102.74 m) × 42 ft 10 in (13.05 m) × 27 ft
8 in (8.43 m). **Eng** Sgl scr, compound
inverted; 2 cyls: 48 in (121.92 cm) and

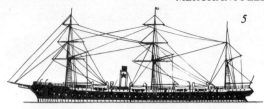

5

86 in (218.44 cm); *Stroke:* 45 in (114.3
cm); 350 HP; *Stm P:* 80 lb; 12 kts. **H**
Iron, 2 decks, 6 holds, fcsle 60 ft (18.29
m); *Pass:* 80 1st, 300 3rd.

1865 Built as *Java* for Cunard.
1877 Engine compounded by Fawcett,
Preston & Co, Liverpool.
1878 Acquired to replace *Russland (4).*
Renamed *Zeeland.* Antwerp-New York
service. Belgian registry.
1889 Sold. Traded as *Zeeland.*
1892 Became sailing vessel *Lord
Spencer.*
1895 Disappeared at sea.

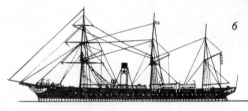

6

6 PERUSIA

Bt 1857 Tod & McGregor, Glasgow; *T:*
3,446 g, 2,207 n. **Dim** 352 ft 7 in
(107.46 m) × 41 ft 6 in (12.64 m) × 27 ft
6 in (8.38 m). **Eng** Sgl scr, compound
inverted; 2 cyls: 57 in (144.78 cm) and
95 in (241.3 cm); *Stroke:* 49 in (124.46
cm); 500 HP; *Stm P:* 60 lb; 12 kts. **H**
Iron, 3 decks and awning deck; *Pass:* 95
1st, 300 3rd.

1857 Built as *Nemesis* for P&O SN Co.
1869 Chartered to Cunard.
1871 Chartered to Inman.
1872 Chartered to Norddeutscher Lloyd
as *Perusia.* Engine compounded by
Rankin & Blackmore, Greenock.
1879 Purchased by Red Star. Antwerp-
New York service.
1880 Sold to P. Denny. Renamed
Nemesis.
1881 Broken up.

7 BELGENLAND (I)

Bt 1879 Barrow SB & E Co, Barrow-in-

Furness; *T:* 3,692 g, 2,364 n. **Dim** 402 ft
10 in (122.78 m) × 40 ft 2 in (12.24
m) × 30 ft 7 in (9.32 m). **Eng** Sgl scr,
compound; 2 cyls: 52 in (132.08 cm)
and 90 in (228.6 cm); *Stroke:* 54 in
(137.16 cm); 600 HP; *Stm P:* 80 lb; 14
kts; By builder. **H** Iron, 3 decks; *Pass:*
100 1st, 400 3rd.

1879 Antwerp-New York. Belgian
registry.
1895 Transferred to American Line.
1904 Sold. Became *Venere.* Italian.
1908 Out of Lloyds Register.

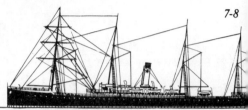

7-8

8 RHYNLAND

Details as *Belgenland (7)* except: *T:*
3,689 g, 2,366 n.

1879 Antwerp-New York. Belgian
registry.
1895 Transferred to American Line.
1906 Sold. Became *Rhyna,* Italy, and
broken up.

9 WAESLAND

Bt 1867 J. & G. Thomson, Glasgow; *T:*
2,960 g. **Dim** 358 ft (109.12 m) × 43 ft
(13.11 m) × 27 ft 9 in (8.46 m). **Eng** Sgl
scr; 2 cyls: 86 in (218.44 cm); *Stroke:* 45
in (114.3 cm); *Stm P:* 25 lb; 9 kts; By
builder. **H** Iron, 2 decks; *Pass:* 430
cabin.

1867 Built as *Russia* for Cunard.
1880 Lengthened to 435 ft (132.59 m)
(9a). *T:* 4,752 g. *Pass:* 100 1st, 1,000
3rd.
1881 Acquired by Red Star. Renamed
Waesland. Placed on the still expanding
Antwerp-New York service.
1895 Transferred to American Line.
Liverpool-Philadelphia service.
1902 Mar 7: Lost in collision with
Harmonides (Houston) off Anglesey,
Wales. Two lives lost.

10 PENNLAND (I)

Bt 1870 J. & G. Thomson, Glasgow; *T:*

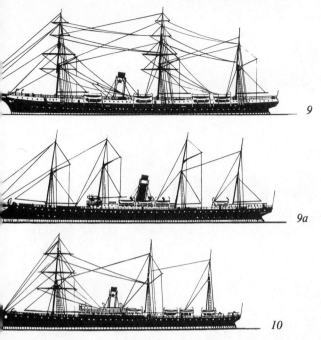

9

9a

10

3,760 g, 2,511 n. **Dim** 361 ft 2 in (110.08 m) × 41 ft 1 in (12.52 m) × 26 ft (7.92 m). **Eng** Sgl scr, compound; 2 cyls: 48 in (121.92 cm) and 84 in (213.36 cm); *Stroke:* 54 in (137.16 cm); 500 HP; *Stm P:* 80 lb; 12 kts; By J. Jack & Co, Liverpool. **H** Iron, 2 decks and spar deck; *Pass:* 100 1st, 450 3rd.

1870 Built as *Algeria* for Cunard.
1881 Engine compounded; 14 kts.
1882 Acquired. Renamed *Pennland.* Placed on Antwerp-New York service to enable the company to maintain weekly sailings in both directions. Belgian registry.
1888 New spar deck added.
1895 Transferred to American Line. Liverpool-Philadelphia service.
1903 Broken up in Italy.

11 NOORDLAND

Bt 1883 Laird Bros, Birkenhead; *T:* 5,212 g, 3,346 n. **Dim** 400 ft (121.92 m) × 47 ft (14.32 m) × 35 ft 4 in (10.77 m). **Eng** Sgl scr, compound; 2 cyls: 48 in (121.92 cm) and 55 in (139.7 cm); *Stroke:* 60 in (152.4 cm); 500 HP; *Stm P:* 80 lb; 13 kts; By builder. **H** Steel, 4 decks, fcsle 77 ft (23.46 m); *Pass:* 100 1st, 500 3rd.

1883 Antwerp-New York service.
1901 Transferred to American Line. Liverpool-Philadelphia service.
1908 Broken up.

12 WESTERNLAND (I)

Bt 1883 Laird Bros, Birkenhead; *T:* 5,736 g, 3,691 n. **Dim** 440 ft (134.11 m) × 47 ft 2 in (14.38 m) × 35 ft 4 in (10.77 m). **Eng** Sgl scr, compound; 2 cyls: 52 in (132.08 cm) and 93 in (236.22 cm); *Stroke:* 66 in (167.64 cm); 700 HP; *Stm P:* 90 lb; 14 kts; By builder. **H** Steel, 4 decks, fcsle 48 ft (14.63 m); *Pass:* 150 1st, 900 3rd.

1883 Antwerp-New York service.

11

12

13

1901 Transferred to American Line. Liverpool-Philadelphia route.
1912 Broken up.

13 FRIESLAND

Bt 1889 J. & G. Thomson, Glasgow; *T:* 6,409 g, 4,675 n. **Dim** 437 ft (133.2 m)×51 ft 2 in (15.6 m)×35 ft (10.67 m). **Eng** Sgl scr, tpl exp; 3 cyls: 35½ in (90.17 cm), 56 in (142.24 cm) and 89 (226.06 cm); *Stroke:* 54 in (137.16 cm); 764 NHP; 3 dbl and 1 sgl ended boilers, 21 furnaces; *Stm P:* 160 lb; 14 kts; By builder. **H** Steel, 4 decks, fcsle 54 ft (16.46 m), poop 42 ft (12.8 m); Pass: 226 1st, 102 2nd, 600 3rd.

Built with a strangely old-fashioned profile. The company's last clipper-bowed vessel and in fact almost the last North Atlantic liner without a straight stem.

1889 Aug 15: Launched for the Antwerp-New York service. Belgian registry.
1905 Transferred to American Line. *T:* 7,116 g.
1910 Became *La Plata,* Italy, but ownership not shown in Lloyds Register.
1912 Broken up.

14 VADERLAND (II)

Bt 1900 John Brown, Clydebank; *T:* 12,018 g, 8,288 n. **Dim** 560 ft 9 in (170.92 m)×60 ft 2 in (18.34 m)×38 ft 2 in (11.63 m). **Eng** Tw scr, quad exp; 2×4 cyls: 31 in (78.74 cm), 44 in (111.76 cm), 62 in (157.48 cm) and 88 in (223.52 cm); *Stroke:* 54 in (137.16 cm); 1,627 NHP; 8 sgl ended boilers, 28 furnaces; *Stm P:* 200 lb; 15 kts; By builder. **H** Steel, 3 decks, fcsle 84 ft (25.6 m), bridge 215 ft (65.53 m), poop 49 ft (14.93 m); *Pass:* 342 1st, 194 2nd, 626 3rd.

Built under British flag. Transferred to Belgian registration when placed on Antwerp-New York service. Reverted to British registry in 1915.

1900 July 12: Launched for Antwerp-New York service.
1915 Became *Southland* (International Nav Co). British. Ran for White Star-Dominion Line. Became troopship for Salonika campaign.
Sept 2: Torpedoed in Aegean Sea but reached port.
1917 June 4: Torpedoed off Irish coast. Four lives lost.

15 ZEELAND (II)

Details as *Vaderland (14)* except: *T:*

14-15

16-17

1,905 g, 7,511 n.
1901 Antwerp-New York. Belgian
registry.
1910-11 Ran for White Star. Liverpool-
Boston.
1915 Became *Northland* (International
Nav Co). British. Became troopship.
1920 Aug 18: Post-war sailings
Antwerp-Southampton-New York.
Renamed *Zeeland*.
1927 Transferred to Atlantic Transport
Line. Renamed *Minnesota*.
1930 Broken up.

16 KROONLAND

Bt 1902 W. Cramp & Son S & EB Co,
Philadelphia; *T:* 12,760 g, 7,927 n. **Dim**
560 ft (170.69 m) × 60 ft 2 in (18.34
m) × 38 ft 5 in (11.71 m). **Eng** Tw scr,
tpl exp; 2 × 3 cyls: 32½ in (82.55 cm),
54 in (137.16 cm) and 89½ in (227.33
cm); *Stroke:* 54 in (137.16 cm); 1,540
NHP; 9 sgl ended boilers, 36 furnaces;
Stm P: 170 lb; 15 kts; By builder. **H**
Steel, 4 decks, fcsle 88 ft (26.82 m),
bridge 273 ft (83.21 m), poop 48 ft
(14.63 m); *Pass:* 350 1st, 200 2nd, 600
3rd.

1902 Placed on Antwerp-New York
service under the American flag.
1916 Operated by American Line.
1920 Apr 14: Resumed post-war sailings
Antwerp-Southampton-New York.
1923 Nov: Sold to Panama Pacific Line.
New York-San Francisco.
1927 Broken up.

17 FINLAND

Details as *Kroonland (16)*.

1902 Antwerp-New York. US registry.
1916 Operated by American Line. New
York-Liverpool.
1920 Apr 28: Resumed service Antwerp-
Southampton-New York.
1923 Transferred to American Line.
New York-Hamburg.
Nov: Sold to Panama Pacific Line. New
York-San Francisco.
1927 Broken up.

18 SAMLAND

Bt 1903 New York SB Corp, Camden,
New Jersey; *T:* 9,710 g, 6,353 n. **Dim**
490 ft (149.35 m) × 58 ft 4 in (17.78
m) × 31 ft 9 in (9.68 m). **Eng** Tw scr, tpl
exp; 2 × 3 cyls: 25 in (63.5 cm), 42½ in
(107.95 cm) and 72 in (182.88 cm);
Stroke: 48 in (121.92 cm); 997 NHP; 2
dbl and 2 sgl ended boilers, 18
furnaces; *Stm P:* 200 lb; 14 kts; By
builder. **H** Steel, 3 decks, bridge 128 ft
(39.01 m).

1903 Built as *Mississippi* for Atlantic
Transport Line.
1906 Acquired by Red Star. Renamed
Samland. Antwerp-Philadelphia.
1911-13 Operated by White Star Line.
Renamed *Belgic*.
1914 Reverted to US flag and *Samland*.
1931 Broken up.

19 GOTHLAND

Bt 1893 Harland & Wolff, Belfast; *T:*
7,669 g, 4,930 n. **Dim** 490 ft 7 in
(149.53 m) × 53 ft 2 in (16.21 m) × 33 ft
6 in (10.21 m). **Eng** Tw scr, tpl exp;
2 × 3 cyls: 26 in (66.04 cm), 42½

18

19

20

(107.95 cm) and 70 in (177.8 cm); *Stroke:* 51 in (129.54 cm); 700 NHP; 14 kts; By builder. **H** Steel, 3 decks, fcsle 61 ft (18.59 m), poop 58 ft (17.68 m); *Pass:* 150 1st, 125 2nd, 600 3rd.

1893 Built as *Gothic* for White Star Line.
1907 Acquired by Red Star. Renamed *Gothland.* Antwerp-Philadelphia.
1911-13 Operated by White Star. Renamed *Gothic.*
1914 Reverted to *Gothland.* Antwerp-New York.
1926 Broken up Bo'ness, Firth of Forth.

20 LAPLAND

Bt 1909 Harland & Wolff, Belfast; *T:* 18,694 g, 13,120 n. **Dim** 605 ft 8 in (184.61 m) × 70 ft 4 in (21.44 m) × 37 ft 4 in (11.38 m). **Eng** Tw scr, quad exp; 2 × 4 cyls: 32½ in (82.55 cm), 47 in (119.38 cm), 68 in (172.72 cm) and 98 in (248.92 cm); *Stroke:* 63 in (160.02 cm); 1,524 NHP; 16 kts; By builder. **H** Steel, 3 decks and shelter deck, fcsle 62 ft (18.9 m), bridge 348 ft (106.07 m); *Pass:* 450 1st, 400 2nd, 1,500 3rd.

1909 Apr: Antwerp-Dover-New York.
1914-19 Operated by White Star Line. Liverpool-New York including some Southampton-New York.
1920 Jan 3: Resumed sailings Antwerp-New York. Belgian registry.
1932-33 Mediterranean cruises.
1933 Oct: Sold to Japan.
1934 Broken up in Japan.

21 BELGENLAND (II)

Bt 1914 Harland & Wolff, Belfast; *T:* 27,132 g, 15,440 n. **Dim** 670 ft 4 in (204.31 m) × 78 ft 4 in (23.87 m) × 44 ft 7 in (13.59 m). **Eng** Tpl scr, tpl exp and LP turbine to centre shaft; 2 × 4 cyls: 35½ in (90.17 cm), 56 in (142.24 cm) and 2 × 64 in (162.56 cm); *Stroke:* 60 in (152.4 cm); 10 dbl ended boilers; *Stm P:* 215 lb; 17 kts; By builder. **H** Steel, 4 decks, bridge and poop 574 ft (174.95 m), upper bridge 371 ft (113.08 m); *Pass:* 500 1st, 500 2nd, 1,500 3rd.

1914 Dec 31: Launched. Laid up incomplete due to the war.
1917 Became *Belgic* for White Star Line. *T:* 24,547 g, 15,440 n. 2 funnels and 3 masts. Cargo vessel only, without

21

21a

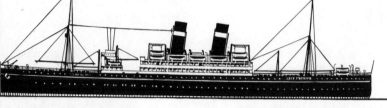

22-23

passenger accommodation.
1923 Apr 4: First voyage as passenger liner *Belgenland (21a)*. Antwerp-Southampton-New York.
1932 Jan 8: Last voyage for Red Star Line.
1935 Became *Columbia* (Atlantic Transport Co of West Virginia).
1936 Broken up Grangemouth, Firth of Forth, Scotland.

22 PITTSBURGH/PENNLAND (II)

For details of this vessel see White Star section, entry *82*.

23 WESTERNLAND (II)

For details of this vessel see White Star section, entry *83*.

Inman Line

History

1850 The Liverpool & Philadelphia Steam Ship Company was founded by the Liverpool ship management of Richardson Brothers & Co. One of the three partners was William Inman. The company purchased, from her builders Tod & McGregor, the *City of Glasgow,* held by some to be the pioneer transatlantic liner. With her the company opened its Liverpool-Philadelphia service.

1851 July: *City of Manchester* added.

1852 To cater for the emigrant trade 400 steerage berths were added to both vessels.

1854 Mar: *City of Glasgow* disappeared at sea without trace.

Sept: The new *City of Philadelphia* was lost on her maiden voyage.

The Crimean War commenced. The French Government chartered *City of Manchester* and two new vessels nearing completion, *City of Baltimore* and *City of Washington.* It was at this time that the two Richardson brothers, being Quakers, withdrew from the company because they disagreed with the policy of chartering the three vessels for trooping purposes. William Inman, who approved the deal, remained and the company henceforth became known as the Inman Line.

1855 The company had no vessels that were not on war service and there was no transatlantic service.

1856 Apr: *City of Baltimore* resumed the Liverpool-Philadelphia run to be joined during the year by *City of Manchester, City of Washington* and the demobilised *Kangaroo,* which had

been purchased in 1854 together with her trooping contract.

Dec 31: *City of Washington* inaugurated calls at New York.

1857 Mar: To cater for the growth of New York traffic the name of the company was changed to the Liverpool, New York and Philadelphia Steam Ship Company. The sailings to New York rapidly predominated so that Philadelphia became a secondary port of call. In this year the company carried 70,000 passengers, one third of all transatlantic travellers.

1858 The Indian Mutiny commenced and *City of Manchester* was recalled for trooping. To replace her the French *Vigo* was purchased, entering service in September.

1859 To cater for the Irish emigrant trade Queenstown (Cobh) was introduced as a port of call. *City of Manchester* made the first Inman call there.

During the winter *Edinburgh* and *Glasgow,* the last two vessels of the Glasgow & North Steam Ship Company, were purchased It was at first thought that a Glasgow service would continue but both vessels were operated from Liverpool, maintaining a weekly service.

1860 Cunard's *Etna* was purchased as the relief vessel.

1861 Sept: *City of New York* (I) commissioned.

1863 An 'extra' service to New York was introduced. This required three vessels. *City of Cork* and *City of London* were new and *African* was purchased and renamed *City of*

Limerick.

1864 Mar: _City of New York_ (I) lost on Daunt's Rock.

1865 July: _Glasgow_ was burnt at sea and foundered.

A feeder service between Halifax and St John's, New Brunswick, commenced. The twice weekly services continued to cater for the boom in transatlantic travel which followed the American Civil War. However, business started to fall off in 1866.

1867 A slump set in. Alternative uses were sought for the 'extra' service vessels. _City of Limerick_ tried the Liverpool-New Orleans route, and _City of Cork_ and _Kangaroo_ were put on an Antwerp-New York service.

The Cunard contract between Liverpool and Halifax and Boston lapsed and in keen bidding William Inman secured a subsidy for a fortnightly service between Queenstown and Halifax. _Etna_ took the first sailing. In the same year the US Post Office awarded the Inman Line a contract between New York-Queenstown-Liverpool.

1869 The US contract, which had been on the basis of payment by category of mail carried, was replaced by an annual subsidy of £35,000 for a weekly service New York-Queenstown-Liverpool.

Mar: _City of Brussels_ entered service. It was also in this year that the company started to lengthen its ships, a practice that Harland & Wolff initiated. Previously the length to beam ratio had been of the order of 8½:1, but now 10:1 became the accepted average for all trading purposes. The ratio of _City of Brussels_ reflected the new practice. Various Inman vessels were lengthened, commencing with _City of Washington._

1870 The 'extra' service was reintroduced with sailings from Liverpool on Thursdays and Saturdays. When the Canadian mail contract expired Halifax ceased to be a port of call. During this year the Inman Line carried 3,600 cabin and 40,500 steerage passengers, a total which exceeded Cunard; in fact Inman's nearest rival was National Line.

1871 Jan: _City of Boston_ disappeared without trace, probably as a result of striking an iceberg.

The White Star Line's transatlantic service commenced and Inman had to think about building ships capable of competing.

1872 _City of Montreal_ entered service. She was intended to help maintain the Inman reputation in the face of the new vessels of White Star.

1873 Saw the arrival of _City of Chester_ and _City of Richmond,_ the first two-funnellers. None of the three new ships became record breakers and the Blue Riband remained with White Star, who had won it in May of the preceding year.

1875 The Inman Steamship Co Ltd was formed, the company entering into a period of collaboration with White Star. Apr: _City of Berlin,_ designed to take the transatlantic record, entered service and at 5,500 tons was the largest steamer on the North Atlantic (_Great Eastern,_ built 1860, was at this time laid up at Milford Haven). She won the record but held it for four months only.

The 'extra' service to New York was ended due to a further slump in travel and continued over-capacity on the route.

1879-80 The slump led to the selling of the smaller ships. _City of London_ went first, followed by _City of Limerick, City of Dublin, City of Bristol_ (ex-_Etna_), _City of Antwerp_ and _City of Brooklyn._ They were disposed of because the size of ships had doubled in ten years and new ships had to be large, fast and comfortable.

1881 _City of Rome_ launched and entered service, where she was a considerable disappointment. William Inman died in July, aged 56, at his home at Upton, Wirral, Cheshire, and therefore did not live to see his dream-ship fail to come up to expectations. Her failure arose from the need to use considerable amounts of iron instead of the steel planned.

1882 _City of Rome_ was handed back to her builders.

1883 Jan: _City of Brussels_ sank after collision in Liverpool Bay. To fill the gap this caused the company purchased the nearly-completed *Vancouver* of Dominion Line, renaming her *City of Chicago*. *City of New York* (II) was sold to Allan Line.

1883-86 To fill the gap caused by *City of Rome*'s failure White Star's *Baltic* was employed in Inman service. *City of Rome* herself was now being operated by Anchor Line.

1884 *City of Paris* (I) sold to French owners.

1886 The Inman Line was now in serious financial difficulties. The older ships had gone and a capital shortage made it difficult to replace them and fulfil the fleet's requirements with modern tonnage. Attempts to raise money failed.

Oct: The company went into voluntary liquidation so that the American International Navigation Company, already owners of Red Star Line and American Line, could acquire the fleet and assets of the Inman Line. This they did, and the International Navigation Co Ltd, registered in England with its head office in Liverpool, took over the fleet. To perpetuate the famous name the operating company became the Inman & International Steamship Co Ltd. Thus despite the predominantly American capital the ships remained under the British flag.

1887 Aug: Misfortune continued to dog the company when *City of Montreal* was destroyed at sea. The fleet was thus reduced to four, of which *City of Berlin* was in Laird's yard being re-engined and modernised and would remain there for four more months. To maintain their service the American Line transferred the *Ohio*. This interchange within the trio of companies started a custom which led to the eventual disappearance of Inman & International.

1888 *City of New York* (III), then the largest steamer in the world, entered service. She was the first large express liner to have twin screws.

1889 Her sister, *City of Paris* (II), was commissioned. She took the Blue Riband back from Cunard's *Etruria* in both directions.

1891 The company needed only four

ships to operate a weekly service to New York with a fifth as standby for overhaul periods. The company owned six, so they sold *City of Richmond*. The fleet now comprised *City of Chester, City of Berlin, City of New York* (III), *City of Paris* (II) and *City of Chicago*.

1892 May 10: For some time it had been hoped to increase the number of US flag carriers on the North Atlantic and an Act of Congress now ensured the transfer of the company's two newest British flag vessels (*City of New York* and *City of Paris*) to US flag registry. In the autumn the contract for the carriage of the mails from New York to Southampton was awarded to Inman & International provided that the vessels employed were all US flag.

July: *City of Chicago* lost near Kinsale.

1893 Feb: The last Liverpool-New York Inman sailing took place. The fleet and service was then transferred to Southampton and the head office was moved to New York, into the American Line offices. All Inman vessels became US flag ships. In order to tidy up the situation the *City* prefixes were dropped and the fleet became *Chester, New York, Paris* and *Berlin*. The last remaining indication of any connection with the great Inman name was that the vessels of the American Line and Red Star Line adopted the black Inman funnel with its perfectly placed white band. The original Inman house flag had disappeared when Inman & International was formed, and to signify the 1893 reformation a new house flag, white with a blue bald eagle thereon, was now introduced. This is the flag which is today flown by the United States Line.

1902 The International Navigation Co of New Jersey, owners of the Red Star Line and American Line, changed its name to the International Mercantile Marine Company, the history of which has been covered under the section on the Red Star Line.

Routes

1850-56 Liverpool-Philadelphia.

1856 Liverpool-New York-Philadelphia.
1857-93 Liverpool-Queenstown (Cobh)-
New York.
1867-70 Liverpool-New Orleans.

1867-68 Antwerp-New York.
1867-70 Queenstown-Halifax with
feeder service to St John, New
Brunswick.

Livery

Funnel Black with broad white band.
Uppers White with some brown
deckhouses.
Hull Black with red waterline.
Masts Buff.
Lifeboats White with red lead coloured
interiors.

Fleet index

Illustrated fleet list

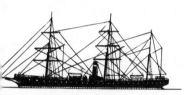

1 CITY OF GLASGOW

Bt 1850 Tod & McGregor, Glasgow; *T:*
1,610 g. **Dim** 258 ft (78.64 m) oa, 237 ft
(72.24 m) × 34 ft (10.36 m) × 25 ft (7.62
m). **Eng** Sgl scr, athwartship beam
geared engine; 2 cyls: 71 in (180.34 cm);
Stroke: 60 in (152.4 cm); 3 sgl ended
boilers; *Stm P:* 10 lb; 9 kts; Propeller
diam 13 ft (3.96 m), 2 bladed. **H** Iron, 1
deck; *Pass:* 52 1st, 85 2nd (400 3rd
added 1852); *Crew:* 70.

*The beam geared engine had two
cylinders on the port side. Two centrally
pivoted beams crossed the ship and were
cranked to a large cog wheel. The
wheel, with a ratio of 3:1, meshed
directly onto the teeth of the propeller
shaft pinion. The stroke took 4 seconds
to give 45 rpm to the screw.*

1850 Made four round voyages for Tod
& McGregor to enable them to gain
experience of vessels in a seaway.
Dec: Acquired by Liverpool &
Philadelphia SS Co (managers
Richardson Brothers & Partners).
Dec 17: Liverpool-Philadelphia in
Inman colours, a white band being
painted on the black funnel.
1851-54 Inman service Liverpool-New
York. Fares: 21 guineas first class, 13
guineas second class.
1852 Passenger accommodation added
for 400 third class. Commanded by

Captain B. E. Matthews (ex-*Great
Eastern*).
1854 Mar 1: Sailed Liverpool-New
York. Disappeared without trace. 480
lost.

2 CITY OF MANCHESTER

Bt 1851 Tod & McGregor, Glasgow; *T:*
1,892 g, 2,125 dwt. **Dim** 274 ft (83.51
m) oa, 339 ft (103.33 m) jib to taffrail,
265 ft (80.77 m) × 37 ft (11.28 m) × 25 ft
(7.62 m). **Eng** Sgl scr, beam geared as
(1); Cyl: 70 in (177.8 cm); *Stroke:* 60 in
(152.4 cm); 400 NHP; *Stm P:* 10 lb; 9
kts. **H** Iron, 1 deck; *Pass:* 150 1st, 400
3rd; *Crew:* 80.

*The two square-rigged masts were of
tubular iron.*

1851 June 14: Launched.
July 26: Maiden voyage Liverpool-
Philadelphia. Captain Campbell.
1854 Chartered by French Government
as Crimean War transport. Marseilles-
Crimea service.
1856 *T:* 2,109 g.
1857 Transport during Indian Mutiny.
1859 Apr: Queenstown (Cobh)
introduced as port of call. First call
made by *City of Manchester*.
1862 Reboilered, 3 dbl ended.
1871 Feb: Sold. Engines removed.
Served as four-masted barque.
1876 Wrecked.

3

3 CITY OF PITTSBURGH

Bt 1851 New York; *T:* 1,500 g. **Dim** 245 ft (74.67 m) × 38 ft (11.58 m) × 22 ft (6.7 m). **Eng** Sgl scr, direct acting; 2 cyls: 71 in (180.34 cm); *Stroke:* 48 in (121.92 cm); 120 HP; *Stm P:* 8 lb; 9 kts. **H** Wood, 1 deck.

1851 This vessel was not owned by Inman Line but they acted as her agents in Liverpool, New York and Philadelphia. Her owners were the New York and San Francisco Steamship Co. Nevertheless she wore Inman colours.
Oct 27: Maiden voyage Philadelphia-Liverpool in 19½ days.
Nov 29: On return voyage lost propeller three days out. Voyage completed under sail and took 45 days.
1852 Inaugurated New York-Philadelphia-San Francisco via Cape Horn service.
Oct 24: Caught fire at Valparaiso. Burnt out and a total loss but no lives lost. Insured for $279,000.

4-6

4 CITY OF PHILADELPHIA

Bt 1855 Tod & McGregor, Glasgow; *T:* 2,368 g. **Dim** 294 ft (89.61 cm) × 39 ft (11.89 m) × 24 ft (7.31 m). **Eng** Sgl scr, beam geared (ratio 3½:1); 2 cyls: 70 in (177.8 cm); *Stroke:* 60 in (152.4 cm); 450 NHP; *Stm P:* 10 lb; 10 kts. **H** Iron, 1 deck, fcsle 75 ft (22.86 m); *Pass:* 200 1st, 400 3rd; *Crew:* 82.

1854 Aug 30: Maiden voyage Liverpool-Philadelphia.
Sept 9: Wrecked Cape Race on maiden voyage. No lives lost.

5 CITY OF BALTIMORE

Details as *City of Philadelphia (4)* except: **Bt** 1855; *T:* 2,368 g. **Dim** Length 326 ft (99.36 m).

1855 Laid down as a sister of *City of Philadelphia* she was lengthened by 30 ft (9.14 m) during construction and 50 cabin class berths added.
Mar 20: Maiden voyage Liverpool-Marseilles to become French Government Crimean War transport. It was the chartering of this vessel to the French which caused the Richardson brothers to withdraw from the firm.
1856 Apr 23: First voyage Liverpool-Philadelphia.
1874 Sold. Renamed *Fivaller* by Hall Line.
1882 Became *Benicarlo*. Spanish.

6 CITY OF WASHINGTON

Details as *City of Philadelphia (4)* except: *T:* 2,380 g. **Dim** Length 319 ft (97.23 m), width 40 ft (12.19 m).

1855 The third Inman-built vessel to be chartered for French Government Crimean War service.
1856 Dec 31: First Inman voyage Liverpool-New York. This marked the opening of the New York service. This arose because *Kangaroo (7)* was frozen in the Delaware river for five weeks, though New York was itself ice free. The New York service initially alternated with Philadelphia.
1869 Lengthened to 358 ft (109.12 m) and modernised. *T:* 2,870 g. Barque-rigged.
1873 July 7: Wrecked Cape Sable. No lives lost.

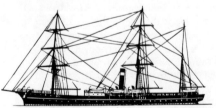

7

7 KANGAROO

Bt 1853 Charles Hill & Co, Bristol; *T:* 1,773 g. **Dim** 257 ft 5 in (78.46 m) × 36 ft 2 in (11.02 m) × 27 ft (8.23 m). **Eng** Sgl scr, oscillating; 2 cyls; 160 HP: *Stm*

P: 8 lb; 9 kts. **H** Iron, 1 deck; *Pass:* 80
1st, 130 2nd.

Kangaroo's *sisters were* Emeu, *which
went to Cunard, and* Dinornis, Black
Swan *and* Menura, *all of which were
sold to the French company Messageries
Imperiales, later Messageries Maritimes,
and were renamed* Indus, Gange *and*
Euphrate *respectively.*

1853 One of five sisters built for
Australasian Pacific Mail SP Co, a
subsidiary of Royal Mail and Pacific
Steam Navigation.
1854 Did not enter service Panama-
Australia but was chartered for Crimean
War service at £100 per day. When, on
May 2, her owners went into liquidation
Inman took her over cum-contract.
1856 July 30: Entered Inman service
Liverpool-Philadelphia. 200 cabin class
berths.
1870 Chartered to E. Bates & Co.
1876 Sold. Converted into cable vessel
by the Telegraph Construction &
Maintenance Co. Same name. Mainmast
removed.
1888 Became *Selamet,* Turkish.
1901 Broken up.

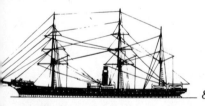

8 VIGO

Bt 1855 John Laird, Birkenhead; *T:*
1,953 g. **Dim** 270 ft (82.29 m) × 35 ft
(10.67 m) × 26 ft (7.92 m). **Eng** Sgl scr,
tw cyl horizontal, direct acting; 2 cyls:
72 in (182.88 cm); *Stroke:* 60 in (152.4
cm); 400 NHP; *Stm P:* 14 lb; 10 kts; By
builder. **H** Iron, 1 deck, fcsle 40 ft
(12.19 m); *Pass:* 200 cabin.

Vigo's *sisters,* Erie *and* Huron, *were
also acquired by Spain and France but
in 1858 were resold to P&O as* Behar
and Ellora.

1854 Laid down as *Huron* for Canadian
Steam Navigation Co.
1855 Acquired on stocks by Vapores
Correos Espanoles Trasatlanticos.

Renamed *Vigo.*
1856 Sold to Compagnie Franco
Americaine, France. Same name.
1858 Acquired by Inman Line to replace
City of Manchester, taken up for Indian
Mutiny service.
Sept 1: First Inman voyage Liverpool-
New York.
1861 Sold to United States Government.
Remained as *Vigo.*
1881 Broken up.

9 EDINBURGH

Bt 1855 Tod & McGregor, Glasgow; *T:*
2,197 g, 1,494 n. **Dim** 300 ft (91.44
m) × 39 ft 8 in (12.09 m) × 25 ft 8 in
(7.82 m). **Eng** Sgl scr, compound; 2
cyls: 44 in (111.76 cm) and 78 in (198.12
cm); *Stroke:* 42 in (106.68 cm); 275 HP;
Stm P: 47 lb; By Laird Bros,
Birkenhead. **H** Iron, 2 decks and spar
deck; *Pass:* 160 cabin, 300 3rd.

1855 Built as *Edinburgh* for Glasgow &
New York Steam Ship Co.
Dec 28: Maiden voyage Glasgow-New
York.
1859 Purchased with *Glasgow* by Inman
Line. Everyone expected her to continue
the Glasgow service.
Nov 23: Entered Liverpool-New York
route. Thereafter only intermittent
Glasgow sailings.
1870 Chartered to E. Bates & Co.
1872 Sold to Telegraph Construction
Co. Converted to cable ship. Same
name. As a cable layer *Edinburgh* had
four cable tanks: No 1 26 ft (7.92 m)
diam × 7 ft 8 in (2.34 m) deep; No 2 32
ft (9.75 m) × 22 ft (6.7 m); No 3 32 ft
(9.75 m) × 22 ft (6.7 m); and No 4 24 ft
(7.31 m) × 12 ft 6 in (3.81 m), = 40,200
cu ft (1,137.66 cu m) of cable.
187? Sold to Dutch owners. Renamed
Amsterdam.
1880 Acquired by Adamson &
Ronaldson for London-Boston service.
Renamed *Edinburgh.*

1887 Sold to Italian Government.
Renamed.
1894 Broken up Italy.

10 GLASGOW

Bt 1851 Tod & McGregor, Glasgow; *T:*
1,962 g. **Dim** 262 ft (79.85 m) × 36 ft
(10.97 m) × 22 ft (6.7 m). **Eng** Sgl scr,
direct acting; 2 cyls; 10 kts. **H** Iron, 2
decks, headroom 7 ft 6 in (2.28 m);
Coal: 600 tons; *Cargo:* 1,500 tons; *Pass:*
160 cabin, 200 3rd.

1851 Built as *Glasgow,* first vessel for
the new Glasgow & New York Steam
Ship Co.
Sept 16: Maiden voyage Glasgow-New
York.
1854-56 Chartered to French
Government for Crimean War service.
1859 Sold to Inman Line with *Edinburgh
(9).* The sale resulted from the loss of
her sister, *New York,* on Mull of
Kintyre; the fortnightly service could
not then be maintained and the trade
did not warrant a new ship.
1860 Feb 22: First Inman voyage.
Liverpool-New York.
1865 July 31: Caught fire at sea. Burnt
out and sank. No lives lost.

11 ETNA

Bt 1855 Caird & Co, Greenock; *T:*
2,215 g. **Dim** 305 ft (92.96 m) × 36 ft 3
in (11.05 m) × 27 ft (8.23 m). **Eng** Sgl
scr, beam geared; 2 cyls; 10 kts; By
Laird Bros, Birkenhead. **H** Iron, 1 deck.

1855 Built for Cunard. Immediately
became Crimean War transport.
1856 Feb 5: Entered Cunard service.
Havre-New York then Liverpool-New
York.
1857 Feb 24: Operated by European and
Australian Royal Mail Co.
Southampton-Malta-Alexandria. Last
sailing Aug 12.

1860 Acquired by Inman Line.
Dec 5: First voyage Liverpool-New York.
1871 Renamed *City of Bristol* after
modernising which included lengthening
to 349 ft 4 in (106.48 m) and increasing
tonnage to 2,655 g, installing extra
passenger space, new boilers and new
compound inverted engines; 2 cyls; 48½
in (123.19 cm) and 84½ in (214.63 cm);
Stroke: 42 in (106.68 cm); 350 HP; *Stm
P:* 60 lb. Width increased to 37 ft 7 in
(11.45 m), depth to 27 ft 1 in (8.26 m).
May 30: First voyage after renaming.
Liverpool-New York.
1880 Sold to J. P. Davies, Liverpool.

12 CITY OF NEW YORK (I)

Bt 1861 Tod & McGregor, Glasgow; *T:*
2,360 g. **Dim** 336 ft (102.41 m) × 40 ft
(12.19 m) × 28 ft (8.53 m). **Eng** Sgl scr,
horizontal trunk; 2 cyls; 350 HP; *Stm
P:* 60 lb; 12 kts; By Laird Bros,
Birkenhead. **H** Iron, 1 deck; *Pass:* 100
1st, 300 3rd.

1861 Sept 11: Maiden voyage Liverpool-
New York.
1864 Mar 29: Wrecked in dense fog on
Daunt Rocks near Queenstown, Ireland,
when she stood in too close to shore.
No lives lost.

13 CITY OF CORK

Bt 1863 Wm Denny & Co, Dumbarton;
T: 1,547 g. **Dim** 265 ft (80.77 m) × 33 ft
(10.06 m) × 24 ft (7.31 m). **Eng** Sgl scr,
oscillating; 2 cyls; 10 kts. **H** Iron, 1
deck; *Pass:* 60 1st, 150 3rd.

1863 Mar 21: Maiden voyage Liverpool-
New York.

1871 Too small and not worth lengthening or modernising. Sold.

14 CITY OF LIMERICK

Bt 1855 Smith & Rodgers, Glasgow; *T:* 1,529 g, 1,040 n. **Dim** 281 ft (85.65 m) × 34 ft 4 in (10.46 m) × 30 ft 4 in (9.25 m). **Eng** Sgl scr, beam geared; 2 cyls; 10 kts. **H** Iron, 1 deck.

1855 Built as *African* for Dizon & Co. British.
1863 Acquired by Inman Line.
May 29: First voyage Liverpool-New York.
1870 Modernised. Lengthened to 331 ft 1 in (100.92 m). *T:* 2,536 g. Compound engines fitted; 2 cyls: 36 in (91.44 cm) and 72 in (182.88 cm); *Stroke:* 42 in (108.68 cm); 250 HP; *Stm P:* 75 lb; 10 kts; By G. Forrester & Co, Liverpool.
1880 Sold to William Ross & Co, Thistle Line. London-New York service.
1882 Jan 8: Disappeared at sea. 43 lost.

15

15 CITY OF LONDON

Bt 1863 Tod & McGregor, Glasgow; *T:* 2,560 g. **Dim** 281 ft 5 in (85.78 m) × 38 ft 8 in (11.78 m) × 29 ft (8.84 m). **Eng** Sgl scr, compound inverted; 2 cyls: 52 in (132.08 cm) and 89 in (226.06 cm); *Stroke:* 48 in (121.92 cm); 450 HP; *Stm P:* 70 lb; 12 kts. **H** Iron, 3 decks; *Pass:* 150 cabin, 400 3rd.

1863 July 8: Maiden voyage Liverpool-New York.
1869 Lengthened to 374 ft (113.99 m) and modernised. *T:* 2,765 g.
1879 Sold to William Ross & Co, Thistle Line, for London-New York route. Two ships were sold, this and the *City of Limerick (14)*. They were delivered at the end of their respective advertised sailings.
1881 Nov 13: Sailed. Disappeared at sea. 41 lost.

16 CITY OF DUBLIN

Bt 1864 Smith & Rodgers, Glasgow; *T:* 2,138 g. **Dim** 318 ft (96.93 m) × 36 ft 3 in (11.05 m) × 29 ft 5 in (8.97 m). **Eng** Sgl scr, beam geared; 2 cyls; 11 kts. **H** Iron, 2 decks; *Pass:* 100 cabin, 400 3rd.

1864 Built as *Hellespont* for British owners. Acquired by Inman Line. Sept 3: First voyage Liverpool-New York.
1873 Became *Quebec* (Dominion Line). Compound engines fitted; Cyls: 46 in (116.84 cm) and 78 in (198.12 cm); *Stroke:* 42 in (106.68 cm); 275 HP; *Stm P:* 60 lb; By Laird Bros, Birkenhead.
1883 Sold. Became *Nautique*. French.
1890 Foundered in North Atlantic.

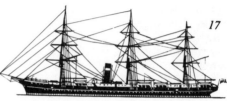

17

17 CITY OF BOSTON

Bt 1865 Tod & McGregor, Glasgow; *T:* 2,278 g. **Dim** 332 ft (101.19 m) oa, 305 ft 5 in (93.09 m) × 35 ft (10.68 m) × 27 ft (8.23 m). **Eng** Sgl scr, compound inverted; 4 cyls; 12 kts. **H** Iron, 2 decks; *Pass:* 100 cabin, 400 3rd.

Entered service ship-rigged. Later converted to barque rig.

1864 Nov 15: Launched.
1865 Feb 8: Maiden voyage Liverpool-New York.
1870 Jan 25: Sailed New York for Liverpool. Disappeared without trace. 177 lives lost.

18 CITY OF NEW YORK (II)

Bt 1865 Tod & McGregor, Glasgow; *T:* 2,642 g. **Dim** 321 ft 6 in (97.99 m) × 39 ft 7 in (12.06 m) × 33 ft (10.06 m). **Eng** Sgl scr, horizontal trunk; 2 cyls: 89 in (226.06 cm); *Stroke:* 42 in (106.68 cm); 12 kts; By builder. **H** Iron, 2 decks; *Coal:* 105 tons per day; *Pass:* 100 cabin, 400 3rd.

1865 Built as *Delaware*. Purchased before completion.
June 7: Maiden voyage Liverpool-New

York.
1871 Lengthened to 375 ft (114.3 m). *T:* 3,081 g, 2,380 n. *Pass:* 150 cabin, 400 3rd.
1879 Compound engines installed.
1883 Sold to Allan Line. Renamed *Norwegian.*
1903 Broken up in Holland.

19 CITY OF DURHAM

Bt 1865 James Laing & Co, Glasgow; *T:* 697 g, 538 n. **Dim** 201 ft (61.26 m) × 28 ft 9 in (8.76 m) × 16 ft 7 in (5.05 m). **Eng** Sgl scr, compound inverted; 2 cyls: 28 in (71.12 cm) and 42 in (106.68 cm); *Stroke:* 30 in (76.2 cm); 120 HP; *Stm P:* 95 lb; 10 kts; By Laird Bros, Birkenhead. **H** Iron, 1 deck, 4 holds.

1865 Aug: Built for feeder service between Halifax and St John, New Brunswick.
1870 Halifax ceased to be an Inman port of call.
1878 Sold to J. Edwards, Liverpool.

20

20 CITY OF PARIS (I)

Bt 1866 Tod & McGregor, Glasgow; *T:* 2,556 g. **Dim** 346 ft (105.46 m) × 40 ft (12.19 m) × 26 ft (7.92 m). **Eng** Sgl scr, horizontal trunk; 2 cyls: 89 in (226.06 cm); *Stroke:* 42 in (106.68 cm); 450 HP; 13 kts. **H** Iron, 2 decks; *Pass:* 150 cabin, 400 3rd.

When built City of Paris *was one of the fastest vessels afloat, closely matched for speed by Cunard's* Scotia.

1866 Mar 21: Maiden voyage Liverpool-New York.
1870 Lengthened to 398 ft (121.31 m). *T:* 3,500 g. *Pass:* 150 cabin, 400 3rd.
1879 Compound engine fitted.
1884 Sold. Became *Tonquin.* French.
1885 Mar: Sunk off Malaga, Spain, in collision.

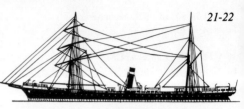

21-22

21 CITY OF ANTWERP

Bt 1867 Tod & McGregor, Glasgow; *T:* 2,391 g, 1,626 n. **Dim** 332 ft (101.19 m) × 39 ft 4 in (11.99 m) × 25 ft 10 in (7.87 m). **Eng** Sgl scr, inverted; 2 cyls: 69 in (175.26 cm); *Stroke:* 36 in (91.44 cm); 550 HP; *Stm P:* 30 lb, 12 kts; By builder. **H** Iron, 2 decks; *Pass:* 150 1st, 400 3rd.

1867 Feb 20: Maiden voyage Liverpool-New York.
1879 Sold. Became *Thanemore* (Johnston Line). British. Fitted with compound engines.
1890 Nov 26: Sailed and disappeared without trace. 43 lives lost. Assumed to have hit one of several icebergs reported in the area.

22 CITY OF BROOKLYN

Details as *City of Antwerp (21)* except: *T:* 2,911 g, 1,980 n. **Dim** Length 354 ft (107.9 m).

1869 Mar 31: Maiden voyage Liverpool-New York.
1879 Sold. Became *Brooklyn* (Dominion Line). British. Lengthened to 400 ft (121.92 m) and fitted with compound engines. *T:* 4,215 g.
1885 Nov 8: Wrecked on Anticosti Island. No lives lost.

23 AJAX

Bt 1867 Tod & McGregor, Glasgow; *T:* 163 g, 133 n. **Dim** 108 ft (32.92 m) × 23 ft 1 in (7.04 m) × 8 ft 10 in (2.69 m). **Eng** Sgl scr, inverted; 2 cyls: 14½ in (36.83 cm); *Stroke:* 18 in (45.72 cm); 30 HP; *Stm P:* 45 lb; 9 kts; By builder. **H** Iron, 1 deck.

1867 Tug at Liverpool.

24 CITY OF HALIFAX

Bt 1868 Watson & Co, Sunderland; *T:* 681 g, 462 n. **Dim** 204 ft 3 in (62.25 m) × 29 ft 10 in (9.09 m) × 17 ft 6 in

25

26

(5.33 m). **Eng** Sgl scr; 2 cyls; 10 kts. **H** Wood with iron beams, 1 deck.

1868 Built for feeder service between Halifax-St John, New Brunswick.
1870 Halifax ceased to be an Inman port of call.
Details of *City of Halifax*'s disposal unknown.

25 CITY OF BRUSSELS

Bt 1869 Tod & McGregor, Glasgow; *T:* 3,747 g, 2,434 n. **Dim** 390 ft (118.87 m) × 40 ft 4 in (12.29 m) × 34 ft 6 in (10.52 m). **Eng** Sgl scr, horizontal trunk, direct acting with surface condenser; 2 cyls: 91½ in (232.41 cm); *Stroke:* 48 in (121.92 cm); 250 HP; *Stm P:* 30 lb; 13 kts; By builder. **H** Iron, 2 decks; *Coal:* 110 tons per day; *Pass:* 150 cabin, 450 3rd.

First transatlantic liner to have steam steering gear; constructed by the Vauxhall Foundry, Liverpool.

1869 Oct 14: Maiden voyage Liverpool-New York.
Dec: Crossed New York-Queenstown (Cobh) in 7 days 22 minutes at average of 14.66 kts, taking record from Cunard's *Russia*. Inman's first record breaker.
1876 Compound tandem engine fitted; 4 cyls: 2 × 48½ in (123.19 cm) and 2 × 84½ in (214.63 cm); *Stroke:* 42 in (106.68 cm); 350 HP; *Stm P:* 60 lb; By Laird Bros, Birkenhead. A forward

second funnel then added.
1883 Jan 7: Collided in fog with Hall Line's *Kirby Hall* at mouth of River Mersey, Liverpool, and sank with loss of ten lives.

26 CITY OF MONTREAL

Bt 1872 Tod & McGregor, Glasgow; *T:* 4,451 g, 2,939 n. **Dim** 419 ft 1 in (127.74 m) × 44 ft (13.41 m) × 34 ft 2 in (10.41 m). **Eng** Sgl scr, compound horizontal; 2 cyls: 60 in (152.4 cm) and 102 in (259.08 cm); *Stroke:* 54 in (137.16 cm); 600 HP; *Stm P:* 50 lb; 13 kts; By builder. **H** Iron, 2 decks; *Pass:* 150 cabin, 450 3rd.

1872 Feb 8: Maiden voyage Liverpool-New York.
1876 Compound inverted engine fitted. Second funnel added. *City of Montreal* had been designed to compete with the new White Star vessels. She was larger but slower and was heavy on fuel—hence her re-engining.
1887 Aug 10: Caught fire and burnt out at sea. Her cargo was more than 8,000 bales of raw American cotton. All passengers and crew rescued by Furness Line's *York City*. At Board of Trade enquiry it was stated that in the previous five months 73 ships carrying cotton had caught fire.

27 CITY OF CHESTER

Bt 1873 Caird & Co, Greenock; *T:* 4,566 g, 2,713 n. **Dim** 444 ft 7 in

27

28

(135.51 m) × 44 ft 2 in (13.46 m) × 34 ft 7 in (10.54 m). **Eng** Sgl scr, compound; 2 cyls: 72in (182.88 cm) and 120 in (304.8 cm); *Stroke:* 66 in (167.64 cm); 750 HP; *Stm P:* 80 lb; By builder. **H** Iron, 2 decks; *Pass:* 132 cabin, 1,310 3rd.

1873 At the time of building the 120 in (304.8 cm) LP cylinder diameter was the largest yet installed.
July 10: Maiden voyage Liverpool-New York.
1893 Became *Chester* (American Line), USA.
1898 Became *Sedgwick* (United States Government) for use as a transport in the war with Spain. Afterwards laid up.
1905 Became *Arizona*. Italian. Then renamed *Neapoletano*.
1907 Apr: Broken up in Italy.

28 CITY OF RICHMOND

Bt 1873 Tod & McGregor, Glasgow; *T:* 4,607 g, 2,840 n. **Dim** 440 ft 8 in (134.31m) × 43 ft 6 in (13.26 m) × 34 ft 1 in (10.39 m). **Eng** Sgl scr, compound inverted, surface condensers; 2 cyls: 76 in (193.04 cm) and 120 in (304.8 cm); *Stroke:* 60 in (152.4 cm); 700 HP; 10

boilers, 30 furnaces; *Stm P:* 65 lb; 15 kts; By builder. **H** Iron, 2 decks, saloon 44 ft (13.41 m) long × beam width; *Pass:* 150 cabin, 1,300 3rd.

1873 Sept 4: Maiden voyage Liverpool-New York. A modified *City of Montreal (26)* with two funnels to increase boiler draft.
1891 Sold.

29 CITY OF BERLIN

Bt 1875 Caird & Co, Greenock; *T:* 5,491 g, 2,957 n. **Dim** 513 ft (156.36 m) oa, 488 ft 7 in (148.94 m) × 44 ft 2 in (13.46 m) × 34 ft 10 in (10.62 m). **Eng** Sgl scr, compound inverted; 2 cyls: 72 in (182.88 cm) and 120 in (304.8 cm); *Stroke:* 72 in (182.88 cm); 850 HP; *Stm P:* 75 lb; By builder. **H** Iron, 3 decks, fcsle 97 ft (29.56 m); *Pass:* 202 cabin, 1,500 3rd; *Crew:* 150.

1874 Oct 27: Launched.
1875-81 The largest North Atlantic liner. Described as 'the finest liner afloat'.
1875 Apr 29: Maiden voyage Liverpool-New York. For four months held the record crossing in both directions, westbound 7 days 18 hours 2 minutes at

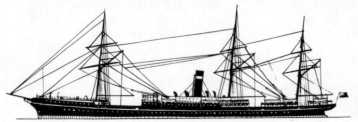

29

_30_

15.21 kts, eastbound 7 days 22 hours at 14.66 kts. The records were both lost to White Star's *Germanic*.
1879 Electric light fitted in dining saloon.
1887 Triple expansion engine fitted by John Laird, Birkenhead, with Howden forced draught furnaces.
1893 Became *Berlin* (American Line), USA.
1898 Became *Meade* (US Government) for war with Spain. Troop transport to Philippines, then training ship at Boston, Massachusetts, until 1918.
1921 Broken up at Philadelphia.

30 CITY OF ROME

Bt 1881 Barrow Shipbuilding Co, Barrow-in-Furness; *T:* 8,415 g, 3,453 n, 13,500 dwt. **Dim** 560 ft (170.69 m) oa, 546 ft (166.42 m) × 52 ft 4 in (15.95 m) × 37 ft (11.28 m). **Eng** Sgl scr, compound inverted, 3 crank tandem; 6 cyls: 3 × 43 in (109.22 cm) and 3 × 86 in (218.44 cm); *Stroke:* 72 in (182.88 cm); 1,500 HP; 8 boilers, 48 furnaces; *Stm P:* 90 lb; 16 kts; By builder. **H** Iron, 4 decks, dining saloon 72 ft (21.94 m) long × beam width × 9 ft high (2.74 m); *Cargo:* 3,800 tons designed, 2,500 tons actual; *Pass:* 520 cabin, 810 3rd.

1881 June 14: Launched. First liner on North Atlantic to have three funnels. Oct 13: Maiden voyage Liverpool-New York. *City of Rome* was designed to be built of steel but due to a steel shortage

iron was used extensively and the ship was slower than the design speed. Her maiden voyage took 9 days 17 hours outward and 8 days 16 hours 45 minutes homeward. She was laid up for the winter of 1881. Improvements were made to her machinery but she was still below specification. In Sept 1882, after only six round voyages, she was returned to her builders. Litigation followed and although by now operated by Anchor Line she remained the property of her builders. William Inman had died in July 1881 so did not live to see the disappointing outcome of his plan to build the finest vessel afloat.
1882 Transferred, after less than a year, to Anchor Line. Same name. As built she had lifeboats nested on the bridge deck, but Anchor Line refitted the ship and sponsored the boats clear of the deck.
1902 Broken up in Germany.

31 CITY OF CHICAGO

Bt 1883 Charles Connell & Co, Glasgow; *T:* 5,202 g, 3,883 n. **Dim** 430 ft 7 in (131.24 m) × 45 ft (13.71 m) × 33 ft 7 in (10.24 m). **Eng** Sgl scr, compound; 3 cyls: 56 in (142.24 cm) and 2 × 80 in (203.2 cm); *Stroke:* 60 in (152.4 cm); 900 HP; *Stm P:* 90 lb; 15 kts; By J. & J. Thomson, Glasgow. **H** Iron; *Pass:* 130 cabin, 840 3rd.

The only straight-stemmed Inman ship.

_31_

32-33

1883 Laid down as *Vancouver* (Dominion Line) but acquired on stocks to replace *City of Brussels (25)*.
Sept 18: Maiden voyage Liverpool-New York.
1892 July 1: Wrecked near Old Head of Kinsale, Southern Ireland. No lives lost.

32 CITY OF NEW YORK (III)

Bt 1888 J. & G. Thomson, Clydebank; *T:* 10,499 g, 5,573 n. **Dim** 527 ft 6 in (160.78 m) × 63 ft 2 in (19.25 m) × 41 ft 10 in (12.75 m). **Eng** Tw scr, tpl exp; 2 × 3 cyls: 45 in (114.3 cm), 71 in (180.34 cm) and 113 in (287.02 cm); *Stroke:* 60 in (152.4 cm); 1,978 NHP; *Stm P:* 150 lb; 19 kts. **H** Iron, fcsle 75 ft (22.86 m), poop 75 ft (22.86 m); *Pass:* 540 cabin, 200 2nd, 1,000 3rd.

Introduced the wider beam-to-length ratio into the fleet. The first twin screw express liner, resulting in the disappearance of sails and square-rigged masts. The saloon's glass roof is visible forward of the bridge.

1888 Aug 1: Maiden voyage Liverpool-New York.
1893 Became *New York* (American Line), USA.
1898 Became *Harvard,* US Government transport.
1903 New quad exp engine fitted. Two funnels.
1913 *Pass:* 700 2nd, 1,000 3rd.
1917-19 Taken over by US Government. Renamed *Plattsburg.*
1921 Sold to Polish Navigation Co. Renamed *New York*. Service New York-

Antwerp-Danzig.
1923 Broken up in Genoa.

33 CITY OF PARIS (II)

Details as *City of New York (32)* except: **Bt** 1889; *T:* 10,669 g, 5,468 n.

1889 Apr 3: Maiden voyage Liverpool-New York.
1890 Nov 25: A propeller shaft snapped approaching Ireland inbound, flooding the engine room. Towed to Queenstown. She was saved by the internal system of watertight bulkheads.
1893 Became *Paris* (American Line), USA.
Mar 25: First voyage Southampton-New York.
1898 Requisitioned by US Government. Renamed *Yale.*
1899 May 21: Went ashore on the Manacles, Cornwall. Salvaged. Rebuilt with two funnels and quad exp engines installed. On completion renamed *Philadelphia.*
1901 Aug 31: Re-entered Southampton-New York service.
1913 *Pass:* 700 2nd, 1,000 3rd.
1917-19 Taken over by US Government. Renamed *Harrisburg.*
1920 Resumed commercial service Southampton-Cherbourg-New York.
Nov: Laid up.
1922 Sold to New York & Naples SS Co. Renamed *Philadelphia.*
July 1: First voyage New York-Gibraltar-Naples. Mutiny broke out and ended voyage at Naples instead of Constantinople as planned. Laid up in Genoa.
1923 Broken up in Genoa, Italy.

Leyland Line

History

1850 Bibby Bros commenced trading between Liverpool and the traditional Mediterranean ports. Amongst their staff was the 28-year-old Frederick R. Leyland who, during the next decade, rose to become a partner in the firm.
1869 The opening of the Suez Canal affected Bibby's business. Within a year the need to diversify was becoming evident. Frederick Leyland wished to seek trading areas either beyond Suez or, following the American Civil War, with the expanding United States.
1872 Talks began by which Leyland would acquire the Bibby vessels.
1873 Jan: 21 steamers and the tug *Camel* were transferred to Frederick Leyland & Co. The new company's trade continued to be to the Mediterranean but plans were commenced to expand its activities.
1874 The fleet contained a number of old ships and these began to be disposed of. During this year *Athenian* (I), *Cairo*, *Crimean* and *Danube* were all sold and the company lost its first ship when *Rhone* went missing.
1875 It was decided to open up services to Boston, the major British companies serving New York and Philadelphia.
1876 Mar 11: *Iberian* (I) inaugurated the company's new route to the USA. *Istrian* and *Illyrian* were her sisters on the route and the three ships operated a fortnightly service.
1877 Later *Bavarian* (I), *Bohemian* (I) and *Bulgarian* were added. *Albanian* (I) was wrecked.
1878 Mar 7: *Assyrian* (I) went aground on Cythera in the Aegean and was abandoned.
1880 *Anatolian* was wrecked at the mouth of the River Mersey. *Sicilian, Venetian* (I), *Castilian* and *Oporto* (I) were sold.
1881 The building of larger replacement ships included the delivery of *Virginian* and *Venetian* (II) (1882). *Cyprian* was lost by storm at sea.
1884 *Illyrian* wrecked.
1885 *Iberian* (I) wrecked.
1887 *Cyrenian* sold.
1888 *Douro* (II) foundered.
1892 Jan: Frederick Leyland died, aged 60.
Nov: Frederick Leyland & Co Ltd was formed, with Christopher Furness and Walter Glynn as managing directors. An effect of the former's appointment was the beginning of a close association between the Leyland and Furness Lines. One of the first collaborations was the inauguration of a joint London-Boston service which was later to have passenger capacity added.
1895 Passenger carriage was introduced, in a modest way, with the delivery of *Victorian, Armenian* and, in 1896, *Cestrian*. They had accommodation for 50 cabin class passengers.
Mar 3: *Venetian* (II) was wrecked near Boston.
1896 The founding of the Wilson's & Furness-Leyland Line Ltd took place. This was an amalgamation of three companies: the Wilson-Hill Line, which had been on the North Atlantic since 1875; the Furness Line, of which Christopher Furness was the principal founder, which operated steamers from

West Hartlepool to America; and the Leyland Line with its London-Boston service. Wilson's and Furness tossed a coin for which name came first in the title. The other activities of Leyland were not affected and the new company chartered its steamers from the respective partners. Five new steamers were built for the new concern.

1899 July: *Winifredian* and *Devonian* (I) (to enter service in 1900), steamers with accommodation for 135 passengers, were placed on the London-Boston route.

Oct: *Armenian* and *Victorian* were used as transports during the Boer War and were out of Leyland service for three years.

Dec 31: The West India & Pacific SS Co was acquired and with it a fleet of 19 vessels. This company's main trading activity was to the Caribbean and Leyland continued to operate their services to the Gulf of Mexico area.

1900 To accommodate the new acquisition the holding company became Frederick Leyland & Co (1900) Ltd. *Favonian* was wrecked and *Ligurian* broken up.

1901 A Liverpool-New York service was inaugurated by five vessels. They were *Canadian, Bohemian* (II), *Georgian, Philadelphian* (I) and *Tampican. Lesbian* broken up. Joint Mediterranean services were operated with G. Papayanni & Co of Liverpool.

1902 Feb 4: The International Mercantile Marine Company was formed and its first British acquisition, in May, was the Leyland concern. This was followed by ownership of the American, Atlantic Transport, Dominion, Red Star and White Star Lines.

July: *Hanoverian* completed for the Liverpool-Boston service. After only three voyages to Boston she was transferred to Dominion Line and renamed *Mayflower*. One other immediate effect of IMMC control was the cessation of Leyland's Mediterranean trade, it being IMMC policy to concentrate on the North Atlantic. The Chairman of Leyland was Mr John R. Ellerman (1862-1933). In

1901 he formed the London, Liverpool and Ocean Shipping Co Ltd which in 1902 became Ellerman Lines Ltd and took over the Mediterranean trade together with an undertaking not to enter the North Atlantic trade for ten years. Initially a blue band was added to the funnel between the pink and black top but this was soon changed to the familiar Ellerman bright buff with white band and black top.

1903 Leyland withdrew from the Liverpool-New York service, which was transferred to White Star together with *Victorian* and *Armenian*. These retained their own names but *American* and *European* became *Cufic* and *Tropic*. IMMC also ceased construction on Leyland's two six-masted liners *Servian* and *Scotian*. They were sold in 1907 to the Hamburg America Line.

1908 The company's name became Frederick Leyland and Company Ltd. *Median, Memphian, Mercian* and *Meltonian* were delivered.

1910 A class of ten ships with 'N' names, commencing with *Nessian,* began to enter service. They were sisters of the 'M' class of 1908. *Virginian* was released for scrapping.

1912 *Cyrenian* broken up in Belgium.

1914 May 3: *Columbian* (I) burnt at sea in the North Atlantic. Ownership of the Furness-Leyland fleet was vested with Leyland.

1915 June 28: *Armenian* was captured by the German submarine *U-24* off Trevose Head, Cornwall, and then torpedoed.

July 30: *Iberian* (II) torpedoed off Fastnet.

Nov 9: *Californian* torpedoed off Cape Matapan.

1916 Dec 14: *Victorian* torpedoed off Malta.

1917 This year of the war proved to be a calamitous one for the Leyland Line. No fewer than 14 of their ships were lost. Unless otherwise stated they were torpedoed:

Feb 4: *Floridian* (II) 200 miles off Land's End.

Feb 20: *Leysian* wrecked seven miles south of Stumble Head en route Belfast-Cardiff.

Mar 8: *Georgian* lost off Cape Sidero.
Mar 13: *Norwegian* (I) managed to beach herself but was a total loss.
Apr 5: *U-59* took *Canadian* off Fastnet, but *Winifredian* reached port safely after striking a mine in the North Sea.
May: *Belgian* (II) was successfully beached but was beyond repair.
May 21: *Colonial* (I) wrecked herself on the Scillies.
June 2: *Cameronian* lost with all hands 50 miles off Alexandria.
June 10: *Anglian* lost off Bishop's Rock.
June 24: *Sylvanian* north-west of Tory Island, Northern Ireland.
July 31: *Orubian* 160 miles north-west of Eagle Island.
Aug 21: *Devonian* (I) off Tory Island.
Oct 8: *Memphian* close to the North Arklow Lighthouse.
Oct 10: *Cambrian* south-west of Start Point.
1918 The final year of the war saw still further ships lost:
Mar 23: *Etonian* off Kinsale, Southern Ireland.
Apr 29: *U-48* finished off the already torpedoed *Kingstonian* by attacking her in Carloforte harbour, Sardinia.
June 25: *Atlantian* (I) off Eagle's Rock.
Oct 19: *Almerian* lost by mine off Licata, Sicily.
Nov 11: Armistice Day, and Leyland was left with 23 vessels including only one passenger ship, the fortunate *Winifredian.*
1919 Three 'War' type standard ships were acquired as war loss replacements. They were *Barbadian* (II), *Belgian* (II) and *Bolivian.*
1920 *Bohemian* (II), having survived the furies of war, was wrecked near Halifax, Nova Scotia. In the same year *Philadelphian* (II) was delivered by Harland & Wolff.
1921 IMMC began a series of post-war consolidations aimed at regrouping their multifarious activities. The first of these affected the British & North American SN Co—the Dominion Line. Their fleet of seven vessels, *Dominion* (II), *Canada, Regina, Cornishman, Welshman, Turcoman* and *Irishman* (II), were all transferred to Leyland

ownership, but outwardly there was no change and the ships continued in Dominion colours and trades. *Bovic* of White Star was also transferred and renamed *Colonian* (II). With her advent *Lancastrian* went to the shipbreakers.

The success of the 'M's and 'N's of 1908-14 prompted the ordering of eight sisters. The first, another 'N', was *Norwegian* (II) but the remaining seven were given names beginning with 'D'. This group was mainly engaged on the old West India & Pacific SS Co's Mexican Gulf routes.
1922 *Winifredian* returned to Leyland's Liverpool-Boston service.
1923 The old *Hanoverian,* so briefly a Leyland ship back in 1902, came back from White Star as *Devonian* (II) to act as consort to *Winifredian. Indian* was broken up.
1924 *Colombian* (II) wrecked near Kinsale, Ireland.
1927 Leyland's two remaining passenger ships went to Red Star's Antwerp-Southampton-New York service.
1928 *Atlantian* (II) was the final ship ever built for Leyland. With her arrival *Oxonian* was broken up.
1929 *Winifredian* and *Devonian* (II) were sold for breaking up after spending some time laid up.

Towards the end of the year the final four Red Star ships were, like Dominion's seven, transferred to Leyland ownership but continued in Red Star colours on Red Star routes. The ships were *Belgenland, Lapland, Pennland* and *Westernland.* This marked the end of the International Navigation Co.
1930 As the economic depression of the 1930s took hold the Leyland group consisted of 28 ships (excluding Red Star).
1932-33 13 of the fleet were broken up. Another seven went to T. & J. Harrison and continued on their Mexican Gulf trades and two more were sold to Greek owners.
1933 IMMC sold the five remaining ships, four of them to the Donaldson Line. They were *Dakotian, Nortonian, Norwegian* (II) and *Nubian. Oranian*

went to L. A. Embericos in 1934 as
Tamesis.
1935 With the disposal of their last ship,
Frederick Leyland & Co Ltd, IMMC's
first acquisition, ceased to exist.

Routes

1873-1902 Liverpool-Mediterranean
ports.
1875-1934 Liverpool-Boston-Philadelphia,
Liverpool-Portland, Maine.

1893-1914 London-Boston.
1900-34 Liverpool/London-Mexican
Gulf ports, especially New Orleans
(West India & Pacific SS Co routes).
1901-3 Liverpool-New York.

Livery

Funnel Pink with black top
Hull Black with red waterline.
Uppers White, deck vents buff.
Masts Biscuit brown.
Lifeboats White.

Fleet index

113

Nessian	101	Oxonian	94	Tagus	58
Nestorian	102			Tampican	72
Nevisian	103	Parisian	121	Texan	65
Nicaraguan	71	Persian	12	Turcoman	128
Nicosian	103	Philadelphian (I)	47		
Ninian	104	Philadelphian (II)	125		
Nitonian	105			Venetian (I)	8
Nortonian	107	Regina	132	Venetian (II)	41
Norwegian (I)	108	Rhone	3	Victorian	49
Norwegian (II)	134	Rimouski	142	Virginian	40
Novian	110	Russian	49		
Nubian	106			Welshman	127
		Scotian	95	West Indian	64
Oporto (I)	22	Scythian	112	William Cliff	69
Oporto (II)	42	Servian	96	Winifredian	60
Oranian	114	Sicilian	7		
Orubian	115	Sylvanian	113	Yucatan	62

Illustrated fleet list

1

1 ATHENIAN (I)

Bt 1854 Smith & Rodgers, Glasgow; *T:* 1,094 g. **Dim** 241 ft 2 in (75.51 m) × 29 ft 5 in (8.97 m) × 20 ft (6.1 m). **Eng** Sgl scr; 2 cyls; 20 HP; 8 kts. **H** Iron, 1 deck.

1854 Built for Elder Dempster (African Steam Navigation Co).
1871 Sold.
1873 Acquired with 21 other vessels by Frederick Leyland. Lengthened to 243 ft 3 in (74.14 m).
1874 Sold. Renamed *Caroline,* H. Ellis, London.

2 BELGIAN (I)

Bt 1855; *T:* 1,989 g. **Eng** Sgl scr; 2 cyls. **H** Iron, 1 deck. No other details available.

1855 Built for Elder Dempster (African Steam Nav Co).
1873 Acquired by Frederick Leyland.

3 RHONE

Bt 1856 Smith & Rodgers, Glasgow; *T:* 1,387 g. **Dim** 257 ft 2 in (73.38 m) × 34 ft 7 in (10.54 m) × 22 ft (6.7 m). **Eng** Sgl scr, simple inverted; 2 cyls. **H** Iron, 1 deck.

1856 Built for Bibby Bros.
1873 Sold to Frederick Leyland.
1874 Reported missing.

4 DANUBE

Details as *Rhone (3)* except: *T:* 1,386 g.
1856 Built for Bibby Bros.
1873 Acquired by F. Leyland.
1874 Sold. Became sailing ship *Charles Dickens.*
1909 Broken up.

5 CAIRO

Bt 1857 T. D. Marshall & Co, South Shields; *T:* 1,465 g. **Dim** 256 ft 2 in (78.08 m) × 35 ft (10.67 m) × 22 ft (6.7 m). **Eng** Sgl scr, simple; 3 cyls. **H** Iron, 1 deck.

1857 Built as *Fred Chapple* (Fred Chapple & Co).
1859 Acquired by Bibby Bros.
1873 Acquired by F. Leyland.
1874 Sold. Became sailing ship *Cairo.*
1876 Reported missing.

6 CRIMEAN

Bt 1857 Smith & Rodgers, Glasgow; *T:* 1,473 g. **Dim** 261 ft 7 in (79.73 m) × 36 ft (10.97 m) × 22 ft (6.7 m). **Eng** Sgl scr, simple; 2 cyls. **H** Iron, 1 deck.

1857 Built as *Crimean* for Levant Co.
1859 Acquired by Bibby Bros.
1873 Taken over by F. Leyland.
1874 Sold. Became sailing vessel *Fritz Reuter.*
1898 Lost.

7 SICILIAN

Bt 1859 E. J. Harland, Belfast; *T:* 1,492 g, 1,015 n. **Dim** 270 ft 6 in (82.45 m) × 33 ft 7 in (10.24 m) × 22 ft 9 in (6.93 m). **Eng** Sgl scr, simple, 2 cyls.

7-8

1859 Built for Bibby Bros.
1873 Taken over by F. Leyland.
1880 Sold. Became *Mayumba,* African SS Co (Elder Dempster). Engine compounded; 2 cyls: 40 in (101.6 cm) and 70 in (177.8 cm); *Stroke:* 36 in (91.44 cm); 250 HP; *Stm P:* 60 lb; 10 kts; By J. Jack Rollo & Co, Liverpool.
1884 Destroyed by fire.

8 VENETIAN (I)

Details as *Sicilian (7)* except: *T:* 1,562 g, 995 n.

1859 Built for Bibby Bros.
1873 Taken over by F. Leyland.
1880 Sold. Became *Landana,* African SS Co (Elder Dempster). Engine compounded as *Sicilian.* Later became *Tarapaca.*
1894 Wrecked.

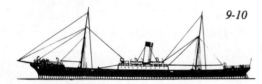

9-10

9 EGYPTIAN

Bt 1861 Harland & Wolff, Belfast; *T:* 2,086 g, 1,356 n. **Dim** 335 ft (102.11 m) × 34 ft 2 in (10.41 m) × 24 ft (7.31 m). **Eng** Sgl scr, simple; 2 cyls: 42 in (106.68 cm); *Stroke:* 42 in (106.68 cm); 450 HP; *Stm P:* 60 lb; 10 kts; By J. Jack Rollo & Co, Liverpool.

1861 Built for Bibby Bros.
1873 Taken over by F. Leyland.
1902 Sold for breaking up.

10 ARABIAN

Details as *Egyptian (9)* except: *T:* 2,066 g, 1,345 n. **Eng** Compounded by addition of 1P cylinder; By McNab & Co, Greenock.

1862 Built for Bibby Bros.
1871 Compound; 4 cyls: 42 in (106.68

cm) and 72 in (182.88 cm); *Stroke:* 42 in (106.68 cm).
1873 Acquired by F. Leyland.
1902 Sold. Broken up.

11 CASTILIAN

Bt 1862 Harland & Wolff, Belfast; *T:* 635 g, 398 n. **Dim** 240 ft (73.15 m) × 24 ft (7.31 m) × 15 ft 6 in (4.72 m). **Eng** Sgl scr, compound inverted; 2 cyls: 28 in (71.12 cm) and 52 in (132.08 cm); *Stroke:* 33 in (83.82 cm); 110 HP; *Stm P:* 60 lb; 10 kts; By J. Jack Rollo & Co, Liverpool. **H** Iron, 1 deck.

1862 Built for Bibby Bros.
1873 Taken over by F. Leyland.
1902 Broken up.

12 PERSIAN

Bt 1863 Harland & Wolff, Belfast; *T:* 2,137 g, 1,404 n. **Dim** 361 ft 9 in (110.26 m) × 34 ft (10.36 m) × 24 ft 4 in (7.42 m). **Eng** Sgl scr, compound inverted; 2 cyls: 42 in (106.68 cm) and 75 in (190.5 cm); *Stroke:* 42 in (106.68 cm); 225 HP; *Stm P:* 60 lb; 10 kts; By J. Jack Rollo & Co, Liverpool. **H** Iron, 2 decks.

1863 Built for Bibby Bros. First straight stem in company.
1873 Taken over by F. Leyland.
1902 Broken up.

13 DOURO (I)

Bt 1864 Harland & Wolff, Belfast; *T:* 556 g, 305 n. **Dim** 195 ft 9 in (59.66 m) × 27 ft 1 in (8.25 m) × 15 ft 7 in (4.75 m). **Eng** Sgl scr, simple; 2 cyls: 42 in (106.68 cm); *Stroke:* 40 in (101.6 cm); 100 HP; *Stm P:* 60 lb; 9 kts. **H** Iron, 1 deck, fcsle 26 ft (7.92 m), poop 114 ft (34.75 m).

1864 Built for Bibby Bros.
1871 2 cyl compound engine installed.
1873 Taken over by F. Leyland.
Became *Alcira* (Not in Lloyds).
Became *Camilla* (Not in Lloyds).
Became *Cephalonia,* owned by A. I. Diakakis, Greece.
Became *Nilos,* owned by N. J. Eustathiadis, Piraeus, Greece.
1927 Dismantled in Greece.

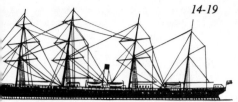

14-19

14 IBERIAN (I)

Bt 1867 Harland & Wolff, Belfast; *T:* 2,890 g, 1,923 n. **Dim** 390 ft (118.87 m) × 37 ft 2 in (11.33 m) × 29 ft 3 in (8.91 m). **Eng** Sgl scr, compound inverted; 2 cyls: 50 in (127 cm) and 88 in (223.52 cm); *Stroke:* 51 in (129.54 cm); 350 HP; *Stm P:* 60 lb; 10 kts; By J. Jack Rollo & Co, Liverpool. **H** Iron, 1 deck.

1867 Built for Bibby Bros.
1873 Taken over by F. Leyland.
1878 2 cyl compound engine installed.
1885 Lost.

15 ILLYRIAN

Details as *Iberian (14)* except: *T:* 2,931 g, 1,923 n.

1867 Built for Bibby Bros.
1873 Taken over by F. Leyland.
1878 4 cyl compound engine installed.

16 ISTRIAN

Details as *Iberian (14)* except: *T:* 2,930 g, 1,923 n.

1867 Built for Bibby Bros.
1873 Taken over by F. Leyland.
1877 4 cyl compound engine installed.
1894 Sold to Furness Withy. Same name.
1895 Broken up.

17 BAVARIAN

Bt 1869 Harland & Wolff, Belfast; *T:* 3,111 g, 2,027 n. **Dim** 400 ft (121.92 m) × 37 ft 2 in (11.33 m) × 28 ft 6 in (8.69 m). **Eng** Sgl scr, simple, 2 cyls. **H** Iron, 1 deck.

1869 Built for Bibby Bros.
1873 Taken over by F. Leyland.
1877 4 cyl compound engine installed; 2 × 2 cyls: 30 in (76.2 cm) and 61 in (154.94 cm); *Stroke:* 54 in (137.16 cm); 350 HP; *Stm P:* 60 lb; 11 kts; By J. Jack Rollo & Co, Liverpool.

18 BOHEMIAN (I)

Details as *Bavarian (17)* except: **Bt** 1870; *T:* 3,113 g, 2,031 n.

1870 Built for Bibby Bros.
1873 Taken over by F. Leyland.
1877 4 cyl compound engine installed.
1881 Wrecked.

19 BULGARIAN

Details as *Bavarian (17)* except: **Bt** 1870; *T:* 3,112 g, 2,029 n.

1870 Built for Bibby Bros.
1873 Taken over by F. Leyland.
1877 4 cyl compound engine installed.
1894 Sold to Furness Withy. Same name.
1895 Broken up.

20 CAMEL

Bt 1868 Wm Denny & Co, Dumbarton; *T:* 33 g, 16 n. **Dim** 50 ft 7 in (15.42 m) × 13 ft 1 in (3.99 m) × 9 ft (2.74 m). **Eng** Sgl scr; 2 cyls. **H** Iron, 1 deck.

1868 Built for Bibby Bros. Tug at Liverpool.
1873 Taken over by F. Leyland.
1885 Sold to foreign owners.

21 ALBANIAN (I)

Bt 1870 Thos Royden & Sons, Liverpool; *T:* 1,417 g. **Dim** 291 ft 9 in (88.92 m) × 31 ft 2 in (9.5 m) × 22 ft 7 in (6.88 m). **Eng** Sgl scr, compound; 2 cyls. **H** Iron, 1 deck.

1870 Built for Bibby Bros.
1873 Taken over by F. Leyland.
1877 Sunk in collision off Great Orme, North Wales.

22 OPORTO (I)

Bt 1870 J. Reid, Port Glasgow; *T:* 565 g, 352 n. **Dim** 201 ft (61.26 m) × 26 ft 2 in (7.97 m) × 15 ft 7 in (4.75 m). **Eng** Sgl scr, compound inverted; 2 cyls: 28 in (71.12 cm) and 51 in (129.54 cm); *Stroke:* 30 in (76.2 cm); 110 HP; *Stm P:* 60 lb; 10 kts.

1870 Built for Bibby Bros.
1873 Taken over by F. Leyland.
1880 Sold.
1902 Sunk by collision. Raised but scrapped.

23 CYPRIAN

Bt 1874 Bowdler Chaffer, Seacombe, Cheshire; *T:* 1,433 g, 941 n. **Dim** 292 ft 2 in (89.05 m) × 30 ft 1 in (9.17 m) × 22 ft 2 in (6.76 m). **Eng** Sgl scr, compound; 2 cyls: 32 in (81.28 cm) and 64 in (162.56 cm); *Stroke:* 36 in (91.44 cm); 170 HP; *Stm P:* 85 lb; 10 kts; By Fawcett, Preston & Co, Liverpool. **H** Iron, 1 deck.

1874 First ship actually built for F. Leyland.
1881 Foundered in storm.

24 CYRENIAN

Details as *Cyprian (23)* except: *T:* 1,432 g, 938 n. **Eng** By J. Jack Rollo & Co, Liverpool.

1874 Built for F. Leyland.
1887 Sold to E. L. Thomas, Liverpool. Renamed *Algeria.*
1912 Broken up in Belgium.

25-26,28-29

25 LESBIAN

Bt 1874 Thos Royden & Sons, Liverpool; *T:* 1,559 g, 1,019 n. **Dim** 302 ft 4 in (92.15 m) × 31 ft 2 in (9.5 m) × 23 ft 2 in (7.06 m). **Eng** Sgl scr, compound inverted; 2 cyls: 37 in (93.98 cm) and 66 in (167.64 cm); *Stroke:* 42 in (106.68 cm); 190 HP; *Stm P:* 60 lb; 10 kts. **H** Iron, 2 decks.

1874 Built for F. Leyland.
1888 Shown as owned by Lesbian SS Co, F. Leyland managers.
1901 Broken up.

26 LIGURIAN

Details as *Lesbian (25)* except: *T:* 1,561 g, 1,016 n.

1874 Built for F. Leyland.
1889 Sunk by collision. Salved.
1894 Sold. Became *Jacinta,* Linea de Vapores Serra, Bilbao, Spain.
1900 Broken up.

27 LISBON

Bt 1874 Thos Royden & Sons,

Liverpool; *T:* 664 g, 416 n. **Dim** 211 ft 5 in (64.44 m) × 26 ft 1 in (7.95 m) × 16 ft (4.87 m). **Eng** Sgl scr, compound inverted; 2 cyls: 28 in (71.12 cm) and 51 in (129.54 cm); *Stroke:* 30 in (76.2 cm); 110 HP; *Stm P:* 60 lb; 9 kts; By J. Jack Rollo & Co, Liverpool. **H** Iron, 1 deck.

1874 Mediterranean service.

28 ASSYRIAN (I)

Bt 1875 Thos Royden & Sons, Liverpool; *T:* 1,617 g, 1,060 n. **Dim** 301 ft 7 in (91.92 m) × 31 ft 2 in (9.5 m) × 23 ft 4 in (7.11 m). **Eng** Sgl scr, compound inverted; 2 cyls: 34 in (86.36 cm) and 68 in (172.72 cm); *Stroke:* 36 in (91.44 cm); 180 NHP; *Stm P:* 90 lb; 10 kts; By J. Jack Rollo & Co, Liverpool. **H** Iron, 2 decks.

1874 Mediterranean service.
1878 Mar 7: Lost on Isle of Elaphonisi, Cythera, Greece.

29 ATHENIAN (II)

Details as *Assyrian (28)* except: *T:* 1,619 g, 1,057 n. **Eng** 190 NHP on same cylinder measurements.

1875 Mediterranean service.

30 ALGERIAN

Bt 1876 Bowdler Chaffer & Co, Seacombe, Cheshire; *T:* 1,757 g. **Dim** 312 ft 4 in (95.1 m) × 31 ft 2 in (9.5 m) × 23 ft 10 in (7.26 m). **Eng** Sgl scr, compound inverted; 2 cyls: 24 in (60.96 cm) and 50 in (127 cm); *Stroke:* 45 in (114.3 cm); 220 HP; *Stm P:* 90 lb; By J. Jones & Sons, Liverpool. **H** Iron, 1 deck.

1876 Mediterranean service.

31 ALSATIAN

Details as *Algerian (30)* except: **Bt** Started by Bowdler Chaffer, completed by F. Leyland; *T:* 1,765 g, 1,158 n.

1877 A strike over pay held up work and Bowdler Chaffer's yard closed. Leyland's therefore completed *Alsatian,* as well as *Anatolian (32)* and *Andalusian (33),* themselves.
1901 Transferred to Ellerman Lines

(J. R. Ellerman & Co).
1907 Broken up.

32 ANATOLIAN

Details as *Algerian (30)* except: *T:*
1,763 g, 1,156 n.
1877 Completed by F. Leyland.
1880 Wrecked Crosby Channel, River
Mersey.

33 ANDALUSIAN

Details as *Algerian (30)* except: *T:*
1,774 g, 1,142 n.
1877 Completed by F. Leyland.
Registered at Sydney, New South Wales.
1902 Transferred to Ellerman Lines.
1909 Broken up.

34 DOURO (II)

Bt 1880 Oswald Mordaunt & Co,
Southampton; *T:* 728 g, 466 n. **Dim**
211 ft 6 in (64.46 m) × 27 ft 2 in
(8.28 m) × 16 ft 7 in (5.05 m). **Eng**
Sgl scr, compound inverted; 2 cyls: 26
in (66.04 cm) and 52 in (132.08 cm);
Stroke: 33 in (83.82 cm); 100 HP; 9 kts;
By builder. **H** Iron, 1 deck.

1880 Entered service. Mediterranean
routes.
1888 Foundered.

35 FALERNIAN

Bt 1880 Oswald Mordaunt & Co,
Southampton; *T:* 2,252 g, 1,479 n. **Dim**
343 ft 5 in (104.67 m) × 34 ft 5 in
(10.49 m) × 23 ft 6 in (7.16 m). **Eng** Sgl
scr, compound; 4 cyls: 2 × 24 in
(60.96 cm) and 2 × 50 in (127 cm);
Stroke: 48 in (121.92 cm); 250 HP; 10
kts; By builder. **H** Iron, 2 decks.

1880 Delivered. Mediterranean
services.
1902 Transferred to Ellerman Lines.

36 FABIAN

Details as *Falernian (35)* except: **Bt**
1881; *T:* 2,248 g, 1,476 n. **Dim** Length
342 ft (104.24 m).

1881 Delivered. Mediterranean
services.

37 FAVONIAN

Details as *Falernian (35)* except: **Bt**
1881; *T:* 2,247 g, 1,476 n. **Dim** Length
342 ft 5 in (104.36 m).

1881 Entered service. Mediterranean
services.
1900 June: Wrecked.

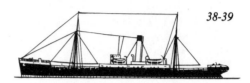

38-39

38 FLAMINIAN

Bt 1880 Palmers & Co, Newcastle; *T:*
2,131 g, 1,391 n. **Dim** 333 ft
(101.5 m) × 33 ft 4 in (10.16 m) ×
23 ft 7 in (7.19 m). **Eng** Sgl scr,
compound inverted; 2 cyls: 24 in
(60.96 cm) and 50 in (127 cm); *Stroke:*
45 in (114.3 cm); 250 HP; 10 kts; By
builder. **H** Iron, 1 deck.

1880 Mediterranean routes.
1902 Transferred to Ellerman Lines.

39 FLAVIAN

Details as *Flaminian (38)* except: *T:*
2,139 g, 1,399 n.

1880 Mediterranean routes.
1902 Transferred to Ellerman Lines.

40

40 VIRGINIAN

Bt 1881 Palmers & Co, Newcastle; *T:*
4,081 g, 2,695 n. **Dim** 422 ft 2 in
(128.68 m) × 40 ft 10 in (12.45 m) ×
28 ft 9 in (8.76 m). **Eng** Sgl scr,
compound inverted; Cyls: 2 × 29 in
(73.66 cm) and 2 × 62 in (157.48 cm);
Stroke: 60 in (152.4 cm); 600 HP; 10
kts. **H** Iron, 3 decks.

1881 Oct: Entered service.
1910 Sold for breaking up.

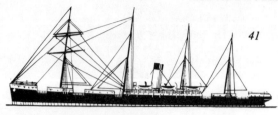

41

41 VENETIAN (II)

Details as *Virginian (40)* except: **Bt**
1882; *T:* 4,055 g, 3,166 n.
1882 Entered service.
1895 Mar 3: Wrecked near Boston,
Massachusetts.

42 OPORTO (II)

Bt 1888 C. J. Bigger, Londonderry,
Northern Ireland; *T:* 739 g, 460 n. **Dim**
212 ft (64.61 m) × 27 ft 1 in (8.25
m) × 16 ft 8 in (5.08 m). **Eng** Sgl scr,
compound; 2 cyls: 16 in (40.64 cm) and
43 in (109.22 cm); *Stroke:* 36 in (91.44
cm); 80 RHP; 10 kts; By J. Rollo &
Sons, Liverpool. **H** Steel, 1 deck, fcsle
23 ft (7.01 m), bridge 59 ft (17.98 m).
1888 Entered service.

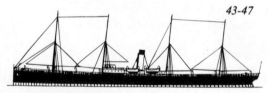

43-47

43 BOSTONIAN (I)

Bt 1888 Harland & Wolff, Belfast; *T:*
4,668 g, 3,030 n. **Dim** 421 ft 8 in (128.52
m) × 43 ft 2 in (13.16 m) × 30 ft 10 in
(9.4 m). **Eng** Sgl scr, tpl exp; 3 cyls: 29
in (73.66 cm), 45 in (114.3 cm) and 74
in (187.96 cm); *Stroke:* 60 in (152.4 cm);
433 NHP; *Stm P:* 150 lb; 12 kts; By
builder. **H** Steel, 3 decks, fcsle 88 ft
(26.82 m), bridge 156 ft (47.55 m), poop
56 ft (17.07 m).
1888 Aug: Delivered.
1899 Operated by Wilson's & Furness-
Leyland Line.

44 COLOMBIAN (I)

Bt 1890 Harland & Wolff, Belfast; *T:*
5,088 g, 3,323 n. **Dim** 442 ft 7 in (134.9
m) × 45 ft 2 in (13.77 m) × 31 ft (9.45
m). **Eng** Sgl scr, tpl exp; Cyls: 30 in

(76.2 cm), 45 in (114.3 cm) and 74 in
(187.96 cm); *Stroke:* 60 in (152.4 cm);
433 NHP; *Stm P:* 150 lb; 12 kts; By
builder. **H** Steel, 3 decks, fcsle 96 ft
(29.26 m), bridge 138 ft (42.06 m), poop
62 ft (18.9 m).
1890 Entered service.
1914 May 3: Burnt at sea 150 miles
south of Sable Island. 18 lost.

45 GEORGIAN

Details as *Colombian (44)* except: *T:*
5,088 g, 3,318 n.
1890 Entered service.
1917 Mar 8: Torpedoed off Cape
Sidero.

46 LANCASTRIAN

Details as *Colombian (44)* except: **Bt**
1891; *T:* 5,120 g, 3,321 n. **H** Fcsle 102
ft (31.08 m), bridge 143 ft (43.58 m),
poop 69 ft (21.03 m).
1891 Entered service.
1920-21 Broken up.

47 PHILADELPHIAN (I)

Details as *Colombian (44)* except: **Bt**
1891; *T:* 5,120 g, 3,322 n. **H** Fcsle 102
ft (31.09 m), bridge 143 ft (43.59 m),
poop 69 ft (21.03 m).
1891 North Atlantic service.

48 MINHO

Bt 1890 J. Jones & Sons, Liverpool; *T:*
835 g, 510 n. **Dim** 211 ft 1 in (64.34
m) × 27 ft (8.23 m) × 16 ft 9 in (5.1 m).
Eng Sgl scr, compound; 2 cyls: 16 in
(40.64 cm) and 43 in (109.22 cm);
Stroke: 24 in (60.96 cm); 80 RHP; 10
kts; By builder. **H** Steel, 1 deck, fcsle 29
ft (8.84 m), bridge 55 ft (16.76 m).
1890 Entered service.
1902 Transferred to Ellerman Lines.

49 VICTORIAN

Bt 1895 Harland & Wolff, Belfast; *T:*
8,825 g, 5,753 n. **Dim** 512 ft 6 in
(156.21 m) × 59 ft 2 in (18.03 m) × 35 ft
(10.67 m). **Eng** Sgl scr, tpl exp; 3 cyls:
31 in (78.74 cm), 52 in (132.08 cm) and
86 in (218.44 cm); *Stroke:* 66 in (167.64
cm); 718 NHP; *Stm P:* 190 lb; 13 kts;

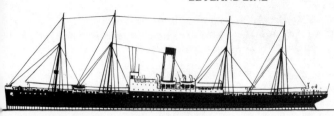

49-52

By builder. **H** Steel, 3 decks, fcsle 109 ft (33.22 m), bridge 208 ft (63.4 m), poop 59 ft (17.98 m); *Pass:* 50 1st.
1895 Passenger carriage introduced. Sept 7: Maiden voyage Liverpool-Boston.
1899 Boer War transport.
1903 Transferred to White Star Line. Liverpool-New York, cargo service.
1914 Renamed *Russian.*
1916 Dec 14: Torpedoed off Malta.

50 ARMENIAN

Details as *Victorian (49)* except: *T:* 8,825 g, 5,754 n.
1895 Sept 28: Maiden voyage Liverpool-Boston.
1899 Boer War transport.
1903 May: Transferred to White Star Line. Cargo service.
1915 June 28: Torpedoed by *U-24* off Trevose Head, Cornwall.

51 CESTRIAN

Details as *Victorian (49)* except: **Bt** 1896; *T:* 8,823 g, 5,753 n.
1896 Liverpool-Boston service.

52 LONDONIAN

Bt 1896 Harland & Wolff, Belfast; *T:* 8,823 g. **Dim** 512 ft (156.05 m) × 59 ft (17.98 m) × 35 ft (10.67 m). **Eng** Sgl scr, tpl exp; Cyls: 22 in (55.88 cm), 36½ in (92.71 cm) and 60 in (152.4 cm); *Stroke:* 48 in (121.92 cm); 499 NHP; *Stm P:* 90 lb; 12 kts; By builder. **H** Steel, 2 decks; *Pass:* 50 1st.
1896 Built as *Idaho* for Wilson's &

Furness-Leyland's Liverpool-Boston service.
1898 Renamed *Londonian.*
Nov 23: Capsized, North Atlantic. 17 lives lost.

53 ANGLIAN

Bt 1896 Alex Stephen & Sons, Glasgow; *T:* 5,532 g, 3,613 n. **Dim** 450 ft (137.16 m) × 49 ft 1 in (14.96 m) × 39 ft 10 in (12.14 m). **Eng** Sgl scr, tpl exp; 3 cyls: 32 in (81.28 cm), 54 in (137.16 cm) and 86 in (218.44 cm); *Stroke:* 54 in (137.16 cm); 660 NHP; *Stm P:* 180 lb; 12 kts; By builder. **H** Steel, 2 decks, fcsle 52 ft (15.85 m), bridge 254 ft (77.42 m), poop 38 ft (11.58 m).
1896 Laid down as *London City* for Furness Withy. Purchased on the stocks. Renamed *Megantic* by the Wilson-Hill Line for their London-New York service.
Renamed *Anglian* and operated by Wilson's & Furness-Leyland Line, London-Boston.
1900 Transferred to Frederick Leyland (1900) Ltd.
1917 June 10: Torpedoed off Bishop's Rock.

54 CAMBRIAN

Bt 1896 Wm Gray & Co, West Hartlepool; *T:* 5,626 g, 3,643 n. **Dim** 450 ft (137.16 m) × 49 ft 1 in (14.96 m) × 39 ft 10 in (12.14 m). **Eng** Sgl scr, tpl exp; 3 cyls: 32 in (81.28 cm), 54 in (137.16 cm) and 86 in (218.44 cm); *Stroke:* 54 in (137.16 cm); 660 NHP; *Stm P:* 180 lb; 12 kts; By Central

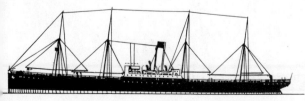

53-54

Marine Engine Works, West Hartlepool.
H Steel, 2 decks, fcsle 52 ft (15.85 m),
bridge 254 ft (77.42 m), poop 38 ft
(11.58 m).
1896 Built for the Wilson-Hill Line.
London-New York service.
1899 Renamed *Bostonian* (II).
1901 Transferred to Frederick Leyland
(1900) Ltd.
1917 Oct 10: Torpedoed south-east of
Start Point.

55 ALMERIAN

Bt 1897 R. Thompson & Sons,
Sunderland; *T:* 2,984 g, 1,910 n. **Dim**
351 ft 6 in (107.14 m) × 42 ft 2 in (12.85
m) × 23 ft 4 in (7.11 m). **Eng** Sgl scr, tpl
exp; 3 cyls: 22 in (55.88 cm), 36 in
(91.44 cm) and 62 in (157.48 cm);
Stroke: 48 in (121.92 cm); 284 NHP;
Stm P: 200 lb; 12 kts; By G. Clark,
Sunderland. **H** Steel, 2 decks, fcsle 36 ft
(10.97 m), bridge 106 ft (32.31 m),
poop 37 ft (11.28 m).
1897 Entered service.
1918 Oct 19: Mined off Licata, Sicily.

56 ALBANIAN (II)

Details as *Almerian (55)* except: *T:*
2,930 g, 1,876 n.
1898 Entered service.
1921 Sold to Hull Beacon SS Co
(Oughtred & Harrison). Same name.
19?? Broken up.

57 ASSYRIAN (II)

Details as *Almerian (55)* except: *T:*

2,890 g, 1,541 n.
1898 Oct: Entered service.
Sold before 1908.

58 TAGUS

Bt 1898 Caledon SB & E Co, Dundee;
T: 937 g, 509 n. **Dim** 220 ft (67.06
m) × 28 ft 7 in (8.71 m) × 16 ft 4 in (4.98
m). **Eng** Sgl scr, compound; 2 cyls: 18
in (45.72 cm) and 48 in (121.92 cm);
Stroke: 36 in (91.44 cm); 88 RHP; *Stm
P:* 160 lb; 9 kts; By builder. **H** Iron, 2
decks, fcsle 33 ft (10.06 m), bridge 79 ft
(24.08 m).
1898 Entered service on Mediterranean
routes.

59 ATLANTIAN (I)

Bt 1899 Armstrong Whitworth & Co,
Newcastle; *T:* 9,355 g, 6,168 n. **Dim** 482
ft (146.91 m) × 57 ft 4 in (17.47 m) × 32
ft 7 in (9.93 m). **Eng** Tw scr, tpl exp; 3
cyls: 21 in (53.34 cm), 35 in (88.9 cm)
and 59 in (149.86 cm); *Stroke:* 48 in
(121.92 cm); 701 NHP; *Stm P:* 186 lb;
13 kts; By Wallsend Slipway. **H** Steel, 2
decks and awning deck, bridge 121 ft
(36.88 m).
1899 Built for West India & Pacific SS
Co.
1900 Taken over by F. Leyland. Used
on the North Atlantic routes.
1918 June 25: Torpedoed off Eagle's
Rock.

60 WINIFREDIAN

Bt 1899 Harland & Wolff, Belfast; *T:*

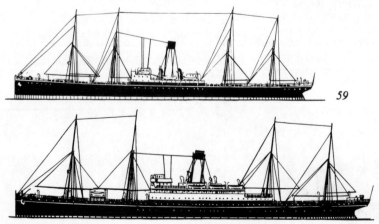

59

60-61

0,428 g, 6,816 n. **Dim** 570 ft (173.74 m)
a, 552 ft 6 in (168.4 m)×59 ft 4 in
18.08 m)×28 ft 10 in (8.79 m); *Dft:* 31
t 6 in (9.6 m). **Eng** Sgl scr, tpl exp; 3
yls: 33 in (83.82 cm), 56 in (142.24 cm)
nd 94 in (238.76 cm); *Stroke:* 66 in
167.64 cm); 5,500 IHP; 2 dbl and 2 sgl
nded boilers; *Stm P:* 200 lb; 14 kts; By
uilder. **H** Steel, 3 decks and shelter
leck, 8 hatches, 820 head of cattle;
Coal: 1,120 tons; *Pass:* 140 1st.

899 July 22: Maiden voyage Liverpool-
Boston. One Boer War trooping run.
914-16 Trooping.
917 Apr: Struck mine in North Sea but
eached port.
918 Returned to Liverpool-Boston
ervice.
927 Transferred to Red Star's
Antwerp-New York route.
929 Broken up in Italy. 30 years old
nd 23 years on the Liverpool-Boston
un.

1 DEVONIAN (I)

Details as *Winifredian (60)* except: *T:*
0,418 g, 6,812 n.
900 Sept 15: Maiden voyage Liverpool-
Boston.
917 Aug 21: Torpedoed off Tory
sland, Donegal, Ireland. Two lives lost.

2 YUCATAN

Bt 1882 Harland & Wolff, Belfast; *T:*
,810 g, 1,793 n. **Dim** 336 ft 6 in
102.56 m)×38 ft 2 in (11.63 m)×26 ft
in (8.03 m). **Eng** Sgl scr, compound;
×2 cyls: 29 in (73.66 cm) and 56 in
142.24 cm); *Stroke:* 42 in (106.68 cm);
39 NHP; 10 kts; By builder. **H** Iron, 2
ecks.
882 Built for West India & Pacific SS
Co Ltd.
900 Purchased with fleet by F.
Leyland.

3 BERNARD HALL

Bt 1880 James Laing, Sunderland; *T:*
,678 g, 1,706 n. **Dim** 338 ft (103.02
m)×38 ft (11.58 m)×26 ft (7.92 m).
Eng Sgl scr, compound; 2 cyls: 29 in
73.66 cm) and 59 in (149.86 cm);
Stroke: 42 in (106.68 cm); 188 NHP; 10

kts; By G. Forrester & Co, Liverpool. **H**
Iron, 2 decks, fcsle 30 ft (9.14 m),
bridge 93 ft (28.35 m).
1880 Built for West India & Pacific SS
Co Ltd.
1900 Taken over by F. Leyland.

64 WEST INDIAN

Details as *Bernard Hall (63)* except: **Bt**
1891; *T:* 2,704 g, 1,706 n.
1891 Built for West India & Pacific SS
Co Ltd.
1900 Taken over by F. Leyland.

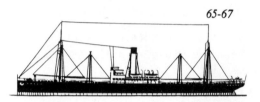

65-67

65 TEXAN

Bt 1883 Harland & Wolff, Belfast; *T:*
3,257 g, 2,077 n. **Dim** 360 ft 7 in
(109.91 m)×41 ft 4 in (12.6 m)×19 ft 4
in (5.89 m). **Eng** Sgl scr, compound; 2
cyls: 40 in (101.6 cm) and 80 in (203.2
cm); *Stroke:* 51 in (129.54 cm); 381
NHP; 10 kts; By builder. **H** Iron, 3
decks.
1883 Built for West India & Pacific SS
Co Ltd.
1900 Taken over by F. Leyland.

66 FLORIDIAN (I)

Details as *Texan (65)* except: **Bt** 1884;
T: 3,257 g, 2,098 n.
1884 Built for West India & Pacific SS
Co Ltd.
1900 Taken over by F. Leyland.

67 COSTA RICAN

Details as *Texan (65)* except: **Bt** 1885;
T: 3,179 g, 2,093 n.
1885 Built for West India & Pacific SS
Co Ltd.
1900 Taken over by F. Leyland.

68 DARIEN

Bt 1888 Barclay, Curle & Co, Glasgow;
T: 3,299 g, 2,178 n. **Dim** 370 ft (112.78
m)×41 ft 2 in (12.55 m)×27 ft (8.23

68-71

m). **Eng** Sgl scr, tpl exp; 3 cyls: 28 in (71.12 cm), 44 in (111.76 cm) and 74 in (187.96 cm); *Stroke:* 51 in (129.54 cm); 391 NHP; 10 kts; By builder. **H** Steel, 3 decks, fcsle 47 ft (14.32 m), bridge 126 ft (38.4 m), poop 42 ft (12.8 m).
1888 Built for West India & Pacific SS Co Ltd.
1900 Taken over by F. Leyland.

69 WILLIAM CLIFF

Details as *Darien (68)* except: *T:* 3,352 g, 2,169 n.
1888 Built for West India & Pacific SS Co Ltd.
1900 Jan 1: Taken over by F. Leyland.

70 LOUISIANIAN

Details as *Darien (68)* except: **Bt** 1891; *T:* 3,642 g, 2,386 n.
1891 Built for West India & Pacific SS Co Ltd.
1900 Taken over by F. Leyland.
1913 Feb: Sold to Italian owners.

71 NICARAGUAN

Details as *Darien (68)* except: *T:* 3,642 g, 2,386 n.
1888 Built for West India & Pacific SS Co Ltd.
1900 Taken over by F. Leyland.

cm); 424 NHP; 13 kts; By builder. **H** Steel, 2 decks.
1889 Built as *Runic* for White Star Line. Livestock carrier.
Feb 21 : Maiden voyage.
1895 Sold to West India & Pacific SS Co Ltd. Renamed *Tampican*.
1900 Jan 1: Transferred to F. Leyland. Liverpool-New York run.
1912 Sold to South Pacific Whaling Co, Oslo. Renamed *Imo*. Whale-oil tanker.
1917 Dec 6: Collided with *Mount Blanc* (CGT) at Halifax, Nova Scotia. The French ship, carrying ammunition, exploded, obliterating the suburb of Richmond. 1,500 killed, 2,000 missing.
1918 Became Norwegian *Guvernoren*.
1921 Nov 30: Wrecked at Port Stanley.

73 CUBAN

Bt 1891 Naval Construction & Armament Co, Barrow-in-Furness; *T:* 4,201 g, 2,728 n. **Dim** 360 ft (109.73 m) × 43 ft 2 in (13.16 m) × 33 ft 8 in (10.26 m). **Eng** Sgl scr, tpl exp; 3 cyls: 27 in (68.58 cm), 44 in (111.76 cm) and 72 in (182.88 cm); *Stroke:* 48 in (121.92 cm); 396 NHP; 2 dbl ended boilers; 12 kts; By builder. **H** Steel, 2 decks.
1891 Nov: Built for West India & Pacific SS Co Ltd.
1900 Taken over by F. Leyland.

74 MEXICAN

Details as *Cuban (73)*.
1891 Built for West India & Pacific SS Co Ltd.
1900 Jan 1: Taken over by F. Leyland.

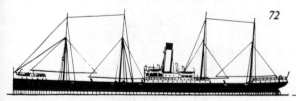

72

75-76

72 TAMPICAN

Bt 1889 Harland & Wolff, Belfast; *T:* 4,833 g, 3,126 n. **Dim** 430 ft 7 in (131.24 m) × 45 ft 2 in (13.77 m) × 30 ft (9.14 m). **Eng** Sgl scr, tpl exp; 3 cyls: 27 in (68.58 cm), 44½ in (113.03 cm) and 74 in (187.96 cm); *Stroke:* 60 in (152.4

75 BARBADIAN (I)

Bt 1893 Naval Construction & Armament Co, Barrow-in-Furness; *T:* 4,501 g, 2,934 n. **Dim** 380 ft 2 in (115.87 m) × 44 ft 2 in (13.46 m) × 26 ft 7 in (8.1 m). **Eng** Sgl scr, tpl exp; 3 cyls: 25½ in (64.77 cm), 42½ in (107.95 cm) and 72 in (182.88 cm); *Stroke:* 51 in (129.54 cm); 437 NHP; 2 dbl ended boilers; 13 kts; By builder. **H** Steel, 3 decks.

1893 Built for West India & Pacific SS Co Ltd.

1900 Jan 1: Taken over by F. Leyland.

76 JAMAICAN

Details as *Barbadian (75)* except: *T:* 2,948 n.

1893 Built for West India & Pacific SS Co Ltd.

1900 Jan 1: Taken over by F. Leyland.

77 AMERICAN

Bt 1895 Harland & Wolff, Belfast; *T:* 8,196 g, 5,407 n. **Dim** 475 ft 10 in (145.03 m) × 55 ft 2 in (16.81 m) × 35 ft 10 in (10.92 m). **Eng** Tw scr, tpl exp; 2 × 3 cyls: 19 in (48.26 cm), 31 in (78.74 cm) and 52 in (132.08 cm); *Stroke:* 48 in (121.92 cm); 375 NHP; 12 kts; By builder. **H** Steel, 3 decks, bridge 95 ft (28.96 m); *Pass:* 40 1st.

1895 Aug 8: Launched. Built as *American* for West India & Pacific SS Co Ltd.
Oct 9: Maiden voyage Liverpool-New Orleans.

1898 Chartered to Atlantic Transport Line.

1900 Jan 1: Taken over by F. Leyland. Same name. Used as Boer War mule transport.

1904 May 21: Sold to White Star Line. Renamed *Cufic.* Liverpool-Sydney.

1914 War service as armed transport.

1917-19 Operated under the Liner Requisition Scheme.

1919-23 Reverted to Australian trade.

1923 Dec: Sold for scrapping to G. Lombardo, Genoa.

1924 Jan 25: Sold to Soc Anon Ligure di Nav a Vapore, Genoa. Renamed *Antartico.*

1927 Sold to Bozzo & Mortola. Renamed *Maria Giulia.*

1930 Apr: Laid up for sale.

1932 Nov: Sold and broken up at Genoa.

78 EUROPEAN

Details as *American (77)* except: *T:*

8,262 g, 5,385 n.

1895 Built as *European* for West India & Pacific SS Co Ltd.
July 9: Maiden voyage Liverpool-New Orleans.

1900 Jan 1: Taken over by F. Leyland. Became Boer War transport.

1904 Sold to White Star Line. Renamed *Tropic* (II). Used on Australian run.

1908 Dec 12: Collided with coaster *Wyoming* off the Skerries.

1917-19 Operated under the Liner Requisition Scheme.

1919 Reverted to Australian run.

1923 Sold to Ditta L. Pittaluga, Italy, as *Tropic.*

1924 Sold to Soc Anon Ligure di Nav a Vapore, Genoa. Renamed *Artico.*

1927 Sold back to Pittaluga. Renamed *Transilvania.*

1933 Broken up at Genoa.

79-80

79 ANTILLIAN

Bt 1898 Caird & Co, Greenock; *T:* 5,613 g, 3,678 n. **Dim** 420 ft 9 in (128.24 m) × 49 ft 2 in (14.99 m) × 21 ft 10 in (6.65 m). **Eng** Sgl scr, tpl exp; 3 cyls: 28 in (71.12 cm), 46 in (116.84 cm) and 77 in (195.58 cm); *Stroke:* 54 in (137.16 cm); 555 NHP; *Stm P:* 180 lb; 12 kts; By builder. **H** Steel, 2 decks, fcsle 76 ft (23.16 m), bridge 115 ft (35.05 m), poop 35 ft (10.67 m); *Pass:* 38 1st.

1898 Built for West India & Pacific SS Co Ltd.

1900 Jan 1: Taken over by F. Leyland.

80 COLOMBIAN (II)

Details as *Antillian (79)* except: *T:* 5,613 g, 3,680 n.

1898 Built as *Colombian* for West India & Pacific SS Co Ltd.

1899 Nov 5: Boer War transport No 39. Took 10th Royal Hussars (Prince of Wales' Own) to South Africa in 28 days.

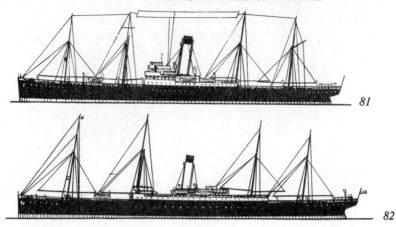

81

82

1900 Jan 1: Taken over by F. Leyland. Renamed *Asian* because *Colombian* (I) *(44)* still in fleet. Cargo only.
1924 Sept 17: Went aground in fog on Stag Rocks, Kinsale, Southern Ireland. Lost.

81 BOHEMIAN (II)

Bt 1900 Alex Stephen, Linthouse, Glasgow; *T:* 8,548 g, 5,542 n. **Dim** 512 ft (156.06 m) × 58 ft 2 in (17.73 m) × 34 ft 4 in (10.46 m). **Eng** Sgl scr, tpl exp; 3 cyls: 32 in (81.28 cm), 54 in (137.16 cm) and 90 in (228.6 cm); *Stroke:* 66 in (167.64 cm); 807 NHP; *Stm P:* 190 lb; 13 kts; By builder. **H** Steel, 3 decks; *Pass:* 60 1st.
1900 Sept 8: Maiden voyage Liverpool-Boston.
1920 Wrecked near Halifax, Nova Scotia.

82 CANADIAN

Bt 1900 Hawthorn Leslie & Co, Newcastle; *T:* 9,301 g, 6,010 n. **Dim** 530 ft (161.54 m) × 59 ft 4 in (18.08 m) × 35 ft 2 in (10.72 m). **Eng** Sgl scr, tpl exp; 3 cyls: 32 in (81.28 cm), 54 in (137.16 cm) and 90 in (228.6 cm); *Stroke:* 66 in (167.64 cm); 805 NHP; 2 dbl and 2 sgl ended boilers; *Stm P:* 200 lb; 13 kts; By

builder. **H** Steel, 3 decks, bridge 214 ft (65.23 m); *Pass:* 60 1st.
1900-3 Liverpool-New York.
1903 Liverpool-Boston sevice.
1917 Apr 5: Torpedoed by *U-59* 47 miles off Fastnet.

83 CALEDONIAN

Bt 1900 Caledon SB & E Co, Dundee; *T:* 4,986 g, 3,212 n. **Dim** 426 ft 6 in (130 m) × 50 ft 4 in (15.34 m) × 28 ft 5 in (8.66 m). **Eng** Sgl scr, tpl exp; 3 cyls: 25 in (63.5 cm), 41½ in (105.41 cm) and 71 in (180.34 cm); *Stroke:* 60 in (152.4 cm); 464 NHP; 4 sgl ended boilers; *Stm P:* 200 lb; 13 kts; By builder. **H** Steel, 3 decks; *Coal:* 732 tons; *Cargo:* 323,000 cu ft (9,146 cu m) grain.
1900 Liverpool-Boston service.

84 DOURO (III)

Bt 1900 Caledon SB & E Co, Dundee; *T:* 1,028 g, 638 n. **Dim** 235 ft (71.63 m) × 30 ft 7 in (9.32 m) × 16 ft 5 in (5 m). **Eng** Sgl scr, compound; 2 cyls: 18 in (45.72 cm) and 48 in (121.92 cm); *Stroke:* 36 in (91.44 cm); 88 RHP; *Stm P:* 160 lb; 9 kts; By builder. **H** Steel, 2 decks, fcsle 37 ft (11.28 m), bridge 82 ft (24.99 m).
1900 Built for Mediterranean service.
1902 Transferred to Ellerman Lines.

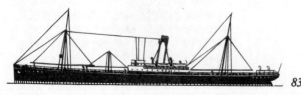

83

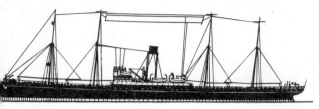

85

85 INDIAN

Bt 1900 Workman Clark & Co, Belfast; *T:* 9,121 g, 5,991 n, 13,613 dwt. **Dim** 482 ft 10 in (147.17 m) × 57 ft 2 in (17.42 m) × 31 ft 11 in (9.73 m). **Eng** Tw scr, tpl exp; 2 × 3 cyls: 21 in (53.34 cm), 35 in (88.9 cm) and 58 in (147.32 cm); *Stroke:* 48 in (121.92 cm); 604 NHP; 2 dbl and 1 sgl ended boilers, 15 furnaces; *Stm P:* 180 lb; 12 kts; By builder. **H** Steel, 2 decks, bridge 113 ft (34.44 m); *Pass:* 60 1st.

1900 North Atlantic service.
1923 Broken up in Germany.

86 IBERIAN (II)

Bt 1900 Sir James Laing & Sons, Sunderland; *T:* 5,223 g, 3,347 n. **Dim** 437 ft (133.2 m) × 48 ft 9 in (14.86 m) × 29 ft 10 in (9.09 m). **Eng** Sgl scr, tpl exp; 3 cyls: 25 in (63.5 cm), 41½ in (105.41 cm) and 71 in (180.34 cm); *Stroke:* 60 in (152.4 cm); 470 NHP; 2 dbl ended boilers; *Stm P:* 200 lb; 12 kts; By J. Dickinson & Sons, Sunderland. **H** Steel, 3 decks and shelter deck, bridge 108 ft (32.92 m).

1900 Entered service.
1915 July 30: Torpedoed off Fastnet.

87 BELGIAN (II)

Bt 1900 Sir James Laing & Sons, Sunderland; *T:* 3,657 g, 2,364 n. **Dim** 382 ft 4 in (116.53 m) × 45 ft 4 in (13.82 m) × 25 ft 10 in (7.87 m). **Eng** Sgl scr, tpl exp; 3 cyls: 24 in (60.96 cm), 40¼ in (102.23 cm) and 68 in (172.72 cm); 366 NHP; *Stm P:* 200 lb; 11 kts; By T. Richardson & Sons, Hartlepool. **H**

Steel, 2 decks, fcsle 43 ft (13.11 m), bridge 132 ft (40.23 m), poop 40 ft (12.19 m).

1900 Entered service.
1917 May: Torpedoed. Reached port but not repaired.

88 ALEXANDRIAN

Bt 1901 Wigham Richardson & Co, Newcastle; *T:* 4,467 g, 2,899 n. **Dim** 411 ft (125.27 m) × 46 ft 8 in (14.22 m) × 27 ft 1 in (8.25 m). **Eng** Sgl scr, tpl exp; 3 cyls: 25 in (63.5 cm), 41½ in (105.41 cm) and 71 in (180.34 cm); *Stroke:* 48 in (121.92 cm); 470 NHP; 2 dbl ended boilers; *Stm P;* 200 lb; 12 kts; By builder. **H** Steel, 2 decks.

1901 Entered service.
1917 Jan: Torpedoed and beached. Salvaged.
19?? Sold to Febo A Bertorello, Genoa. Same name.
1926 Broken up.

89 COLONIAN (I)

Bt 1901 Hawthorn Leslie & Co, Newcastle; *T:* 6,440 g, 4,141 n. **Dim** 450 ft 6 in (137.31 m) × 54 ft 2 in (16.51 m) × 30 ft 7 in (9.32 m). **Eng** Sgl scr, tpl exp; 3 cyls: 27 in (68.58 cm), 45½ in (115.57 cm) and 76 in (193.04 cm); *Stroke:* 60 in (152.4 cm); 552 NHP; *Stm P:* 200 lb; 12 kts. **H** Steel, 3 decks and shelter deck, bridge 126 ft (38.4 m); *Pass:* 12 1st.

1901 Entered service.
1917 May 21: Wrecked on North Bishop Rocks, Scilly Isles, en route Boston-London.

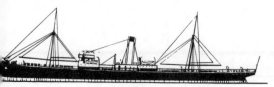

88

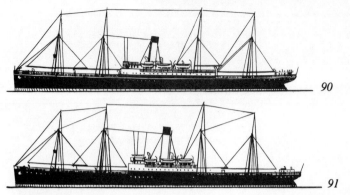

90

91

90 KINGSTONIAN

Bt 1901 Hawthorn Leslie & Co,
Newcastle; *T:* 6,564 g, 4,207 n. **Dim** 467
ft (142.34 m) × 53 ft 8 in (16.36 m) × 31
ft 7 in (9.63 m). **Eng** Sgl scr, tpl exp; 3
cyls: 31 in (78.74 cm), 52 in (132.08 cm)
and 86 in (218.44 cm); *Stroke:* 60 in
(152.4 cm); 674 NHP; 2 dbl and 2 sgl
ended boilers; *Stm P:* 200 lb; 13 kts; By
builder. **H** Steel, 3 decks; *Pass:* 40 1st.

1901 Entered service.
1918 April 11: Torpedoed by *U-68* in
Mediterranean. Towed to Carloforte,
Sardinia.
Apr 29: Torpedoed by *U-48* at
Carloforte and lost.

91 CALIFORNIAN

Bt 1902 Caledon SB & E Co, Dundee;
T: 6,223 g, 4,038 n. **Dim** 447 ft 7 in
(136.42m) × 53 ft 9 in (16.38 m) × 30 ft 6
in (9.3 m). **Eng** Sgl scr, tpl exp; 3 cyls:
26 in (66.04 cm), 43½ in (110.49 cm)

and 74 in (187.96 cm);*Stroke:* 60 in
(152.4 cm); 518 NHP; *Stm P:* 200 lb; 14
kts; By builder. **H** Steel, 3 decks, bridge
115 ft (35.05 m); *Pass:* 35 1st.

1902 Entered service.
1915 Nov 9: Torpedoed off Cape
Matapan.

92 ETONIAN

Bt 1898 Furness Withy & Co, West
Hartlepool; *T:* 6,438 g, 4,135 n. **Dim**
475 ft 6 in (144.93 m) × 52 ft 4 in (15.95
m) × 23 ft 2 in (7.06 m). **Eng** Sgl scr, tpl
exp; 3 cyls: 32 in (81.28 cm), 54 in
(137.16 cm) and 90 in (228.6 cm);
Stroke: 66 in (167.64 cm); 842 NHP; 2
dbl and 2 sgl ended boilers; *Stm P:* 200
lb; 13 kts; By Central Marine
Engineering Works, West Hartlepool. **H**
Steel, 3 decks; *Pass:* 30 1st.

1898 Built as *Chicago* for Wilson Line
(Thomas Wilson, Sons & Co).
Transferred to Wilson's & Furness-
Leyland Line. Renamed *Etonian.*

92

93

1918 Mar 23: Torpedoed off Kinsale.

93 HANOVERIAN

Bt 1902 Hawthorn Leslie & Co, Newcastle; *T:* 13,518 g, 8,663 n. **Dim** 582 ft (177.39 m) × 60 ft 4 in (18.39 m) × 38 ft 4 in (11.68 m). **Eng** Tw scr, tpl exp; 2 × 3 cyls: 28 in (71.12 cm), 47½ in (120.65 cm) and 80 in (203.2 cm); *Stroke:* 60 in (152.4 cm); 1,269 NHP; *Stm P:* 200 lb; 15 kts; By builder. **H** Steel, 3 decks; *Pass:* 150 1st, 600 3rd.
1902 July 19: Maiden voyage Liverpool-Boston. Three round voyages.
1903 Transferred to Dominion Line. Renamed *Mayflower*. Transferred to White Star Line. Renamed *Cretic*.
1923 Returned to Leyland Line. Renamed *Devonian* (II) and returned to Liverpool-Boston service. Her original name was not resumed because of the war association with Hanover.
1927 Served in Leyland colours on Red Star Line's Antwerp-Southampton-New York run.
1929 Broken up at McLellan's yard, Bo'ness, Firth of Forth.

94 OXONIAN

Bt 1898 Chas Connell & Co, Glasgow; *T:* 6,306 g, 4,072 n. **Dim** 459 ft (139.9 m) × 52 ft 6 in (16 m) × 31 ft (9.45 m). **Eng** Sgl scr, tpl exp; 3 cyls: 28 in (71.12 cm), 47½ in (120.65 cm) and 78 in (198.12 cm); *Stroke:* 60 in (152.4 cm); 608 NHP; *Stm P:* 200 lb; 12 kts; By D. Rowan, Glasgow. **H** Steel, 2 decks; *Pass:* 12.

1898 Built as *Pinemore* for Johnston Line.
1902 Purchased by F. Leyland and renamed *Oxonian*.
1928 Broken up.

95 SCOTIAN

Bt 1903 Harland & Wolff, Belfast; *T:* 18,074 g, 11,223 n. **Dim** 599 ft (182.57 m) × 68 ft 2 in (20.78 m) × 48 ft 4 in (14.73 m). **Eng** Tw scr, quad exp; 2 × 4 cyls: 25 in (63.5 cm), 36 in (91.44 cm), 52½ in (133.35 cm) and 75 in (190.5 cm); *Stroke:* 54 in (137.16 cm); 827 NHP; 14 kts; By builder. **H** Steel, 4 decks and awning deck, bridge 166 ft (50.6 m); *Pass:* 200 1st, 150 2nd, 3,006 3rd.
1903 Ordered by Wilson's & Furness-Leyland Line. Work suspended when company decided not to enter North Atlantic passenger trade.
1907 Sold to Hamburg America Line. Renamed *President Lincoln* after provisionally being named *Brooklyn*. June 1: Maiden voyage Hamburg-Plymouth-New York.
1917 Seized at New York by US Government. Served without change of name.
1918 May 31: Torpedoed and sunk. 26 lives lost.

96 SERVIAN

Details as *Scotian (95)* except: *T:* 18,072 g, 11,112 n.
1903 Ordered by Wilson's & Furness-Leyland Line. Work suspended when

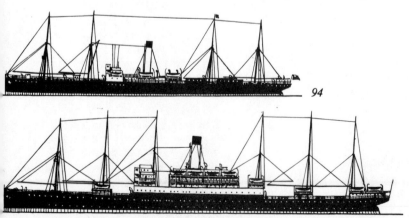

94

95-96

company decided not to enter North Atlantic passenger trade.
1907 Sold to Hamburg America Line. Renamed *President Grant* after provisionally being named *Berlin*. Sept 14: Maiden voyage Hamburg-Plymouth-New York.
1914 Laid up in New York.
1917 Seized by US Government. Sailed as *President Grant.*
1924 Became *Republic,* United States Lines.
1931-45 US Army transport.
1952 Broken up at Baltimore.

97-110

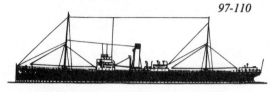

97 MEDIAN

Bt 1908 Harland & Wolff, Belfast; *T:* 6,296 g, 4,065n. **Dim** 400 ft 4 in (122.02 m) × 52 ft 4 in (15.95 m) × 26 ft 10 in (8.18 m). **Eng** Sgl scr, quad exp; 4 cyls: 23½ in (59.69 cm), 34½ in (87.63 cm), 49 in (124.46 cm) and 70 in (177.8 cm); *Stroke:* 51 in (129.54 cm); 350 NHP; 2 dbl ended boilers; *Stm P;* 215 lb; 12 kts; By builder. **H** Steel, 2 decks and shelter deck, forward bridge 35 ft (10.67 m), after bridge deck 52 ft (15.85 m).
1908 Entered service.
1933 Broken up in UK.

98 MEMPHIAN

Details at *Median (97)* except: *T:* 6,305 g, 4,066 n.
1908 Entered service.
1917 Oct 8: Torpedoed off North Arklow Lighthouse.

99 MERCIAN

Details as *Median (97)* except: *T:* 6,305 g, 4,066 n.
1908 Entered service.
1933 Broken up in UK.

100 MELTONIAN

Details as *Median (97)* except: **Bt** 1909 Harland & Wolff, Belfast; *T:* 6,306 g, 4,065 n.

1909 Entered North Atlantic service.
1933 Broken up in UK.

101 NESSIAN

Details as *Median (97)* except: **Bt** 1912 Scotts SB & E Co, Greenock; *T:* 6,276 g, 4,012 n.
1912 Entered Liverpool-Caribbean service.
1933 Broken up in Italy.

102 NESTORIAN

Details as *Median (97)* except: **Bt** 1912 Scotts SB & E Co, Greenock; *T:* 6,395 g, 4,089 n.
1912 Entered Liverpool-Caribbean service.
1917 Jan 2: Wrecked south of Cape Clear Island en route Galveston-Liverpool.

103 NICOSIAN

Details as *Median (97)* except: **Bt** 1912 D. & W. Henderson & Co, Glasgow; *T:* 6,369 g, 4,097 n.
1912 Laid down and launched as *Nicosian.* Renamed *Nevisian.* Same company.
1933 Broken up in Italy.

104 NINIAN

Details as *Median (97)* except: **Bt** 1912 Hawthorn Leslie & Co, Newcastle; *T:* 6,385 g, 4,068 n.
1912 North Atlantic service.
1933 Broken up in Italy.

105 NITONIAN

Details as *Median (97)* except: **Bt** 1912 Hawthorn Leslie & Co, Newcastle; *T:* 6,381 g, 4,066 n.
1912 North Atlantic service.
1933 Broken up in Italy.

106 NUBIAN

Details at *Median (97)* except: **Bt** 1912 Hawthorn Leslie & Co, Newcastle; *T:* 6,384 g, 4,067 n.
1912 Entered Leyland service to Boston.
1934 Sold to Donaldson Line. Same name. Bristol Channel-Canada service.
1935 July: Broken up in Italy.

107 NORTONIAN

Details as *Median (97)* except: **Bt** 1913
D. & W. Henderson, Glasgow; *T:* 6,387
g, 4,097 n.

1913 Placed on Boston service.
1934 Sold to Donaldson Line. Same
name. Bristol Channel-Canada service.
1935 Broken up in Italy.

108 NORWEGIAN (I)

Details as *Median (97)* except: **Bt** 1913
Caledon SB & E Co, Dundee; *T:* 6,327
g, 4,056 n.

1913 Placed on Boston service.
1917 Mar 13: Torpedoed off Cork.
Beached but total loss.

109 NAPERIAN

Details as *Median (97)* except: **Bt** 1914
Napier & Miller, Glasgow; *T:* 6,410 g,
4,101 n.

1914 Entered service.
1933 Broken up in Italy.

110 NOVIAN

Details as *Median (97)* except: **Bt** 1914
D. & W. Henderson & Co, Glasgow; *T:*
6,368 g, 4,096 n.

1914 North Atlantic service.
1933 Broken up in Italy.

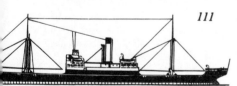

111

111 FLORIDIAN (II)

Bt 1913 Short Bros, Sunderland; *T:*
4,777 g, 3,024 n. **Dim** 385 ft (117.35
m) × 51 ft 6 in (15.7 m) × 27 ft 6 in
(8.38 m). **Eng** Sgl scr, tpl exp; 3 cyls: 26
in (66.04 cm), 43 in (109.22 cm) and 71
in (180.34 cm); *Stroke:* 48 in (121.92
cm); 393 NHP; *Stm P:* 180 lb; 11½ kts.
H Steel, 2 decks.

1913 Entered service.
1917 Feb 4: Torpedoed 200 miles west
of Fastnet. Five killed. The captain,
chief engineer and wireless operator
were taken prisoner.

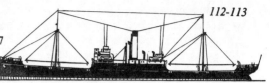

112-113

112 SCYTHIAN

Bt 1913 Ropner & Sons, Stockton-on-
Tees; *T:* 4,865 g, 3,028 n. **Dim** 390 ft
(118.87 m) × 50 ft 6 in (15.39 m) × 28 ft
(8.53 m). **Eng** Sgl scr, tpl exp; 3 cyls: 26
in (66.04 cm), 43 in (109.22 cm) and 71
in (180.34 cm); *Stroke:* 48 in (121.92
cm); 392 NHP; 3 sgl ended boilers; *Stm
P:* 180 lb; 12 kts; By Blair & Co,
Stockton. **H** Steel, 2 decks, fcsle 37 ft
(11.28 m), bridge 115 ft (35.05 m), poop
33 ft (10.06 m).

1913 Entered service.
1930 Broken up.

113 SYLVANIAN

Details as *Scythian (112)* except: **Bt** 1913
Ropner & Sons, Stockton-on-Tees; *T:*
4,858 g, 3,010 n.

1914 Aug: Entered service.
1917 June 24: Torpedoed north-west of
Tory Island.

114 ORANIAN

Bt 1914 Napier & Miller, Glasgow; *T:*
3,942 g, 2,448 n. **Dim** 365 ft 2 in (111.3
m) × 47 ft 9 in (14.55 m) × 27 ft (8.23
m). **Eng** Sgl scr, tpl exp; 3 cyls: 25½ in
(64.77 cm), 42½ in (107.95 cm) and 72
in (182.88 cm); *Stroke:* 48 in (121.92
cm); 449 NHP; 3 sgl ended boilers; *Stm
P:* 200 lb; 12 kts; By Dunsmuir &
Jackson, Glasgow. **H** Steel, 2 decks,
fcsle 67 ft (20.42 m), bridge 140 ft
(42.67 m), poop 38 ft (11.58 m).

1914 North Atlantic routes.
1934 Mar: Became *Tamesis*, Greek.
L.A. Embericos.

115 ORUBIAN

Details as *Oranian (114)* except: **Bt** 1914
Scotts SB & E Co, Greenock; *T:* 3,876
g, 2,412 n.

1914 North Atlantic routes.
1917 July 31: Torpedoed 160 miles
north-west of Eagle Island.

116 **BOSTONIAN** (III)

Bt 1915 Harland & Wolff, Belfast; *T:* 6,225 g, 3,964 n. **Dim** 399 ft 1 in (121.64 m) × 52 ft 2 in (15.9 m) × 33 ft 10 in (10.31 m). **Eng** Sgl scr, oil engine; 12 cyls: 25 in (63.5 cm); *Stroke:* 33½ in (85.09 cm); 534 NHP; 12 kts; By Burmeister & Wain. **H** Steel, 2 decks.

1915 Built as *Bostonian.* Sold to Glen Line and renamed Glengyle.
1923 Sold to Pacific Steam Nav. Renamed *Lautaro.*
1947 Became *River Swift* of Jenny SS Co, London.
1948 Caught fire at Rio de Janeiro and not repaired.
1949 Broken up.

117 **CAMERONIAN**

Bt 1914 J. Frerichs & Co, Einswarden, Germany; *T:* 5,861 g. **Dim** 428 ft 5 in (130.58 m) × 55 ft (16.76 m) × 29 ft (8.84 m). **Eng** Sgl scr, quad exp; 10½ kts. **H** Steel, 2 decks.

1914 Built as *Kamerun* for Hamburg America Line.
1915 Found deserted in the Kamerun River, West Africa, by HMS *Cumberland.* A Naval prize-crew sailed her to Liverpool, where she arrived Feb 1. The prize-crew turned her over to Leyland.
1917 June 2: Torpedoed 50 miles north-west of Alexandria. All 63 aboard lost. She was carrying mules, escorted by 32 Army personnel, to Alexandria.

118 **HURONIAN**

Bt 1915 D. & W. Henderson & Co, Glasgow; *T:* 8,755 g, 5,634 n. **Dim** 475 ft 7 in (144.96 m) × 58 ft 1 in (17.7 m) × 37 ft 6 in (11.43 m). **Eng** Tw scr, quad exp; 2 × 4 cyls: 22½ in (57.15 cm), 32¼ in (81.92 cm), 47 in (119.38 cm) and 67 in (170.18 cm); *Stroke:* 48 in (121.92 cm); 855 NHP; 2 dbl and 2 sgl ended boilers; *Stm P:* 215 lb; 14 kts; By builder. **H** Steel, 2 decks, bridge 125 ft (38.1 m).

1915 Apr: Completed.
1932 Broken up in Italy.

119 **LEYSIAN**

Bt 1906 Armstrong Whitworth & Co, Newcastle; *T:* 4,703 g, 2,999 n. **Dim** 400 ft (121.92 m) × 52 ft (15.85 m) × 27 ft (8.23 m). **Eng** Sgl scr, tpl exp; 3 cyls: 27 in (68.58 cm), 45 in (114.3 cm) and 75 in (190.5 cm); *Stroke:* 48 in (121.92 cm); 477 NHP; 3 sgl ended boilers; *Stm P:* 180 lb; 10 kts; By North East Marine Engineering Co, Newcastle. **H** Steel, 2 decks.

1906 Built as *Serak* for Deutsche-Dampfsfahrts Kosmos, Germany.
1916 Became *Leysian.*
1917 Feb 20: Wrecked seven miles south of Stumble Head Lighthouse en route Belfast-Cardiff.

120 **MONTCALM**

Bt 1897 Palmers Co, Newcastle; *T:* 7,082 g, 5,357 n. **Dim** 445 ft (135.64 m) × 52 ft 6 in (16 m) × 27 ft 7 in (8.41 m). **Eng** Sgl scr, tpl exp; 3 cyls: 30 in (76.2 cm), 50½ in (128.27 cm) and 81½ in (207.01 cm); *Stroke:* 54 in (137.16 cm); 664 NHP; 3 dbl ended boilers; *Stm P:* 180 lb; 12 kts; By builder. **H** Steel, 2 decks and shelter deck.

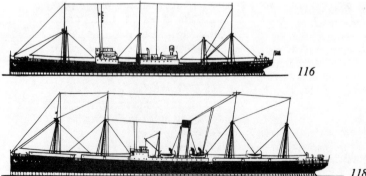

116

118

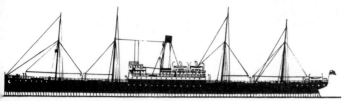

121

1897 Built for Elder Dempster.
1903 Taken over by Canadian Pacific Railway with the Elder Dempster Canadian routes.
1914 One of six ships acquired by the Admiralty.
1916 Operated by F. Leyland.
1917 Sold to Anglo Saxon Petroleum. Renamed *Crenella*.

121 PARISIAN

Bt 1899 Alex Stephen & Co, Glasgow; *T:* 7,548 g, 4,848n. **Dim** 483 ft 7 in (147.4 m) × 57 ft (17.37 m) × 32 ft 8 in (9.96 m). **Eng** Sgl scr, tpl exp; 3 cyls: 30 in (76.2 cm), 50 in (127 cm) and 83 in (210.82 cm); *Stroke:* 60 in (152.4 cm); 690 NHP; *Stm P:* 165 lb; 12 kts. **H** Steel, 2 decks; *Pass:* 60 1st.

1899 Built as *Bethania* for Hamburg America Line.
1916 Captured by Royal Navy. Awarded to F. Leyland. Renamed *Parisian*, her port of registry being Kingston, Jamaica.
1918 Sold. Renamed *Esther Dollar* (Dollar SS Co, USA).
1930 Became *Chief Skidegate*, Canadian American Line.
1934 Became *Taihoku Maru*, Azuma Shinko KK.
1944 Sunk by US submarine.

122 BARBADIAN (II)

Bt 1919 Swan Hunter & Wigham Richardson, Newcastle; *T:* 5,289 g, 3,266 n. **Dim** 412 ft (125.58 m) oa, 400 ft 2 in (121.97 m) × 52 ft 5 in (15.98 m) × 28 ft 5 in (8.66 m). **Eng** Sgl scr, tpl exp; 3 cyls: 27 in (68.58 cm), 44 in (111.76 cm) and 73 in (185.42 cm); *Stroke:* 48 in (121.92 cm); 517 NHP; 3 sgl ended boilers; *Stm P:* 180 lb; By builder. **H** Steel, 2 decks, fcsle 40 ft (12.19 m), bridge 113 ft (34.44 m), poop 49 ft (14.93 m).

1919 Apr 16: Launched. Built as Standard 'B' Type *War Tapir*, Yard No 1101. Acquired by Leyland. Renamed *Barbadian*.
1933 Nov: Sold to Greece. Renamed *Axios*.
1944 Mar 28: Wrecked off Sandheads en route Port Okha-Calcutta with cement.

122-124

123 BELGIAN (III)

Details as *Barbadian (122)* except: *T:* 5,287 g, 3,228 n.
1919 Aug 29: Launched. Laid down as Standard 'B' Type. Completed as *Belgian*.
1934 Sold to Achille Lauro. Renamed *Amelia Lauro*.
1940 June: Seized at Immingham on Italy's entry into war. Renamed *Empire Activity*.
1943 Oct 3: Ran onto Peckford Reef, Sir Charles Hamilton Sound, Newfoundland, and sank.

124 BOLIVIAN

Details as *Barbadian (122)* except:
Bt 1919 Irvines SB & DD Co, West Hartlepool; *T:* 5,116 g, 3,154 n.
1919 Feb 18: Launched. Built as Standard 'B' Type *War Otter* (II).
1920 Mar: Renamed *Bolivian* on completion, after lying incomplete for six months.
1935 Became *Alfios*, N.G. Livanos, Piraeus, Greece.
1946 Apr 25: Went ashore at East Spit, Sable Island, in ballast en route Glasgow-Halifax, Nova Scotia. Constructive loss.

125 PHILADELPHIAN (II)

Bt 1920 Harland & Wolff, Belfast; *T:*

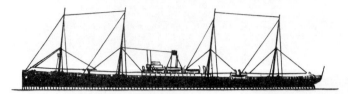

6,586 g, 4,059 n. **Dim** 412 ft 7 in (125.75 m) × 55 ft 9 in (16.99 m) × 34 ft 5 in (10.49 m). **Eng** Sgl scr, 2 steam turbines; 678 NHP; 3 water-tube boilers; 14 kts; By builder. **H** Steel, 1 deck and shelter deck, fcsle 40 ft (12.19 m).

1920 Feb: The last vessel built by Harland & Wolff for Leyland.
1933 Broken up.

126 CORNISHMAN

Bt 1891 Harland & Wolff, Belfast; *T:* 5,749 g, 3,678 n. **Dim** 460 ft 9 in (140.44 m) × 49 ft 1 in (14.96 m) × 30 ft 10 in (9.4 m). **Eng** Tw scr, overlapping propellers, tpl exp; 2 × 3 cyls: 22½ in (57.15 cm), 36½ in (92.71 cm) and 60 in (152.4 cm); *Stroke:* 48 in (121.92 cm); 499 NHP; 13 kts; By builder. **H** Steel, 1 deck, 10 watertight compartments.

1891 Feb 11: Launched. Built as *Nomadic* for White Star. Livestock carrier.
Apr 24: Maiden voyage.
1899 Transport No 34 during Boer War.
1903 Sold to Dominion Line, initially as *Nomadic*.
1904 Renamed *Cornishman*.
1921 Transferred from Dominion Line to F. Leyland. Same name. (A number of Dominion vessels were transferred, on paper only, to Frederick Leyland & Co. They continued to operate in Dominion colours and on Dominion routes.)
1926 Broken up by Wards at Hayle, Cornwall, for £10,500.

127 WELSHMAN

Details as *Cornishman (126)* except: *T:* 5,730 g, 3,670 n.

1891 Built as *Tauric* for White Star.
May 16: Maiden voyage Liverpool-New York.
1903 Sold to Dominion Line.
Mar 12: First voyage, Liverpool-

Portland, as *Tauric.*
1904 Renamed *Welshman*.
1921 Transferred from Dominion Line to F. Leyland. Same name.
1929 Broken up at Bo'ness, Firth of Forth.

128 TURCOMAN

Bt 1892 Harland & Wolff, Belfast; *T:* 5,829 g, 3,683 n. **Dim** 445 ft (135.64 m) × 49 ft 2 in (14.99 m) × 30 ft 1 in (9.17 m). **Eng** Tw scr, tpl exp; 2 × 4 cyls: 20 in (50.8 cm), 2 × 31 in (78.74 cm) and 52 in (132.08 cm); *Stroke:* 42 in (106.68 cm); 429 NHP; *Stm P:* 180 lb; 11 kts; By builder. **H** Steel, 2 decks and shelter deck, fcsle 52 ft (15.84 m), bridge 98 ft (29.87 m), poop 55 ft (16.76 cm).

1892 Built as *Lord Erne*. Registered as owned by Harland & Wolff but operated by Irish Shipowners Ltd of Belfast.
1899 Renamed *Turcoman* and sold to the British & North Atlantic SN Co (Dominion Line).
1921 Transferred from Dominion Line to F. Leyland. Same name.
1926 May: Broken up in Italy.

129 DOMINION

Bt 1894 Harland & Wolff, Belfast; *T:* 6,976 g, 4,402 n. **Dim** 445 ft 6 in (135.79 m) × 50 ft 2 in (15.29 m) × 29 ft 10 in (9.09 m). **Eng** Tw scr, tpl exp; 2 × 3 cyls: 22½ in (57.15 cm), 36½ in (92.71 cm) and 60 in (152.4 cm); *Stroke:* 48 in (121.92 cm); 499 NHP; 12 kts; By builder. **H** Steel, 3 decks, fcsle 102 ft (31.09 m), bridge 207 ft (63.09 m), poop 58 ft (17.68 m); *Pass:* 200 1st, 170 2nd, 750 3rd.

1894 Built as *Prussia* for Hamburg America Line.
1898 Acquired by Dominion Line. Renamed *Dominion*.
May 7: Entered Liverpool-Montreal service.

130

1914-18 War service. Store ship and supply vessel.
1918 Dec 2: Re-entered commercial service Liverpool-Portland, Maine.
1919 Converted to cargo only.
1921 Feb 26: Transferred to F. Leyland ownership with the remainder of the Dominion fleet. Continued on the Liverpool-Portland route in Dominion colours.
1922 Sold to A. Sonenberg, Germany, for scrapping.

130 CANADA

Bt 1896 Harland & Wolff, Belfast; *T:* 9,684 g, 5,668 n. **Dim** 500 ft 5 in (152.53 m) × 58 ft 2 in (17.73 m) × 38 ft 10 in (11.84 m). **Eng** Tw scr, tpl exp; 2 × 3 cyls: 28½ in (72.39 cm), 47½ in (120.65 cm) and 77 in (195.58 cm); *Stroke:* 54 in (137.16 cm); 873 NHP; 12 kts. **H** Steel, 4 decks; *Pass:* 150 1st, 400 3rd.
1896 Oct 1: Maiden voyage Liverpool-Quebec-Montreal.
Dec 23: Winter service Liverpool-Boston.
1899-1902 Boer War transport.
1903 Apr 22: Reverted to Liverpool-Quebec-Montreal service. *T:* 9,413 g.
1914-18 Requisitioned as troopship.
1918 Re-entered winter service to Portland, Maine. *Pass:* 463 cabin, 755 3rd.
1921 Transferred to F. Leyland ownership. Continued in Dominion colours.
1926 Aug 13: Last voyage to Montreal before sale to Italian shipbreakers.

131 IRISHMAN

Bt 1899 Harland & Wolff, Belfast; *T:* 9,540 g, 6,139 n. **Dim** 500 ft 7 in (152.58 m) × 62 ft 5 in (19.02 m) × 34 ft (10.36 m). **Eng** Tw scr, quad exp; 2 × 4 cyls: 21¼ in (53.97 cm), 31½ in (80.01 cm), 46 in (116.84 cm) and 66 in (167.64 cm); *Stroke:* 48 in (121.92 cm); 604 NHP; 12 kts. **H** Steel, 4 decks.
1899 Built for Dominion Line's North Atlantic cattle and general services.
1921 Transferred from Dominion Line.
1924 Broken up in Germany.

132 REGINA

For details of this vessel see Dominion section, entry *47*.

133 COLONIAN (II)

Bt 1892 Harland & Wolff, Belfast; *T:* 6,583 g, 4,230 n. **Dim** 470 ft (143.26 m) × 53 ft 1 in (16.18 m) × 23 ft 10 in (7.26 m). **Eng** Tw scr, tpl exp; 2 × 3 cyls: 22½ in (57.15 cm), 36½ in (92.71 cm) and 60 in (152.4 cm); *Stroke:* 48 in (121.92 cm); 499 NHP; 13 kts; By builder. **H** Steel, 3 decks; *Coal:* 50 tons per day.
1892 Built as *Bovic* for White Star Line.
June 28: Launched.
Aug 22: Maiden voyage Liverpool-New York.
1914 Manchester-New York. Masts and funnel lopped to pass under Manchester Ship Canal bridges.
1917-19 Government service.
1922 Transferred from White Star. Renamed *Colonian*.
1928 Broken up in Rotterdam.

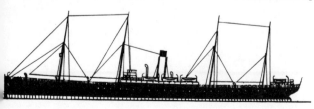

133

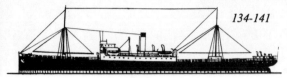

134-141

134 NORWEGIAN (II)

Bt 1921 Caledon SB & E Co, Dundee; *T:* 6,357 g, 4,018 n. **Dim** 400 ft 2 in (121.97 m) × 52 ft 5 in (15.98 m) × 35 ft (10.67 m). **Eng** Sgl scr, quad exp; 4 cyls: 23½ in (59.69 m), 34 in (86.36 cm), 49 in (124.46 cm) and 70 in (177.8 cm); *Stroke:* 51 in (129.54 cm); 644 NHP; *Stm P:* 215 lb; 14 kts. **H** Steel, 2 decks and shelter deck, bridge 143 ft (43.59 m).

Only Dorelian (141) *and* Norwegian *had mainmast rising out of a deckhouse.*

1921 North Atlantic cargo service.
1934 Sold to Donaldson. Same name. Bristol Channel-Canada route.
1954 Sold to Cia de Nav Almirante, Panama. Renamed *Maria Elaine.*
1959 Dec 30: Arrived Osaka, Japan, for breaking up.

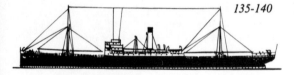

135-140

135 DAKARIAN

Details as *Norwegian (134)* except:
Bt 1921 D. W. Henderson, Glasgow; *T:* 6,426 g, 4,065 n.
1921 North Atlantic cargo service.
1933 Sold to T. & J. Harrison. Same name.
1939 Sold to Ben Line. Renamed *Benvannoch.*
1946 Sold to Andrew Weir. Renamed *Birchbank.* Sold to Japan. Renamed *Shunkei Maru,* Kato Sempaku KK.

136 DAKOTIAN

Details as *Norwegian (134)* except:
Bt 1922 D. W. Henderson, Glasgow; *T:* 6,426 g, 4,065 n.
1922 North Atlantic cargo service.
1934 Sold to Donaldson. Same name.
1940 Nov 21: Mined in Dale Roads, Milford Haven.

137 DARIAN

Details as *Norwegian (134)* except: **Bt** 1922 D. W. Henderson, Glasgow; *T:* 6,434 g, 4,065 n.
1922 North Atlantic cargo service.
1933 Sold to T. & J. Harrison. Same name.
1939 Sold to Ben Line. Renamed *Benvrackie.*
1941 May 13: Torpedoed in North Atlantic.

138 DAYTONIAN

Details as *Norwegian (134)* except: **Bt** 1922 D. W. Henderson, Glasgow; *T:* 6,434 g, 4,066 n.
1922 North Atlantic cargo service.
1933 Sold to T. & J. Harrison. Same name.
1942 Mar 13: Torpedoed off Florida.

139 DAVISIAN

Details as *Norwegian (134)* except: **Bt** 1923 D. W. Henderson, Glasgow; *T:* 6,433 g, 4,065 n.
1922 North Atlantic cargo service.
1933 Sold to T. & J. Harrison. Same name.
1940 July 10: Sunk by German raider No 21 *Widder.*

140 DELILIAN

Details as *Norwegian (134)* except: **Bt** 1923 D. W. Henderson, Glasgow; *T:* 6,423 g, 4,064 n.
1923 North Atlantic cargo service.
1933 Sold to T. & J. Harrison.
1936 Sold to Donaldson. Same name.
1954 Feb: Broken up at Port Glasgow by Smith & Houston Ltd.

141 DORELIAN

Details as *Norwegian (134)* except: **Bt** 1923 Caledon SB & E Co, Dundee; *T:* 6,431 g, 4,069 n.
1923 North Atlantic cargo service.
1933 Sold to T. & J. Harrison. Same name.
1936 Sold to Donaldson. Same name.
1954 Feb: Broken up at Dalmuir by W. H. Arnot Young & Co.

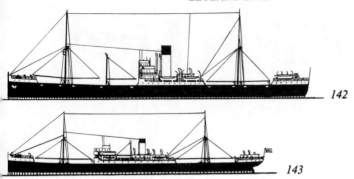

142

143

142 **RIMOUSKI/BOSTONIAN** (IV)

Bt 1918 Harland & Wolff, Belfast; *T:* 8,950 g, 5,590 n. **Dim** 460 ft 4 in (140.31 m) × 58 ft 4 in (17.78 m) × 37 ft 4 in (11.38 m). **Eng** Tw scr, quad exp; 2 × 4 cyls: 20½ in (51.35 cm), 29½ in (74.93 cm), 42 in (106.68 cm) and 61 in (154.94 cm); *Stroke:* 48 in (121.92 cm); 516 NHP; 14 kts; By builder. **H** Steel, 4 decks, fcsle 53 ft (16.15 m), bridge 130 ft (39.62 m), poop 39 ft (11.89 m), cruiser stern.

1918 Completed for Dominion Line but operated by Leyland. Designed as a passenger liner, *Rimouski* was completed and used as a cargo transport. She was never converted back to her original role.
1919 Used on White Star-Dominion Line cargo services.
1927 Renamed *Bostonian* (IV) on transfer from Dominion Line.
1932 Broken up in Italy.

143 **ATLANTIAN** (II)

Bt 1928 Caledon SB & E Co, Dundee; *T:* 6,549 g, 4,016 n. **Dim** 414 ft 7 in (126.36 m) × 54 ft 7 in (16.64 m) × 33 ft 9 in (10.29 m). **Eng** Sgl scr, quad exp; 4 cyls: 27 in (68.58 cm), 39 in (99.06 cm), 56 in (142.24 cm) and 80 in (203.2 cm); *Stroke:* 54 in (137.16 cm); 777 NHP; 4 sgl ended boilers; *Stm P:* 215 lb; 14 kts; By builder. **H** Steel, 2 decks, fcsle 40 ft (12.19 m), bridge 150 ft (45.72 m), poop 41 ft (12.5 m).

1928 The last ship built for Leyland.
1933 Sold to T. & J. Harrison. Same name.
1951 Sold to Japan. Renamed *Hakusan Maru.*

Dominion Line

History

1870 Jan: The Liverpool & Mississippi
Steamship Company was formed to
develop the increasingly important trade
between the cotton growing areas of the
Southern United States and the
Lancashire mills. The company's
backers appointed as managers Flinn,
Main & Montgomery, who for some
time had been gaining experience on the
South Atlantic trade with sailing packets
and steamers. In addition they possessed
a wide range of agents with trading
connections in the Mississippi basin. For
the service two new steamers were
ordered.
Oct 6: The maiden sailing was taken by
St Louis, followed a month later by
Crescent City. Four sister ships were
then ordered aimed at introducing a
fortnightly service.
1871 Feb 8: Misfortune struck when
Crescent City went aground at Galley
Head, Ireland, and was lost on the
inbound leg of her maiden voyage.
Nov 18: *Memphis,* the first of the four
new sisters, was delivered.
1872 May 4: Next *Mississippi* sailed, but
she opened the new and important
Canadian route.
June 7: *Vicksburg* joined the fleet.
Cargo commitments were good and the
loss of *Crescent City* left a gap which
was filled on Sept 3 by the purchase of
Hamburg America's pioneer
Hammonia, which was sailing under
Allan Line colours as *Belgian.* She
appears initially to have been chartered;
at any rate, she retained her Allan
name.
Dec 11: *Texas* joined the fleet; her

winter route was to Portland, Maine.
The entry into the Canadian service
seems to have been the result of
requests from Flinn, Main &
Montgomery's Canadian connections,
and the sailings were advertised under
the name 'Dominion Line'. To recognise
the company's Canadian interests its
name was changed on Aug 29 to the
Mississippi & Dominion Steamship Co
Ltd. Queenstown (Cobh) became a port
of call.
The New Orleans competition was
stepped up during 1872. Allan Line
retaliated with a New Orleans service,
which was not successful, and the new
State Line service from Glasgow was
inaugurated by their *Louisiana.*
1873 The change in trading emphasis
became clearer when Inman's *City of
Dublin* was purchased and renamed
Quebec. Belfast was introduced as a
port of call.
Oct 1: *Missouri* lost on Gingerbread
Shoal, Bahamas.
1874 Apr 29: *Dominion* (I) entered
service, followed on July 15 by *Ontario.*
No further new ships would ever bear
Southern States names.
1875 June 1: *Vicksburg* ran into an
iceberg off Newfoundland and was lost,
reducing the fleet to seven vessels. That
summer the company maintained a
weekly Canadian service only at the
expense of transferring ships from the
New Orleans route. A replacement for
Vicksburg was necessary.
1876 Dominion went again to Hamburg
America and this time took over
Bavaria, without change of name.

1877 Feb 6: *Bavaria* was burnt out at
sea. The company bridged the gap with
chartered tonnage. *Borussia,* also
'Hapag', was purchased; she was sister
to *Bavaria.* Still consolidating their
position the fourth of the early Clyde-
built Hamburg America vessels was
acquired, this time the *Teutonia.* The
fleet by the end of 1877 had become *St
Louis, Memphis, Mississippi, Texas,
Quebec, Dominion* (I), *Ontario,
Borussia* and *Teutonia,* a total of nine
ships.
1879 Feb 25: *Memphis* was lost near
Corunna.
June 20: *Brooklyn,* formerly Inman's
City of Brooklyn, entered service to
replace *Memphis.*
 Charles Connell delivered *Montreal*
and *Toronto* but disaster again struck in
December when *Borussia* foundered at
sea with heavy loss of life.
1880 *Ottawa* (I) was completed, but her
career ended within the same 12 months
when she was wrecked on Nov 22 at
Cape La Roche.
1883 *Vancouver* (I) was sold on the
stocks to the Inman Line, who had lost
their *City of Brussels* in January.
Dominion immediately ordered a
replacement.
1884 *Vancouver* (II) entered service. She
bore a strange resemblance to her main
rival, the Allan Line's *Parisian,* though
she was not only slower but less
luxurious too.
1885 A share of the Canadian Mail
contract was obtained.
1886 The Canadian summer services
now called at either Belfast or
Londonderry.
1891 *Labrador* entered service.
1894 Dec 12: At a general meeting of
the shareholders it was agreed to
transfer the management of the
Mississippi & Dominion SS Co to
Richards, Mills & Co in place of Flinn,
Main & Montgomery. The new
managers were already owners of the
British & North Atlantic Steam
Navigation Co whose five cargo
steamers had been running between
Liverpool and Boston under the
management of the Warren Line. These
ships were now progressively transferred

to the Dominion fleet. The six were
Roman, Norseman (I), *Ottoman,
Angloman, Cambroman* and also
Scotsman, then being built and having
passenger accommodation.
1896 *Canada* was delivered, obviously
for the Canadian service.
1898 Hamburg America Line's *Prussia*
was bought and renamed *Dominion* (II),
whilst *New England* was delivered by
Harland & Wolff.
1899 *Lord Erne* was purchased and
renamed *Turcoman.*
Mar 1: *Labrador* was wrecked on
Skerryvore, to be followed on Sept 22
by the four-year old *Scotsman.*
1900 The new *Commonwealth* entered
the Liverpool-Boston service. ATL's
Michigan became *Irishman* (II) in
exchange for *Irishman* (I).
1902 Feb 4: The International
Mercantile Marine Company was
formed. They acquired the shares of
Frederick Leyland first, then the
Dominion, American, Atlantic
Transport, Red Star and White Star
Lines. A process of re-allocating the
passenger ships followed under the
name Steamship Amalgamation Plan.
At first it seemed likely that Dominion
would carry the main passenger banner
on the non-New York routes, especially
with the delivery of *Merion* (owned by
the American Line) and the transfer
from Leyland, in early-1903, of
Hanoverian, which was renamed
Mayflower, and from Red Star of
Kensington and *Southwark.*
Vancouver (II) inaugurated the
Boston-Azores-Gibraltar-Naples-Genoa
service.
1903 *Columbus* was also delivered to
Dominion for their Liverpool-Boston
route. However, IMMC decided that
White Star should serve the USA and
Dominion Canada. There followed, in
short order, a number of transfers and
changes. *Canada,* following Boer War
service, reverted to the St Lawrence
service with *Dominion* (II). *New
England* was sold to the Allan Line,
Commonwealth became White Star's
Canopic, Merion went back to the
American Line with a black funnel and
a white band (that was rather too thin

for her tall funnel), *Mayflower* was
renamed *Cretic* by White Star and
Columbus, after but two voyages,
emerged as *Republic*. *Kensington* and
Southwark stayed at the Canadian
berth. In reverse *Cufic* had become
Manxman, Tauric had become
Welshman and *Nomadic* ended up as
Cornishman. During the year the
Canadian Pacific Railway Co purchased
Elder Dempster's Canadian routes and
interests. They were to become
formidable competitors.
1904 *Ottawa* (II), formerly White Star's
cherished *Germanic*, came over from the
American Line for the Canadian route,
whilst *Vancouver* (II) returned from her
Boston-Mediterranean route.
1908 Two large replacement Canadian
liners were laid down as *Albany* and
Alberta but were both transferred to
White Star and saw service as *Megantic*
and *Laurentic* (I). The move was
dictated by the need to compete with the
entry of the Canadian Pacific Railway
Co on the Canadian routes with their
new ships, *Empress of Britain* and
Empress of Ireland. A combined
service, known as the 'White Star-
Dominion Joint Service', was mounted.
This brought White Star into Canadian
waters, a fact that was strongly resented
by the non-IMMC existing carriers,
particularly the Allan Line.
1910 *Vancouver* (II), *Kensington* and
Southwark (1911) were scrapped and
Ottawa (II) sold.
1911 *Canada* was the sole remaining
Dominion ship on the Canadian service.
She ran in consort with White Star's
Laurentic, Megantic and *Teutonic*.
1914 *Canada* became a troopship and
Dominion's passenger services ceased.
Actually Red Star's *Zeeland* and
Vaderland became *Northland* and
Southland in 1915 and maintained the
route, although *Southland* was later
sunk.
1916 Mar 24: *Englishman* torpedoed.
1917 *Norseman* (II) torpedoed in
Mudros Harbour.
1918 The Dominion passenger liner
Regina was completed as a cargo ship
together with *Rimouski*, which never
actually entered Dominion service and

whose career can be found set out in the
Leyland illustrated fleet list.
1919 *Manxman* foundered in the North
Atlantic.
1921 The remaining Dominion ships,
now all owned by the British North
Atlantic SN Co, were transferred by
IMMC to Leyland Line ownership. The
ships transferred were *Canada,
Dominion* (II), *Regina, Welshman,
Cornishman, Irishman* (II), *Turcoman*
and *Rimouski*. The transferred ships
continued their Dominion services
uninterrupted under the same 'White
Star-Dominion Line Joint Service'.
1924 *Irishman* (II), participant in the
strange swopping of ships back in 1900,
was broken up in Holland.
1926 *Cornishman* went home to be
scrapped—at Hayle, Cornwall. *Canada*
went too, aged 30, this time to Italy.
With her departure the Joint Service
name was replaced with a new title,
'White Star Line (Canadian Services)',
and so departed from the public scene
the name Dominion Line. And in the
same year White Star itself was acquired
by the Royal Mail Steam Packet Co.
1929 The final Dominion ship was
Welshman, and she was finally broken
up at Bo'ness, Firth of Forth.

Routes

1870-1914 Liverpool-New Orleans
(cargo).
1872-1926 Liverpool-Queenstown
(Cobh)-Quebec-Montreal.
1872-1926 Liverpool / Bristol
(Avonmouth)-Halifax-Portland (Maine)
/ Philadelphia.
1885-88 Bristol (Avonmouth)-New
Orleans (cargo).
1886-96 Liverpool-Belfast /
Londonderry-Quebec-Montreal.
1888-1914 Liverpool-Cobh-Baltimore
(winter service).
1896-1929 Liverpool-Boston.
1902-10 Boston-Mediterranean (winter
service).
A particular problem for the Canadian
services was the winter closure, by ice,
of the St Lawrence seaway. This
produced seasonal services and several

short term attempts to find winter
employment for the Canadian vessels.

Livery

Funnel Red with a white band, one red
band width below the black top.
Hull Black, mainly with white fcsle,
bridge and poop. Red waterline.
Uppers White, deck vents white.
Masts Buff.
Lifeboats White.

Fleet index

Illustrated fleet list

1 ST LOUIS

Bt 1870 Rollo Clover & Co, Birkenhead; *T:* 1,827 g, 1,228 n. **Dim** 301 ft 3 in (91.82 m)×35 ft (10.67 m)×17 ft 4 in (5.28 m). **Eng** Sgl scr, compound; 2 cyls: 22 in (55.88 cm) and 65 in (165.1 cm); *Stroke:* 35 in (88.9 cm); 200 HP; *Stm P:* 60 lb; 10 kts. **H** Iron, 1 deck; *Pass:* 50 cabin, 500 3rd.

1870 Oct 6: Maiden voyage Liverpool-New Orleans.
1872 June 12: Took the company's second Canadian service, Liverpool-Quebec-Montreal.
1882 Sold. Re-engined at Hull by C.D. Holmes & Co. Owned by T. Baker & Son, Cardiff.
1889 Renamed *Cheang Chew*. Owned by Khoo Syn Thwak, Singapore.

2 CRESCENT CITY

Bt 1870 Archibald McMillan, Dumbarton; *T:* 2,017 g, 1,420 n. **Dim** 316 ft (96.32 m)×35 ft 2in (10.72 m)×17 ft 8 in (5.38 m). **Eng** Sgl scr, compound inverted; 2 cyls: 45½ in (115.57 cm) and 80 in (203.2 cm); *Stroke:* 42 in (106.68 cm); 300 HP; *Stm P:* 60 lb; 11 kts. **H** Iron, 1 deck; *Pass:* 75 cabin, 500 3rd.

Very similar to Memphis *class.* 'Crescent City' *is the nickname for New Orleans.*

1870 Nov 10: Maiden voyage Glasgow-Liverpool-New Orleans.
1871 Feb 8: Wrecked on Galley Head, Ireland, inward bound on maiden voyage.

3-6

3 MEMPHIS

Bt 1871 Archibald McMillan, Dumbarton; *T:* 2,485 g, 1,595 n. **Dim** 327 ft (99.67 m)×38 ft 2 in (11.63 m)×25 ft 4 in (7.72 m). **Eng** Sgl scr, compound inverted; 2 cyls: 45½ in (115.57 cm) and 80 in (203.2 cm); *Stroke:* 42 in (106.68 cm); 300 HP; *Stm P:* 60 lb; 11 kts; By J. & J. Thomson, Glasgow. **H** Iron, 2 decks, 4 holds, fcsle 40 ft (12.19 m), poop 60 ft (18.29 m); *Pass:* 80 cabin, 600 3rd.

1871 Nov 18: Maiden voyage Liverpool-New Orleans.
1872 July 3: Took over Canadian service from *St Louis (1)*, Liverpool-Quebec-Montreal. Canadian run in summer, New Orleans in winter.
1879 Feb 25: Wrecked near Corunna, Spain.

4 MISSISSIPPI

Bt 1872 Archibald McMillan, Dumbarton; *T:* 2,159 g, 1,371 n. **Dim** 320 ft 6 in (97.69 m)×35 ft (10.67 m)×25 ft (7.62 m). **Eng** Sgl scr, compound inverted; 2 cyls: 42 in (106.68 cm) and 75 in (190.5 cm); *Stroke:* 42 in (106.68 cm); 275 HP; *Stm P:* 60 lb; By J. Jack, Rollo & Co, Liverpool. **H** Iron, 2 decks, fcsle 46 ft (14.02 m), poop 48 ft (14.63 m); *Pass:* 80 cabins, 600 3rd.

Memphis *class but dimensions, engine, poop and fcsle differ.*
1872 May 4: Maiden voyage Liverpool-Quebec-Montreal. Inaugurated the Dominion service to Canada, a monthly summer service.
1874 Apr 20: Grounded near Cape Florida. Salvaged.
1883 Avonmouth-Canada service.
1888 Sold. Renamed *Sicilia.* Owned Goodyear & Co, British.
1895 Oct: Wrecked off Trevose Head.

5 VICKSBURG

Details as *Memphis (3)* except: *T:* 2,484 g, 1,592 n.
1872 June 7: Maiden voyage Glasgow-Quebec-Montreal.
Aug 8: Grounded St Lawrence. Refloated.
1874 Canadian service in summer, Boston and Portland in winter.
1875 Jan 1: Collided with iceberg off Newfoundland. 47 lost.

6 TEXAS

Details as *Memphis (3)* except: *T:* 2,372 g, 1,509 n. **Dim** Length 325 ft 6 in (99.21 m).
1872 Dec 11: Maiden voyage Liverpool-Boston-Portland.
1873 Apr 16: Summer Canadian run Liverpool-Quebec-Montreal.
1894 June 4: Wrecked near Cape Race. No lives lost.

7 QUEBEC

Bt 1864 Smith & Co, Glasgow; *T:* 2,138 g, 1,403 n. **Dim** 318 ft (96.93 m) × 36 ft 3 in (11.05 m) × 29 ft 6 in (8.99 m).
Eng Sgl scr, compound inverted; 2 cyls: 46 in (116.84 cm) and 78 in (198.12 cm); *Stroke:* 42 in (106.68 cm); 275 HP; *Stm P:* 60 lb; 10 kts; By Laird Bros, Birkenhead. **H** Iron, 2 decks; *Pass:* 60 cabin, approx 400 3rd.
1864 Laid down as *Hellespont* for W. Dixon, British. Acquired on the stocks.
Sept 3: Renamed *City of Dublin,* Inman Line. Liverpool-New York.
1873 Sold to Dominion Line. Renamed *Quebec.* Liverpool-Quebec-Montreal. Replacement for *Missouri (8),* lost Oct 1.

1883-88 On Avonmouth berth.
1888 Sold. Renamed *Nautique.* Owned by Bossiere Fréres & Cie, France.
1890 Feb 10: Foundered in the North Atlantic.

8-11

8 MISSOURI

Bt 1855 Caird & Co, Greenock; *T:* 2,259 g, 1,465 n. **Dim** 280 ft (85.34 m) × 38 ft 7 in (11.76 m) × 25 ft (7.62 m). **Eng** Sgl scr, geared oscillating; 2 cyls: 67 in (170.18 cm); *Stroke:* 72 in (182.88 cm); 250 HP; *Stm P:* 60 lb; 10 kts. **H** Iron, 2 decks; *Pass:* 54 1st, 146 2nd, 310 3rd; *Crew:* 77.
1855 Built as *Hammonia* for Hamburg America Line.
1864 Became *Belgian,* Allan Line.
1872 Sept 3: Acquired. Two voyages as *Belgian.*
1873 Feb 5: First voyage as *Missouri,* Liverpool-New Orleans.
Oct 1: Wrecked on Gingerbread Shoal, Bahamas. No lives lost.

9 BAVARIA

Details as *Missouri (8)* except: *T:* 2,131 g, 1,346 n.
1857 Built as *Petropolis* for Hamburg Brasilienische.
1858 Acquired by Hamburg America. Renamed *Bavaria.*
Nov 1: First voyage Hamburg-Southampton-New York.
1871 Engine compounded by C.A. Day & Co, London.
1876 Acquired by Dominion Line. Continued as *Bavaria.* Replacement vessel for *Vicksburg (5).*
1877 Feb 6: Burnt out at sea. All saved.

10 BORUSSIA

Details as *Missouri (8)* except: **Bt** 1854; *T:* 2,075 g, 1,320 n. **Dim** Length 292 ft (89 m).
1854 Built as *Borussia* for Hamburg America. Chartered to British

144

Government for repatriating troops after Crimean War.

1856 June 1: Took Hapag's first Hamburg-New York service.
1857 Southampton introduced as a port of call.
1877 July 14: Purchased by Dominion Line. Placed on the Liverpool-Quebec-Montreal route. A replacement for *Bavaria (9)*, lost earlier in the year.
1879 Dec 2: Foundered at sea. 165 lost. Only 26 survived.

11 TEUTONIA

Details as *Missouri (8)* except: **Bt** 1856; *T:* 2,266 g, 1,451 n. **Dim** Length 296 ft 1 in (90.25 m).

1856 Built as *Teutonia* for Hamburg Brasilienische.
1859 July 15: First voyage for Hamburg America Line. Hamburg-Southampton-New York.
1871 Engine compounded by Reihers, Hamburg; 12 kts.
1877 Purchased by Dominion Line for the Liverpool-New Orleans service as *Teutonia.*
1880 Transferred to Canadian and New England services.
1882 Sold to Francesca Costa, Italy. Renamed *Regina.*
1889 Renamed *Piemontese* by Costa, then in 1890 *Regina* again.
1891 Became *Mentana* of Schiaffino, Italy.
1894 Broken up at Spezia.

12 DOMINION (I)

Bt 1874 Archibald McMillan, Dumbarton; *T:* 3,176 g, 2,032 n. **Dim** 335 ft (102.11 m) × 38 ft 5 in (11.71 m) × 25 ft 7 in (7.8 m). **Eng** Sgl scr, compound inverted; 2 cyls: 47 in (119.38 cm) and 84 in (213.36 cm); *Stroke:* 45 in (114.3 cm); 300 HP; *Stm P:* 70 lb; 11 kts; By J. Jack, Rollo & Co, Liverpool. **H** *Pass:* 80 cabin, 600 3rd.

1874 Apr 29: Maiden voyage Liverpool-Quebec-Montreal.
1883-94 Avonmouth service.
1890 Tpl exp engines fitted.
1895 Sold to E. Thirkell & Co, Liverpool.
1896 Jan 4: Wrecked at Berehaven.

13 ONTARIO

Details as *Dominion (12)* except: *T:* 3,175 g, 2,017 n. **Dim** Length 335 ft 7 in (102.29 m). **Eng** 350 HP, but other details identical; By J. & J. Thomson, Glasgow.

1874 July 15: Maiden voyage Liverpool-Quebec-Montreal.
1885-94 Avonmouth-Canada berth.
1895 Laid up.
1896 Broken up.

14 BROOKLYN

Bt 1869 Tod & McGregor, Glasgow; *T:* 4,215 g. **Dim** 354 ft 4 in (108 m) × 42 ft 6 in (12.95 m) × 26 ft 10 in (8.18 m). **Eng** Sgl scr, horizontal trunk; 2 cyls: 71 in (180.34 cm); *Stroke:* 42 in (106.68 cm); 450 HP; *Stm P:* 30 lb; 13 kts; By builder. **H** Iron, 2 decks; *Pass:* 80 cabin, 400 3rd.

1869 Built as *City of Brooklyn,* Inman Line.
1879 June 20: Acquired by Dominion Line. Placed on the Liverpool-Quebec-Montreal service. Lengthened to 400 ft (121.92 m) and rebuilt with compound engines.
1885 Nov 8: Wrecked on Anticosti Island. No lives lost.

15-16

15 MONTREAL

Bt 1879 Chas Connell & Co, Glasgow; *T:* 3,308 g, 2,160 n. **Dim** 329 ft 6 in (100.43 m) × 39 ft 4 in (11.99 m) × 32 ft 8 in (9.96 m). **Eng** Sgl scr, compound inverted; 2 cyls: 45 in (114.3 cm) and 80 in (203.2 cm); *Stroke:* 48 in (121.92 cm); 375 HP; *Stm P:* 75 lb; 12 kts; By J. & J. Thomson, Glasgow. **H** Iron, 3 decks; *Pass:* Cabin and 3rd.

1879 Oct 27: Maiden voyage Glasgow-Liverpool-New Orleans.
1880 Apr 23: Liverpool-Quebec-Montreal service.
1889 Aug 4: Wrecked on Belle Isle. No lives lost.

16 TORONTO

Details as *Montreal (15)* except: *T:* 2,583 g, 1,668 n. **Dim** Depth registered as 25 ft 2 in (7.67 m), which also accounts for differing tonnages on otherwise identical measurements.
1879 Nov: Maiden voyage Liverpool-Quebec-Montreal.
1894 Aug 3: Last voyage to Montreal from Liverpool.
Oct: Sold to G. B. Laverello, Genoa. Renamed *Pina*.
1897 Broken up in Italy.

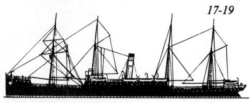

17-19

17 OTTAWA (I)

Bt 1880 Chas Connell, Glasgow; *T:* 3,712 g. **Dim** 359 ft 7 in (109.6 m) × 40 ft 3 in (12.27 m) × 24 ft 10 in (7.57 m). **Eng** Sgl scr, compound inverted; 2 cyls: 48 in (121.92 cm) and 87 in (220.98 cm); *Stroke:* 54 in (137.16 cm); 500 HP; *Stm P:* 80 lb; 12 kts; By J. & J. Thomson, Glasgow. **H** Iron, 3 decks and awning deck, 6 holds, fcsle 46 ft (14.02 m), bridge 134 ft (40.84 m); *Pass:* Cabin and 3rd.
1880 Placed on Canadian run, Liverpool-Quebec-Montreal.
Nov 22: Wrecked on Cape La Roche. All saved.

18 SARNIA

Details as *Ottawa (17)* except: *T:* 3,726 g, 2,422 n. **Dim** Length 360 ft 7 in (109.91 m).
1882 Sept 7: Maiden voyage Liverpool-Quebec-Montreal.
1894 Sept 28: Last voyage to Montreal.
1896 Sold to Furness Withy. Same name. Masts reduced to two.
1897 Broken up in Italy.

19 OREGON

Details as *Sarnia (18)* except: *T:* 3,712 g, 2,407 n.
1883 Sept 28: Maiden voyage Liverpool-Halifax-Portland (Maine).
1896 Sold to Furness Withy. Same name. Masts reduced to two.
1897 Broken up in Italy by G. Tardy, Genoa.

20 VANCOUVER (II)

Bt 1884 Chas Connell & Co, Glasgow; *T:* 5,141 g. **Dim** 430 ft 7 in (131.24 m) × 45 ft (13.72 m) × 33 ft 7 in (10.24 m). **Eng** Sgl scr, compound; 3 cyls: 58 in (147.32 cm) and 2 × 80 in (203.2 cm); *Stroke:* 66 in (167.64 cm); 1,000 HP; *Stm P:* 90 lb; 14 kts; By J. & J. Thomson, Glasgow. **H** Iron, 4 decks, 7 holds, bridge 188 ft (57.3 m); *Pass:* 100 cabin, 250 2nd, 800 3rd (max 1,262).

The first Vancouver *was sold on the stocks to the Inman Line and became their* City of Chicago. *Dominion immediately placed a repeat order.*

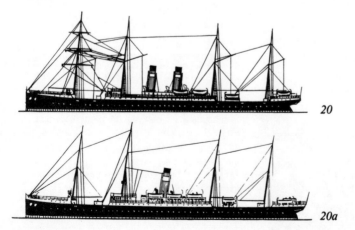

20

20a

1884 Entered Liverpool-Quebec-Montreal service.
1893 Modernised *(20a)*. Sgl funnel and tpl exp engines fitted; 15 kts.
1896 Aug: Collided with *Lake Ontario* (Beaver Line).
1902 Boston-Mediterranean service.
1904 Reverted to Liverpool-Quebec-Montreal run.
1905 Became relief vessel.
1910 Broken up by T. W. Ward.

21

21 LABRADOR

Bt 1891 Harland & Wolff, Belfast; *T:* 4,737 g. **Dim** 401 ft (122.22 m) × 47 ft 2 in (14.38 m) × 28 ft (8.53 m). **Eng** Sgl scr, tpl exp; 3 cyls: 22 in (55.88 cm), 30½ in (77.47 cm) and 48 in (121.92 cm); *Stroke:* 48 in (121.92 cm); 390 NHP; *Stm P:* 80 lb; 15 kts; By builder. **H** Steel, 2 decks; *Pass:* 100 1st, 50 2nd, 1,000 3rd.

1891 Aug 20: Maiden voyage Liverpool-Quebec-Montreal.
1899 Mar 1: Wrecked on Skerryvore. No lives lost.

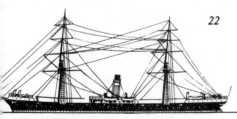

22

22 HAMILTON

Bt 1869 Palmers & Co, Newcastle; *T:* 3,121 g, 2,209 n. **Dim** 345 ft 6 in (105.31 m) × 43 ft 5 in (13.23 m) × 35 ft 1 in (10.69 m). **Eng** Sgl scr; 2 cyls: 40 in (101.6 cm); *Stroke:* 60 in (152.4 cm); 250 HP; 11 kts. **H** Iron, 2 decks.

1869 Built as *Nevada* for Liverpool & Great Western SS Co, the Guion Line. Feb 2: Maiden voyage Liverpool-New York.
1881 Compound inverted engines fitted:

2 cyls: 40 in (101.6 cm) and 80 in (203.2 cm); 400 HP; By G. Forrester & Co, Liverpool. *T:* 3,617 g, 2,355 n.
1893 Sold to Dominion Line. Renamed *Hamilton* and registered as owned by the Hamilton SS Co.
1896 Sold to S. L. Dodd, Bristol. Broken up.

23 ROMAN

Bt 1884 Laird Bros, Birkenhead; *T:* 4,572 g, 2,848 n. **Dim** 405 ft (123.44 m) × 43 ft 7 in (13.28 m) × 17 ft 7 in (5.36 m). **Eng** Sgl scr, compound; 2 cyls: 48 in (121.92 cm) and 85 in (215.9 cm); *Stroke:* 60 in (152.4 cm); 479 NHP; 3 dbl ended boilers, 18 furnaces; *Stm P:* 80 lb; 10 kts; By builder. **H** Iron, 3 decks and awning deck, fcsle 46 ft (14.02 m), poop 106 ft (32.31 m), 4 masts.

1884 Liverpool-New York service. Owned by British & North Atlantic SN Co. Managed by Warren Line.
1894 Transferred to the Dominion Line when British & North Atlantic SN acquired the company.
1910 Feb: Sold to J. J. King. Broken up at Troon.

24 NORSEMAN (I)

Bt 1882 Laird Bros, Birkenhead; *T:* 4,450 g, 2,834 n. **Dim** 392 ft (119.48 m) × 44 ft (13.41 m) × 25 ft 4 in (7.72 m). **Eng** Sgl scr, compound; 2 cyls: 48 in (121.92 cm) and 85 in (215.9 cm); *Stroke:* 60 in (152.4 cm); 486 NHP; 3 dbl ended boilers; 10 kts; By builder. **H** Iron.

1882 Owned by British & North Atlantic SN Co. Liverpool-Boston service.
1894 Transferred to the Dominion Line.
1899 Mar 28: Stranded near Marblehead, Massachusetts. Refloated but sold for scrap.

25 SCOTSMAN

Bt 1895 Harland & Wolff, Belfast; *T:* 6,041 g, 5,730 n. **Dim** 470 ft 7 in (143.43 m) × 49 ft 2 in (14.99 m) × 31 ft 10 in (9.7 m). **Eng** Tw scr, tpl exp; 2 × 3 cyls: 22 in (55.88 cm), 36½ in (92.71 cm) and 60 in (152.4 cm); *Stroke:* 48 in (121.92 cm); 499 NHP; *Stm P:* 90 lb; 13 kts; By builder. **H** Steel, 3 decks; *Pass:*

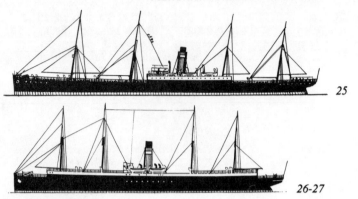

25

26-27

100 1st, 130 2nd.
1895 Nov 28: Maiden voyage Liverpool-
Halifax-Portland.
1899 Sept 22: Wrecked Belle Isle Straits.
13 lost.

26 OTTOMAN

Bt 1890 Laird Bros, Birkenhead; *T:*
4,843 g, 3,010 n. **Dim** 403 ft 8 in
(123.04 m) × 45 ft 7 in (13.89 m) × 25 ft
2 in (7.67 m). **Eng** Sgl scr, tpl exp; 3
cyls: 31 in (78.74 cm), 50 in (127 cm)
and 78 in (198.12 cm); *Stroke:* 60 in
(152.4 cm); 526 NHP; 3 dbl ended
boilers, 18 furnaces; *Stm P:* 150 lb; 11
kts; By builder. **H** Steel, 3 decks and
spar deck, fcsle 49 ft (14.93 m), bridge
99 ft (30.17 m), poop 49 ft (14.93 m).
1890 Built for British & North Atlantic
SN Co. Managed by Warren Line.
1896 Transferred to Dominion Line.
1911 Broken up at Preston by T. W.
Ward.

27 ANGLOMAN

Details as *Ottoman (26)* except: **Bt** 1892;
T: 4,892 g, 3,040 n.
1892 Built for British & North Atlantic
SN Co. Managed by Warren Line.
Liverpool-Boston service.
1896 Transferred to Dominion Line.

Feb 9: Wrecked on Skerries, Anglesey.
1897 Aug: Wreck sold for £115 and
broken up as she lay.

28 CANADA

Bt 1896 Harland & Wolff, Belfast; *T:*
8,800 g, 5,701 n. **Dim** 500 ft 4 in (152.5
m) × 58 ft 2 in (17.73 m) × 31 ft 1 in
(9.47 m). **Eng** Tw scr, tpl exp; 2 × 3
cyls: 28½ in (72.39 cm), 47½ in (120.65
cm) and 77 in (195.58 cm); *Stroke:* 54 in
(137.16 cm); 873 NHP; 15 kts; By
builder. **H** Steel, 3 decks; *Pass:* 200 1st,
200 2nd, 800 3rd.
1896 Oct 1: Maiden voyage Liverpool-
Quebec-Montreal.
Dec 23: Winter service Liverpool-
Boston.
1899-1902 Boer War transport.
1903 Apr 22: Reverted to Liverpool-
Quebec-Montreal service. *T:* 9,413 g.
1914-18 Requisitioned as troopship.
1918 Re-entered winter route service to
Portland, Maine. *Pass:* 463 cabin, 755
3rd.
1926 Aug 13: Last voyage to Montreal
before sale to Italian shipbreakers.

29 DOMINION (II)

Bt 1894 Harland & Wolff; *T:* 6,618g,
4,251 n. **Dim** 445 ft 6 in (135.79 m) × 50
ft 2 in (15.29 m) × 29 ft 10 in (9.09 m).

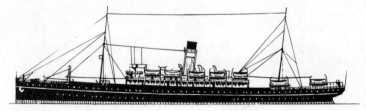

28

29

Eng Tw scr, tpl exp; 2×3 cyls: 22½ in (57.15 cm), 36½ in (92.71 cm) and 60 in (152.4 cm); *Stroke:* 48 in (121.92 cm); 499 NHP; 14 kts; By builder. **H** Steel, 3 decks; *Pass:* 200 1st, 170 2nd, 750 3rd.
1894 Built as *Prussia* for Hamburg America Line.
1898 Acquired by Dominion Line. Renamed *Dominion*.
May 7: Entered Liverpool-Montreal service.
1914-18 War service. Storeship and supply vessel.
1918 Dec 2: Re-entered commercial service Liverpool-Portland, Maine.
1919 Converted to cargo only.
1921 Feb 26: Final Dominion Line voyage.
1922 Broken up by A. Sonenberg, Hamburg.

30 NEW ENGLAND

Bt 1898 Harland & Wolff, Belfast; *T:* 11,394 g, 7,416 n. **Dim** 550 ft 4 in (167.74 m)×59 ft 4 in (18.08 m)×35 ft 10 in (10.92 m). **Eng** Tw scr, tpl exp; 2×4 cyls: 30 in (76.2 cm), 50 in (127 cm) and 2×58 in (147.32 cm); *Stroke:* 54 in (137.16 cm); 985 NHP; 16 kts; By builder. **H** Steel, 3 decks; *Pass:* 200 1st,

200 2nd, 800 3rd.
1898 Built for British & North American SN Co.
June 30: Maiden voyage Liverpool-Boston.
1903 Transferred to Allan Line. Renamed *Scandinavian*.
1923 Broken up at Emden by Klasmann and Lentze.

31 IRISHMAN (I)

Bt 1898 Harland & Wolff, Belfast; *T:* 8,001 g, 6,118 n. **Dim** 490 ft 6 in (149.5 m)×56 ft 4 in (17.17 m)×25 ft (7.62 m). **Eng** Tw scr, tpl exp; 2×3 cyls: 19 in (48.26 cm), 31 in (78.74 cm) and 52 in (132.08 cm); *Stroke:* 48 in (121.92 cm); 478 NHP; *Stm P:* 180 lb; 12 kts; By builder. **H** Steel, 2 decks and spar deck.
1898 Built as *Monmouth* for Elder Dempster's Canadian services. Sold to Dominion Line. Renamed *Irishman*.
1900 Transferred to Atlantic Transport Line. Renamed *Michigan*.
1902 Transferred to National Line. Same name.
1914 Sold to E. Modiano, Trieste. Renamed *Candido*.
1927 Broken up in Italy.

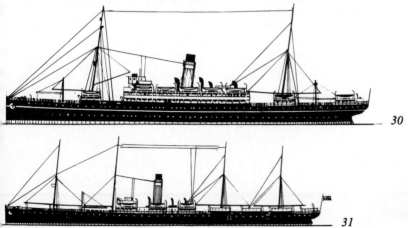

30

31

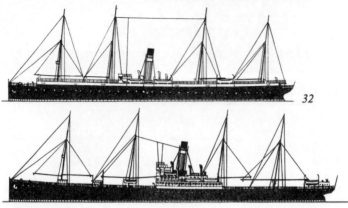

32

33

32 TURCOMAN

Bt 1892 Harland & Wolff, Belfast; *T:*
5,610 g, 3,647 n. **Dim** 445 ft (135.63
m) × 49 ft 2 in (14.99 m) × 30 ft 1 in
(9.17 m). **Eng** Tw scr, tpl exp; 2 × 3
cyls: 19 in (48.26 cm), 31 in (78.74 cm)
and 52 in (132.08 cm); *Stroke:* 48 in
(121.92 cm); 429 NHP; *Stm P:* 180 lb;
12 kts; By builder. **H** Steel, 2 decks,
fcsle 52 ft (15.85 m), bridge 98 ft (29.87
m), poop 55ft (16.76 m).
1892 Built for Irish Shipowners Ltd as
Lord Erne.
1899 Purchased by Dominion Line.
Renamed *Turcoman.*
1921 Transferred to Frederick Leyland.
Same name.
1926 Broken up in Italy.

33 IRISHMAN (II)

Bt 1899 Harland & Wolff, Belfast; *T:*
9,510 g, 6,158 n. **Dim** 500 ft 7 in
(152.58 m) × 62 ft 4 in (19 m) × 34 ft
(10.36 m). **Eng** Tw scr, quad exp; 2 × 4
cyls: 21¼ in (53.97 cm), 31½ in (80.01
cm), 46 in (116.84 cm) and 66 in (167.64
cm); *Stroke:* 48 in (121.19 cm); 604
NHP; *Stm P:* 165 lb; 13 kts; By builder.
H Steel, 3 decks.
1899 Built as *Michigan* for Atlantic
Transport Line.
1900 Transfered to Dominion Line.

Renamed *Irishman.*
1921 Transferred to Frederick Leyland.
Same name.
1924 Broken up in Holland.

34 CAMBROMAN

Bt 1892 Laird Bros, Birkenhead; *T:*
5,517 g, 3,552 n. **Dim** 429 ft 10 in
(131.01 m) × 46 ft 4 in (14.12 m) × 30 ft
1 in (9.17 m). **Eng** Sgl scr, tpl exp; 3
cyls: 30½ in (77.47 cm), 48 in (121.92
cm) and 78 in (198.12 cm); *Stroke:* 60 in
(152.4 cm); 533 NHP; 2 dbl and 2 sgl
ended boilers; *Stm P:* 160 lb; 12 kts; By
builder. **H** Steel, 3 decks, fcsle 48 ft
(14.63 m), bridge and poop 250 ft (76.2
m).
1892 Built for British & North American
Steam Navigation. Warren Line
managers. Cargo vessel only.
1894 Transferred with management to
British & North American fleet.
1899 Converted to a passenger ship to
replace *Sarnia (18)* which had to be sold
for scrap. *Pass:* 100 1st, 50 2nd.
1902 Operated on the Boston-
Mediterranean service.
1910 Broken up in Germany.

35 COMMONWEALTH

Bt 1900 Harland & Wolff, Belfast; *T:*
12,097 g, 7,717 n. **Dim** 578 ft 4 in

34

35

(176.28 m) × 59 ft 4 in (18.08 m) × 35 ft 8 in (10.87 m). **Eng** Tw scr, tpl exp; 2 × 4 cyls: 29½ in (74.93 cm), 50 in (127 cm) and 2 × 58 in (147.32 cm); *Stroke:* 54 in (137.16 cm); 988 NHP; 16 kts; By builder. **H** Steel, 3 decks; *Pass:* 250 1st, 250 2nd, 800 3rd.

1900 Oct 4: Maiden voyage Liverpool-Boston.
1903 Transferred to White Star Line. Renamed *Canopic.*
1904 Jan 14: First voyage Liverpool-Boston.
1905-22 New York-Fiume service except during 1914-18.
1922 Nov 18: First voyage Bremen-Southampton-Halifax-New York route.
1925 Broken up by T. W. Ward, Briton Ferry.

36 MANXMAN

Bt 1888 Harland & Wolff, Belfast; *T:* 4,639 g, 3,122 n. **Dim** 430 ft 8 in (131.27 m) × 45 ft 2 in (13.77 m) × 30 ft (9.14 m). **Eng** Sgl scr, tpl exp; 3 cyls: 27 in (68.58 cm), 44½ in (113.03 cm) and 74 in (187.96 cm); *Stroke:* 60 in (152.4 cm); 424 NHP; 13 kts; By builder. **H** Steel, 2 decks, fcsle 48 ft (14.63 m), bridge 80 ft (24.38 m), poop 48 ft (14.63 m).

1888 Oct 10: Launched as *Cufic,* White Star's first livestock carrier. 1,000 cattle.
Dec 8: Maiden voyage Liverpool-New York.
1896 Chartered to Cia Trasatlantica. Renamed *Neustra Senora de Guadaloupe.*
1898 Reverted to White Star as *Cufic.*
1902 Transferred to Dominion Line. Renamed *Manxman.*
1915 Sold to R. Lawrence, Montreal. Same name.
1917 British Government service.
1919 Sold to Universal Transport Co Ltd, New York. Same name.
Dec 18: Foundered in North Atlantic. 45 lives lost.

37 MERION

Bt 1902 John Brown & Co, Clydebank; *T:* 11,621 g, 7,459 n. **Dim** 530 ft 6 in (161.7 m) × 59 ft 2 in (18.03 m) × 27 ft 2 in (8.28 m). **Eng** Tw scr, tpl exp; 2 × 3 cyls: 29 in (73.66 cm), 46½ in (118.11 cm) and 75 in (190.5 cm); *Stroke:* 51 in (129.54 cm); 893 NHP; *Stm P:* 160 lb; 14 kts. **H** Steel, 3 decks, bridge 150 ft (45.72 m); *Pass:* 150 2nd, 1,700 3rd.

1902 Mar 8: Maiden voyage Liverpool-Boston.
1903 Mar 5: Last voyage for Dominion Line. Transferred to American Line for whom she was originally built.
Apr: Liverpool-Philadelphia service.
1914 Purchased by British Admiralty. Converted to resemble battleship HMS *Tiger.*
1915 May 30: Torpedoed in Aegean Sea.

38 MAYFLOWER

Bt 1902 Hawthorn Leslie, Newcastle; *T:* 13,507 g, 8,663 n. **Dim** 582 ft (177.39 m) × 60 ft 4 in (18.39 m) × 38 ft 4 in

37

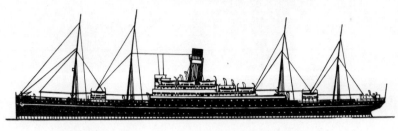

38

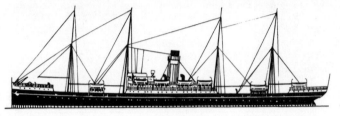

39-40

(11.68 m). **Eng** Tw scr, tpl exp; 2 × 3
cyls: 28 in (71.12 cm), 47½ in (120.65
cm) and 80 in (203.2 cm); *Stroke:* 60 in
(152.4 cm); 1,269 NHP; *Stm P:* 180 lb;
15 kts; By builder. **H** Steel, 3 decks;
Pass: 800 2nd.

1902 Built as *Hanoverian* for Frederick
Leyland.
July 19: Maiden voyage Liverpool-
Boston. Made three round voyages only.
1903 Apr 9: Transferred by the
International Mercantile Marine Co to
Dominion Line service. Renamed
Mayflower. Liverpool-Boston service.
Served in Dominion Line colours for
seven round voyages.
Nov 26: Became *Cretic,* White Star.
Liverpool-Boston.
1904-22 Oct: New York-Mediterranean
service except 1914-18.
1923 Became *Devonian* (F. Leyland).
Liverpool-Boston.
1927 Transferred to Red Star Line's
Antwerp-Southampton-New York
service.
1929 Broken up at Bo'ness, Firth of
Forth, by P. & W. MacLellan.

39 KENSINGTON
For details of this vessel see American
Line section, entry *18.*

40 SOUTHWARK
For details of this vessel see American
Line section, entry *17.*

41 COLUMBUS
Bt 1903 Harland & Wolff, Belfast; *T:*
15,378 g, 9,742 n. **Dim** 570 ft (173.74
m) × 67 ft 8 in (20.62 m) × 24 ft (7.31
m). **Eng** Tw scr, quad exp; 2 × 4 cyls: 29
in (73.66 cm), 41½ in (105.41 cm), 61 in
(154.94 cm) and 87 in (220.98 cm);
Stroke: 60 in (152.4 cm); 1,180 NHP;
Stm P: 180 lb; 16 kts. **H** Steel, 5 decks;
Pass: 160 1st, 1,000 3rd.

1903 Oct 1: Maiden voyage Liverpool-
Boston. Two round voyages.
Transferred by International Mercantile
Marine to White Star. Renamed
Republic.
1904 Jan 14: Liverpool-Boston service.
1909 Jan 23: Sunk in head-on collision
with *Florida* (Lloyd Italiano). No lives
lost. *Florida* lost her bows but survived.

41

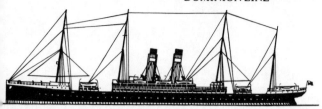

42

42 OTTAWA (II)

Bt 1875 Harland & Wolff, Belfast; *T:*
5,071 g, 2,991 n. **Dim** 455 ft (138.68
m) × 45 ft 2 in (13.77 m) × 34 ft (10.36
m). **Eng** Sgl scr, tpl exp; 3 cyls: 35½ in
(90.17 cm), 58 in (147.32 cm) and 96 in
(243.84 cm); *Stroke:* 69 in (175.26 cm);
765 NHP; 15 kts; By builder. **H** Iron, 3
decks, poop 50 ft (15.24 m); *Pass:* 200
1st, 1,500 3rd.

1875 July 15: Launched.
May 20: Maiden voyage Liverpool-New
York as *Germanic,* White Star.
1895 Re-engined by builder.
1899 Feb 16: Capsized at her berth in
New York. Refitted.
1904 Transferred to American Line.
Southampton-Cherbourg-New York
service.
1905 Transferred to Dominion Line for
Liverpool-Quebec-Montreal service.
Renamed *Ottawa.*
1910 Sold to Turkey. Renamed
Gul Djemal.
1915 May 3: Torpedoed by HMS *E.14*
in Sea of Marmora. Salved.
1920-21 Nov: Operated by Ottoman-
America Line. Istanbul-New York. Also
New York-Naples-Istanbul-Varna-
Constanza-Odessa.
1928 Name spelled *Gulcemal.*
1945-50 Used as floating hotel.
1950 Broken up, 75 years old, at
Messina, Sicily.

43 ALBANY

1908 Laid down for Dominion Line as
the largest vessel to date for their
Canadian service. Transferred by
International Mercantile Marine to

White Star service and renamed before
launching. Launched as *Megantic.*
Operated under the 'White Star-
Dominion Joint Service'.

44 ALBERTA

1908 Laid down for Dominion Line.
Launched as *Laurentic* (I). Details as
Albany (43).

45 WELSHMAN

Bt 1891 Harland & Wolff, Belfast; *T:*
5,728 g, 3,665 n. **Dim** 460 ft 9 in
(140.44 m) × 49 ft 1 in (14.96 m) × 30 ft
10 in (9.4 m). **Eng** Tw scr, overlapping
tpl exp; 2 × 3 cyls; 22½ in (57.15 cm),
36½ in (92.71 cm) and 60 in (152.4 cm);
Stroke: 48 in (121.92 cm); 499 NHP; 13
kts. **H** Steel, 2 decks, 10 watertight
compartments; *Crew:* 45.

1891 Entered service as *Tauric* (White
Star). Livestock carrier.
1903 Sold to Dominion Line. Initially
served as *Tauric.*
1904 Renamed *Welshman.*
1921 July: Transferred to Frederick
Leyland. Same name.
1929 Dec: Sold and broken up at
Bo'ness, Firth of Forth, by P. & W.
MacLellan.

46 CORNISHMAN

Details as *Welshman (45)* except: *T:*
5,749 g, 3,685 n.

1891 Entered service as *Nomadic* (White
Star). Livestock carrier.
1903 Sold to Dominion Line. Initially
served as *Nomadic.*
1904 Renamed *Cornishman.*
1921 July: Transferred to Frederick

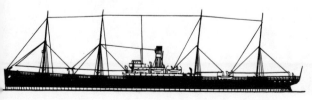

45-46

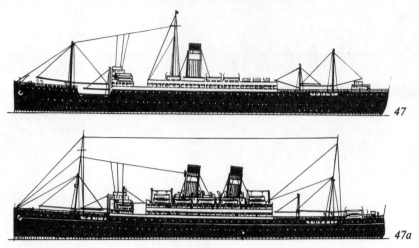

_47_

_47a_

Leyland. Same name.
1926 Mar 12: Arrived for breaking up at Hayle, Cornwall, by T. W. Ward.

47 REGINA

Bt 1918 Harland & Wolff, Belfast; _T:_ 16,313 g, 9,874 n. **Dim** 575 ft 3 in (175.34 m) × 67 ft 8 in (20.62 m) × 41 ft 2 in (12.55 m). **Eng** Tpl scr, 2 tpl exp and one sgl reduction geared turbines; 2 × 4 cyls: 28 in (71.12 cm), 44 in (111.76 cm) and 2 × 49½ in (125.73 cm); _Stroke:_ 54 in (137.16 cm); 15 kts; By builder. **H** Steel, 4 decks; _Pass:_ 600 cabin, 1,700 3rd.

1918 Completed, hurriedly, as cargo vessel _(47)._
1922 Mar 16: First voyage after being rebuilt as passenger ship _(47a)._ Liverpool-Halifax-Portland, Maine.
1929 Became _Westernland,_ Red Star. Antwerp-Southampton-New York.
1930 _Pass:_ 350 cabin, 350 tst, 800 3rd.
1935 Transferred to Arnold Bernstein. Same name and service.
1939 Sold to Holland America Line. Remained _Westernland._
1943 Purchased by British Admiralty as repair ship.

1947 Broken up at Blyth, Northumberland.

48 NORSEMAN (II)

Bt 1897 Harland & Wolff, Belfast; _T:_ 9,545 g, 6,128 n. **Dim** 500 ft 8 in (152.6 m) × 62 ft 4 in (19 m) × 33 ft 10 in (10.31 m). **Eng** Tw scr, quad exp; 2 × 4 cyls: 21¼ in (53.97 cm), 32½ in (82.55 cm), 46 in (116.84 cm) and 66 in (167.64 cm); _Stroke:_ 48 in (121.92 cm); 604 NHP; _Stm P:_ 180 lb. **H** Steel, 3 decks and shelter deck, bridge 110 ft (33.53 m).

1897 Built as _Brasilia_ for Hamburg America Line.
1900 Became _Norseman_, Dominion Line.
1910 June 7: Chartered to Aberdeen Line until Jan 1914.
1917 Torpedoed and sunk at Mudros Harbour. Raised but broken up by Societa Italiana di Salvataggi de Navegazione.

49 ENGLISHMAN

Bt 1891 Harland & Wolff, Belfast; _T:_ 5,257 g, 3,345 n. **Dim** 430 ft (131.06

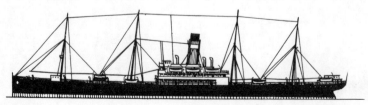

_48_

m) × 47 ft (14.32 m) × 37 ft 10 in (11.53 m). **Eng** Tw scr, tpl exp; 2 × 3 cyls: 19 in (48.26 cm), 31 in (78.74 cm) and 52 in (132.08 cm); *Stroke:* 42 in (106.68 cm); 350 NHP; *Stm P:* 180 lb; 13 kts. **H** Steel, 3 decks and shade deck.
1891 Built as *Ionia* for City of Liverpool. SN Co (D. & W. MacIver, managers).
1892 Oct: Purchased by Elder Dempster. Renamed *Montezuma* and chartered to Atlantic Transport Line, London-New York.

1893 Reverted to Elder Dempster. Liverpool-Quebec-Montreal.
1898 Sold to Union Line. Renamed *Sandusky*.
1899 Sold to Dominion Line. Renamed *Englishman*.
1916 Mar 24: Torpedoed en route Avonmouth-Portland.

50 **RIMOUSKI**

For details of this vessel see Leyland section, entry *142*.

Atlantic Transport Line

History

1881 The Atlantic Transport Line (ATL) was founded by Bernard N. Baker, a director of the already flourishing Baltimore Storage and Lighterage Co. He joined forces with the Pennsylvania Railway Co, who still hankered after establishing Philadelphia as the leading eastern seaboard port in the United States which would thereby feed their rail network. Back in 1872 the company had essayed the Atlantic trade by their participation in the American Line, but their investment had not prospered and the disposal of their interests was openly mooted and, in 1884, was realised when the International Navigation Co acquired the company.

But one thing was clear from their experience: namely, that it was cheaper to operate under the British flag than the American. The trick was to use US capital to found and operate a British-registered concern and to involve a sound but energetic British shipbroking agent to provide the necessary tonnage. The chosen agents were Hooper & Williams of London who injected two things vital to success. The first was money, which pledged their dedication, and the second was the advice that ownership was better, in Britain, than chartering. *Surrey,* launched on Apr 16 1881, was their first ship, followed by *Suffolk.*

1882 The ATL commenced operations with their managing agents now named Hooper, Murrell & Williams. The company chose London as its base port, and ATL came closer than anyone else to establishing London as a premier transatlantic seaport. It was to take a full half century for them to be proved wrong in their choice. Their destination ports were on the US East Coast. Their third vessel, *Sussex,* was delivered.

1884 Jan 4: *Surrey* collided with the German steamer *Uranus* off Bishop's Rock but both survived.

1885 Dec 17: *Sussex* was lost on Bryher in the Scilly Isles inward bound from Baltimore for London.

1886 The managing firm was restructured with the senior partner, Mr A. S. Williams, forming Williams, Torrey & Field. New ships were ordered and these were given North American state names beginning with 'M'. *Maryland* (I) was the first to be delivered.

Sept 28: *Suffolk* went ashore at the Old Lizard Head and was lost.

1887 *Montana* (I) delivered. The second ship of the year was *Minnesota* (I), their first 'Harland & Wolffer'.

1888 A replacement for *Sussex* and *Suffolk* but laid down and delivered as *Swansea* but was renamed *Maine* (I) to conform to the new house style. At the same time *Surrey* became *Michigan* (I), but she was sold in the following year to Christopher Furness.

1889 *Missouri* (I) delivered.

Apr 6: The passengers and crew of Thingvalla's foundering *Denmark* were rescued in mid-Atlantic by *Missouri.*

1890 *Michigan* (II) and *Mississippi* (I) were commissioned.

1892 Mar: *Massachusetts* (I) entered service with her sister *Manitoba* arriving in the following month. Both had passenger accommodation for 80 persons. ATL's initial move into the passenger trade was modest but significant for future policy and building.

One interesting aspect of ATL was their habit of renaming chartered ships with temporary names also commencing with 'M'. Some of these came from Elder Dempster, who also used 'M' for many of their Canadian vessels.

1896 Wilson's & Furness-Leyland Line was founded to operate a London-New York service. The effect was to drive National Line out of business and ATL purchased the company's goodwill and fleet (two ships, *America* and *Europe*). To complement them *Michigan* (II) and *Mississippi* (I) were transferred and scheduled to run in consort with them.

Two new ships arrived. They were *Mohawk* (I) and *Mobile* (I). Their names denoted that the company had run out of 'M' states but still retained the now traditional 'M' initial letter.

1897 Hamburg America's *Persia* was acquired, mainly because she was practically a sister ship to the *Massachusetts* (I) class and was thereby an easily assimilated fifth vessel. ATL renamed her *Minnewaska* (I).

1898 The Spanish-American War broke out following the sinking at Havana of the USS *Maine*. The United States urgently needed troop transports and purchased no fewer than seven ATL ships. In addition ATL gifted *Missouri* to the US Navy for conversion into a hospital ship. The seven vessels transferred to Government service, with their 'American Civil War Officers' renamings, were *Michigan* (II) *(Kilpatrick), Mississippi* (I) *(Buford), Manitoba (Logan), Massachusetts* (I) *(Sheridan), Mohawk* (I) *(Grant), Mobile* (I) *(Sherman)* and *Minnewaska* (I) *(Thomas). Missouri* (I) became the hospital ship *Egbert*.

The effect on ATL's position was critical. They had only four small ships with which to carry on their considerable business. But against the background of the Spanish-American War Bernard Baker had bid for the four new ships of Wilson's &

Furness-Leyland and at a final £968,000 the offer was accepted. *Alexandra* was renamed *Menominee, Boadicea* became *Marquette, Cleopatra* the *Mohegan* and *Victoria* was rechristened *Manitou.* To add cargo capacity *British Crown* came from British Shipowners Co and was renamed *Mackinaw* while White Star's *Belgic* became *Mohawk* (II).

The recovery of ATL was thus swift and remarkable, and the price paid by the US Government enabled ATL to replenish their fleet and still be in pocket on the deal.

However, 1898 had highlighted in the United States the fact that ATL, an American company, was effectively a British-owned and operated concern with all the implications thereof. The solution was to reverse the process, and the Atlantic Transport Company of West Virginia was formed to acquire the assets of ATL, meaning its ships, and to build and own American flag vessels. Because of the still advantageous economics the current fleet was to continue to be registered under the British flag but control was undisputedly American. The first action of the new group was to order four 13,000-tonners from Harland & Wolff.

Oct 14: *Mohegan,* on her second voyage under her new name, ran aground on the Manacles. At least ten miles off course at the time, she struck the rocks a glancing blow which opened up her hull and within ten minutes she had sunk, drowning 106 of those aboard.

1899 In October the Boer War led to *Mohawk* (II) becoming a transport. She never returned to ATL ownership.

Michigan (III) delivered.

1900 This year saw a curious exchange of two ships between ATL and Dominion Line. *Michigan* (III), less than a year old, was swopped for Dominion's two-year old *Irishman* (I) and took the name *Michigan* (IV). Not to be outdone, Dominion renamed *Michigan* (III) — *Irishman*(II)!

May 10: *Minneapolis,* first of the new 13,000-ton class, sailed from London to New York.

Aug 11: *Minnehaha* entered service.

1902 Feb 4: The International Mercantile Marine Company was formed with a capital of $120 million.

May 24: The Steamship Amalgamation

Plan was adopted whereby the group was to acquire the shares and assets of Atlantic Transport Line, White Star, Dominion, American Line, Red Star Line and the Leyland Line. Harland & Wolff, Belfast, was appointed shipbuilder to the concern, but not exclusively. Special provision was made to enable ships to be constructed in America.

July 12: *Minnetonka* (I), third of the 13,000-ton quartet, entered service. The fourth was *Minnewaska* (II) and, being delivered after the Steamship Amalgamation Plan, she was transferred to White Star and renamed *Arabic*.

Two ships were laid down at the Camden yard of the New York Shipbuilding Co and named *Minnekahda* (I) and *Minnelora,* but prior to entering service they were both sold to the Pacific Mail SS Co and renamed *Manchuria* and *Mongolia*. Strangely enough, as we shall see, in 1916 both eventually became ATL ships.

1903 United States' yards delivered four sedate 12-knotters with limited passenger accommodation. They were *Maine* (II), *Missouri* (II), *Massachusetts* (II) and *Mississippi* (II). All four were sold within a decade, being outmoded by subsequent buildings, although the last of the four, *Mississippi* (II), was remodelled and became *Samland* of Red Star.

1907 Two of National Line's four remaining ships, *America* and *Europe,* were transferred to the parent company and renamed *Memphis* and *Mobile* (II).

1908 *Memphis* broken up at Bo'ness, Firth of Forth.

1909 *Minnewaska* (III) was delivered, thereby making up the originally ordered London-New York quartet. Their passage time of ten days was not of record beating proportions but the IMMC policy was to major on comfort, reliability and regularity.

1910 Apr 18: *Minnehaha* stranded in fog on the Scilly Isles, where she remained for a month before being floated off minus much of her cargo.

1911 *Mobile* (II) sold to Norwegian owners for further trading.

1913 *Maine* (III) was acquired second-hand but three new ships, *Maryland* (II), *Mississippi* (III) and *Missouri* (III) arrived from Harland & Wolff. *Mississippi* was

fitted with a pair of Burmeister & Wain oil engines and was one of the earliest motorships. *Montana* (I) sold to Italian owners.

1914 The First World War began and ATL passenger ships were used for trooping duties. *Manhattan* and *Michigan* (IV) came from the National Line, and with their transfer the separate existence of that company ceased.

1915 Apr: The IMMC went into liquidation and was placed by its creditors in the hands of a Receiver, Mr P. A. Franklin, who was assisted in arranging new finance by the banker F. W. Scott. Under their astute guidance the company so recovered that at the end of the first year the future of the concern was reasonably secure. But the return on the investment was inadequate and the diverse component parts of the group did not warrant the injection of large sums of additional finance, especially during wartime.

Oct 23: *Marquette* was sunk in the Aegean by *U-35*.

1916 Mar 23: *Minneapolis* was torpedoed in the Mediterranean, also by *U-35*.

Nov 29: *Minnewaska* (III) fell victim to a mine off the Greek island port of Mudros in the Aegean.

The Pacific Mail Co had ceased in 1915 and IMMC re-acquired the two intended ATL liners *Manchuria* (ex-*Minnekahda* (I)) and *Mongolia* (ex-*Minnelora*) and, in 1916, allocated them to ATL of West Virginia as war loss replacements.

1917 Mar 23: *Maine* (II) torpedoed off Berry Head, Brixham.

Sept 7: *Minnehaha* torpedoed near Fastnet. *Minnekahda* (II), laid down in 1914 as a twin-funnelled passenger ship, was completed as an enormous cargo carrier for use on the North Atlantic.

1918 Jan 30: *Minnetonka* (I) torpedoed by *U-64* in the Mediterranean.

Sept 1: *Mesaba* (I) sunk by a German submarine in St George's Channel near Tuskar Rock.

Nov 11: Armistice day.

1919 *Minnesota* (II) was purchased from the Great Northern Railway Co, and to accommodate her name ATL's ageing *Minnesota* (I) of 1887 was renamed *Mahopac*. She was employed on the European emigrant service where her accommodation for 3,000 passengers was of enormous benefit. *Mesaba* (II), ex-*War Icarus,* acquired.

1920 *Minnekahda* (II) was taken to Quincy, Massachusetts, and given 2,150 emigrant berths. She joined *Minnesota* (II) on the emigrant traffic. *Maine* (IV), *Montana* (II) and *Montauk* acquired. *Manitou* was transferred to the Red Star Line.

1922 Following the restrictions imposed by the Dillingham Immigration Restrictions Act *Minnesota* (II) was laid up whilst *Minnekahda* (II) was converted to 750 tourist class.

1923 *Minnesota* (II) and *Mackinaw* were broken up in Germany and *Mahopac* in Holland. *Minnewaska* (IV), 21,716 tons, was delivered as one of a replacement pair for the wartime losses of the passenger fleet.

1924 *Minnetonka* (II), a slightly larger sister to *Minnewaska* (IV), was delivered. These two ships were constructed with a huge cargo capacity topped by passenger accommodation for 370. The passenger capacity indicated the failure of London to challenge either Liverpool or Southampton and the cargo capacity was really too vast to be handled at passenger disembarkation points.

1925 *Mesaba* (II) was transferred to White Star and renamed *Delphic.*

1926 *Menominee* went to Italy for breaking up but *Michigan* (IV), the old Dominion Line's *Irishman,* was sold to Commodore Modiana for a further brief career.

1927 *Manhattan* scrapped in Italy. Red Star's *Zeeland* was transferred and renamed *Minnesota* (III).

1929 The clouds of depression were gathering and passenger traffic from London declined. *Minnesota* (III) went to the scrap-yard whilst the American Dollar SS Co took both *Manchuria* and *Mongolia* for further service on the Pacific.

1931 With the depression severely affecting North Atlantic trade IMMC decided to sell ATL's passenger fleet as soon as the opportunity arose. The decision marked the beginning of the final phase of ATL, for whom no new ships were built.

1932 *Maine* (IV) became Russia's *Skala.*

1933 *Maryland* (II), *Mississippi* (III) and *Missouri* (III) were all sold for scrapping.

1934 After two of the shortest careers of any large passenger liners *Minnetonka* (II) and *Minnewaska* (IV), both less than ten years old, went for breaking up. Their very early demise probably demonstrates more than any other maritime event the drastic effect of the depression on the less well-ensconced shipping concerns. IMMC's pockets were not deep enough to support the ships and, in any case, their original design proved with hindsight to have been a massive mistake. They fetched only £35,000 each, the cost of a good house today.

The end of these two ships was also the end of the Atlantic Transport Line Ltd of London. However, ATL of West Virginia still remained and late in the year they actually acquired from IMMC Red Star's *Belgenland,* which was renamed *Columbia.* She was given a white hull but retained Red Star's black funnels with a white band.

1935 *Columbia* arrived in New York, flying the US flag, with plans to commence a cruise service from New York-Panama-Los Angeles-San Francisco. After less than ten voyages she was laid up.

Montana (II) and *Montauk* were broken up in Italy. Both had been laid up for about six years.

1936 May 4: *Columbia* arrived in Scotland for breaking up at Bo'ness. She was the final ATL ship and the company thereafter ceased to exist.

Routes

1882-1934 London-Philadelphia, London-Baltimore, London-New York.

Livery

Funnel Darkish red with a hint of brown, black top.

Hull Black, brown-red waterline.

Uppers White with light brown deck fittings.

Masts Milk chocolate brown.

Lifeboats White.

Fleet index

Illustrated fleet list

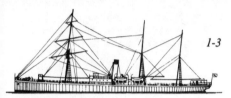

1-3

1 SURREY

Bt 1881 William Gray & Co, West
Hartlepool; *T:* 2,949 g, 1,384 n. **Dim** 300 ft
(91.44 m) × 40 ft 2 in (12.24 m) × 24 ft 6 in
(7.47 m). **Eng** Sgl scr, compound inverted;
2 cyls: 40 in (101.6 cm) and 75 in (190.5
cm); *Stroke:* 45 in (114.3 cm); 250 NHP; 3
sgl ended boilers; *Stm P:* 75 lb; 10 kts; By
Blair & Co, Stockton-on-Tees. **H** Iron,
1 deck and spar deck.

1881 Apr 16: Launched. Owned by Atlantic
Transport Company, managed by Hooper
& Williams.
1884 Jan 4: Collided with German *Uranus*
off Bishop's Rock. Repaired.
1888 Renamed *Michigan* (I). Sold to
Williams, Torrey & Field's Bernard SS Co.
1889 Sold to Christopher Furness. Same
name.
Sold to R. L. Gilchrist.
1890 Sold to Charles Lilburn.
Sold to C. A. Beyts, later Beyts Craig & Co.
1893 Sold to Wilhelm Wilhelmsen, Norway,
still as *Michigan*.
1900 Sold to Luckenbach SS Co, USA.
Renamed *Harry Luckenbach*. Oil in bulk.
1918 Jan 6: Torpedoed by *U-84* in Bay of
Biscay, north-west of Penmarch.

2 SUFFOLK

Details as *Surrey (1)* except: **Bt** 1882 by R. &
H. Green, Blackwall; *T:* 2,924 g, 1,379 n.

1881 Dec 23: Launched.
Owned by Hooper, Murrell & Williams.
1886 Sept 28: Wrecked on the Lizard
carrying two passengers, 38 crew and 161
steers. Ran into fog off Lizard in calm
weather. The captain, W. H. Williams,
went to the forward bridge but the ship
grounded at 6 kts. All saved and many
steers swam ashore.
Oct: Wreck broke up and capsized.

3 SUSSEX

Details as *Surrey (1)* except: **Bt** 1882
Wigham Richardson, Newcastle-upon-
Tyne; *T:* 2,795 g, 1,290 n.

1882 Owned by Hooper, Murrell &
Williams.
1885 Dec 17: Wrecked Scilly Isles on Maiden
Bower Ledge en route Baltimore-London.

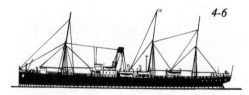

4-6

4 MARYLAND (I)

Bt 1886 William Gray, West Hartlepool; *T:*
2,773 g, 1,814 n. **Dim** 320 ft (97.54 m) × 41
ft (12.5 m) × 25 ft 7 in (7.8 m). **Eng** Sgl scr,
tpl exp; 3 cyls: 25¾ in (65.4 cm), 42 in
(106.68 cm) and 68 in (172.72 cm); *Stroke:*
45 in (114.3 cm); 310 NHP; 2 dbl ended
boilers; *Stm P:* 150 lb; 12 kts; By Central
Marine Works, West Hartlepool.

Sister ships were Maine (5), Missouri (6)
and Montana (7).

1886 Nov: Delivered. Entered London-Baltimore service.
1912 Sold to Italy. Renamed *Redentore* by B. Degregori, Genoa.
1913 May 1: Wrecked en route Misurata-Tolmetta, Tripoli. Stranded 15 miles from port. Broke in three.

5 MAINE (I)

Details as *Maryland (4)* except: **Bt** 1887; *T:* 2,816 g, 1,813 n. **Dim** Length 315 ft 2 in (96.06 m). **Eng** Cyls: 24½ in (62.23 cm), 40 in (101.6 cm) and 65 in (165.1 cm); *Stroke:* 42 in (106.68 cm).

1887 July: Built as *Swansea* for company.
1888 Renamed *Maine* to conform to 'M' nomenclature.
1900 Fitted out as hospital ship for Boer War.
1902 Presented by ATL to Royal Navy as permanent hospital ship. HMHS *Maine*.
1914 June 17: Wrecked on Island of Mull.

6 MISSOURI (I)

Details as *Maine (5)* except: *T:* 2,903 g, 1,822 n.

1889 Apr: On second voyage took *Danmark* (Thingvalla Line) in tow. She had lost her propeller and sank next day, but all 800 passengers were rescued. *Missouri* jettisoned some cargo to carry them.
1898 Presented to US Government as hospital ship USS *Egbert.*
1902 Renamed *Stanley Dollar,* Dollar SS Co managers. Actually owned by B.H.A. Michaelson, St Thomas, West Indies.
1904 Renamed *Missouri.* Owned by Stanley Dollar Co Ltd, Victoria, British Columbia.
1905 Renamed *Stanley Dollar.* Same owners.
Sept 6: Stranded at Katsuura, Japan, and became a total loss. Caused by an uncharted rock.

7

7 MONTANA (I)

Details as *Maryland (4)* except: **Bt** 1887; *T:* 2,840 g, 1,812 n.

1887 Nov: Delivered. Cattle carrier.

Liverpool-Baltimore service.
1913 Sold to Italy. Renamed *Resurrezione* by B. Degregori, Genoa.
1926 Broken up.

8 MINNESOTA (I)

Bt 1887 Harland & Wolff, Belfast; *T:* 3,216 g, 2,080 n. **Dim** 345 ft 6 in (105.31 m) × 40 ft 10 in (12.45 m) × 26 ft 7 in (8.1 m). **Eng** Sgl scr, tpl exp; 3 cyls: 24½ in (62.23 cm), 37 in (93.98 cm) and 64 in (162.56 cm); *Stroke:* 48 in (121.92 cm); 291 NHP; *Stm P:* 160 lb; 12 kts. **H** Steel, 2 decks.

1887 Nov 22: Ran trials. Cattle carrier. Liverpool-Baltimore route.
1918 Renamed *Mahopac.* Same owners.
1926 Sept: Broken up at Rotterdam.

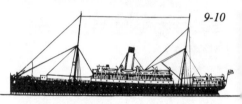

9-10

9 MICHIGAN (II)

Bt 1890 Harland & Wolff, Belfast; *T:* 3,722 g. **Dim** 370 ft 8 in (113 m) × 44 ft 2 in (13.46 m) × 26 ft 7 in (8.1 m). **Eng** Sgl scr, tpl exp; 3 cyls: 25½ in (64.77 cm), 42 in (106.68 cm) and 70 in (177.8 cm); *Stroke:* 51 in (129.54 cm); 350 NHP; *Stm P:* 175 lb; 13 kts; By builder. **H** Steel, 2 decks.

1890 Entered service.
1896 Transferred to National Line. Same name.
1898 Sold to US Government. Became US Transport *Kilpatrick.*
1921 Became *Acropolis,* Stephenidis, Benas & Co Inc, New York. Piraeus-New York. Second funnel added.
1923 Sold to Booras SN Co. Renamed *Washington.*
1924 Sold to United States & China SS Co. Renamed *Great Canton.*
Broken up in Italy.

10 MISSISSIPPI (I)

Details as *Michigan (9)* except; *T:* 3,732 g.
1890 Entered service.
1896 Transferred with *Michigan* to National Line. Same name.

1898 Became US Transport *Buford* (in which guise she is shown in the drawing; as originally built she had four masts).
1923 Sold to F. Linderman, San Francisco. Same name.
1928 Sold to Alaskan Siberian Nav Co.
1929 Sold for breaking up.

11 MANITOBA

Bt 1892 Harland & Wolff, Belfast; *T:* 5,672 g, 4,166 n. **Dim** 445 ft (135.64 m) × 49 ft 2 in (14.99 m) × 30 ft (9.14 m). **Eng** Tw scr, tpl exp; 2 × 3 cyls: 22½ in (57.15 cm), 36½ in (92.71 cm) and 60 in (152.4 cm); *Stroke:* 48 in (121.92 cm); 611 NHP; *Stm P:* 175 lb; 13 kts; By builder. **H** Steel, 3 decks, bridge 152 ft (46.33 m), poop 45 ft (12.72 m); *Pass:* 80 1st.

1892 Apr: Maiden voyage London-New York.
1898 Became US Army Transport *Logan*.
1923 Sold to E. T. Winston, Savannah, Georgia. Renamed *Candler*.
1924 Broken up.

12 MASSACHUSETTS (I)

Details as *Manitoba (11)* except: *T:* 5,673 g.

1892 Mar: Delivered.
1898 Sold to US Government. Renamed *Sheridan*.
1910 Wrecked near Barnegat Light.

13 MOHAWK (I)

Details as *Manitoba (11)* except: *T:* 5,658 g.

1892 Built for Elder Dempster. London-New York route.
1896 Oct: Purchased. Operated on same route.
1898 Became US Army Transport *Grant*.
1904 Converted by US Army into a dredger. Renamed *Chinook*.

14 MOBILE (I)

Bt 1893 Harland & Wolff, Belfast; *T:* 7,271 g, 4,166 n **Dim** 445 ft 6 in (135.79 m) × 50 ft 2 in (15.29 m) × 29 ft 8 in (9.04 m). **Eng** Tw scr, tpl exp; 2 × 3 cyls: 22½ in (57.15 cm), 36½ in (92.71 cm) and 60 in (152.4 cm); *Stroke:* 48 in (121.92 cm); 499 NHP; *Stm P:* 165 lb; 14 kts; By builder. **H** Steel, 3 decks, Bridge 152 ft (46.33 m), poop 45 ft (13.72 m); *Pass:* 80 1st, 1,800 3rd.

1893 Built for Elder Dempster.
Jan 20: Maiden voyage London-New York.
1896 Purchased by Atlantic Transport Line. Used on same route.
1898 Sold to US Government. Became US Transport *Sherman*.
1923 Sold to Los Angeles SS Co. Renamed *Calawaii*. Los Angeles-Honolulu service.
1933 Broken up in Japan.

15 MINNEWASKA (I)

Bt 1894 Harland & Wolff, Belfast; *T:* 7,008 g, 4,462 n. **Dim** 445 ft 6 in (135.79 m) × 50 ft 2 in (15.29 m) × 29 ft 10 in (9.09 m). **Eng** Tw scr, tpl exp; 2 × 3 cyls: 22½ in (57.15 cm), 36½ in (92.71 cm) and 60 in (152.4 cm); *Stroke:* 48 in (121.92 cm); 499 NHP; *Stm P:* 165 lb; 14 kts; By builder. **H** Steel, 3 decks, fcsle 102 ft (31.09 m), bridge 207 ft (63.09 m), poop 58 ft (17.68 m); *Pass:* 80 1st, 1,800 3rd.

Her sister, Hapag's Prussia *(I), became* Dominion *of the Dominion Line in 1897.*

1894 Built as *Persia* for Hamburg America Line. Hamburg-New York route.
1897 Purchased and renamed *Minnewaska*. London-New York.
1898 Sold to US Government. Became US Transport *Thompson* for use during the Philippines Mutiny.
1929 Broken up.

16 MENOMINEE

Bt 1897 Alex Stephen & Sons, Linthouse, Glasgow; *T:* 6,918 g, 4,441 n. **Dim** 492 ft

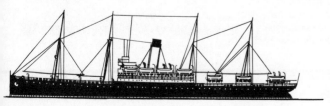

11-13

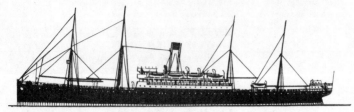

16-20

(149.96 m) oa, 475 ft (144.78 m) ×
52 ft 3 in (15.92 m) × 31 ft 3 in (9.52 m).
Eng Sgl scr, tpl exp; 3 cyls: 32 in (81.28 cm),
54 in (137.16 cm) and 90 in (228.6 cm);
Stroke: 66 in (167.64 cm); 770 NHP,
4,300 IHP; 2 dbl and 2 sgl ended boilers;
Stm P: 190 lb; 13½ kts; By builder.
H Steel, 3 decks, 10 bulkheads, 7 holds;
Coal: 1,100 tons; *Pass:* 120 1st.
1897 Built as *Alexandra* for Wilson's &
Furness-Leyland Line.
1898 Purchased and renamed
Menominee. Actually took one voyage for
Atlantic Transport Line as *Alexandra* on
July 14.
1902 June 14: Last voyage for Atlantic
Transport Line. Then ran for Red Star Line
on Antwerp-Philadelphia service.
1926 Broken up in Italy.

17 MARQUETTE

Details as *Menominee (16)* except:
T: 7,057 g, 4,536 n.

1898 Built as *Boadicea* for Wilson's &
Furness-Leyland Line. Purchased and
renamed *Marquette.* Actually undertook
one voyage as *Boadicea* on July 7, London-
New York.
1901 On Red Star Line's Antwerp-
Philadelphia route.
1915 Oct 23: Sunk by *U-35* in Aegean. 29
lives lost.

18 MOHEGAN

Details as *Menominee (16)* except: **Bt** 1898
Earle's SB Co, Hull; *T:* 6,889 g, 4,494 n.
1898 Built as *Cleopatra* for Wilson's &
Furness-Leyland Line. Purchased by
Atlantic Transport Line and renamed
Mohegan. Actually took one sailing as
Cleopatra on July 31, London-New York.
Oct 13: First voyage as *Mohegan.*
Oct 14: Ran ashore on the Manacles and
became a total loss. 106 lives lost in a calm
sea on a clear night.

19 MANITOU

Details as *Menominee (16)* except: **Bt** 1897
Furness Withy & Co, West Hartlepool;
T: 6,849 g, 4,384 n. **Eng** By T. Richardson
& Sons, Hartlepool.

1898 Maiden voyage London-New York.
Built as *Victoria* for Wilson's & Furness-
Leyland Line. Acquired by Atlantic
Transport Line.
Sept 4: Ran for one voyage as *Victoria* and
was then renamed *Manitou.* London-New
York service.
1902 June: Transferred to Red Star route
Antwerp-Philadelphia.
1920 Renamed *Poland.* Transferred to Red
Star management. 1,106 third class
accommodation added.
1922 On White Star's Bremen-Quebec-
Montreal route with *Vedic.* After three
round voyages laid up.
1925 Sold for breaking up for £18,000.
Renamed *Natale* for last voyage.

20 MESABA (I)

Details as *Menominee (16)* except: **Bt** 1898;
T: 6,833 g, 4,423 n. **Eng** 772 NHP.

1898 Built as *Winifreda* for Wilson's &
Furness-Leyland Line.
July 21: Acquired with sisters. Took one
voyage for Atlantic Transport Line as
Winifreda, then renamed *Mesaba.*
1909 Became reserve steamer when
Minnewaska (37) entered service.
1918 Sept 1: Torpedoed in St George's
Channel between South Wales and Ireland.

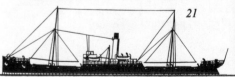

21

21 MACKINAW

Bt 1891 Harland & Wolff, Belfast;
T: 3,204 g, 2,050 n. **Dim** 345 ft 6 in
(105.31 m) × 40 ft 10 in (12.45 m) ×

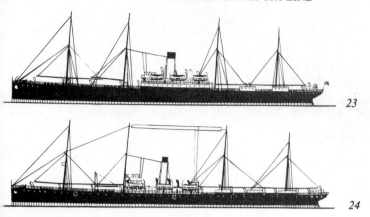

23

24

26 ft 7 in (8.1 m). **Eng** Sgl scr, tpl exp; Cyls: 23 in (58. 42 cm), 37 in (93.98 cm) and 64 in (162.56 cm); *Stroke:* 48 in (121.92 cm); 302 NHP; 2 dbl ended boilers; By builder. **H** Steel, 2 decks, fcsle 46 ft (14.02 m), bridge 94 ft (28.65 m), poop 38 ft (11.58 m).

1891 Built as *British Crown* for British Shipowners Co.
1897 Acquired by Atlantic Transport Line. Renamed *Mackinaw.*
1923 Sold to Gebrudder Beerman and broken up in Germany.

22 MOHAWK (II)

Bt 1885 Harland & Wolff, Belfast; *T:* 4,212 g, 2,695 n. **Dim** 420 ft 4 in (128.11 m) × 42 ft 5 in (12.93 m) × 29 ft 4 in (8.94 m). **Eng** Sgl scr, 2 tandem compound; 2 × 2 cyls: 43 in (109.22 cm) and 86 in (218.44 cm); *Stroke:* 60 in (152.4 cm); 500 HP; *Stm P:* 70 lb; 14 kts; By builder.

1885 Jan 3: Launched as *Belgic,* illustrated in White Star section, entry *20.*
July 7: Handed over. Built to operate under charter to Occidental & Oriental on their Pacific route.
Nov 28: Maiden voyage San Francisco-Yokohama-Hong Kong.
1898 Ended San Francisco service.
1899 Sold to Atlantic Transport Line. Renamed *Mohawk.*
Sept 7: First voyage London-New York.
Dec: Became Boer War transport.
1903 Broken up at Garston, Mersey.

23 MICHIGAN (III)

Bt 1899 Harland & Wolff, Belfast;

T: 9,510 g, 6,158 n. **Dim** 500 ft 8 in (152.6 m) × 62 ft 5 in (19.02 m) × 34 ft (10.36 m). **Eng** Tw scr, quad exp; 2 × 4 cyls: 21 ¼ in (53.98 cm), 31 ½ in (80.01 cm), 46 in (116.84 cm) and 66 in (167.64 cm); *Stroke:* 48 in (121.92 cm); 604 NHP; *Stm P:* 165 lb; 12 kts; By builder. **H** Steel, 3 decks.

1899 Laid down as *Belgia* for Hamburg America Line. Purchased on the stocks and renamed *Michigan.*
1900 Transferred to Dominion Line and renamed *Irishman.* Continued in Dominion service. Managed by Frederick Leyland & Co.
1924 Sold to Dutch shipbreakers.

24 MICHIGAN (IV)

Bt 1898 Harland & Wolff, Belfast; *T:* 8,001 g, 6,118 n. **Dim** 490 ft 6 in (149.5 m) × 56 ft 4 in (17.17 m) × 25 ft (7.62 m). **Eng** Tw scr, tpl exp; 2 × 3 cyls: 19 in (48.26 cm), 31 in (78.74 cm) and 52 in (132.08 cm); *Stroke:* 48 in (121.92 cm); 478 NHP; *Stm P:* 165 lb; 12 kts; By Fawcett, Preston & Co, Liverpool. **H** Steel, 2 decks.

This vessel had the rather rare distinction of not having its engine built by Harland & Wolff themselves.

1898 May: Maiden voyage Liverpool-New Orleans as *Monmouth* of Elder Dempster. Cattle carrier. Transferred after one voyage to Dominion Line. Renamed *Irishman.* Employed on London-New York service.
1900 Transferred from Dominion Line. Renamed *Michigan* (IV) to replace *Michigan* (III) *(23).*

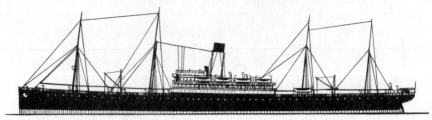

25-27

1902 Transferred to National Line. Same name.
1914 Absorbed back into Atlantic Transport Line (thereby ending National Line).
1926 Sold to E. Modiano, Trieste. Renamed *Candido*.
1927 Broken up in Italy.

25 MINNEAPOLIS

Bt 1900 Harland & Wolff, Belfast; *T:* 13,448 g, 8,631 n. **Dim** 600 ft 7 in (183.06 m) × 65 ft 6 in (19.96 m) × 39 ft 7 in (12.06 m). **Eng** Tw scr, quad exp; 2 × 4 cyls: 30 in (76.2 cm), 43 in (109.22 cm), 63 in (160.02 cm) and 89 in (226.06 cm); *Stroke:* 60 in (152.4 cm); 1,227 NHP; *Stm P:* 180 lb; 16 kts; By builder. **H** Steel, 4 decks and shelter deck; *Pass:* 250 1st.

1900 May 10: Maiden voyage London-New York.
1915 Transport.
1916 Mar 23: Torpedoed by *U-35* in the Mediterranean.

26 MINNEHAHA

Details as *Minneapolis (25)* except: *T:* 13,443 g, 8,637 n.

1900 Aug 11: Maiden voyage London-New York.
1910 Apr 18: Stranded on Scilly Isles. Refloated safely after a month ashore during which most of cargo was removed piecemeal.
1917 Sept 7: Torpedoed 12 miles off Fastnet.

27 MINNETONKA (I)

Details as *Minneapolis (25)* except: **Bt** 1902; *T:* 13,440 g, 11,839 n.

1902 July 12: Maiden voyage London-New York.
1918 Jan 30: Torpedoed by *U-64* in the Mediterranean.

28 MINNEWASKA (II)

Bt 1903 Harland & Wolff, Belfast; *T:* 15,801 g, 10,062 n. **Dim** 600 ft 7 in (183.06 m) × 65 ft 6 in (19.96 m) × 47 ft 7 in (14.5 m). **Eng** Tw scr, quad exp; 2 × 4 cyls: 30 in (76.2 cm), 43 in (109.22 cm), 63 in (160.02 cm) and 89 in (226.06 cm); *Stroke:* 60 in (152.4 cm); 1,228 NHP; *Stm P:* 180 lb; 16 kts; By builder. **H** Steel, 4 decks; *Pass:* 350 1st.

1902 Dec 18: Launched.
1903 Laid down as *Minnewaska* but transferred to White Star on the stocks. Renamed *Arabic*.
June 26: Maiden voyage Liverpool-New York as *Arabic*.
1905 Liverpool-Boston service regularly except when relieving on Liverpool-New York route.
1915 Aug 19: Torpedoed off Southern Ireland. 44 lives lost.

29 MINNEKAHDA (I)

Bt 1903 New York SB Co, Camden, New Jersey; *T:* 13,639 g, 8,750 n. **Dim** 600 ft (182.88 m) × 65 ft 4 in (19.91 m) × 31 ft 1 in (9.47 m). **Eng** Tw scr, quad exp; 2 × 4 cyls: 30 in (76.2 cm), 43 in (109.22 cm),

28

29-30

31-34

63 in (160.02 cm) and 89 in (226.06 cm);
Stroke: 60 in (152.4 cm); 1,923 NHP; 4 dbl
and 4 sgl ended boilers; *Stm P:* 215 lb;
16 kts; By builder. **H** Steel, 4 decks, bridge
204 ft (62.18 m); *Coal:* 3,443 tons; *Cargo:*
557,000 cu ft (15,763 cu m) bulk and
34,700 cu ft (982 cu m) refrig; *Pass:*
250 1st, 800 3rd; *Crew:* 220.
1904 Laid down as *Minnekahda* but
completed in May as *Manchuria* for Pacific
Mail SS Co. For her resumed Atlantic
Transport Line career see *Manchuria (43)*.

30 MINNELORA

Details as *Minnekahda (29)*.

1904 Laid down as *Minnelora* but
completed as *Mongolia* for Pacific Mail SS
Co. For her resumed Atlantic Transport
Line career see *Mongolia (44)*.

31 MAINE (II)

Bt 1903 Maryland Steel Co, Sparrow's
Point, Baltimore; *T:* 7,959 g, 5,077 n.
Dim 492 ft (149.96 m) × 58 ft 3 in (17.75 m)
× 31 ft 10 in (9.7 m). **Eng** Tw scr, tpl exp;
2 × 3 cyls: 25 in (63.5 cm), 42½ in (107.95 cm)
and 72 in (182.88 cm); *Stroke:* 48 in
(121.92 cm); 935 NHP; 2 dbl and 2 sgl
ended boilers; *Stm P:* 200 lb; 12 kts; By
builder. **H** Steel, 3 decks, bridge 125 ft
(38.1 m).

1903 May: Completed.
1906 Sold to American-Hawaiian SS Co as
Maine.
1907 Renamed *Virginian*. Same company.

32 MISSOURI (II)

Details as *Maine (31)* except: *T:* 7,914 g,

5,077 n.

1903 Dec: Completed.
1906 Sold to American-Hawaiian SS Co as
Missouri.
1908 Renamed *Missourian*. Same company.

33 MASSACHUSETTS (II)

Details as *Maine (31)* except: **Bt** 1903 New
York SB Co, Camden, New Jersey;
T: 7,913 g, 5,131 n. **Dim** Length 490 ft
(149.35 m). **Eng** 997 NHP, although cyls
and stroke same as *Maine*. **H** Bridge 128 ft
(39.01 m).

1911 Sold to American-Hawaiian SS Co.
Renamed *Kansan*.
1917 Sunk by submarine in Bay of Biscay.

34 MISSISSIPPI (II)

Details as *Massachusetts (33)* except:
T: 9,710 g, 6,353 n.

1906 Transferred to Red Star Line.
Renamed *Samland*.
1911 Became *Belgic*, White Star.
1913 Returned to Red Star. Renamed
Samland. Cargo only.
1931 Apr: Sold to Italian shipbreakers.

35 MEMPHIS

Bt 1891 Gourlay Bros, Dundee; *T:* 5,158 g,
3,340 n. **Dim** 435 ft (132.59 m) × 46 ft 4 in
(14.12 m) × 25 ft 2 in (7.67 m). **Eng** Sgl
scr, tpl exp; 3 cyls: 30 in (76.2 cm), 48 in
(121.92 cm) and 79 in (200.66 cm); *Stroke:*
60 in (152.4 cm); 516 NHP; 3 dbl ended
boilers; *Stm P:* 180 lb; 12 kts; By builder.
H Steel, 2 decks.

1891 Cattle carrier. Built as *America* for

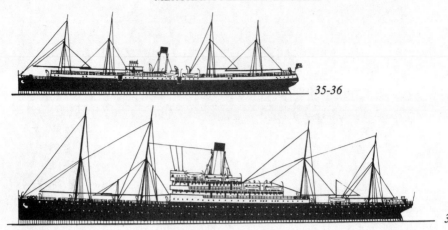

35-36

37

National Line. Liverpool-New York service.
1903 Went ashore on Sable Island. Refloated. Uninsured.
1907 Transferred to Atlantic Transport Line and renamed *Memphis*.
1908 Broken up at Bo'ness, Firth of Forth.

36 MOBILE (II)

Details as *Memphis (35)* except: *T:* 5,302 g, 3,400 n.

1891 Cattle carrier. Built as *Europe* for National Line. Liverpool-New York service.
1907 Transferred to Atlantic Transport Line and renamed *Mobile*.
1911 Sold to Akties Quilimane, Larvik. Renamed *Thoger*. Whaling.
1914 Renamed *Guvernoren*.
1915 Jan 22: Burnt at sea south of Shetland Islands.

37 MINNEWASKA (III)

Bt 1909 Harland & Wolff, Belfast; *T:* 14,317 g, 8,878 n. **Dim** 600 ft 4 in (182.98 m) × 65 ft 5 in (19.94 m) × 39 ft 7 in (12.06 m). **Eng** Tw scr, quad exp; 2 × 4 cyls: 30 in (76.2 cm), 43 in (109.22 cm), 63 in (160.02 cm) and 89 in (226.06 cm); *Stroke:* 60 in (152.4 cm); 1,222 NHP; *Stm P:* 200 lb; By builder. **H** Steel, 4 decks and shelter deck; *Pass:* 340 1st.

1909 Maiden voyage London-New York.
1915 Became troop transport.
1916 Nov 29: Mined near Mudros, Suda Bay in the Aegean. Beached but beyond repair. Broken up locally as she lay. The

mine was laid by the German submarine *UC-23*.

38 MAINE (III)

Bt 1905 D. & W. Henderson & Co, Glasgow; *T:* 3,617 g, 2,338 n. **Dim** 361 ft (110.03 m) × 46 ft 2 in (14.07 m) × 17 ft 6 in (5.33 m). **Eng** Sgl scr, tpl exp; 3 cyls: 24 in (60.96 cm), 40 in (101.6 cm) and 67 in (170.18 cm); *Stroke:* 45 in (114.3 cm); 363 NHP; *Stm P:* 185 lb; 11 kts; By builder. **H** Steel, 1 deck and spar deck, fcsle 46 ft (14.02 m), bridge 200 ft (60.96 m), poop 31 ft (9.45 m).

1905 Built as *Sierra Blanca* for Sierra Blanca SS Co (Thompson, Anderson & Co).
1913 Sold to Frederick Leyland for £38,500 but with intention of Atlantic Transport Line operating her. Renamed *Maine*.
1917 Mar 23: Torpedoed off Berry Head, Brixham, Devon.

39-41

39 MARYLAND (II)

Bt 1913 Harland & Wolff, Govan, Glasgow; *T:* 4,731 g, 2,962 n. **Dim** 370 ft (112.78 m) × 50 ft 2 in (15.29 m) × 31 ft (9. 45 m). **Eng** Sgl scr, quad exp; 4 cyls: 24½ in (62.23 cm), 35 in (88.9 cm), 50 in (127 cm) and 73 in (185.42 cm); *Stroke:* 54 in (137.16 cm); 392 NHP; 4 sgl ended boilers; 10 kts; By builder. **H** 5 holds, 10

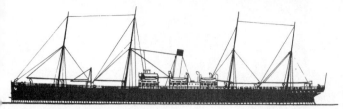

42

winches; *Coal:* 904 tons at 40 tons per day; *Cargo:* 396,155 cu ft (11,213 cu m).

1913 Entered service. Cattle carrier only. Displacement 10,190 tons.
1933 Aug: Sold for breaking up. P. & W. MacLellan, Bo'ness, Firth of Forth.

40 MISSISSIPPI (III)

Details as *Maryland (39)* except: *T:* 4,738 g, 2,936 n. **Eng** Motorship; 2,800 IHP; By Burmeister & Wain. *Fuel:* 578 tons oil at 10.8 tons per day (economical compared with coal); *Cargo:* 416,747 cu ft (11,796 cu m).

1913 First British motorship on North Atlantic.
1933 Aug: Sold for breaking up. P. & W. MacLellan, Bo'ness, Firth of Forth.

41 MISSOURI (III)

Details as *Maryland (39)* except: **Bt** 1914; *T:* 4,697 g, 2,949 n. *Cargo:* 399,975 cu ft (11,321 cu m).

1914 Entered service. Cattle and cargo carrier.
1933 Oct 2: Sold for breaking up. P. & W. MacLellan, Bo'ness, Firth of Forth.

42 MANHATTAN

Bt 1898 Harland & Wolff, Belfast; *T:* 8,115 g, 6,236 n. **Dim** 490 ft 6 in (149.5 m) × 56 ft 3 in (17.14 m) × 25 ft (7.62 m). **Eng** Tw scr, tpl exp; 2 × 3 cyls: 19 in (48.26 cm), 31 in (78.74 cm) and 52 in (132.08 cm); *Stroke:* 48 in (121.92 cm); 478 NHP; *Stm P:* 165 lb; 12 kts; By Fawcett, Preston & Co, Liverpool. **H** Steel,

2 decks and spar deck.

1898 Built for Atlantic Transport Line's North American cattle and cargo service, London-New York route. Following the acquisition of the National Line shares *Manhattan* was transferred over to bring their fleet strength up to four.
1914 With the ending of National Line's London-New York service she was absorbed back into Atlantic Transport.
1927 Sold to Italian shipbreakers.

43 MANCHURIA

For details see *Minnekahda (29)*.

1904 Laid down as *Minnekahda*. Completed as *Manchuria* for Pacific Mail SS Co.
1916 Acquired. Transferred to London-New York run. Same name.
1919-23 New York-Hamburg run for American Line.
1923 Chartered to Panama Pacific Line. New York-Panama Canal-San Francisco.
1929 Sold to Dollar SS Co. Renamed *President Johnson. T:* 15,543 g.
1940 Renamed *Tagus,* Tagus Nav Co SA, Panama.
1947 Renamed *Santa Cruz.* Same company. Chartered to the Italia Line.
1952 Broken up at Savona, Italy.

44 MONGOLIA

For details see *Minnekahda (29)*.

1904 Laid down as *Minnelora (30)*. Completed as *Mongolia* for Pacific Mail SS Co.

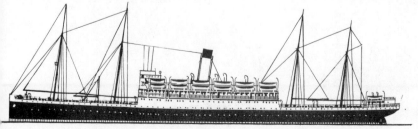

43-44

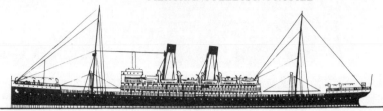

45-46

1916 Acquired. London-New York service. Same name.
1919-23 New York-Hamburg service for American Line.
1923 Chartered to Panama Pacific Line. New York-Panama Canal-San Francisco service.
1929 Sold to Dollar SS Co. Renamed *President Fillmore*. *T:* 15,575 g.
1931-40 Laid up.
1940 Sold. Renamed *Panamanian*. Cia Transatlantica Centroamericana SA.
1949 Broken up at Hong Kong.

45 KOREA

Bt 1901 Newport News SB & DD Co, Newport News; *T:* 11,276 g, 5,651 n. **Dim** 551 ft 7 in (168.12 m) × 63 ft 2 in (19.25 m) × 40 ft 9 in (12.42 m). **Eng** Tw scr, quad exp; 2 × 4 cyls: 35 in (88.9 cm), 50 in (127 cm), 70 in (177.8 cm) and 100 in (254 cm); *Stroke:* 66 in (167.64 cm); 1,625 NHP; 6 dbl and 2 sgl ended boilers; *Stm P:* 180 lb; By builder. **H** Steel, 3 decks, fcsle 72 ft (21.94 m), bridge 245 ft (74.68 m), poop 112 ft (34.14 m); *Coal:* 2,976 tons; *Pass:* 300 1st.

Portside views of this ship show two open bridge decks. The starboard side had the lower deck plated over, providing a passageway to the best cabins.

1901 Built for Pacific Mail SS Corp. San Francisco-Yokohama-Hong Kong.
1915 Aug 12: Sold with rest of fleet to Atlantic Transport Line. Same name.
1915-16 Used on New York-London service with name and nationality on sides.
1916 Sold to Toyo Kisen Kaisha. Renamed

Korea Maru. Transpacific route.
1927 Service taken over by Nippon Yusen Kaisha. Same name.
1930 Laid up.
1934 Aug: Sold for breaking up in Japan.

46 SIBERIA

Details as *Korea (45)* except: *T:* 11,284 g, 5,655 n.

1901 Built for Pacific Mail SS Corp. San Francisco-Yokohama-Hong Kong.
1915 Aug 12: Sold with rest of fleet to Atlantic Transport Line. Same name.
1915-16 New York-London service. Sailed in Atlantic Transport Line colours with name and nationality on sides.
1916 Sold to Toyo Kisen Kaisha. Renamed *Siberia Maru*.
1927 Service taken over by Nippon Yusen Kaisha. Same name.
1930 Laid up.
1935 Jan: Sold for breaking up in Japan.

47 CHINA

Bt 1889 Fairfield Co, Glasgow; *T:* 5,060 g, 3,186 n. **Dim** 440 ft 4 in (134.21 m) × 48 ft 1 in (14.65 m) × 32 ft 9 in (9.98 m). **Eng** Sgl scr, tpl exp; 3 cyls: 40 in (101.6 cm), 66 in (167.64 cm) and 106 in (269.24 cm); *Stroke:* 72 in (182.88 cm); 953 NHP; 6 dbl and 1 sgl ended boilers; *Stm P:* 120 lb; 17 kts; By builder. **H** Steel, 3 decks, 4 holds, 4 masts, fcsle 58 ft (17.68 m), bridge 220 ft (67.06 m), poop 56 ft (17.07 m); *Coal:* 1,960 tons; *Pass:* 139 1st, 33 2nd, 519 3rd.

1889 Built for Pacific Mail SS Co. San Francisco-Yokohama route.

47

48

1915 Aug 12: Sold with rest of fleet to Atlantic Transport Line. Not required so registered in name of John Barneson as being for sale.
Oct: Sold to China Mail SS Corp of San Francisco. Same name.
1925 Broken up.

48 MINNEKAHDA (II)

Bt 1917 Harland & Wolff, Belfast; *T:* 17,281 g, 10,844 n. **Dim** 620 ft 6 in (189.13 m) × 66 ft 5 in (20.24 m) × 47 ft 3 in (14.4 m). **Eng** Tpl scr, 2 tpl exp and LP turbine to centre shaft; 2 × 3 cyls: 30 in (76.2 cm), 47½ in (120.65 cm) and 2 × 54 in (137.16 cm); *Stroke:* 54 in (137.16 cm); *Stm P:* 185 lb; 16 kts; By builder. **H** Steel, 4 decks and shelter deck, bridge 285 ft (86.87 m).

When at sea the four stump masts could be folded onto the deck.

1917 Completed as cargo vessel only. No passengers.
1919 Jan 18: First commercial voyage. London-New York. Cargo only.
1920 To American flag, Atlantic Transport Line of West Virginia. *Pass:* 2,150 3rd.
1921 Mar 31: New York-Hamburg run for American Line. Third class only.
1924-25 Back to London-New York for Atlantic Transport Line. *Pass:* 750 1st, 1,150 3rd.
1931 Last voyage. Laid up.
1936 Broken up at Dalmuir.

49 MINNESOTA (II)

Bt 1904 Eastern SB Co, New London,

Connecticut; *T:* 20,718 g, 13,324 n. **Dim** 622 ft (189.58 m) × 73 ft 6 in (22.4 m) × 41 ft 6 in (12.65 m). **Eng** Tw scr, tpl exp; 2 × 3 cyls: 29 in (73.66 cm), 51 in (129.54 cm) and 89 in (226.06 cm); *Stroke:* 57 in (144.78 cm); 2,293 NHP; *Stm P:* 250 lb; 14 kts. **H** Steel, 4 decks.

Coal fired. Very uneconomical until reboilered in 1916. The steering of this ship was also poor; she veered badly at slow speeds. During her career the promenade deck was extended forward to the mainmast and lifeboats added. Her sister was Dakota *of the Great Northern SS Co.*

1904 Built for Great Northern SS Co, Seattle-Yokohama-Hong Kong.
1911 Broke both propeller shafts 17 miles out from Yokohama.
1916 Operated by Atlantic Transport Line on London-New York service. Reboilered.
1920 Passenger accommodation closed off. Cargo only. London-New York.
1922 Laid up in New York.
1923 Nov: Sold out of service.
1924 Broken up in Germany.

50 MESABA (II)

Bt 1918 Harland & Wolff, Govan, Glasgow; *T:* 8,002 g, 4,905 n. **Dim** 465 ft (141.73 m) oa, 450 ft (137.16 m) × 58 ft 3 in (17.75 m) × 29 ft 1 in (8.86 m). **Eng** Sgl scr, tpl exp; 3 cyls: 26½ in (67.31 cm), 44 in (111.76 cm) and 73 in (185.42 cm); *Stroke:* 48 in (121.92 cm), 5,500 HP; 3 dbl ended boilers; 13 kts; By builder. **H** Steel, fcsle 43 ft (13.11 m), poop 31 ft (9.45 m); *Pass:* 12.

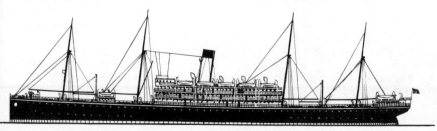

49

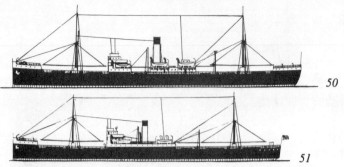

50

51

1918 Sept 19: Launched as *War Icarus,* 'G' type Standard ship. Completed Nov, the only one completed in wartime.
1919 May 5: Maiden voyage for Atlantic Transport Line.
1925 Sold to White Star. Renamed *Delphic.*
1933 Sold to Clan Line. Renamed *Clan Farquhar.*
1948 July 8: Broken up at Milford Haven.

51 MAINE (IV)

Bt 1920 Harland & Wolff, Belfast;
T: 6,600 g, 4,073 n. **Dim** 412 ft 7 in
(125.75 m) × 55 ft 8 in (16.97 m) ×
34 ft 5 in (10.49 m). **Eng** Sgl scr, tpl exp;
3 cyls: 27 in (68.58 cm), 44 in (111.76 cm)
and 73 in (185.42 cm); *Stroke:* 48 in
(121.92 cm); 517 NHP; 3 sgl ended boilers;
Stm P: 180 lb; 12 kts; By builder. **H** Steel,
fcsle 40 ft (12.19 m).

1919 Nov 27: Launched as *War Riddle.*
1920 Built as wartime standard 'N' type.
Completed as *Maine.* No curves were used
in her construction and no rolled plates.
Box shaped. Stern was V-shaped. Lost
rudder on maiden voyage. Salved by
Carrigan Head (Head Line).
1927 Laid up at Southend.
1932 Sold to Arthur Stott & Co, Newcastle,
for £8,000. Resold by them, for £12,000, to
Russia. Renamed *Skala.*
1955 Broken up.

52 MONTANA (II)

Bt 1919 New York SB Corp, Camden, New
Jersey; *T:* 7,772 g, 4,829 n. **Dim** 419 ft 6 in
(127.86 m) × 56 ft 6 in (17.22 m) × 30 ft 2 in
(9.19 m). **Eng** Sgl scr, quad exp; 4 cyls: 24 in
(60.96 cm, 36 in (91.44 cm), 51 in (129.54 cm)
and 75 in (190.5 cm); *Stroke:* 51 in
(129.54 cm); 577 NHP; 3 sgl ended boilers;

Stm P: 220 lb; By builder. **H** Steel, 2 decks,
bridge 77 ft (23.47 m).

1919 Built as *Defender* for United States
Shipping Board.
1920 Acquired by Atlantic Transport Line.
Renamed *Montana.*
1930 Laid up.
1935 May: Broken up in Italy by Cantieri
Metallurgica della Venezia e Giulia.

53 MONTAUK

Details as *Montana (52)* except: Forward
bridge 27 ft (8.23 m).

1919 Built as *Champion* for United States
Shipping Board.
1920 Acquired by Atlantic Transport Line.
Renamed *Montauk.*
1930 Laid up.
1935 May: Broken up in Italy by Cantieri
Metallurgica della Venezia e Giulia.

54 MINNEWASKA (IV)

Bt 1923 Harland & Wolff, Belfast;
T: 21,716 g, 13,418 n. **Dim** 600 ft 8 in
(183.08 m) × 80 ft 5 in (24.51 m) × 49 ft 5 in
(15.06 m). **Eng** Tw scr, 4 sgl reduction geared
Brown-Curtis steam turbines; 15,000 SHP;
Stm P: 220 lb; 16 kts; By builder. **H** Steel,
3 decks and shelter deck, fcsle 83 ft
(25.3 m), bridge 233 ft (71.02 m); *Cargo:*
1,000,000 cu ft (28,317 cu m); *Pass:*
369 1st.

At the time the largest cargo carrier afloat.

1923 Mar 22: Launched.
Sept 1: Maiden voyage London-New York.
1932 Transferred to Red Star's Antwerp-
Southampton-New York route.
Painted in Red Star colours; this marked
the end of the Atlantic Transport Line
funnel. *Pass:* 400 tst.
1933 Sept 28: Last voyage. Laid up at
Antwerp.

54-55

1934 Sold to Douglas & Ramsey, Port Glasgow, for £35,000 for breaking up. Dec 10: Arrived Tail of the Bank. Beached and broken up.

55 **MINNETONKA** (II)

Details as *Minnewaska (54)* except: *T:* 21,998 g, 13,526 n.

1924 May 3: Maiden voyage London-New York.
1932 Placed on the Antwerp-Southampton-New York services of the Red Star Line. Painted in Red Star colours.
1933 Oct 14: Last voyage. Laid up at Antwerp.
1934 Nov: Broken up at Bo'ness, Firth of Forth, by MacLellan. £35,000.

56 **MINNESOTA** (III)

Bt 1901 John Brown, Clydebank; *T:* 11,667 g, 7,335 n. **Dim** 561 ft 7 in (171.17 m) × 60 ft 2 in (18.34 m) × 38 ft 2 in (11.63 m). **Eng** Tw scr, quad exp; 2 × 4 cyls: 31 in (78.74 cm), 44 in (111.76 cm), 62 in (157.48 cm) and 88 in (223.52 cm); *Stroke:* 54 in (137.16 cm); 1,627 NHP; *Stm P:* 200 lb; 15 kts; By builder. **H** Steel, 3 decks,

fcsle 84 ft (25.6 m), bridge 215 ft (65.53 m), poop 49 ft (14.93 m).

1901 Built as *Zeeland* for Red Star Line. Antwerp-New York.
1910-11 Operated by White Star. Liverpool-Boston.
1915 Renamed *Northland* on White Star-Dominion service. Troopship.
1920 Aug 18: Resumed Antwerp-Southampton-New York service. Renamed *Zeeland*.
1927 Became *Minnesota* on the London-New York service. Managed by F. Leyland & Co.
1929 Oct: Sold to T. W. Ward Ltd for breaking up at Inverkeithing, Firth of Forth. Broken up in 1930.

57 **COLUMBIA**

Bt 1914 Harland & Wolff, Belfast; *T:* 27,132 g, 15,352 n. **Dim** 670 ft 5 in (204.34 m) × 78 ft 5 in (23.9 m) × 44 ft 7 in (13.59 m). **Eng** Tpl scr, 2 tpl exp with LP turbine to centre shaft; 2 × 4 cyls: 35½ in (90.17 cm), 56 in (142.24 cm) and 2 × 64 in (162.56 cm); *Stroke:* 60 in (152.4 cm); *Stm P:* 215 lb; 16 kts; By

56

57

builder. **H** Steel, 4 decks, fcsle and bridge 574 ft (174.95 m), upper bridge 371 ft (113.08 m); *Pass:* 500 1st, 500 2nd, 1,500 3rd

1914 Dec 31: Launched. Construction work stopped for two years.

1917 Entered service as *Belgic,* White Star. Cargo only.

1923 Apr 4: First voyage as *Belgenland.* Antwerp-Southampton-New York.

1932 Jan 8: Final voyage on Antwerp-Southampton-New York route.

1935 Renamed *Columbia* and owned by the Atlantic Transport Line of West Virginia. US flag. The ship was not used on transatlantic service but was placed on the New York-San Francisco route of Panama Pacific, which was operated as a cruise.

1936 Apr: Broken up at Bo'ness, Firth of Forth. On last transatlantic voyage flew British flag.

White Star Line

History

1845 The origins of the great company which was to become universally known as the White Star Line were laid in 1845 when John Pilkington entered business on his own account. Aged 25, he was the son of Christopher Pilkington, the founder of Pilkington Brothers.

John Pilkington was joined in his shipbroking business by another 25-year-old, Henry Threlfell Wilson, who had been apprenticed to Thomas Harrison of the celebrated Liverpool firm T. & J. Harrison who are still in existence as shipowners today. The offices of Pilkington and Wilson were located at Prince's Building, 26 North John Street, Liverpool, and the two young men acted as brokers for sailing vessels employed on the Canadian and American routes.

1846 Feb 26: The brig *Elizabeth* took their first sailing, to Montreal. She was chartered by the firm and represented their first trading venture, broking itself being a commission or fee-paid occupation.

1849 The first ship owned by the two partners was the three-masted barque *Iowa* of 879 g tons. In June advertisements appeared in the Liverpool newspapers announcing sailings by the 'White Star Line of Boston Packets', the announced ports of call being Boston, New York, New Orleans and Charleston.

1851 Gold was discovered in Australia and the first shipment arrived in Britain as proof. This resulted in the commencement of the Australian Gold-Rush and thousands of hopeful miners sought passage in search of their fortunes. For Pilkington and Wilson the opportunity was too good to miss and they decided that the White Star house flag should invade Australian waters.

1852 May: The White Star Line of Australian Packets began to advertise sailings to the Australian gold-fields by the sailing vessels *Bhurtpoor, Blanche, Dundonald* and *Phoenix*. Unfortunately *Bhurtpoor* was lost on the coast of Ireland near Wexford and it was, in fact, her replacement the *Ellen* which took their first sailing to Australia on July 13.

1853 Late in the year, in an effort to establish themselves as the leaders in the packet trade to Australia, White Star took onto their books the new ship *Tayleur*. A fully-rigged iron ship of 1,997 tons, she had been newly-built by Tayleurs of Bank Quay, Warrington, Cheshire, for the Liverpool owner Charles A. Moore. She cost £34,000 and was, at the time, the largest ship yet built in England.

1854 Jan: The maiden sailing of *Tayleur* was a festive occasion for Merseyside, but disaster struck when, just two days out from Liverpool, the ship was wrecked in broad daylight on Lambay Island in Dublin Bay. Of those aboard 282 were saved but tragically 276 persons were drowned. The subsequent Board of Enquiry found 'culpable neglect by the owners Charles Moore & Co.'

May: *Red Jacket* entered service under the White Star flag. She was faster than any sailing ship or, for that matter, any steamer on the Australian run. She normally made the voyage to Melbourne in 70 days.

1856 Dec 31: At the end of the year John

Pilkington resigned from the White Star partnership to return to the family business of Pilkington Brothers. The friendship between he and Henry Wilson remained and they continued to collaborate together. A shareholder in the partnership was James Chambers, the brother-in-law of Henry Wilson. He took the place of John Pilkington and, in accordance with the practice of the times, the name of the concern was changed to H. T. Wilson & Chambers.

1863 The first steam-driven ship for the partnership was the *Royal Standard,* built at Palmers yard at Jarrow.

In those days, during the gold-rush to Australia, speed was all important – after all, the gold might be worked out before the emigrant prospectors arrived. Money was therefore to be made by the firm which could promise faster passages than its competitors, and Henry Wilson, in his determination to beat his rivals, built or chartered only the largest and fastest of sailing ships. He sacrificed the commerciality of cargo loads for speed. A crisis developed in the partnership when Henry Wilson, as senior partner, went so far as to guarantee, under penalty, to make the passage to Melbourne in 68 days. James Chambers was so alarmed about his liability, as a partner, that he withdrew from the company and set up business on his own as James Chambers & Co, a shipowning Liverpool concern that was to survive, albeit in a somewhat modest way, for another century.

1865 Henry Threlfell Wilson was joined by John Cunningham, and the style of the organisation changed to Wilson & Cunningham as managers of the White Star Line of Packets. Both men were instinctive commercial gamblers and they pressed on with their aim to capitalise on their Australian business and to gain a premier position in the market. To dominate any market involves risks and both men took them.

1867 By the autumn of this year the partners owed their bankers, the Royal Bank of Liverpool, the alarming sum of £527,000. There was no prospect of raising more capital and the chances of repaying the sum were remote.

1868 Jan 18: After an agonising appraisal of their position the partnership was forced into liquidation. The assets were realised and finally Thomas H. Ismay, then aged 30, purchased the name 'White Star', together with the red burgee flag with its superimposed white star and the goodwill of the concern, for the sum of £1,000. T. H. Ismay & Co already operated a fleet of sailing ships and in addition Thomas Ismay was a director of the white-funnelled National Steam Navigation Company, which already owned and operated several substantial North Atlantic liners. It was the ambition of young Thomas Ismay that his venture with the White Star name should not only encompass a fleet of North Atlantic steamers but a fleet that was comprised of the most modern vessels on the service.

The story has it that Ismay expounded his ideas, during a game of billiards, to Gustav Schwabe, the Liverpool ship financier. Schwabe was the uncle of another up-and-coming young industrialist, Gustav Wolff, who was then the junior partner of the Belfast shipbuilding yard of Harland & Wolff. Gustav Schwabe came up with a proposal: if Ismay agreed to have the ships built by Harland & Wolff, and also permitted the design to be devised by that company, then he would ensure that the financial backing was forthcoming. It was on this basis that the deal was concluded.

1869 Sept 6: The Oceanic Steam Navigation Company was registered with a capital of £400,000 comprising 400 shares of £1,000 each. The head office of the new concern was to be at 10 Water Street, Liverpool, and amongst the shareholders was to be found not only Thomas Ismay but also Gustav Schwabe. Despite the company's official title it was forever to be known as the White Star Line. An order was immediately placed with Harland & Wolff for four ships.

The founding concern of T. H. Ismay & Co also remained in business and continued to operate sailing ships, mainly to Australia. These too were labelled White Star Packets and also flew the White Star burgee house flag.

1870 In order to strengthen the management William Imrie, who had served his apprenticeship alongside Ismay, joined the concern and the title of the managing agents became Ismay, Imrie & Co. This renamed concern was appointed manager of all the group's vessels both steam and sail, with William Imrie concentrating upon the latter.
Aug 27: *Oceanic* (I), first of the company's new steamers, was launched at Belfast. Her yard number was 73. The contract with Harland & Wolff was new and different. The ships were to be constructed from only the best materials available and no fixed price was quoted. Instead the payment was to be on the basis of 'cost plus an agreed profit margin'. In return Harland & Wolff agreed to build no competitive ships. The clause concerning competitive ships was carefully drawn up; Harland & Wolff could build for any owner provided they and White Star were mutually satisfied that the vessel was not going to be, or likely to be, used in competition with current White Star ships.

Because of their earlier Australian connections contemporary shipping commentators speculated that the four new ships were really intended for the Australian route. Liverpool, they argued, already had the ships of the Cunard, Inman, Guion and National Lines on the New York run, and between them these had such a grip on the market that any newcomer could have little chance of wresting away a sufficient share of the market. But the fact that Thomas Ismay intended to enter the highly competitive North Atlantic market is conclusively demonstrated by the bunker capacities of the four new ships and the two subsequent, larger vessels.

1871 Mar 2: *Oceanic* (I) left Liverpool on her maiden voyage for New York carrying only 64 passengers. Shortly before sailing she developed engine trouble and was forced to return to her Liverpool berth. A delay of two weeks ensued before the much-advertised first sailing could be resumed.
June 8: *Atlantic* entered service.
Sept 14: The third of the quartet, *Baltic* (I) set sail for New York. By the end of

the year these three fine ships were becoming a familiar sight on both sides of the Atlantic, but their passenger lists were poor and they were bottom of the league table of carryings. Breaking into the transatlantic business was proving to be as difficult as the experts had predicted.

Partially to offset the North Atlantic problem, but also to diversify into new areas opened up by the inauguration of the Suez Canal in 1869, Ismay, Imrie & Co purchased two ships being built by Thomas Royden at Liverpool. These were named *Asiatic* (I) and *Tropic* (I) and were employed on the Calcutta route. The use of the '-ic' endings was now clearly established. One other quirk of the owners was that their ships were launched without the traditional naming ceremony; the reception of the ship in Liverpool was instead used as the occasion to celebrate the new arrival.

1872 Feb 1: *Republic* (I), the last of the initial quartet, set sail on her maiden voyage to New York. White Star intended to operate a weekly service to New York and this required five ships. Almost from their inception they began the habit of ordering ships in pairs, and all from Harland & Wolff, and after their initial order Ismay and Imrie had contracted for two more North Atlantic liners that were improved versions of the original four. The first of these to enter service was *Adriatic* (I) on Mar 11, and to her fell the distinction of wresting from Cunard the transatlantic record when in May she dispossessed the sleek paddler *Scotia* of the record which she had held since 1866.

Adriatic made the westbound crossing in 7 days 23 hours 17 mins at 14.52 kts average and the travelling public began to take serious note of these yacht-like ships with the black-topped buff funnels. During the year negotiations with the Mersey Docks & Harbour Board resulted in White Star being allocated a permanent berth at the West Waterloo dock.

With the advent of *Celtic* (I) in October the company decided to challenge William Wheelwright's Pacific Steam Navigation Co's hold on the South

American run.

Oct 5: *Republic* (I) sailed for Valparaiso via Cape Horn to inaugurate the White Star South American route. She was followed by the transfer of *Asiatic* (I) and *Tropic* (I) from their Indian berth.

PSNC's reaction to this competition was to advertise weekly sailings.

Dec: To meet the growing demands for funds the capital of the company was increased to £750,000.

1873 Jan: *Baltic* (I) averaged over 15 kts on the eastbound passage and established a new transatlantic record. By now the speed and comfort of the new company's ships had moved them into the position of the leading carrier on the route.

A pair of sisters, *Gaelic* (I) and *Belgic* (I), were acquired on the stocks. Both vessels were placed on the Pacific Steam Navigation's South American route to Valparaiso via Cape Horn.

Apr 1: *Atlantic* was lost outside Halifax, Nova Scotia, with the loss of 588 lives out of 920 aboard. Her stormy passage from Liverpool had been such a struggle that coal supplies were running short. As a precaution course was set for Halifax but in continuous gales the vessel grounded on the rocks to become the worst North Atlantic disaster yet.

1874 The steamer service to South America was terminated. *Asiatic* (I) and *Tropic* (I) were sold and *Gaelic* (I) with *Belgic* (I) were transferred to a London-New York cargo service.

June 25: *Britannic* (I), an enlarged two-funnelled version of the *Oceanic* (I) class, entered service. She was 1½ kts faster and had her propeller especially lowered below keel level, the idea being to give greater thrust.

1875 May 30: *Germanic,* sister to *Britannic,* left Liverpool on her maiden voyage. Her advent left a ship spare and *Oceanic,* with *Gaelic* and *Belgic,* was chartered to the Occidental & Oriental SS Co for a service San Francisco-Hong Kong.

1876 Nov: *Britannic* took the westbound record from Inman's *City of Berlin* with 7 days 13 hours 11 mins at 15.43 kts average. The eastbound record was broken in February, by *Germanic,* but only until December when *Britannic* took

7 days 12 hours 47 mins at 15.94 kts.

1877 Apr: *Germanic* wrested the record from her sister in 7 days 11 hours 37 mins at 15.76 kts.

1881 *Arabic* (I) and *Coptic* entered service on the Pacific routes but made a few settling in voyages on the Atlantic before assuming their designated services.

1882 Guion's *Alaska* took the westbound transatlantic record from *Germanic.* Her average speed was 16.04 kts. 70 years later the *United States* would more than double this at 34.51 kts (and 3½ days).

1883 *Ionic* (I) and *Doric* (I) were built for the New Zealand joint service with Shaw, Savill & Albion, with the New Zealand Shipping Co acting as White Star's agents.

1885 *Belgic* (II) and *Gaelic* (II) built for the Pacific route San Francisco-Yokohama-Hong Kong.

Cunard's *Etruria* took the westbound record from Guion's *Alaska.*

1887 *Umbria,* sister of *Etruria,* became the record holder.

1888 White Star entered the cattle business with *Cufic* (I) and *Runic* (I), nicknamed the 'cattle boats'.

1889 *Teutonic* and her sister *Majestic* (I) (1890) were White Star's answer to the competition from Cunard's faster *Umbria* and *Etruria* and Inman's splendid *City of New York* and *City of Paris,* which in May and September took and retook the westbound records with a triumphant average speed of 20.01 kts.

1891 Aug: *Teutonic* did the passage from Queenstown (Cobh) to Sandy Hook (2,778 miles) in 5 days 16 hours 31 mins at an average speed of 20.35 kts. This was to be White Star's last record breaker and never again was one of their vessels to recover the Blue Riband. The livestock carriers *Nomadic* (I) and *Tauric* were delivered.

1892 *Naronic,* yet a further livestock ship, was delivered for what was to be but a very brief career. Her sister *Bovi* followed a month later.

1893 Feb 11: *Naronic* left Liverpool for New York and was never seen again.

Gothic was delivered for the New Zealand service.

1894 Jan: *Cevic,* a cattle-boat, entered service.

1895 The largest livestock carrier yet built was *Georgic* (I), built as a replacement for *Naronic*.

1897 *Delphic* (I) built for the New Zealand service. Norddeutscher Lloyd introduced their record breaker *Kaiser Wilhelm der Grosse* with her two pairs of funnels.

1898 The 13,000 ton *Cymric* started off as an even larger cattle-boat, designed to carry passengers as well as cattle. But public opinion was manifesting itself against this practice and *Cymric*'s cattle space was transformed into emigrant steerage accommodation.

1899 White Star launched their *Oceanic* (II). She was the first ship to exceed the almost legendary *Great Eastern* in length but not yet, be it noted, in tonnage. She also adhered to White Star's new policy of moderate speed allied to comfort plus punctuality and reliability. *Oceanic* was capable of a remarkably steady 19 kts which gave her a six-day crossing time from Queenstown to Sandy Hook. The record holder, *Kaiser Wilhelm der Grosse,* did the slightly longer journey from Cherbourg in 5 days 20 hrs. But in bad weather White Star ships slowed down, while the record breakers pursued schedules which drove them relentlessly through the most turbulent seas. This feature of personal comfort before speed paid handsome dividends to White Star over the next 30 years.

Afric, Medic and *Persic* were delivered for a new service Liverpool-Capetown-Sydney, carrying 320 passengers. *Britannic* (I) was used as a Boer War transport.

1900 *Runic* (II) and *Suevic* were the last and slightly different pair, as will be seen from the drawings, for the Australian route.

1901 Apr 4: *Celtic* (II) was launched as the largest ship in the world and the first to exceed 20,000 gross tons as well as *Great Eastern*'s own 18,915 grt. Despite this claim to fame *Celtic* had no intention of becoming a record contestant; her service speed was a lowly 16 kts.

1902 The shares of the company were acquired by the International Mercantile Marine Co together with those of five other lines: American, Atlantic

Transport, Dominion, Leyland and Red Star. White Star was undoubtedly the most prestigious unit of the group and initially the focal point of attention. In the middle of the year IMMC adopted their Steamship Amalgamation Plan which was to have far-reaching effects on the constituent lines. One immediate conclusion was that IMMC saw concentrating on the North Atlantic as its main role. Leyland Line had a strong Mediterranean trade which was siphoned off to form today's Ellerman Lines, and White Star were substantial operators to both New Zealand and Australia. In fact during the first 12 months of the IMMC takeover *Athenic, Corinthic* and *Ionic* (II) were delivered for the New Zealand trade. IMMC's North Atlantic policy led White Star to begin an even closer collaboration with Shaw Savill & Albion until their interchangeable ships were indistinguishable.

1903 Feb 11: *Cedric,* with her name pronounced 'seedric', a sister to *Celtic* (II), entered service.

July: At the end of her Boer War trooping duties *Britannic* (I) was, after some hesitation, sold for scrap.

IMMC had now declared their policy of giving to White Star the Liverpool-New York and Boston main trunk services, plus the Mediterranean route from New York, with Dominion having Canada and Atlantic Transport sailing out of London. It was further decreed that the best of the group's fleet should concentrate on New York. Thus to replace *Britannic* Atlantic Transport's new *Minnewaska* emerged as White Star's *Arabic* (II). From the Dominion Line came *Canopic* ex-*Commonwealth, Romanic* ex-*New England, Republic* (II) ex-*Columbus* and *Cretic* ex-*Mayflower*. In addition Leyland injected four of their vessels; *Victorian* and *Armenian* without changes of name, and *American,* which became *Cufic* (II), and *European,* which was renamed *Tropic* (II). In November *Romanic* took the first New York-Azores-Gibraltar-Naples-Genoa sailing in place of Dominion's *Vancouver* (II).

1904 *Baltic* (II) was commissioned. She became the largest ship afloat but only by the stratagem of lengthening her by 20 ft

(6.1 m) during construction. She sailed on June 29 from Liverpool-New York.

1905 *Germanic* was transferred to the Dominion Line and renamed *Ottawa*.

1907 *Adriatic* (II) arrived, last of the big four and sister to *Baltic* (II), and with her arrival this group of ships was transferred to a Southampton-Cherbourg-New York service. They were planned to be replaced by four very large ships over a period of five years.

1909 Two ships, *Alberta* and *Albany,* laid down for the Dominion Line's Canadian service, became White Star's *Laurentic* (I) and *Megantic*. This marked the inauguration of the 'White Star-Dominion Line Joint Service' which was to survive until 1926.

Jan 23-24: *Republic* (II) was lost en route New York-Naples by collision with Lloyd Italiano's *Florida*. Assistance, in the form of *Baltic* (II) was summoned by wireless telegraphy for the first time.

1910 *Zeeland* was transferred for just over a year to White Star to replace *Republic*.

1911 June 14: *Olympic* (II) left Southampton for New York. She was the largest ship in the world at 45,234 grt. Her speed was a modest 21 kts compared with Cunard's record-breaking *Mauretania*'s 26 kts. The arrival of *Olympic* released *Adriatic* (II) to return to the Liverpool station.

Aug 30: Red Star's *Samland* became *Belgic* (III) on her transfer to White Star.

1912 Jan: *Romantic* was sold to Allan Line and became *Scandinavian*.

Apr 10: *Titanic,* virtually a sister ship to *Olympic* (II), left Southampton on her maiden voyage for New York.

Apr 14: After striking an iceberg a long and fatal gash in the hull resulted in the loss of the ship and 1,503 lives in what was the worst disaster at sea yet.

Olympic was subsequently returned to Harland and Wolff and modified to accommodate safety precautions which included the installation of an inner skin to the hull. The regulations on lifeboats were also modified and *Olympic* emerged with a greatly increased number. To replace *Titanic* the ageing *Majestic* (I) was placed on the Southampton berth pending the arrival of *Britannic* (II), then under construction.

1913 Hamburg America Line's *Imperator* became the largest ship in the world. *Gothic* reverted to Red Star and to her prior name, *Gothland*. *Ceramic* entered the Australian service.

1914 *Vaderland* and *Zeeland* were transferred from Red Star to White Star to replace *Majestic* (I) on the Southampton route. They made their first voyages after the outbreak of the First World War. Construction on *Britannic* (II) temporarily ceased. *Cedric, Celtic* (II), *Oceanic* (II) and *Teutonic* were taken over for duties as armed merchant cruisers.

Sept 8: *Oceanic* was wrecked on the Shetlands.

Oct: *Lapland* transferred from Red Star to make good the absence of *Cedric* and *Celtic* from the Liverpool station.

1915 *Britannic* (II) was completed as a hospital ship. Because of their German-sounding names *Vaderland* became *Southland* and *Zeeland* was rechristened *Northland*.

June 28: *Armenian* sunk by *U-24* off Cornwall.

Aug 19: *Arabic* (II) sunk by *U-24* off Kinsale.

1916 Feb: The hospital ship *Britannic* (II) sank in the Aegean in Zea Channel. She is thought to have struck a mine.

Dec 10: The German raider *Moewe* captured and sank *Georgic* (I) 600 miles out from Cape Race.

Dec 14: *Russian* (ex-*Victorian)* torpedoed off Malta.

Cevic left the fleet for conversion to an oil tanker and became *Bayol*.

1917 Red Star Line had ordered their flagship *Belgenland* in 1913 and in 1917 she was completed as an enormous cargo ship and named *Belgic* (IV) for White Star management.

Jan 25: *Laurentic* (I) was sunk by two mines off Northern Ireland. The subsequent salvage of her bullion was a notable feat.

Feb 2: *Afric* sunk by torpedo.

Apr 7: Holland America's *Statendam* had been completed as *Justicia* with the intention of her being operated by Cunard, her name indicating that she was to fill the gap left by the sinking of

Lusitania, but in the event it was White Star that was able to muster a crew for her and to them she was allocated.
Aug 17: *Delphic* (I) was torpedoed 135 miles from Bishop's Rock.
Sept 4: *Southland* (ex-*Vaderland)* sunk clear of Tory Island.
1918 July 10: *Vedic* joined the fleet.
July 19: *Justicia* torpedoed by *U-64* off Skeryvore.
Sept: *Persic* torpedoed but not sunk.
1919 Mar 13: *Bardic,* ex-*War Priam,* placed on the Australian route.
July: *Canopic* and *Cretic* reopened the New York-Mediterranean service.
Sept: *Adriatic* and *Lapland* restarted the Southampton-Cherbourg-New York run.
1920 Jan: *Gallic* (II), ex-*War Argus,* was placed on the Australian cargo run.
July: *Olympic* (II), now an oil burner, returned to her Southampton station. *Lapland* returned to Red Star's Antwerp-Southampton-New York route. She in turn was replaced by the new *Pittsburgh.*
1921 Royal Mail began a service Southampton-New York with four steamers, *Orbita, Orca, Orduna* and the ex-German liner *Ohio,* a move which presaged the take-over of White Star five years later. *Belgic* (IV) was completed at Harland & Wolff as per her original 1914 design and became again Red Star's *Belgenland.*
Sept: *Arabic* (III), ex-Norddeutscher Lloyd's *Berlin,* replaced *Canopic* on the Mediterranean route. *Haverford* came on to the Liverpool-Philadelphia service for a year.
1922 *Bovic* became *Colonian* of Leyland. *Columbus* joined White Star as *Homeric,* but more important Hamburg America's giant *Bismarck,* the world's largest ship, was purchased and became the *Majestic* (II). *Vedic* and *Poland* (Red Star) began a joint emigrant service from Bremen to Canada. later *Canopic* and *Pittsburgh* (Red Star) took the route. *Poland* was operated by White Star for one summer season.
1923 *Doric* (II) was delivered for the Canadian services and *Regina* joined her from the Dominion Line.
1925 *Bardic* sold and replaced by *Delphic* (II). *Canopic* was broken up at Briton Ferry. *Pittsburgh* was transferred to Red Star.
1926 White Star's German services were terminated due to the re-emergence of the major German lines, Norddeutscher Lloyd and Hamburg America. With the withdrawal for scrapping of Dominion's *Canada* the 'White Star-Dominion Line Joint Service' ended and was replaced by 'White Star Line (Canadian Services)'.
Nov: The Royal Mail Steam Packet Co acquired the shares of the Oceanic Steam Navigation Co and IMMC thus parted with the White Star Line, which again became British-owned. Royal Mail's *Ohio* and *Orca* were transferred and renamed *Albertic* and *Calgaric. Zealandic* was sold to the Aberdeen Line and renamed *Mamilius.*
1927 Apr 22: *Albertic* was placed on the Liverpool-Quebec-Montreal route.
July: *Persic* broken up in Holland.
Nov: *Laurentic* (II) was commissioned.
1928 Jan: *Medic* was sold and converted into the whale factory ship *Hektoria,* and in May *Athenic* followed to become *Pelagos. Albertic* and *Megantic* opened up a service London-Havre-Southampton-Quebec-Montreal. For the New York service *Oceanic* (III) was laid down to replace *Homeric* but the gathering depression caused the cancellation of the contract.
Oct: *Suevic* followed *Medic* and *Athenic* in being converted into a whale factory ship, ending up as *Skytteren.*
Dec 10: *Celtic* (II) was wrecked on Roches Point near Cobh.
During 1928 Belfast and Glasgow were added as ports of call on the Canadian service out of Liverpool.
1929 *Regina* returned to the Red Star Line and was soon renamed *Westernland.*
1930 May: *Runic* (II) also became a whaler and took the name *New Sevilla.*
June: The new motor vessel *Britannic* (III) joined the Liverpool-New York service.
1931 *Corinthic* and *Arabic* (III) both went to the scrap-yard.
1932 Jan 11: *Cedric* sold for shipbreaking.
June: *Georgic* (II) joined her sister *Britannic* (III).
Nov: *Cufic* (II) went to Genoese breakers.

1933 Jan: *Baltic* (II) left on the long final voyage to Japanese breakers. She was later followed by *Megantic. Gallic* (II) and *Delphic* (II), however, were sold to the Clan Line for further trading. *Tropic* (II) was scrapped in Italy and *Albertic* was laid up and went to Osaka early in the following year.

1934 Feb: Agreement was finally reached between Cunard, White Star and the British Government for the formation of Cunard-White Star Ltd, of which Cunard held 62%. To look after the interests of the White Star shareholders the Oceanic Steam Navigation Realisation Co Ltd was formed. IMMC (by now in the form of the United States Lines) was one of the creditors. The new concern gave up any stake in the Australian services and *Ceramic* was disposed of to Shaw Savill and Albion. *Vedic* was sold for breaking up and White Star's contributions to the new company were *Homeric, Majestic* (II) and *Olympic* (II) on the Southampton-New York service, *Britannic* (III) and *Georgic* (II) on the Liverpool-New York route, and *Laurentic* (II) and *Doric* (II) on the Canadian berth together with the veteran *Adriatic* (II) which lasted only until the November, when she was broken up.

1935 *Olympic* (II) was withdrawn from service and scrapped. *Doric* (II) had the misfortune to collide with *Formigny* and was subsequently broken up along with *Calgaric.*

1936 *Majestic* (II) ended her days as HMS *Caledonia* at Rosyth whilst *Homeric* was dismantled round the corner at Inverkeithing.

1939 *Britannic* (III) and *Georgic* (II) both became troopships for the duration. *Laurentic* (II) had her main mast and after deckhouses removed and was converted into an armed merchant cruiser.

1940 Nov 3: *Laurentic* (II) was torpedoed by Otto Kretschmer in *U-99.*

1941 *Georgic* (II) was tremendously badly damaged by bombs at Suez but was painstakingly repaired and returned to service.

1947 Cunard purchased the outstanding 38% of Cunard-White Star Ltd.

1948 *Britannic* (III) returned to the North Atlantic complete with White Star funnels.

1949 Cunard took over all the activities of Cunard-White Star and White Star as a name disappeared, but the two remaining ships continued in White Star livery.

1956 Feb 1: *Georgic* (II) arrived at Faslane at the end of her career.

1960 Dec: *Britannic* (II), White Star's final vessel, arrived at Inverkeithing and with her demise ended one of the greatest-ever names in shipping.

Routes

Some of the terminating dates are approximate because services tended to fade rather than be ended at any specific time.

1872-1960 Liverpool-New York (later with Queenstown (Cobh) as a port of call), Liverpool-Boston/Philadelphia.

1899-1934 Liverpool-Melbourne-Sydney via the Cape.

1883-1926 Liverpool-New Zealand ports via the Cape.

1874-1914 London-New York (cargo).

1872-73 Liverpool-Valparaiso via Cape Horn.

1872-73 Liverpool-Suez-Calcutta.

1875-83 San Francisco-Yokohama-Hong Kong.

1888-1926 Livestock carrying.

1903-9 New York-Azores-Gibraltar-Naples-Genoa.

1907-34 Southampton-Cherbourg-New York.

1909-39 Liverpool-Belfast/Glasgow-Quebec-Montreal.

1922-26 Hamburg/Bremen-Quebec-Montreal.

1928-30 London-Havre-Southampton-Quebec-Montreal.

Livery

Funnel Bright buff with black top.
Hull Black with yellow band one strake down.
Uppers White, ventilators white, inside of cowls red.
Masts Funnel colour.
Lifeboats White.

Fleet index

Illustrated fleet list

1

1 ROYAL STANDARD

Bt 1863 Palmers Bros & Co, Jarrow; *T:*
2,033 g, 1,598 n. **Dim** 255 ft (77.72 m)
× 40 ft (12.19 m) × 27 ft 6 in (8.38 m).
Eng Sgl scr, auxiliary steam; 2 cyls.
H Iron, 2 decks, 5 holds; *Pass:* 40 1st,
800 steerage.

1863 Aug: Launched. Built for H. T.
Wilson & Chambers and operated by
them under the White Star flag.
Nov 23: Maiden voyage Liverpool-
Melbourne. Captain J. E. Allen (who
died during voyage).
1864 Apr 4: Hit iceberg 14 days
homeward from Melbourne. Repaired at
Rio de Janeiro. Captain G. H. Dowell.
1866 May 23: One voyage Liverpool-New
York.
Sept 27: Last steamer voyage to
Melbourne.
1867 Converted to sail after being sold to
Liverpool syndicate.
1869 Oct 10: Wrecked on coast of Brazil,
near Cape St Thomé.

2 SIRIUS

Bt 1865 C. W. Earle & Co, Hull; *T:*
620 g, 491 n. **Dim** 203 ft 6 in
(62.03 m) × 26 ft 1 in (7.95 m) × 16 ft
(4.87 m). **Eng** Sgl scr, compound; 2 cyls:
28 in (71.12 cm) and 51 in (129.54 cm);
Stroke: 39 in (99.06 cm); 205 NHP;
9 kts. **H** Iron, 1 deck.

1865 Feb: Launched. Built for H. T.
Wilson & Chambers for Mediterranean
service.
1866 Jan: Sold foreign. Renamed
Columbia.
1868 Purchased by Anchor Line.
Renamed *Scandinavia.*
1869 Mar: Opened Leith-Christiansand-
Christiania (Oslo)-Gothenburg feeder
service for Anchor's New York run.
Winter Mediterranean routes.
1872 Lengthened to 258 ft (78.64 m). *T:*
1,138 g.
1876 Engine re-compounded by D. & W.
Henderson, Glasgow.
1888 Aug: Sold Christopher Furness.
Renamed *Columbia.*
1890 Sold J. Meek. Renamed *Sirius.*
1893 Sold Olivier & Co, USA.
1894 Sold C. Nelson, Hawaii. Renamed
Kahului.
1897 Sold. Renamed *Cleveland.*
Registered San Francisco.
1900 Oct: Wrecked.

3-6

3 OCEANIC (I)

Bt 1871 Harland & Wolff, Belfast;
T: 3,707 g, 2,350 n. **Dim** 470 ft 4 in
(143.35 m) × 40 ft 10 in (12.46 m) × 31 ft
(9.44 m). **Eng** Sgl scr, compound; 4 cyls:
2 × 41 in (104.14 cm) and 2 × 78 in
(198.12 cm); *Stroke:* 60 in (152.4 cm);

00 NHP; 12 boilers, 24 furnaces; *Stm P:* 5 lb; 14½ kts; By Maudsley, Son & Field, London; Arranged in tandem so that one could operate in case of a breakdown in the other. **H** Iron, 1 deck, 0 watertight bulkheads, length to beam ratio 10:1 in place of the normal 8:1; *Coal:* 65 tons per day; *Pass:* 166 1st, ,000 3rd; *Crew:* 143.

The first class saloon, measuring 80 ft 24.38 m) × 40 ft (12.19 m), was midships and there were separate saloon chairs for each passenger. Every cabin had a port-hole and the ship had two bridal suites. Fares: Saloon £16.16s.0d ingle, £28.7s.0d return; Steerage 6.6s.0d.

870 Aug 27: Launched. Cost £120,000.
871 Feb 26: Arrived at Liverpool 'more like an Imperial yacht than a passenger essel'.
Mar 2: Maiden voyage Liverpool-New York. Commanded by Captain Digby Murray (later knighted). *Oceanic* carried only 64 passengers while Cunard's parallel sailing by *Calabria* took 300. Shortly after sailing she developed engine trouble due to overheated bearings and returned to Liverpool.
Mar 16: Voyage resumed.
872 *Oceanic* returned to Harland & Wolff and a turtle-decked fcsle was added, 72 ft (21.94 m). Extra boilers with extra bunker space were also installed.
875 Mar 11: Last sailing Liverpool-New York. Chartered to Occidental & Oriental SS Co of San Francisco for service San Francisco-Yokohama-Hong Kong.
882 Aug 22: Collided off the Golden Gate, San Francisco, with the coastal liner *City of Chester*. 16 lives lost.
895 May 17: Arrived Belfast for re-engining. After a survey the plan was abandoned. Sold for £8,000 for breaking up on the River Thames.

ATLANTIC

Details as *Oceanic (3)*.

870 Dec 1: Launched.
871 June 8: Maiden voyage Liverpool-New York.
873 Apr 1: On her 19th voyage *Atlantic* was wrecked off Meaghers Head, near Halifax, Nova Scotia, during heavy weather. She was commanded by Captain J. A. Williams. The passenger list comprised 28 saloon class, 577 (including 78 children) third class, and 184 steerage who had joined at Queenstown. The total on board was therefore 862, of whom 585 were drowned. Allegations were made of a coal shortage having caused the loss but these were denied.

5 BALTIC (I)

Details as *Oceanic (3)* except: *T:* 2,209 n.

1871 Mar 8: Launched as *Pacific* but renamed *Baltic* because of the superstition which prevailed following the loss of the Collins liner *Pacific* 15 years earlier.
Sept 14: Maiden voyage Liverpool-New York.
1873 Jan: gained the Blue Riband, crossing the Atlantic in 7 days 20 hours 9 minutes at an average speed of 15.09 kts.
1883 Chartered to the Inman Line, and again in 1885-86.
1888 Sold to the Holland America Line for £35,000 and renamed *Veendam*. Had been laid up in Birkenhead prior to the sale.
Nov 3: First voyage Rotterdam-New York.
1898 Feb 6: Struck a derelict in the North Atlantic and foundered, without loss of life.

6 REPUBLIC (I)

Details as *Oceanic (3)* except: *T:* 3,707 g, 2,187 n. **Eng** By G. Forrester & Co, Liverpool.

1871 July 4: Launched.
1872 Feb 1: Maiden voyage Liverpool-New York.
Oct 5: First voyage Liverpool-Bordeaux-Vigo-Lisbon-Rio de Janeiro-Montevideo-Valparaiso, then Chilean and Peruvian coastal resorts.
1885 Collided with Cunard Line's *Aurania*.
1888 Second class added.
1889 June: Sold for £35,000 to Holland America Line. Renamed *Maasdam*. Triple expansion engines fitted.
1890 Mar 15: Placed on Rotterdam-New York service.
1902 Sold to La Veloce, Italy. Renamed

Vittoria. Later renamed *Citta di Napoli,* same company.
1910 Broken up at Genoa.

7 ASIATIC (I)

Bt 1871 Thos Royden & Sons, Liverpool; *T:* 2,122 g. **Dim** 326 ft 5 in (99.49 m) × 35 ft 2 in (10.72 m) × 25 ft 7 in (7.8 m). **Eng** Sgl scr, compound; 2 cyls: 40 in (101.6 cm) and 80 in (203.2 cm); *Stroke:* 36 in (91.44 cm); 250 HP; *Stm P:* 70 lb; 12 kts; By Laird Bros, Birkenhead. **H** Iron, 1 deck; *Pass:* 10 1st.

1871 Purchased on the stocks. Placed in the Calcutta trade.
1873 Sold to African SS Co (Elder Dempster). Renamed *Ambriz.*
1893 In Elder Dempster service Liverpool-New Orleans. Reboilered.
1895 Still as *Ambriz* became coal hulk at Diego Suarez.
1903 Wrecked on coastal passage to Majunga.

8 TROPIC (I)

Details as *Asiatic (7).*

1871 Purchased on the stocks. Placed on the Calcutta trade from Liverpool.
1872 Nov 5: First voyage Liverpool-South American ports-Valparaiso.
1873 June 4: Last South American voyage. Sold. Became *Federico,* J. Serra y Font, Bilbao.
1886 Sold to Cia de Nav La Flecha, Bilbao. Same Name.
1904 Broken up at Lytham St Annes, Lancashire.

9-10

9 ADRIATIC (I)

Bt 1872 Harland & Wolff, Belfast; *T:* 3,888 g, 2,458 n. **Dim** 452 ft (137.77 m) oa, 437 ft 2 in (133.25 m) × 40 ft 10 in (12.45 m) × 31 ft (9.44 m). **Eng** Sgl scr, compound; 4 cyls: 2 × 41 in (104.14 cm) and 2 × 78 in (198.12 cm); *Stroke:* 60 in

(152.4 cm); 600 HP; 24 furnaces; *Stm P:* 65 lb; By Maudsley, Son & Field, London. **H** Iron, 2 decks, steam steering by Forester & Co, height of mainmast 150 ft (45.72 m); *Pass:* 50 1st, 50 2nd, 800 3rd.

This ship was fitted for gas, in place of candles and oil lamps, by Porter & Co of London. There were 30 jets in the saloon. The idea was a failure due to leaks caused by the workings of the vessel in a seaway.

1871 Oct 17: Launched.
1872 Mar 11: Maiden voyage Liverpool-New York.
May: Took the westbound record from Cunard's *Scotia.*
1874 Oct: Collided with Cunard's *Parthia.*
1875 Mar: Ran down and sank schooner *Columbus.*
Dec: Ran down and sank sailing vessel *Harvest Queen.*
1878 July 19: Ran down and sank brigantine *G.A. Pike* off Tuskar Rock. Five lost.
1888 Second class added.
1899 Feb 12: Went for breaking up at Preston, Lancs.

10 CELTIC (I)

Details as *Adriatic (9)* except: **Bt** 1872; *T:* 3,867 g, 2,439 n. **Eng** By G. Forrester & Co, Liverpool.

1872 Laid down as *Arctic* but renamed because of the loss of the Collins Line *Arctic.*
June 8: Launched as *Celtic.*
Oct 24: Maiden voyage Liverpool-New York.
1883 Jan: Towed into Liverpool by *Britannic (14)* with broken propeller shaft.
1887 May 19: Collided with *Britannic* in fog 300 miles west of Sandy Hook.
1893 Apr 6: Became *Amerika,* Thingvalla Line.
May 27: First voyage Copenhagen-New York. Danish flag.
1898 Broken up.

11 GAELIC (I)

Bt 1873 Harland & Wolff, Belfast; *T:* 2,685 g. **Dim** 370 ft (112.77 m) × 36 ft 4 in (11.07 m) × 27 ft 10 in (8.48 m). **Eng**

gl scr, compound inverted; 2 cyls: 47 in
119.38 cm) and 84 in (213.36 cm);
troke: 45 in (114.3 cm); 300 HP; *Stm P:*
5 lb; 12 kts; By builder. **H** Iron, 2
ecks; *Pass:* 40 saloon.

873 Acquired on the stocks for South
American service.
an 29: Maiden voyage Liverpool-
'alparaiso.
875 May 29: Chartered to Occidental &
Oriental SS Co for San Francisco-Japan
ervice.
883 Sold for £30,000 to Cia de Nav La
'lecha, Bilbao. Renamed *Hugo.*
896 Sept 24: Stranded on Terschelling
ands. Became a constructive loss.
Refloated and broken up in Amsterdam.

2 BELGIC (I)
Details as *Gaelic (11)* except: **Bt** 1874;
: 2,652 g, 1,716 n. **Eng** 350 HP; By
. Jack Rollo & Co, Liverpool.

874 Acquired for South American service.
Ran in consort with *Gaelic (11).*
875 San Francisco-Japan route for
Occidental & Oriental SS Co.
883 Sold. Became *Goefredo,* Portugal.
884 Wrecked River Mersey.

 13

3 TRAFFIC (I)
Bt 1873 Speakman, Runcorn, Cheshire;
: 155 g, 83 n. **Dim** 101 ft 9 in (31.01 m) ×
3 ft 7 in (7.19 m) × 9 ft 7 in (2.92 m).
Eng Sgl scr; 2 cyls: 20 in (50.8 cm);
troke: 20 in (50.8 cm); *Stm P:* 12 lb;
kts; By W. P. Galton, Manchester.
H Wood.

872 Sept 22: Launched.
873 Baggage tender at Liverpool.
896 Sold. Became *Traffic,* Liverpool
ighterage Co.
919 Engine removed. Converted to dumb
·arge.
941 May 5: Sunk in air attack on
.iverpool. Salved. Returned to service.
955 Broken up on Tranmere Beach,
Mersey.

4 BRITANNIC (I)
Bt 1874 Harland & Wolff, Belfast;

 *14-15*

T: 5,004 g, 3,152 n. **Dim** 455 ft (138.68 m)
× 45 ft 2 in (13.77 m) × 33 ft 8 in (10.26 m).
Eng Sgl scr, 2 sets tandem compound; 2 × 2
cyls: 48 in (121.92 cm) and 83 in (210.82 cm);
Stroke: 60 in (152.4 cm); 4,900 IHP, 760 HP;
8 boilers, 32 furnaces; *Stm P:* 70 lb; 16 kts;
By Maudsley, Son & Field, Lambeth. **H** Iron,
2 decks, 8 watertight compartments; *Pass:*
220 1st, 1,500 3rd; *Crew:* 135.

*Initially fitted with adjustable propeller
shaft which could be raised or lowered to
increase thrust. Not successful in practice
and removed after nine voyages.*

1873 Designed by Sir E. J. Harland.
Engines designed by Mr Charles Sells. Cost
£200,000. Laid down as *Hellenic* but
renamed before launch.
1874 Feb 3: Launched.
June 25: Maiden voyage Liverpool-New
York. Held westbound and eastbound
records, both passages in less than 7½ days.
1881 Collided with and sank *Julia* off
Belfast.
July: Stranded in fog at Kilmore, Ireland.
1887 May 19: Collided with *Celtic (10)* in
fog 200 miles off Sandy Hook. Returned to
New York.
1889 Collided with and sank brig *Czarawitz*
in Liverpool Bay.
1899 Aug 16: Final transatlantic voyage,
then became Boer War troopship as
Transport No 62.
1900 Nov 12: Painted white for voyage to
represent Great Britain at inauguration of
Australian Commonwealth.
1902 Oct: Sent to Belfast for re-engining
and reboiling but condemned after
examination.
1903 July: Sold for £11,500 for scrapping.
Aug 11: Left in tow for breaking up at
Hamburg.

15 GERMANIC
Details as *Britannic (14)* except:
T: 5,008 g, 3,150 n.

15a

1874 July 15: Launched. Designed by Sir
E. J. Harland. Cost £200,000.

1875 May 30: Maiden voyage Liverpool-
New York.

1876 Feb: Record westbound passage 7 days
15 hours 17 minutes. Averaged 15.79 kts.

1877 Apr: Record eastbound passage 7 days
11 hours 37 minutes. Averaged 15.76 kts.

1895 Triple expansion engine fitted by
Harland & Wolff. Modernised. Funnels
heightened, extra deck *(15a)*. First ship to
use Liverpool floating landing stage.

1899 Feb 16: Capsized at her New York
berth due to weight of ice on decks.

1903 Sept 23: Last voyage for White Star.

1904 Became *Germanic* (American Line) on
Southampton-New York berth. Sold to
Dominion Line and converted to emigrants
only.

1905 Jan 5: Renamed *Ottawa.* Liverpool-
Quebec-Montreal service.

1909 Laid up.

1910 Sold to Government of Turkey as
transport. Renamed *Gul Djemal.*

1915 May 3: Torpedoed by HMS *E.14* in
Sea of Marmora. Raised.

1920-21 Transferred to Ottoman-America
Line emigrant service. Mediterranean and
Black Sea ports to New York. Later Black
Sea only.

1928 Name revised to *Gulcemal* (Turkiye).

1949 Store ship at Istanbul.

1950 Floating hotel.

Oct 29: Left Istanbul in tow for Messina for
breaking up.

16 **ARABIC** (I)

Bt 1881 Harland & Wolff, Belfast;
T: 4,368 g, 2,788 n. **Dim** 430 ft 2 in

(131.12 m) × 42 ft 2 in (12.85 m) ×
31 ft 6 in (9.6 m) **Eng** Sgl scr, compound;
4 cyls: 2 × 32 in (81.28 cm) and 2 × 71 in
(180.34 cm); *Stroke:* 60 in (152.4 cm);
550 HP; *Stm P:* 65 lb; 13 kts; By J. Jack
& Co, Liverpool. **H** Steel, 2 decks;
Pass: 180 1st, 900 3rd.

1881 Apr 30: Launched as *Asiatic* (II).
Handed over as *Arabic.* Built to operate for
Occidental & Oriental SS, San Francisco.
Sept 10: Maiden voyage Liverpool-New
York. Made three round voyages on this
route.

1882 Transferred to Pacific routes.

1887-88 Liverpool-New York service.
Second class berths added.

1888-89 Returned to Occidental & Oriental
services.

1890 Sold to Holland America Line for
£65,000. Renamed *Spaarndam.*
Mar 29: First voyage Rotterdam-New York.

1901 Aug: Broken up at Preston,
Lancashire.

17 **COPTIC**

Details as *Arabic (16)* except: *T:* 4,367 g,
2,789 n.

1881 Aug 10: Launched. Built for San
Francisco-Yokohama-Hong Kong service
of Occidental & Oriental.
Nov 16: Maiden voyage Liverpool-New
York.

1882 Mar: Took up Pacific station.

1884 Refrigeration plant fitted.
Liverpool-New Zealand service.

1895 Returned to Occidental & Oriental
services.

1906 Sold to Pacific Mail. Renamed *Persia.*

16-19

Pacific services.
1915 Sold to Toyo Kisen Kaisha. Renamed *Persia Maru*. Same routes.
1924 Laid up at Yokohama.
1926 Broken up at Osaka.

18 IONIC (I)

Bt 1883 Harland & Wolff, Belfast; *T:* 4,753 g, 3,070 n. **Dim** 439 ft 10 in (134.06 m) oa, 427 ft 7 in (130.33 m) × 44 ft 2 in (13.46 m) × 28 ft 10 in (8.79 m). **Eng** Sgl scr, 2 compound tandem; 4 cyls: 2 × 32 in (81.28 cm) and 2 × 71 in (180.34 cm); *Stroke:* 60 in (152.4 cm); 500 HP; *Stm P:* 70 lb; By builder. **H** Steel, 3 decks; *Pass:* 70 1st.

1883 Jan 10: Launched. Chartered to New Zealand Shipping Co.
Apr 26: Maiden voyage London-Wellington. Record 43 days 22 hours 5 minutes.
1884 Sailed for New Zealand on White Star-Shaw Savill joint service.
1894 Extensive refit. Externally yards were removed and funnel heightened. Quad exp engine; Cyls: 28 in (71.12 cm), 40 in (101.6 cm), 56½ in (143.51 cm) and 80 in (203.2 cm); 16 kts.
1899 Dec: Last voyage London-New Zealand with troops' horses for Boer War.
1900 Apr: Chartered Spanish Government for the repatriation of troops after their war with the USA.
Sold for £47,000 Aberdeen Line. Renamed *Sophocles*.
1908 Apr: Broken up at Morecambe, Lancashire.

19 DORIC (I)

Details as *Ionic (18)* except: *T:* 4,784 g, 3,071 n. **Dim** 440 ft 10 in (134.37 m) oa.

1883 Mar 10: Launched. Built for New Zealand trade. Chartered to New Zealand Shipping Co.
July 26: Maiden voyage London-Wellington.
1885 Served on White Star-Shaw Savill joint service.
1896 Chartered to Occidental & Oriental SS Co for San Francisco-Yokohama-Hong Kong service.
1906 Sold to Pacific Mail SS Co. Renamed *Asia*.
1911 Apr 23: Wrecked in fog on Hea Chu

Island near Wenchow, South China, en route Hong Kong-San Francisco. No lives lost.

20-21

20 BELGIC (II)

Bt 1885 Harland & Wolff, Belfast; *T:* 4,212 g, 2,695 n. **Dim** 420 ft 4 in (128.12 m) × 42 ft 5 in (12.93 m) × 29 ft 4 in (8.94 m). **Eng** Sgl scr, 2 tandem compound; 4 cyls: 2 × 43 in (109.22 cm) and 2 × 86 in (218.44 cm); *Stroke:* 60 in (152.4 cm); 500 HP; *Stm P:* 70 lb; 14 kts; By builder.

1885 Jan 3: Launched.
July 7: Handed over. Built to operate under charter to Occidental & Oriental on their Pacific route.
Nov 28: Maiden voyage San Francisco-Yokohama-Hong Kong.
1898 Final San Francisco service.
1899 Sold to Atlantic Transport Line. Renamed *Mohawk*.
Sept 7: First voyage London-New York.
Dec: Became Boer War transport.
1903 Broken up at Garston, Mersey.

21 GAELIC (II)

Details as *Belgic (20)* except: *T:* 4,206 g, 2,691 n.

1885 Feb 28: Launched. Built to operate under charter to Occidental & Oriental SS Co.
Nov 10: Maiden voyage San Francisco-Yokohama-Hong Kong.
1904 Apr: Final San Francisco voyage.
1905 Sold to Pacific Steam Nav Co, Liverpool. Renamed *Callao*.
1907 Broken up at Briton Ferry.

22 TEUTONIC

Bt 1889 Harland & Wolff, Belfast; *T:* 9,984 g, 4,269 n. **Dim** 582 ft (177.39 m) oa, 565 ft 8 in (172.42 m) × 57 ft 8 in (17.58 m) × 39 ft 5 in (12.01 m). **Eng** Tw scr, overlapping, tpl exp; 2 × 3 cyls: 43 in (109.22 cm), 68 in (172.72 cm) and 110 in

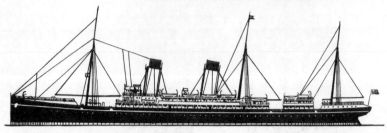

22-23

(279.4 cm); *Stroke:* 60 in (152.4 cm); 1,875 NHP; 20 kts; **H** Siemens-Martin Steel, 3 decks, 13 bulkheads; *Pass:* 300 1st all in separate cabins, 190 2nd, 1,000 3rd.

Designed for conversion to armed merchant cruiser. Funnels placed far enough apart to enable the saloon to be placed in between.

1889 Jan 19: Launched. Designed by the Hon A. H. Carlisle who was also responsible for *Olympic* and *Titanic*. Handed over in July.
Aug 1: Attended Spithead Naval Review as the first armed merchant cruiser. Inspected by the Kaiser and the Prince of Wales.
Aug 7: Maiden voyage Liverpool-Queenstown-New York.
1890 Aug: Took westbound record 5 days 19 hours 5 minutes, then 5 days 16 hours 31 minutes at 20.35 kts.
1897 Took part in Diamond Jubilee Naval Review at Spithead.
1898 Collided at New York with US Transport *Berlin*.
1907 Sailings transferred to Southampton.
1913 Masts reduced to two. First class discontinued.
1914 Sept 20: Became armed merchant cruiser, 10th Cruiser Squadron.
1918 Troopship UK-Egypt service.
1921 Laid up in Cowes Roads. Sold and broken up at Emden, Germany.

23 MAJESTIC (I)

Details as *Teutonic (22)* except: **Bt** 1890; *T:* 9,965 g, 4,270 n.

1889 June 29: Launched.
1890 Mar 22: Handed over.

Apr 2: Maiden voyage Liverpool-Queenstown-New York.
1891 July: Took westbound record 5 days 18 hours 8 minutes at 20.1 kts average.
1899 Boer War transport.
1902-3 Refitted at Belfast. Masts reduced to two; a new mainmast was fitted and the mizzen removed.
1907 Terminal transferred to Southampton.
1911 Became the reserve vessel.
1912 Returned to service after loss of *Titanic*.
1914 May 5: Arrived for breaking up at Morecambe.

24 CUFIC (I)

Bt 1888 Harland & Wolff, Belfast; *T:* 4,639 g, 3,122 n. **Dim** 430 ft 8 in (131.27 m) × 45 ft 2 in (13.77 m) × 30 ft (9.14 m). **Eng** Sgl scr, tpl exp; 3 cyls: 27 in (68.58 cm), 44½ in (113.03 cm) and 74 in (187.96 cm); *Stroke:* 60 in (152.4 cm); 424 NHP; 13 kts; By builder. **H** 2 decks, fcsle 48 ft (14.63 m), bridge 80 ft (24.38 m), poop 48 ft (14.63 m).

1888 Oct 10: Launched. White Star's first livestock carrier, 1,000 head. The first shipment of live cattle across the Atlantic was in July 1874 by *European* (H. N. Hughes & Nephew).
Dec 8: Maiden voyage Liverpool-New York.
1896 Chartered to Cia Transatlantica as *Nuestra Senora de Guadaloupe*.
1898 Returned to White Star. Renamed *Cufic*.
1901 Sold to Dominion Line. Renamed *Manxman*.

24-25

1915 Sold to R. Lawrence, Montreal. Same name.
1917 British Government service.
1919 Sold to Universal Transport Co Ltd, New York, still as *Manxman*.
Dec 18: Foundered in North Atlantic. 45 lives lost.

25 RUNIC (I)

Details as *Cufic (24)* except: **Bt** 1889; *T:* 4,833 g, 3,126 n.

1889 Feb 21: Maiden voyage Liverpool-New York. Livestock carrier, 1,000 head.
1895 May: Sold to West India & Pacific SS Co. Renamed *Tampican*.
1899 Dec 31: Transferred with rest of fleet to F. Leyland & Co. Same name. Reboilered. Liverpool-New York.
1912 Sold to H. E. Moss, Liverpool.
1913 Sold to South Pacific Whaling Co, Oslo (then Christiania). Renamed *Imo*. Converted to whale-oil tanker for Antarctic whaling service.
1917 Dec 6: 8.45 am. Collided with *Mont Blanc* (CGT) at Halifax, Nova Scotia. 17 minutes later the French ship's cargo of ammunition exploded. The blast was felt 120 miles away and obliterated the suburb of Richmond. Casualties totalled 1,500 killed, 2,000 missing, and 8,000 injured. 3,000 houses were destroyed.
1918 Became Norwegian *Guvernoren*.
1921 Oct 26: Left Sandfjord.
Nov 30: Grounded in fog 20 miles from Port Stanley. Lost.

26 NOMADIC (I)

Bt 1891 Harland & Wolff, Belfast; *T:* 5,749 g, 3,678 n. **Dim** 460 ft 9 in (140.44 m) × 49 ft 1 in (14.96 m) × 30 ft 10 in (9.4 m). **Eng** Tw scr, overlapping, tpl exp; 2 × 3 cyls: 22½ in (57.15 cm), 36½ in (92.71 cm) and 60 in (152.4 cm); *Stroke:* 48 in (121.92 cm); 499 NHP; 13 kts; By builder. **H** Steel, 10 watertight compartments; *Coal:* 50 tons per day; *Crew:* 45.

1891 Feb 11: Launched. Built as livestock carrier.
Apr 4: Completed.
Apr 24: Maiden voyage Liverpool-New York.
1899 Store ship and horse transport during Boer War as *Transport No 34*.
1903 Sold to Dominion Line. Initially served as *Nomadic*.
1904 Renamed *Cornishman*.
1921 Transferred to Frederick Leyland. Same name.
1926 Mar: Sold for scrapping for £10,500.
Mar 12: Arrived Hayle, Cornwall, for breaking up.

27 TAURIC

Details as *Nomadic (26)* except: *T:* 5,728 g, 3,665 n.

1891 Mar 12: Launched. Built as livestock carrier.
May 16: Maiden voyage Liverpool-New York.
1903 Sold to Dominion Line.
Mar 12: First voyage Liverpool-Portland as *Tauric*.
1904 Renamed *Welshman*.
1921 Transferred to Frederick Leyland. Same name.
1929 Dec: Broken up at Bo'ness, Firth of Forth.

28 NARONIC

Bt 1892 Harland & Wolff, Belfast; *T:* 6,594 g, 4,225 n. **Dim** 470 ft 1 in (143.26 m) × 53 ft 1 in (16.18 m) × 23 ft 10 in (7.26 m). **Eng** Tw scr, 2 tpl exp; 2 × 3 cyls: 22½ in (57.15 cm), 36½ in (92.71 cm) and 60 in (152.4 cm); *Stroke:* 48 in (121.92 cm); 499 NHP; 13 kts. **H** Steel, 3 decks; *Fuel:* 50 tons per day; *Pass:* 150 1st.

1892 May 26: Launched.
July 15: Maiden voyage Liverpool-New York. Livestock carrier. Cost £121,685.
1893 Feb 11: Left Liverpool for New York and disappeared. 74 lives lost. Two empty *Naronic* lifeboats were found 40N 47.37W.

26-27

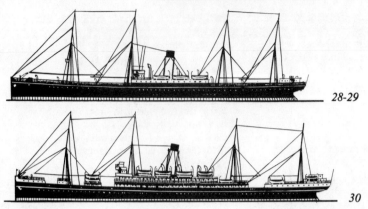

28-29

30

The Board of Trade enquiry did not establish how the vessel was lost. It was her seventh voyage.

29 BOVIC

Details as *Naronic (28)* except:
T: 6,583 g, 4,230 n.

1892 June 28: Launched. Built as livestock carrier.
Aug 22: Maiden voyage Liverpool-New York.
1914 Manchester-New York sailings introduced. Masts lopped to funnel height to pass under Manchester Ship Canal bridges.
1917-19 Requisitioned for Government service.
1922 Jan 16: Transferred to Frederick Leyland. Renamed *Colonian*.
1928 Broken up at Rotterdam.

30 GOTHIC

Bt 1893 Harland & Wolff, Belfast;
T: 7,755 g, 4,975 n. **Dim** 490 ft 8 in (149.56 m) × 53 ft 2 in (16.21 m) × 33 ft 5 in (10.19 m). **Eng** Tw scr, 2 tpl exp; 2 × 3 cyls: 26 in (66.04 cm), 42½ in (107.95 cm) and 70 in (177.8 cm); *Stroke:*51 in (129.54 cm); 700 NHP; 14 kts; **H** Steel, 3 decks, fcsle 61 ft (18.58 m), poop 58 ft (17.68 m); *Pass:* 104 1st, 114 3rd, raised to 250 in 1906.

1892 June 28: Launched.
1893 Dec 30: Maiden voyage London-Wellington, New Zealand. Largest ship to enter Port of London. Broke record.
1906 Wool cargo caught fire. Beached and flooded at Cattewater, Plymouth.
1907 Refitted after fire. Transferred to Red Star Line as *Gothland*. Antwerp-

Philadelphia service.
1911-13 Returned to White Star. Renamed *Gothic*. Australian and New Zealand run.
1913 Back to Red Star Line. Reverted to *Gothland*.
1914 June: Ashore on Gunner Rocks, Scilly Isles. Repaired Southampton.
1921 May: Took a turn for White Star as *Gothland*.
1925 Mar: Last voyage for Red Star Antwerp-Philadelphia.
1926 Jan: Sold for £16,000 for breaking up. Arrived Bo'ness, Firth of Forth.

31

31 MAGNETIC

Bt 1891 Harland & Wolff, Belfast;
T: 619 g, 122 n. **Dim** 170 ft 6 in (51.97 m) × 32 ft (9.75 m) × 16 ft (4.88 m). **Eng** Tw scr, 2 tpl exp; 2 × 3 cyls: 17 in (43.18 cm), 27 in (68.58 cm) and 43 in (109.22 cm); *Stroke:* 28 in (71.12 cm); 195 NHP; 13½ kts; By builder. **H** Steel, 1 deck; *Pass:* 1,200 plus their baggage.

1891 June 6: Delivered. Passenger tender at Liverpool. Fresh water replenisher. Fitted for towing and used as company tug.
1897 June: Accompanied *Teutonic (22)* as tender to Diamond Jubilee Spithead Naval Review.
1925 Oct 3: Caught fire Liverpool. Beached at Tranmere. Restored.
1932 Dec: Sold to Alexandra Towing Co. Renamed *Ryde*.
1934 Stationed Llandudno for coastal excursions.
1935 Aug: Broken up at Port Glasgow.

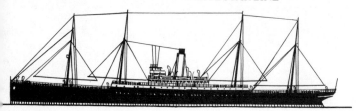

32

32 CEVIC

Bt 1894 Harland & Wolff, Belfast;
T: 8,301 g, 5,403 n. **Dim** 523 ft (159.41 m) oa,
500 ft (152.4 m) × 60 ft (18.29 m) × 38 ft
(11.58 m). **Eng** Tw scr, 2 tpl exp; 2 × 3 cyls:
23½ in (59.69 cm), 38½ in (97.79 cm) and
64 in (162.56 cm); *Stroke:* 48 in (121.92 cm);
568 NHP; 13 kts; By builder. **H** Steel,
2 decks.

1893 Sept 25: Launched.
1894 Jan: Maiden voyage Liverpool-New
York. Livestock carrier.
1908 Australian service via Cape and
experimentally via Suez.
1914 Dec 1: Converted into dummy of
battleship HMS *Queen Mary.*
1915 Apr: Patrolled off New York after
the raider *Kronprinz Wilhelm* had applied
for internment by seeking refuge in New
York harbour.
1916 Converted to oil tanker with circular
tanks. Fleet auxiliary. Renamed *Bayol.*
1917 Transferred to Shipping Controller.
Renamed *Bayleaf.* Managed by Lane &
McAndrews.
1920 June 9: Sold to Anglo-Saxon
Petroleum Co (Shell). Renamed *Pyrula.*
Became depot ship at New York.
1925 Became Shell hulk at Curacao. Same
name.
1933 July 25: Sold for breaking up at
Genoa.

33 PONTIC

Bt 1894 Harland & Wolff, Belfast;
T: 395 g, 210 n. **Dim** 150 ft 6 in (45.87 m) ×
26 ft 1 in (7.95 m) × 11 ft 1in (3.38 m). **Eng**
Sgl scr, tpl exp; 3 cyls: 13 in (33.02 cm),

33

21 in (53.34 cm) and 34 in (86.36 cm);
Stroke: 24 in (60.96 cm); 6 RHP; 10½ kts;
H Steel, 1 deck; Water boat: 11,000 gallons
(50,000 litres).

1894 Feb 3: Launched. Baggage tender at
Liverpool.
Apr 13: Completed. Captain Ponting.
1919 Oct 9: Sold to Rea Towing Co,
Liverpool, for £5,100. Used for similar
duties on the River Mersey.
1925 Jan 23: Sold to John Donaldson,
Glasgow, for breaking up. Reprieved and
used as sand ballast carrier.
1930 Broken up Clyde.

34 GEORGIC (I)

Bt 1895 Harland & Wolff, Belfast;
T: 10,077 g, 6,570 n. **Dim** 558 ft 8 in
(170.28 m) × 60 ft 4 in (18.39 m) × 36 ft
(10.97 m). **Eng** Tw scr, tpl exp; 2 × 3 cyls:
24 in (60.96 cm), 39½ in (100.33 cm) and
65½ in (166.37 cm); *Stroke:* 51 in
(129.54 cm); 612 NHP; 13 kts; **H** Steel, 3
decks, fcsle 104 ft (31.7 m), bridge 229 ft
(69.8 m), poop 68 ft (20.73 m); *Pass:* 10 1st.

1895 June 22: Launched. Built as
replacement for *Naronic (28).*
Aug 16: Maiden voyage Liverpool-New
York. The largest livestock carrier yet built.
1916 Dec 10: Captured and sunk by
German raider *Moewe* 600 miles off Cape
Race. She was carrying 1,200 horses and
10,000 barrels of oil. Philadelphia-Brest.

34

36

35 DELPHIC (I)

Bt 1897 Harland & Wolff, Belfast;
T: 8,273 g, 5,401 n. **Dim** 475 ft 10 in
(145.03 m) × 55 ft 3 in (16.84 m) ×
35 ft 10 in (10.92 m). **Eng** Tw scr, tpl exp;
2 × 3 cyls: 19 in (48.26 cm), 31 in (78.74 cm)
and 52 in (132.08 cm); *Stroke:* 48 in
(121.92 cm); 375 NHP; 12 kts; By builder.
H Steel, 3 decks, bridge 125 ft (38.1 m);
Pass: 21 1st.

1897 Jan 5: Launched.
June 17: Maiden voyage Liverpool-New
York.
Aug: Transferred to the London berth for
New Zealand service.
1899 Boer War transport.
1917 Aug 17: Torpedoed and sunk 135
miles from Bishop's Rock. Five lives lost.

36 CYMRIC

Bt 1898 Harland & Wolff, Belfast;
T: 13,096 g, 8,201 n. **Dim** 585 ft 6 in
(178.46 m) × 64 ft 4 in (19.61 m) × 37 ft 10 in
(11.53 m). **Eng** Tw scr, quad exp; 2 × 4
cyls: 25½ in (64.77 cm), 36½ in (92.71 cm),
53 in (134.62 cm) and 75½ in (191.77 cm);
Stroke: 54 in (137.16 cm); 838 NHP;
14½ kts; By builder. **H** Steel, 3 decks,
fcsle 104 ft (31.7 m), bridge 257 ft (78.33 m),
poop 67 ft (20.42 m); *Pass:* 258 1st,
1,160 3rd.

Originally intended as an enlarged Georgic
*(34) she was altered during building to omit
the cattle space. This was extended and
turned into steerage class. The concept of
carrying passengers and cattle together was*
by now becoming unpopular.

1897 Oct 12: Launched.
1898 Feb 11: Maiden voyage Liverpool-
New York.
1899 Boer War transport. Two voyages.
1903 Liverpool-Boston service.
1916 May 8: Torpedoed and sunk by *U-20*
140 miles WNW of Fastnet Rock. Five lives
lost.

37 OCEANIC (II)

Bt 1899 Harland & Wolff, Belfast;
T: 17,274 g, 6,996 n. **Dim** 705 ft
(214.88 m) oa, 685 ft 8 in (209 m) ×
68 ft 4 in (20.83 m) × 44 ft 6 in (13.56 m).
Eng Tw scr, 2 tpl exp; 2 × 4 cyls: 47½ in
(120.65 cm), 79 in (200.66 cm) and 2 × 93 in
(236.22 cm); *Stroke:* 72 in (182.88 cm);
28,000 IHP; 15 dbl ended boilers; *Stm P:*
192 lb; 19 kts; **H** Steel, fcsle 130 ft (39.62 m),
poop 75 ft (22.86 m); *Coal:* 480 tons per day;
Pass: 410 1st, 300 2nd.

First vessel to exceed length of Great
Eastern, *but not her tonnage.*

1899 Jan 14: Launched.
Sept 6: Maiden voyage Liverpool-New
York. Largest liner in the world.
1901 Sept: Collided with and sank steamer
Kincora in fog off Tuskar Rock. Seven lives
lost.
1905 Mutiny aboard.
1907 Transferred to Southampton terminal.
1914 Commissioned as armed merchant
cruiser, 10th Cruiser Squadron.
Sept 8: Wrecked on Foula Island,
Shetlands.

37-38

38 OLYMPIC (I)

This ship was to have been a sister of *Oceanic (37)*. However, the death of T. H. Ismay in 1899 led to the abandonment of the project.

39 AFRIC

Bt 1899 Harland & Wolff, Belfast; *T:* 11,948 g, 7,804 n, 15,400 dwt. **Dim** 565 ft (172.21 m) oa, 550 ft 2 in (167.69 m) × 63 ft 4 in (19.3 m) × 39 ft 10 in (12.14 m). **Eng** Tw scr, quad exp; 2 × 4 cyls: 22 in (55.88 cm), 31½ in (80.01 cm), 46 in (116.84 cm), and 67 in (170.18 cm); *Stroke:* 51 in (129.45 cm); 642 NHP, 5,400 IHP; 4 dbl and 1 sgl ended boilers; 13½ kts; By builder. **H** Steel, 3 decks, 7 holds, 21 derricks, fcsle 55 ft (16.76 m), bridge 107 ft (32.61 m), poop 57 ft (17.37 m); *Coal:* 3,000 tons at 80 tons per day; *Cargo:* 12,500 cu ft (354 cu m) refrig for 100,000 carcasses; *Pass:* 320 cabin, 1920: 260 cabin.

1898 Nov 16: Launched for Australian routes.
1899 Feb 8: Maiden voyage Liverpool-New York. After maiden voyage she returned to Harland & Wolff for improvements.
Sept 9: First voyage Liverpool-Capetown-Sydney. Carried troops for Boer War.
1917 Feb 2: Torpedoed and sunk SSW of Eddystone Lighthouse by *UC66*. 22 dead.

40 MEDIC

Details as *Afric (39)* except: *T:* 11,985 g, 7,825 n.

1898 Dec 15: Launched.

1899 Aug 3: Maiden voyage Liverpool-Sydney via Capetown. On her return voyage carried Australian men and horses to South Africa for Boer War service.
1917 Oct 27: Operated under the Liner Requisition Scheme until Mar 26, 1919.
1928 Jan: Sold to N. Bugge, Tonsberg, and converted by H. C. Grayson, Birkenhead, into whale factory ship. Renamed *Hektoria*.
1942 Sept 11: Torpedoed and sunk by *U-608* in North Atlantic whilst in use as a British Ministry of War Transport oil tanker.

41 PERSIC

Details as *Afric (39)* except: *T:* 11,973 g, 7,819 n.

1899 Sept 7: Launched.
Nov 16: Handed over.
Dec 7: Maiden voyage Liverpool-Sydney via Capetown. Carried troops for Boer War. Her rudder broke at Capetown and the voyage was delayed.
1900 Oct 26: Rescued crew of burning sailing schooner *Madura*.
1917-19 Operated under Liner Requisition Scheme.
1918 Sept: Torpedoed off Sicily but reached port. Repaired.
1927 July 7: Sold for £25,000 and left Mersey for breaking up at Hendrik Ido Ambacht, Holland.

42 RUNIC (II)

Details as *Afric (39)* except: *T:* 12,482 g, 8,097 n.
Hull superstructure layout differed from that of Afric.

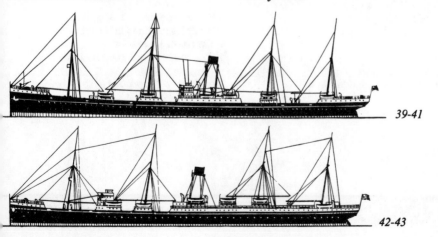

39-41

42-43

195

1900 Oct 25: Launched.
Dec 22: Handed over.
1901 Jan 19: Maiden voyage Liverpool-
Sydney via the Cape.
Nov 25: Towed disabled *Dunottar Castle*
(Union Castle) into Dakar.
1917-19 Operated under the Liner
Requisition Scheme.
1928 Nov 3: Collided with HMS *London*
off Gourock Pier, Clyde.
1929 Dec: Last White Star voyage.
1930 May: Sold to Chr Salveson's Sevilla
Whaling Co and converted into a whale
factory ship. Renamed *New Sevilla*.
1940 Oct 20: Torpedoed and sunk by
U-138 off Galway, Ireland. Two lives lost.

43 SUEVIC

Details as *Afric (39)* except: *T:* 12,531 g,
8,026 n.

1900 Dec 8: Launched.
1901 Mar 23: Maiden voyage Liverpool-
Sydney via the Cape of Good Hope.
1907 Mar 17: Stranded in fog on Stag Rock,
near the Lizard, homeward bound. Wreck
cut in two and stern towed off. A new 212 ft
(64 m) fore part was built at Harland &
Wolff and joined up. *Suevic* was out of
service for 18 months at Southampton. The
ship surgery on *Suevic* was, at the time, the
largest rebuilding operation ever
undertaken. Virtually half the ship was
renewed. Had it not been for the excellent
condition of the undamaged stern and
engines the ship would have been scrapped.
1917-19 Operated under Liner Requisition
Scheme.
1920 Feb 2: Resumed commercial sailings to
Australia. *Pass:* 266 2nd.
1928 Oct: Sold to Yngar Hvistendahl
Finnvhal A/S, Tonsberg, for £35,000.
Converted at Kiel to whale factory ship.
Renamed *Skytteren*.
1940 Apr: Interned at Gothenburg.

1942 Apr 1: Scuttled at Maseskjaer,
Sweden, when intercepted by German Navy
during an attempt by the crew to escape to
Britain.

44 CELTIC (II)

Bt 1901 Harland & Wolff, Belfast;
T: 21,035 g, 13,449 n. **Dim** 700 ft
(213.36 m) oa, 680 ft 10 in (207.52 m) ×
75 ft 4 in (22.96 m) × 44 ft 1 in (13.44 m).
Eng Tw scr, quad exp; 2 × 4 cyls: 33 in
(83.82 cm), 47½ in (120.65 cm), 68½ in
(173.99 cm) and 98 in (248.92 cm);
Stroke: 63 in (160.02 cm); 1,524 NHP;
16 kts; By builder. **H** Steel, 4 decks, fcsle
105 ft (32 m), bridge 334 ft (101.8 m),
poop 81 ft (24.69 m); *Coal:* 280 tons per
day; *Cargo:* 17,000 tons; *Pass:* 347 1st,
160 2nd, 2,350 3rd.

The first vessel to exceed Great Eastern *of
1860 in tonnage, 20,904 g, against 18,915 g.
By accepting 3 kts less speed than the 19 kts
of which she was capable she operated on
only 260 tons of coal per day and was
therefore highly economical.*
This class of four, comprising Celtic,
Cedric (45), Baltic (46) *and* Adriatic
(47), *was built for comfort not speed. It was
company policy to leave speed to Cunard
and Norddeutscher Lloyd.*
1901 Apr 4: Launched.
July 11: Handed over.
July 26: Maiden voyage Liverpool-New
York.
Feb: Took a five-week New York-
Mediterranean cruise.
1914 Oct 20: Commissioned as an armed
merchant cruiser.
1916 Jan: Became a troopship.
1917 Feb 15: Mined in the Irish Sea.
Repaired at Liverpool.
1917-19 Operated under the Liner
Requisition Scheme.
1918 Mar 2: Torpedoed in the Irish Sea. Six

44-45

lives lost. Repaired at Belfast.
1920 Jan: Resumed commercial service
Liverpool-New York.
1925 Apr 21: Collided in the Irish Sea with
Hampshire Coast (Coast Lines). *Celtic*
suffered only superficial damage and
Hampshire Coast made port safely.
1927 Jan 29: Collided off Long Island with
the US *Anaconda* (US Shipping Board).
1928 Cabin class only, 2,500.
Dec 10: When entering Cobh harbour in a
gale *Celtic* was driven ashore on Roches
Point. Remained ashore and eventually
became a total loss. The wreck was sold to
Petersen and Albeck, Copenhagen, and
dismantled as she lay.
1933 Demolition completed.

45 CEDRIC

Details as *Celtic (44)* except: **Bt** 1903;
T: 21,035 g, 13,520 n.
Name pronounced 'Seedric'.

1902 Aug 21: Launched.
1903 Jan 31: Handed over.
Feb 11: Maiden voyage Liverpool-New
York.
1914-15 Armed merchant cruiser in the 10th
Cruiser Squadron.
1915-16 Troopship.
1917-19 Taken over by the Government
under the Liner Requisition Scheme.
1918 Jan 29: Collided at the Mersey Bar
with the *Montreal* of Canadian Pacific,
which sank.
1931 Sept 5: Last voyage Liverpool-New
York.
1932 Jan 11: Sold for £22,150 to Wards,
Inverkeithing. Left for breaking up.

46 BALTIC (II)

Bt 1904 Harland & Wolff, Belfast;
T: 23,876 g, 15,295 n, 19,710 dwt. **Dim**
729 ft (222.2 m) oa, 709 ft 2 in (216.15 m) ×
75 ft 7 in (23.04 m) × 52 ft 7 in (16.03 m);

Dft:37 ft 4 in (11.38 m). **Eng** Tw scr, quad
exp; 2 × 4 cyls: 33 in (83.82 cm), 47½ in
(120.65 cm), 68½ in (173.99 cm) and 98 in
(248.92 cm); *Stroke:* 63 in (160.02 cm);
1,524 NHP; 16 kts. **H** Steel, 4 decks and
shelter deck; *Pass:* 365 1st, 160 2nd, 2,000
3rd; *Crew:* 560.

1903 Nov 21: Launched. In order to make
her the largest ship she was lengthened by
20 ft (6.1 m) during construction, which
added 2,840 grt. This made her slower in
service and she had to be modified.
1904 June 29: Maiden voyage Liverpool-
New York.
1909 Jan: Rescued survivors of collision
between *Republic (49)* and *Florida* (Lloyd
Italiano).
1914-18 Troopship.
1929 Dec 6: Rescued crew of schooner
Northern Lights off Newfoundland.
1932 Sept 17: Last voyage Liverpool-New
York. Laid up.
1933 Jan: Sold.
Feb 17: Left Liverpool for Osaka, Japan,
for breaking up.

47 ADRIATIC (II)

Details as *Baltic (46)* except: **Bt** 1907;
T: 24,541 g, 15,438 n. **Eng** cyls: 35½ in
(90.17 cm), 51 in (129.54 cm), 73½ in
(186.69 cm) and 104 in (264.16 cm).

1906 Sept 20: Launched on the same day as
Cunard's *Mauretania*.
1907 May 8: Maiden voyage Liverpool-New
York.
Terminal transferred to Southampton.
1911 Reverted to Liverpool-New York
route.
1917-18 Operated under the Liner
Requisition Scheme.
1919 Sept 3: Resumed commercial service
Southampton-New York.
Pass: 400 1st, 460 2nd, 1,320 3rd.
1922 Aug 11: Three killed in coal bunker

48

explosion at her Liverpool berth.
1933 Cruising.
Aug 31: Laid up.
1934 Mar 24: Last voyage Liverpool-New York, then cruising ex-Liverpool.
Nov: Sold for £48,000.
Dec 19: Left Liverpool for Osaka, Japan.
1935 Mar 5: Arrived Osaka for scrapping.

48 CRETIC

Bt 1902 Hawthorn Leslie & Co, Hebburn; *T:* 13,507 g, 8,663 n. **Dim** 582 ft (177.39 m) × 60 ft 3 in (18.36 m) × 38 ft 4 in (11.68 m). **Eng** Tw scr, tpl exp; 2 × 3 cyls: 28 in (71.12 cm), 47½ in (120.65 cm) and 80 in (203.2 cm); *Stroke:* 60 in (152.4 cm); 1,269 NHP; 3 dbl and 3 sgl ended boilers; 15 kts; By builder. **H** Steel, 3 decks; *Pass:* 260 1st, 250 2nd, 1,000 3rd.

1902 Built as *Hanoverian* for Frederick Leyland & Co.
July 19: Maiden voyage Liverpool-Boston.
1903 Transferred to Dominion Line. Renamed *Mayflower*.
Apr 9: First voyage Liverpool-Boston. Transferred to White Star. Renamed *Cretic*.
Nov 26: First voyage Liverpool-Boston as *Cretic*.
1904 New York-Mediterranean service.
1917-19 Operated under Liner Requisition Scheme.
1923 Sold to Frederick Leyland. Renamed *Devonian*.
1927-28 Operated by Red Star Line, Antwerp-Southampton-New York.
1928 Mar 9: Last voyage. Laid up.
1929 Broken up at Bo'ness, Firth of Forth.

49 REPUBLIC (II)

Bt 1903 Harland & Wolff, Belfast; *T:* 15,378 g, 9,742 n. **Dim** 570 ft (173.74 m) × 67 ft 8 in (20.62 m) × 24 ft (7.32 m). **Eng** Tw scr, quad exp; 2 × 4 cyls: 29 in (73.66 cm), 41½ in (105.41 cm), 61 in (154.94 cm) and 87 in (220.98 cm); *Stroke:* 60 in (152.4 cm); 1,180 NHP; 16 kts. **H** Steel, 5 decks; *Pass:* 1,200.

1903 Feb 26: Launched. Built as *Columbus* for Dominion Line.
Oct 1: Maiden voyage Liverpool-Boston. Transferred to White Star. Renamed *Republic*.
1909 New York-Mediterranean service.
Jan 23: 5.40 am. Collided 175 miles from Nantucket Lightship, outward bound New York-Naples, with *Florida* (Lloyd Italiano), inbound to New York. *Republic* sank next day. Four lives were lost. Wireless was used for the first time from a vessel in distress. All the passengers (250 first class and 211 steerage) were transferred to the *Florida*. Later the crew followed. A small salvage party remained aboard, under Captain Sealby, until 8 pm Jan 24 when *Republic* was abandoned and sank.

50 ROMANIC

Bt 1898 Harland & Wolff, Belfast; *T:* 11,394 g, 7,416 n. **Dim** 550 ft 4 in (167.74 m) × 59 ft 4 in (18.08 m) × 35 ft 10 in (10.92 m). **Eng** Tw scr, tpl exp; 2 × 4 cyls: 30 in (76.2 cm), 50 in (127 cm) and 2 × 58 in (147.32 cm); *Stroke:* 54 in (139.16 cm); 985 NHP; 15 kts. **H** Steel, 3 decks; *Pass:* 1,090.

49

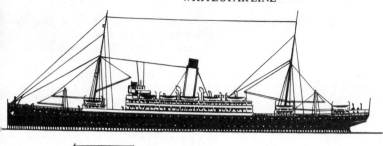

50

51

1898 Apr 7: Launched. Built as *New England* for Dominion Line.
June 30: Maiden voyage Liverpool-Boston.
1903 USA-Mediterranean service.
1912 Jan: Sold to Allan Line. Renamed *Scandinavian*.
1915 The Allan Line was taken over by Canadian Pacific.
1922 Laid up.
1923 July: Sold for breaking up. Scrapped at Hamburg.

51 ARABIC (II)

Bt 1903 Harland & Wolff, Belfast; *T:* 15,801 g, 10,062 n. **Dim** 600 ft 8 in (183.08 m) × 65 ft 6 in (19.96 m) × 47 ft 7 in (14.5 m). **Eng** Tw scr, quad exp; 2 × 4 cyls: 30 in (76.2 cm), 43 in (109.22 cm), 63 in (160.02 cm) and 89 in (226.06 cm); *Stroke:* 60 in (152.4 cm); 16 kts. **H** Steel, 4 decks; *Pass:* 200 1st, 200 2nd, 1,000 3rd.

1902 Laid down as *Minnewaska* for Atlantic Transport Line.
1903 Dec 18: Launched as *Arabic*.
June 26: Maiden voyage Liverpool-New York.
1905 Liverpool-Boston service. Alternated thereafter with New York at approx two-

yearly intervals.
1913 First class omitted.
1915 Aug 19: Torpedoed and sunk by *U-24* off Old Head of Kinsale, Ireland. 44 lives lost.

52 ATHENIC

Bt 1902 Harland & Wolff, Belfast; *T:* 12,234 g, 7,833 n. **Dim** 500 ft 4 in (152.5 m) × 63 ft 4 in (19.28 m) × 45 ft (13.72 m). **Eng** Tw scr, quad exp; 2 × 4 cyls: 22 in (55.88 cm), 31 ½ in (80.01 cm), 46 in (116.84 cm) and 68 in (172.72 cm); *Stroke:* 48 in (121.92 cm); 641 NHP; 14 kts. **H** Steel, 4 decks; *Pass:* 121 1st, 117 2nd, 450 3rd.

1901 Aug 17: Launched.
1902 Feb 14: Maiden voyage London-Wellington, New Zealand.
1917-19 Operated under the Liner Requisition Scheme.
1920 May 3: Rescued passengers from *Munamar* (Munsen Line) in Pacific.
1927 Oct: Last voyage London-Wellington.
1928 May: Sold for £33,000 to Brunn & Von de Lippe (Hvalfangerselskapet Pelagos A/S), Tonsberg. Converted at South Bank on Tees to whale factory ship. Renamed *Pelagos*.

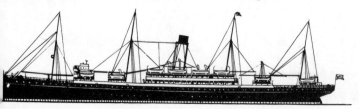

52-54

1962 Sold to S. F. Brunn and broken up at Hamburg.

53 CORINTHIC

Details as *Athenic (52)* except:
T: 12,367 g, 7,832 n.

1902 Apr 10: Launched.
Nov 20: Maiden voyage London-Wellington.
1917-19 Operated under the Liner Requisition Scheme.
1931 Aug: Last voyage to New Zealand.
Dec 16: Sold for £10,250 to Hughes Bolckow for scrapping at Blyth.

54 IONIC (II)

Details as *Athenic (52)* except:
T: 12,352 g, 7,826 n.

1903 May 22: Launched. Maiden voyage London-Wellington.
1917-19 Operated under the Liner Requisition Scheme.
1927 Rescued the crew of the fishing vessel *Daisy*.
1932 Transferred to Shaw Savill & Albion when Cunard took over the North Atlantic services.
1936 Dec: Last voyage to New Zealand.
1937 Jan: Sold for £31,500 for breaking up in Japan.

55 VICTORIAN

Bt 1895 Harland & Wolff, Belfast;
T: 8,825 g, 5,753 n. **Dim** 512 ft 6 in (156.21 m) × 59 ft 3 in (18.06 m) × 35 ft (10.67 m). **Eng** Sgl scr, tpl exp; 3 cyls: 31 in (78.74 cm), 52 in (132.08 cm) and 86 in (218.44 cm); *Stroke:* 66 in (167.64 cm); 718 NHP; 3 dbl and 2 sgl ended boilers; *Stm P:* 190 lb; 13 kts; By builder. **H** Steel, 3 decks, fcsle 109 ft (33.22 m), bridge 208 ft (63.4 m), poop 59 ft (17.98 m); *Pass:* 60 2nd.

1895 Built for Frederick Leyland & Co (illustrated in Leyland section, entry *49*).

Sept 7: Maiden voyage Liverpool-Boston.
1899-1902 Boer War transport.
1903 Transferred to White Star Line. Liverpool-New York.
1904 White Star cargo service.
1914 Renamed *Russian*.
1916 Dec 14: Torpedoed and sunk off Malta.

56 ARMENIAN

Details as *Victorian (55)* except:
T: 8,825 g, 5,754 n.

1895 Built for Frederick Leyland & Co.
Sept 28: Maiden voyage Liverpool-Boston.
1899-1902 Boer War transport.
1903 May: Transferred to White Star Line.
1904 White Star cargo service.
1915 June 28: Torpedoed and sunk by *U-24* off Trevose Head, Cornwall. She was captured by *U-24,* and the crew were allowed to abandon ship before the submarine torpedoed her.

57 CUFIC (II)

Bt 1895 Harland & Wolff, Belfast;
T: 8,249 g, 5,444 n. **Dim** 475 ft 10 in (145.03 m) × 55 ft 2 in (16.81 m) × 35 ft 10 in (10.92 m). **Eng** Tw scr, tpl exp; 2 × 3 cyls: 19 in (48.26 cm), 31 in (78.74 cm) and 52 in (132.08 cm); *Stroke:* 48 in (121.92 cm); 375 NHP; 11 kts; By builder. **H** Steel, 3 decks, bridge 95 ft (28.96 m).

1895 Aug 8: Launched. Built as *American* for West India & Pacific SS Co.
Oct 9: Maiden voyage Liverpool-New Orleans.
1898 Chartered to Atlantic Transport Line.
1900 Jan 1: Sold to Frederick Leyland & Co as *American*. Became Boer War transport.
1904 Sold to White Star. Renamed *Cufic* (II).
May 21: First voyage Liverpool-Sydney.
1914 War service as transport. Armed.
1917-19 Operated under Liner Requisition Scheme.
1919-23 Reverted to Australian trade.

55-56

1923 Dec: Sold to G. Lombardo for scrapping at Genoa.
1924 Jan 25: Sold to Soc Anon Ligure di Nav a Vapore, Genoa. Renamed *Antartico*.
1927 Sold to Bozzo & Mortola. Renamed *Maria Giulia*.
1930 Apr: Laid up for sale.
1932 Nov: Sold and broken up at Genoa.

58 TROPIC (II)

Details as *Cufic (57)* except: **Bt** 1896; *T:* 8,262 g, 5,412 n.

1896 Built as *European* for West India & Pacific SS Co.
July 9: Maiden voyage Liverpool-New Orleans.
1900 Jan 1: Sold to Frederick Leyland & Co. Taken over as Boer War transport.
1904 Sold to White Star. Renamed *Tropic* (II). Australian run.
1908 Dec 12: Collided with coaster *Wyoming* off Skerries.
1917-19 Operated under Liner Requisition Scheme.
1919 Reverted to Australian services.
1923 Sold to Ditta L. Pittaluga as *Tropic*.
1924 Sold to Soc Anon Ligure di Nav a Vapore. Renamed *Artico*.
1927 Sold back to Pittaluga and renamed *Transilvania*.
1933 Broken up at Genoa.

59 GALLIC (I)

Bt 1894 John Scott & Co, Kinghorn; *T:* 461 g, 185 n. **Dim** 150 ft (45.72 m) × 28 ft 2 in (8.59 m) × 10 ft 2 in (12.25 m). **Eng** Pad, compound; 4 cyls: 2 × 22 in (55.88 cm) and 2 × 40 in (101.6 cm); *Stroke:* 48 in (121.92 cm); 177 NHP; By builder. **H** Steel, 1 deck; *Pass:* 1,200 and their baggage.

1894 Built for Corporation of Birkenhead as Mersey ferry *Birkenhead* (III). Their last paddler.
1907 Mar: Sold to White Star. Renamed *Gallic*. Stationed at Cherbourg as tender pending the completion of *Nomadic (66)* and *Traffic (67)*. This followed the opening of the Southampton terminal.
1913 Broken up at Garston, River Mersey.

60 CANOPIC

Bt 1900 Harland & Wolff, Belfast; *T:* 12,268 g, 7,712 n. **Dim** 578 ft 4 in (176.28 m) × 59 ft 4 in (18.08 m) × 35 ft 9 in (10.9 m). **Eng** Tw scr, tpl exp; 2 × 4 cyls: 29½ in (74.93 cm), 50 in (127 cm) and 2 × 58 in (147.32 cm); *Stroke:* 54 in (137.16 cm); 988 NHP; 16 kts; By builder. **H** Steel, 3 decks; *Pass:* 250 1st, 250 2nd, 800 3rd.

1900 May 31: Launched. Built as *Commonwealth* for Dominion Line.
Oct 4: Maiden voyage Liverpool-Boston.
1903 Sold to White Star and renamed *Canopic*.
Jan 14: First voyage Liverpool-Boston.
1904 Transferred to New York-Mediterranean service.
1917-19 Operated under Liner Requisition Scheme.
1922 May 13: First voyage Liverpool-Quebec-Montreal.
Nov: On Bremen-Southampton-Halifax berth, later Hamburg.
1925 Broken up at Briton Ferry.

61 LAURENTIC (I)

Bt 1908 Harland & Wolff, Belfast; *T:* 14,892 g, 9,255 n. **Dim** 550 ft 4 in (167.74 m) × 67 ft 3 in (20.5 m) × 41 ft 2 in (12.55 m). **Eng** Tpl scr, 2 tpl exp and 1 LP turbine; 2 × 4 cyls: 30 in (76.2 cm), 46 in (116.84 cm) and 2 × 53 in (134.62 cm); 4 cyls to each tpl exp eng driving outer shafts plus one LP turbine connected to

59

60

61-62

centre shaft; *Stroke:* 54 in (137.16 cm);
1,180 NHP; 17 kts; By builder; Steam
turbine by J. Brown & Co, Greenock.
H Steel, 3 decks; *Pass:* 230 1st, 430 2nd,
1,000 3rd.

1908 Sept 9: Launched. Laid down as
Alberta for Dominion Line but launched as
Laurentic.
1909 Apr 29: Maiden voyage Liverpool-
Quebec-Montreal.
1911 Held the record for Canadian route,
return voyage time of 13 days 4 hours.
1914 Became Canadian Government
transport.
1917 Jan 25: Hit two mines off Northern
Ireland near Lough Swilley en route
Liverpool-Halifax with £5 million gold
bullion aboard. Capsized and sank in 120 ft
of water with loss of 354 lives out of 475
aboard. Later £4,958,000 of the gold was
recovered by salvage, considered to be a
brilliant feat on the part of Naval divers
under Commander G. C. Damant.
1924 Finally only 25 out of 3,211 bars of
gold were not recovered after 5,000 dives at
a cost of only £128,000.

62 MEGANTIC

Details as *Laurentic (61)* except: *T:*14,878 g,
9,183 n. **Eng** Tw scr, propulsion by
2 conventional quad exp; 2 × 4 cyls: 29 in
(73.66 cm), 42 in (106.68 cm), 61 in
(154.94 cm) and 87 in (220.98 cm); *Stroke:*
60 in (152.4 cm); 1,180 NHP.

1908 Laid down as *Albany* for Dominion
Line.
Dec 10: Launched as *Megantic.*
1909 June 17: Maiden voyage Liverpool-
New York.
1914-17 Troopship.
1917-19 Operated under Liner Requisition
Scheme.
1919 Returned to Canadian service.
1924 Converted to cabin class only.
1927 Trooping service to China.
1928 On London berth.

1931 Liverpool-Quebec-Montreal route.
July: Laid up in Rothesay Bay.
1933 Feb: Left for Osaka for breaking up.

63 ZEELAND

Bt 1901 John Brown, Clydebank;
T: 11,905 g, 7,511 n. **Dim** 561 ft 7 in
(171.17 m) × 60 ft 2 in (18.34 m) × 38 ft 2 in
(11.63 m). **Eng** Tw scr, quad exp; 2 × 4 cyls:
31 in (78.74 cm), 44 in (111.76 cm), 62 in
(157.48 cm) and 88 in (223.52 cm);
Stroke: 54 in (137.16 cm); 1,627 NHP;
8 sgl ended boilers; *Stm P:* 100 lb; 15 kts;
By builder. **H** Steel, 3 decks, fcsle 84 ft
(25.6 m), bridge 215 ft (65.53 m), poop
49 ft (14.93 m); *Pass:* 342 1st, 194 2nd,
626 3rd.

1900 Nov 24: Launched.
1901 Built for Red Star Line (illustrated in
Red Star section, entry *15*).
Apr 13: Maiden voyage Antwerp-New
York.
1910 Apr 11: Transferred to White Star's
Liverpool-Boston route to replace *Republic
(49).*
1911 Sept 14: Returned to Red Star.
1914 Sept: Back to White Star. Liverpool-
New York then Canadian route.
1915 Renamed *Northland.* Used as
troopship.
1920 Aug: Resumed Red Star sailings
Antwerp-Southampton-New York and
renamed *Zeeland.*
1927 Sold to Atlantic Transport Line.
Renamed *Minnesota.*
1930 Broken up at T. Ward, Inverkeithing,
Firth of Forth.

64 OLYMPIC (II)

Bt 1911 Harland & Wolff, Belfast;
T: 45,234 g, 20,847 n. **Dim** 825 ft 6 in
(259.84 m) × 92 ft 6 in (28.19 m) × 59 ft 6 in
(18.13 m), keel to bridge 104 ft (31.7 m),
keel to funnel top 175 ft (53.34 m). **Eng** Tpl
scr, 2 tpl exp and 1 LP turbine; 2 × 4 cyls:
54 in (137.16 cm), 84 in (213.36 cm) and

2 × 97 in (246.38 cm); *Stroke:* 75 in (190.5 cm); 6,906 RHP; 21 kts; By builder. **H** Steel, 5 full decks, fcsle 127 ft (38.71 m), bridge 540 ft (164.59 m), poop 76 ft (23.16 m); *Pass:* 735 1st, 675 2nd, 1,030 3rd. *Drawing appears on page 206.*

1908 Dec 16: Laid down.
1910 Oct 20: Launched.
1911 June 14: Maiden voyage Southampton-New York.
Sept 20: Collided with HMS *Hawke* in Solent. *Olympic* blamed.
1912-13 Returned to Harland & Wolff for six months for safety rebuilding after the loss of *Titanic (70)*. New tonnage 46,439 g.
1914 Oct: Attempted, unsuccessfully, to tow the mined battleship HMS *Audacious* to port.
1915 Trooping duties.
1918 May 12: Rammed and sank *U-130* near the Lizard.
1920 Refitted and converted to oil burning. June 25: Resumed service Southampton-New York.
1924 Mar 22: When leaving New York collided with Furness-Bermuda Line's *Fort St George.*
1928 Second class renamed tourist class.
1934 May 16: Rammed and sank Nantucket Lightship in fog. Eight lives lost on lightship.
Taken over by Cunard-White Star following the merger of the two companies.
1935 Mar 27: Last voyage Southampton-New York then laid up at Southampton.
Sept: Sold for breaking up at Jarrow to relieve unemployment.
1937 Sept: Hulk towed to Inverkeithing, Firth of Forth, for final demolition.

65 BELGIC (III)

Bt 1903 New York Shipbuilding Corporation, Camden, New Jersey; *T:* 9,748 g, 7,393 n. **Dim** 490 ft 5 in (149.48 m) × 58 ft 2 in (17.73 m) × 39 ft 5 in (12.01 m). **Eng** Tw scr, tpl exp; 2 × 3 cyls: 25 in

(63.5 cm), 42½ in (107.95 cm) and 72 in (182.88 cm); *Stroke:* 48 in (121.92 cm); 997 NHP; 2 dbl and 2 sgl ended boilers; *Stm P:* 200 lb; 14 kts; By builder. **H** Steel, 3 decks and shelter deck, bridge 128 ft (39.01 m)

1903 Built as *Mississippi* for Atlantic Transport Line.
1906 Transferred to Red Star Line. Renamed *Samland.* Placed on Antwerp-New York run.
1911 Aug 30: Transferred to White Star. Renamed *Belgic.* Operated on Australian service. *T:* 10,151 g.
1913 Reverted to Red Star. Renamed *Samland.* Antwerp-New York.
1931 Broken up at Ghent, Belgium.

66

66 NOMADIC (II)

Bt 1911 Harland & Wolff, Belfast; *T:* 1,273 g, 806 n. **Dim** 220ft 8 in (67.26 m) × 37 ft 1 in (11.3 m) × 12 ft 5 in (3.78 m). **Eng** Tw scr, compound; 2 × 2 cyls: 13½ in (34.29 cm) and 27 in (68.58 cm); *Stroke:* 18 in (45.72 cm); 52 NHP; 12 kts. **H** Steel, 2 decks; *Pass:* 1,200 and their baggage.

1911 Apr 25: Launched. Tender based at Cherbourg. For operating and crewing purposes registered in the name of Geo Aug Laniece.
1927 Transferred to Cie Cherbougeoise de Transbordement, Paris. Same name.
1934 Sold to Soc Cherbourgeoise de Remorquage et de Sauvetage, Cherbourg. Renamed *Ingenieur Minard.* (Black funnel, red band).
1940-45 War service in England.
1945 Returned to Cherbourg.
1968 Sold. Broken up.

67 TRAFFIC (II)

Bt 1911 Harland & Wolff, Belfast; *T:* 675 g.

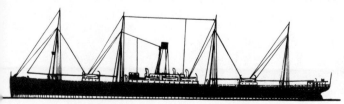

65

67

Dim 175 ft 7 in (53.52 m) × 35 ft 1 in
(10.69 m) × 12 ft 4 in (3.76 m). **Eng** Tw
scr, compound; 2 × 2 cyls: 12 in (30.48 cm)
and 24 in (60.96 cm); *Stroke:* 15 in
(38.1 cm); 36 NHP; 12 kts; By builder. **H**
Steel, 2 decks; *Pass:* 1,200 and their baggage.

1911 Apr 27: Launched.
May 27: Handed over. Stationed at
Cherbourg as a tender. Registered in the
name of Geo Aug Laniece.
1927 Ownership transferred to Compagnie
Cherbourgeoise de Transbordement, Paris.
1934 Sold to Soc Cherbourgeoise de
Remorquage et de Sauvetage and renamed
Ingenieur Riebell.
1940 June: Scuttled at Cherbourg. Raised
by the Germans.
1941 Jan 17: Sunk in German Naval service
during action in Channel.

68 CERAMIC

Bt 1913 Harland & Wolff, Belfast;
T: 18,495 g, 11,729 n. **Dim** 655 ft 1in
(199.67 m) × 69 ft 5 in (21.16 m) × 43 ft 8 in
(13.31 m). **Eng** Tpl scr, 2 tpl exp and LP
turbine on centre shaft; 2 × 4 cyls: 26½ in
(67.31 cm), 42 in (106.68 cm) and 2 × 47½ in
(120.65 cm); *Stroke:* 51 in (129.54 cm);
1,400 NHP; 15½ kts; By builder. **H** Steel,
3 decks, bridge 371 ft (113.08 m); *Pass:*
820 cabin.

1912 Dec 11: Launched.
1913 July 24: Maiden voyage Liverpool-
Australia.

1914-17 Trooping.
1917-19 Operated under Liner Requisition
Scheme.
1934 Transferred to Shaw Savill & Albion
when the White Star Line merged with
Cunard.
1936 Modernised. External appearance
slightly changed.
1940 Feb: Troopship.
1942 Dec 6: Torpedoed and sunk by *U-515*
west of Azores on passage Liverpool-South
Africa-Australia. 655 lives lost. One
survivor picked up by *U-515.*

69 ZEALANDIC

Bt 1911 Harland & Wolff, Belfast; *T:* 8,090 g,
5,172 n. **Dim** 477 ft 6 in (145.52 m) × 63 ft 1 in
(19.23 m) × 31 ft 6 in (9.6 m). **Eng** Tw scr,
quad exp; 4 cyls: 22 in (55.88 cm), 31½ in
(80.01 cm), 46 in (116.84 cm) and 65½ in
(166.37 cm); *Stroke:* 48 in (121.92 cm);
596 NHP; 13 kts; By builder. **H** Steel, fcsle
81 ft (24.69 m), bridge 221 ft (67.36 m),
poop 40 ft (12.19 m).

1911 June 29: Launched.
Oct 30: Maiden voyage Liverpool-
Wellington.
1913 Jan 22: Left New Zealand with a
record wool cargo for London.
Chartered by Western Australian
Government as emigrant carrier.
1917-19 Operated under Liner Requisition
Scheme.
1923 Took disabled sailing ship *Garthsnaid*
into Melbourne in tow.
1926 June: Sold to Aberdeen Line.
Renamed *Mamilius.*

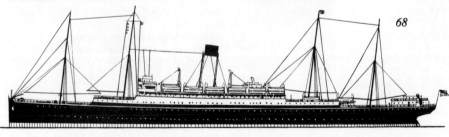

68

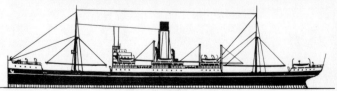

69

1932 Sold to Shaw Savill & Albion. Renamed *Mamari.*
1939 Sold to Admiralty. Converted into dummy version of aircraft carrier HMS *Hermes.*
1941 June 4: Beached and lost near Cromer after air attack.

70 TITANIC

Bt 1912 Harland & Wolff, Belfast; *T:* 46,329 g. **Dim** 825 ft 6 in (259.84 m) × 92 ft 6 in (28.19 m) × 59 ft 6 in (18.13 m). **Eng** Tpl scr, 2 sets with LP turbine to centre shaft; 2 × 4 cyls: 54 in (137.16 cm), 84 in (213.36 cm) and 2 × 97 in (246.38 cm); *Stroke:* 75 in (190.5 cm); 6,900 NHP; 21 kts; By builder. **H** Fcsle 130 ft (39.62 m) bridge 560 ft (170.69 m), poop 76 ft (23.16 m); *Pass:* 905 1st, 564 2nd, 1,134 3rd; *Crew:* 900.

1911 May 31: Launched.
1912 Apr 2: Handed over.
Apr 10: Maiden voyage Southampton-Cherbourg-Cobh-New York. Commanded by Captain Smith. 1,316 passengers.
Apr 14: 11.40 pm. *Titanic* struck an iceberg with a glancing blow which opened up a 300 ft gash spanning five watertight bulkheads. Her design called for her to float with any 4 flooded. Though there were 2,208 people aboard lifeboats were available for only 1,178, which met the Board of Trade requirements of the time. There were, however, over 3,000 life-jackets and 48 lifebuoys, but the water was freezingly cold.
Apr 15: 12.05 am. The lifeboats were swung out. The 'CQD' signal was sent out.
12.45 am. Radio Officer Phillips changed the signal to SOS, the new distress signal. It was the first time it had been used.
Cunard's *Carpathia* signalled she was coming at full speed, but only eight miles away the lights of a still unidentified ship could be seen by *Titanic*. This ship rendered no assistance and sailed on. (At the time Leyland's *Californian* under Captain S. Lord was accused, but other sources name a sealer, *Samson.*)
1.10 am. *Titanic* began settling by the head.
1.27 am. The engine rooms flooded and all motive power failed.
1.50 am. The last lifeboat pulled away, many of them having left only partly filled because so many thought the ship to be unsinkable. When the last boat left there

remained aboard over 1,500 persons, including 688 of her 900 crew. As she up-ended and slid under bow first the Reverend Thomas Byles led many in hymns and prayer.
2.15 am. When submerged up to the second funnel all lights went out.
2.20 am. *Titanic* disappeared. 1,503 died and only 705 survived.

71 BRITANNIC (II)

Details as *Titanic (70)* except: **Bt** 1915; *T:* 48,158 g. **H** Completed with 2,000 hospital beds.

After Olympic (64) *and* Titanic *a third ship was projected as* Gigantic, *but she was instead christened* Britannic *because* Gigantic *resembled* Titanic's *ill-fated name too closely.*

1915 Dec 8: Handed over and commissioned as a hospital ship. Painted in International Red Cross colours.
Dec 12: Maiden voyage to Alexandria.
1916 Nov 21: Sunk by mine or torpedo in Zea Channel, Aegean Sea. 21 lives lost. The ship was racked by a violent explosion below the bridge and became the largest ever British Merchant service loss.

72 VADERLAND

Bt 1900 John Brown, Clydebank; *T:* 11,899 g, 7,490 n. **Dim** 560 ft 8 in (170.89 m) × 60 ft 2 in (18.34 m) × 38 ft 2 in (11.63 m). **Eng** Tw scr, quad exp; 2 × 4 cyls: 31 in (78.74 cm), 44 in (111.76 cm), 62 in (157.48 cm) and 88 in (223.52 cm); *Stroke:* 54 in (137.16 cm); 1,627 NHP; 8 sgl ended boilers; *Stm P:* 200 lb; 15 kts; By builder. **H** Steel, 3 decks, fcsle 84 ft (25.6 m), bridge 215 ft (65.53 m), poop 49 ft (14.93 m); *Pass:* 342 1st, 194 2nd, 626 3rd.

1900 July 12: Launched. Built for International Navigation Co (illustrated in Red Star section, entry *14*).
Dec 8: Maiden voyage Antwerp-Southampton-New York.
1914 Transferred to White Star.
Sept 3: First voyage New York-Southampton.
1915 Because her name was German-sounding *Vaderland* was renamed *Southland* and transferred to White Star-Dominion Line's Liverpool-Quebec-

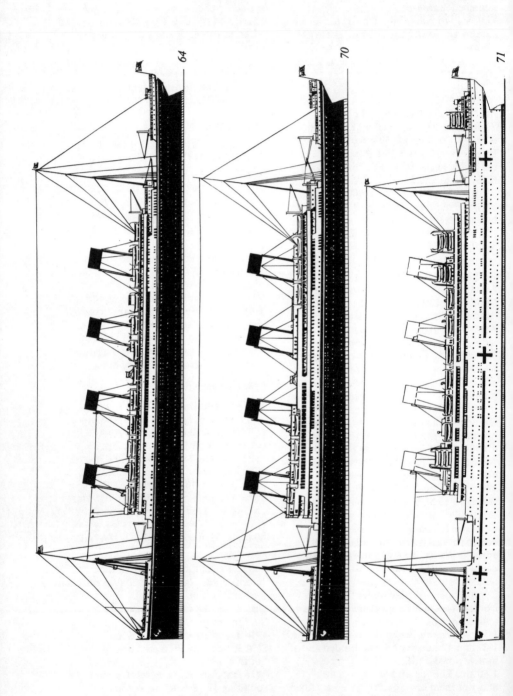

Montreal service. Became troopship.
Sept 2: Torpedoed in Aegean but reached port.
1917 Sept 4: Torpedoed and sunk 140 miles north-west of Tory Island, Ireland. Four lives lost.

73 LAPLAND

Bt 1908 Harland & Wolff, Belfast; *T:* 18,565 g, 11,607 n. **Dim** 605 ft 8 in (184.61 m) × 70 ft 4 in (21.44 m) × 37 ft 4 in (11.38 m). **Eng** Tw scr, quad exp; 2 × 4 cyls: 32½ in (82.55 cm), 47 in (119.38 cm), 68 in (172.72 cm) and 98 in (248.92 cm); *Stroke:* 63 in (160.02 cm); 2,343 NHP; 8 dbl ended boilers; *Stm P:* 215 lb; 17 kts; By builder. **H** Steel, 3 decks, fcsle 62 ft (18.9 m), bridge 348 ft (106.07 m); *Pass:* 450 1st, 400 2nd, 1,500 3rd.

1908 June 8: Launched. Built for Red Star Line (illustrated in Red Star section, entry *20*).
Sept 4: Maiden voyage Antwerp-Dover-New York.
1914 Oct 29: Transferred to White Star's Liverpool-New York service.
1917 Apr: Mined Liverpool Bay off Mersey Bar. Reached Liverpool.
June: Became troopship. Operated under Liner Requisition Scheme.
1919 Southampton-New York service.
Nov 26: Last White Star voyage.
1920 Returned to Red Star. Antwerp-Southampton-New York route. *T:* 18,565 g.
1924 Dec: Collided in River Scheldt with *Java*.
1926 Mainly engaged on cruising.
1932 June 11: Last North Atlantic voyage. Laid up at Antwerp.
1933 Sold for £30,000 for breaking up in Japan.

74 BELGIC (IV)

Bt 1917 Harland & Wolff, Belfast; *T:* 24,547 g,
15,352 n. **Dim** 670 ft 5 in (204.34 m) × 78 ft 5 in (23.9 m) × 44 ft 7 in (13.59 m). **Eng** Tpl scr, tpl exp and LP turbine to centre shaft; 2 × 4 cyls: 35½ in (90.17 cm), 56 in (142.24 cm) and 2 × 64 in (162.56 cm); *Stroke:* 60 in (152.4 cm); *Stm P:* 215 lb; 17 kts; by builder **H** Steel, 4 decks, bridge and poop 574 ft (174.95 m), upper bridge 371 ft (113.08 m); *Pass:* approx 100 1st.

Drawing shows her in wartime 'dazzle' camouflage.

1914 Dec 31: Launched as *Belgenland* for Red Star Line. Remained incomplete at Belfast.
1917 June 21: Completed as cargo vessel. Handed to White Star by International Mercantile Marine but remained registered under International Navigation Co ownership. Liverpool-New York run.
1919 Repatriated US troops to New York.
1921 Returned to Belfast for completion to original design.
1923 Apr 4: First voyage Antwerp-New York as Red Star Line's *Belgenland* (illustrated in Red Star section, entry *21*). *T:* 27,132 g.
1932-33 Laid up Antwerp, then cruising, then laid up again.
1935 Sold to Atlantic Transport Co of West Virginia. Renamed *Columbia*. White hull.
1936 Sold for breaking up at Bo'ness, Firth of Forth.

75 JUSTICIA

Bt 1917 Harland & Wolff, Belfast; *T:* 32,234 g, 19,801 n. **Dim** 740 ft 6 in (225.7 m) × 86 ft 5 in (26.34 m) × 43 ft 1 in (13.13 m). **Eng** Tpl scr, tpl exp and 1 LP turbine to centre shaft; 2 × 4 cyls: 35½ in (90.17 cm), 56 in (142.24 cm) and 2 × 64 in (162.56 cm); *Stroke:* 60 in (152.4 cm); 12 dbl ended boilers; *Stm P:* 215 lb; 18 kts; By builder. **H** Steel, 4 decks, fcsle and bridge 619 ft (188.67 m), promenade

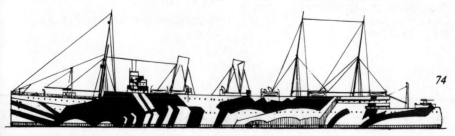

74

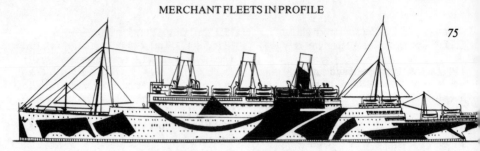

deck 430 ft (131.06 m); *Pass:* 4,000 troops.
Drawing shows her in wartime 'dazzle' camouflage.

1912 Laid down for Holland America Line.
1914 July 9: Launched as *Statendam* but requisitioned by British Government for completion as troopship.
1917 Apr 7: Assigned to White Star management. The name *Justicia* indicated an original intention to allocate her to Cunard. However, they had manning problems whereas White Star could assemble *Britannic (71)*'s crew for her use.
1918 July 19: Torpedoed by *U-64* 20 miles from Skerryvore. Remained afloat and taken in tow but torpedoed again next day and sank. Ten lives lost.

76 GALLIC (II)

Bt 1918 Workman Clark & Co, Belfast; *T:* 7,914 g, 4,888 n. **Dim** 465 ft (141.73 m) oa, 450 ft (137.16 m) × 58 ft 4 in (17.78 m) × 29 ft 1 in (8.86 m). **Eng** tw scr, tpl exp; 2 × 3 cyls: 26½ in (67.31 cm), 44 in (111.76 cm) and 73 in (185.42 cm); *Stroke:* 48 in (121.92 cm); 5,500 HP; 3 dbl ended boilers; 13 kts; By builder. **H** Steel, 2 decks and shelter deck, fcsle 43 ft (13.11 m), poop 31 ft (9.45 m).

1918 Dec: Built as *War Argus* for Shipping Controller. Standard 'G' type, of which 22 were built.
1920 Jan: Purchased by White Star. Renamed *Gallic.* Entered Australian cargo service.
1933 Sold for £53,000 to Clan Line. Became *Clan Colquhoun.*
1947 Sold to Zarata SS Co, Panama.

Renamed *Ioannis Livanos.*
1949 Renamed *Jenny* by Zarata.
1952 Sold to Djakarta Lloyd. Renamed *Imam Bondjol.* Later renamed *Djatinegra.*
1955 Sold for breaking up in Japan.
Dec: Went ashore near Manila en route for Osaka.
1956 Feb 21: Refloated.
June: Broken up at Hong Kong.

77 BARDIC

Details as *Gallic (76)* except: **Bt** Harland & Wolff, Belfast; *T:* 8,010 g, 4,920 n. **Eng** HP cyl: 27 in (68.58 cm); By builder.

1918 Dec 19: Launched as *War Priam* for Shipping Controller.
1919 Mar 13: Purchased by White Star. Renamed *Bardic.*
Mar 18: First voyage Liverpool-New York.
1919-21 Operated by Atlantic Transport Line.
1921 Returned to White Star. Deployed on Australian service.
1924 Aug 31: Stranded in fog off Stag Rock, Lizard. Refloated.
1925 Sold to Aberdeen Line. Renamed *Hostilius.*
1926 Renamed *Horatius.* Same company.
1932 Transferred to Shaw Savill. Renamed *Kumara.*
1937 Sold to J. Latsis, Piraeus. Renamed *Marathon.*
1941 Nov 9: Sunk by German *Scharnhorst* north-east of Cape Verde.

78 DELPHIC (II)

Details as *Gallic (76)* except: *T:* 8,006 g, 4,905 n.

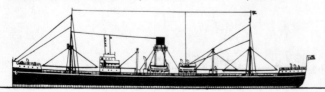

76-78

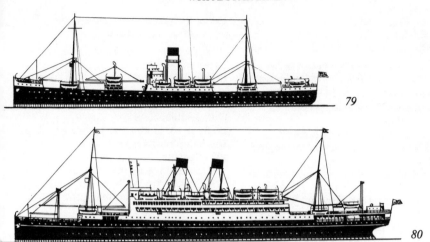

79

80

1918 Sept 19: Launched as *War Icarus* for
Shipping Controller.
1919 Purchased by Atlantic Transport
Line. Renamed *Mesaba*.
1925 Transferred to White Star. Renamed
Delphic. On Australian run.
1933 Sold to Clan Line for £53,000.
Renamed *Clan Farquhar*.
1948 July: Broken up at Milford Haven,
Wales.

79 VEDIC

Bt 1918 Harland & Wolff, Belfast; *T:* 9,332 g,
5,519 n. **Dim** 460 ft 6 in (140.36 m) × 58 ft 4 in
(17.78 m) × 37 ft 4 in (11.38 m). **Eng** Tw scr,
4 steam turbines double reduction geared;
6,000 HP; 14 kts; By builder. **H** Steel, 3 decks,
fcsle 53 ft (16.15 m), bridge 130 ft (39.62 m),
poop 53 ft (16.15 m); *Pass:* 1,250 3rd.

1917 Dec 18: Launched.
1918 July 10: Handed over.
July 11: Maiden voyage Belfast-Clyde-
Boston, there taken over as troopship.
Dec 28: First voyage for White Star
Glasgow-Boston route.
1919 Sept: Used for the repatriation of
British troops from Russia.
Sept 19: Aground on Orkneys. Safely
refloated.
1920 Refitted at Middlesbrough. Canadian
emigrant trade. *Pass:* 1,250 3rd.
1925 Refitted for Australian migrant
service. Largely on Salvation Army charter.
1934 Sold for £10,400 and broken up at
Rosyth, Firth of Forth.

80 ARABIC (III)

Bt 1908 A. G. Weser, Bremen; *T:* 16,786 g,
9,057 n. **Dim** 590 ft 2 in (179.83 m) × 69 ft 7 in
(21.21 m) × 38 ft 10 in (11.84 m). **Eng** Tw scr,
quad exp; 2 × 4 cyls: 34 in (86.36 cm), 48½ in
(123.19 cm), 69¾ in (175.89 cm) and 111 in
(281.94 cm); *Stroke:* 63 in (160.02 cm);
2,127 NHP; *Stm P:* 220 lb; 17 kts. **H** Steel,
3 decks; *Pass:* 266 1st, 246 2nd, 2,700 3rd.

1908 Nov 7: Launched. Built as *Berlin* for
Norddeutscher Lloyd. New York-
Mediterranean service.
1914 German Naval minelayer.
Oct: Responsible for loss of HMS
Audacious (see *Olympic (64)* entry).
Nov 17: Interned at Trondheim, Norway.
1919 Surrendered to Britain. Placed under
P&O management.
1920 Sold to White Star and refitted at
Portsmouth Dockyard.
1921 Sept 7: Renamed *Arabic*. First voyage
Southampton-New York then New York-
Mediterranean.
1924 *Pass:* 500 cabin, 1,200 3rd.
1925-29 On Antwerp-Southampton-New
York service of Red Star.
1927 Apr: In Red Star colours.
1930 Reverted to White Star. *Pass:* 177
cabin, 319 tst, 823 3rd.
1931 Broken up at Genoa. Realised
£17,500.

81 MAJESTIC (II)

Bt 1914 Blohm & Voss, Hamburg;
T: 56,551 g, 26,249 n. **Dim** 915 ft 6 in
(279.04 m) × 100 ft 1 in (30.5 m) × 56 ft 2 in

(17.12 m). **Eng** Quad scr, 8 steam turbines; 23 kts; By builder. **H** Steel, 6 decks; *Pass:* 700 1st, 545 2nd, 850 3rd.

Of her two near-sisters Imperator *became* Berengaria *(Cunard) and* Vaterland *became* Leviathan *(United States Lines).*

1913 Laid down for Hamburg America Line by the Kaiser.
1914 June 20: Launched as *Bismarck.*
1914-18 Remained at Hamburg incomplete. The world's largest ship.
1919 Assigned as part of war reparations to Britain.
1922 Completed as *Bismarck* but purchased by a joint Cunard-White Star consortium with *Imperator* (later *Berengaria*).
May 10: Renamed *Majestic.* Maiden voyage Southampton-Cherbourg-New York. She was only renamed after delivery to Southampton.
1928 Refitted and reboilered.
1934 Taken over by Cunard-White Star in the merger.
1936 Feb 13: Last voyage Southampton-Cherbourg-New York.
May: Sold to Thos W. Ward for £115,000 for breaking up.
July: Sold to Admiralty and converted into an Artificer Cadets' ship. Converted by Thornycroft, Southampton. Renamed HMS *Caledonia.* Funnels shortened by removal of black tops. Thereafter left in White Star colours.
1937 Apr: Based at Rosyth. 2,000 cadets.
1939 Sept: Scheduled for a refit, vacated by cadets.
Sept 29: Caught fire, burnt out and sank at her moorings.
1940 Mar: Sold again to Thos W. Ward for breaking up at Inverkeithing. Salvage commenced.
1943 July 17: Refloated and towed the five miles round to Ward's for final scrapping.

82 PITTSBURGH

Bt 1922 Harland & Wolff, Belfast; *T:* 16,322 g, 9,856 n. **Dim** 601 ft (183.18 m) oa, 575 ft 4 in (175.36 m) × 67 ft 9 in (20.65 m) × 40 ft 10 in (12.45 m). **Eng** Tpl scr. 2 tpl exp and 1 LP turbine to centre shaft; 2 × 4 cyls: 28 in (71.12 cm), 44 in (111.76 cm) and 2 × 49½ in (125.73 cm); *Stroke:* 54 in (137.16 cm);

15 kts; By builder. **H** Steel, 4 decks; *Pass:* 600 cabin, 1,500 3rd.

1913 Nov: Laid down for the American Line
1920 Nov 17: Launched and then completed in White Star colours.
1922 June 6: Maiden voyage Liverpool-Philadelphia.
1925 Jan 28: In Red Star service Antwerp-Southampton-New York.
1926 Renamed *Pennland* (II).
Feb 18: First voyage in new name.
1935 Sold to Arnold Bernstein, Hamburg. Operated Antwerp-Southampton-Halifax-New York as Red Star Line.
1939 June: Sold to Holland America Line. Same name and service.
1940 Troopship. Operated by Britain under Dutch control.
1941 Apr 25: Bombed and sunk in Gulf of Athens.

83 REGINA

Details as *Pittsburgh (82)* except: **Bt** 1918; *T:* 16,313 g, 9,874 n. *Pass:* 350 cabin, 350 tst, 800 3rd.
1913 Laid down for Dominion Line.
1917 Apr 19: Launched and completed as troopship in 1918.
1920-22 Finished to original design at Belfast. Appeared in Dominion Line colours. *Pass:* 631 cabin, 1,824 3rd.
1923 Mar 16: First voyage 'White Star-Dominion Joint Service'. Liverpool-Quebec-Montreal.
1925 Appeared in White Star colours.
1929 Transferred to Red Star Line Antwerp-Southampton-New York.
1930 Renamed *Westernland.* Same route.
1934-35 Laid up. Then sold to Arnold Bernstein's Red Star Line.
1939 Sold to Holland America Line. Same route. Same name.
1940 After outbreak of war escaped to England and served as HQ ship to exiled Dutch Government.
July: Became troopship.
1943 Became Destroyer Depot ship.
1946 Sold to Chr Salvesen, Leith, for conversion to whale factory ship. Plan abandoned.
1947 July 15: Sold for breaking up at Blyth, Northumberland.

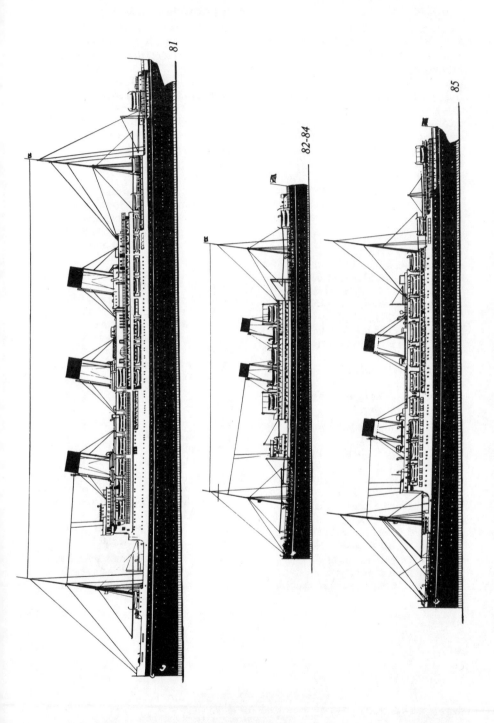

81

82-84

85

84 DORIC (II)

Details as *Pittsburgh (82)* except: **Bt** 1923; *T:* 16,484 g, 9,870 n. **Eng** 4 sgl reduction geared turbines to 2 shafts.

1922 Aug 8: Launched.
1923 July 6: Maiden voyage Liverpool-Quebec-Montreal.
1933 Cruising from Liverpool.
1935 Sept 5: Damaged in a collision off north coast of Portugal with the French liner *Formigny* (Chargeurs Reunis).
Oct: The company decided that *Doric* was not worth repairing. Sold for £35,000 and broken up at Newport, Monmouthshire.

85 HOMERIC

Bt 1922 F. Schichau, Danzig; *T:* 34,351 g, 18,058 n. **Dim** 751 ft (228.9 m) × 83 ft 3 in (25.37 m) × 48 ft 7 in (14.81 m). **Eng** Tw scr, tpl exp; 2 × 4 cyls: 53 in (134.62 cm), 83 in (210.82 cm) and 2 × 96½ in (245.11 cm); *Stroke:* 71 in (180.34 cm); 3,152 NHP; *Stm P:* 230 lb; 19 kts; By F. Schichau's Elbing Works. **H** Steel, 5 decks, bridge 675 ft (205.74 m); *Pass:* 529 1st, 487 2nd, 1,750 3rd.
White Star had listed a Homeric *as being under construction in 1913, but she existed only on paper. The name was now bestowed on this purchased vessel.*

1913 Dec 17: Launched as *Columbus* for Norddeutscher Lloyd.
1920 Surrendered to Britain. Purchased by White Star.
1922 Jan 31: Arrived from Germany. Converted to oil fuel. Renamed *Homeric*.
Feb 15: Maiden voyage Southampton-Cherbourg-New York.
1930 *Pass:* 523 1st, 841 cabin, 314 3rd.
1932 June 1: Last voyage on North Atlantic. Thereafter cruising.
1935 Sept: Laid up off Ryde.
1936 Feb 27: Broken up at Inverkeithing.

86 LAURENTIC (II)

Bt 1927 Harland & Wolff, Belfast; *T:* 18,724 g, 11,103 n. **Dim** 600 ft (182.88 m) oa, 578 ft 2 in (176.22 m) × 75 ft 5 in (22.99 m) × 40 ft 7 in (12.37 m). **Eng** Tpl scr, tpl exp and 2 LP turbines; 4 cyls: 29 in (73.66 cm), 46 in (116.84 cm) and 2 × 52 in (132.08 cm); *Stroke:* 54 in (137.16 cm); *Stm P.* 220 lb; 16 kts; By builder. **H** Steel, 4 decks and shelter deck; *Pass:* 594 cabin, 406 tst, 500 3rd.

1927 June 16: Launched.
Nov 12: Maiden voyage Liverpool-Quebec-Montreal.
1932 Oct 3: Collided with *Lurigethan* (H. E. Moss) in Belle Isle Strait. Both survived.
1935 Aug 18: Collided in fog in Irish Sea with Blue Star's *Napier Star*. Six lives lost.
Dec: Laid up in Southampton Water after a cruising spell.
1936 Sept: Used to transport troops to Palestine. One voyage.
1938 Moved to Falmouth and laid up.
1939 Converted to armed merchant cruiser. Most of after superstructure removed.
1940 Nov 3: Torpedoed off Bloody Foreland in Western Approaches by *U-99,* captained by Germany's greatest U-boat ace Otto Kretschmer.

87 CALGARIC

Bt 1918 Harland & Wolff, Belfast; *T:* 16,063 g, 9,614 n. **Dim** 550 ft 4 in (167.74 m) × 67 ft 4 in (20.52 m) × 43 ft (13.11 m). **Eng** Tpl scr, 2 tpl exp and 1 LP turbine to centre shaft; 2 × 4 cyls: 26½ in (67.31 cm), 42 in (106.68 cm) and 2 × 47½ in (120.65 cm); *Stroke:* 51 in (129.54 cm); 6 dbl ended boilers; *Stm P:* 215 lb; 16 kts; By builder. **H** Steel, 2 decks; *Pass:* 100 cabin, 500 3rd.

1918 Jan: Launched as *Orca* for Pacific Steam Nav Co. Completed as cargo vessel without passenger accommodation.

86

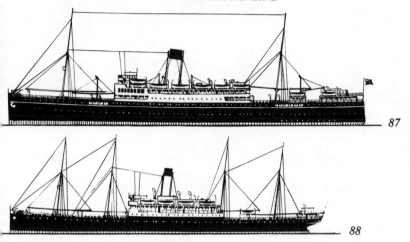

87

88

Returned in the autumn and completed.
1923 Jan 1: Transferred to Royal Mail
Steam Packet Co. Same name. Used on
Hamburg-Southampton-New York route.
1927 Sold to White Star. Renamed
Calgaric.
May 4: First voyage Liverpool-Quebec-
Montreal.
1929-31 Transferred to London-
Southampton-Quebec-Montreal run.
1933 Laid up at Milford Haven.
1935 Sold for £31,000. Broken up at
Rosyth.

88 POLAND

Bt 1898 Furness Withy, West Hartlepool;
T: 8,282 g, 4,834 n. **Dim** 475 ft 6 in
(144.93 m) × 52 ft 2 in (15.9 m) × 31 ft 1 in
(9.47 m). **Eng** Sgl scr, tpl exp; 3 cyls: 32 in
(81.28 cm), 54 in (137.16 cm) and 90 in
(228.6 cm); *Stroke:* 66 in (167.64 cm); 763
NHP; 2 dble and 2 sgl ended boilers; *Stm P.*
190 lb; 13 kts; By T. Richardson & Sons,
West Hartlepool. **H** Steel, 3 decks, fcsle 93 ft
(28.35 m), bridge 230 ft (70.1 m), poop
86 ft (26.21 m); *Pass:* 120 1st.

1897 July 31: Launched.

1898 Built as *Victoria* for Wilson's &
Furness-Leyland Line.
June 6: Maiden voyage London-New York.
Sept 4: Became *Manitou* (Atlantic
Transport Line).
1902-14 Ran for Red Star Line on Antwerp-
Philadelphia route.
1920 Renamed *Poland* by Red Star.
1922 Apr 26: Transferred to White Star
Line. Bremen-Southampton-Quebec-
Montreal service. On closure of St
Lawrence River for the winter she was laid
up.
1925 Sold. Renamed *Natale*. Broken up in
Italy.

89 HAVERFORD

Bt 1901 John Brown, Clydebank; *T:* 11,635 g,
7,493 n. **Dim** 531 ft (161.85 m) × 59 ft 2 in
(18.03 m) × 27 ft 2 in (8.28 m). **Eng** Tw scr,
tpl exp; 2 × 3 cyls: 29 in (73.66 cm), 46½ in
(118.11 cm) and 75 in (190.5 cm); *Stroke:*
51 in (129.54 cm); 893 NHP; *Stm P:* 160 lb;
14 kts; By builder. **H** Steel, 3 decks, bridge
150 ft (45.72 m); *Pass:* 150 2nd, 1,700 3rd.

Sister of American Line's Merion.

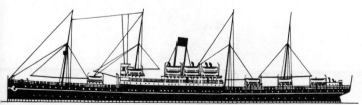

89

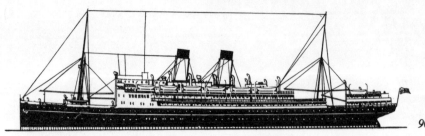

90

1901 Built as *Haverford* for American Line. Liverpool-Philadelphia service.
1921 Apr 1: Owned by the International Mercantile Marine Co and transferred to White Star's Liverpool-Philadelphia service.
1922 Operated again by American Line on Hamburg-New York route.
1924 Dec: Sold and broken up in Italy in 1925.

90 ALBERTIC

Bt 1923 A. G. Weser, Bremen; *T:* 18,940 g, 10,234 n. **Dim** 590 ft 9 in (180.1 m) × 72 ft (21.94 m) × 37 ft 7 in (11.45 m). **Eng** Tw scr, quad exp; 2 × 4 cyls: 34 in (86.36 cm), 49 in (124.46 cm), 63 in (160.02 cm), 69¾ in (177.16 cm) and 102 in (259.08 cm); 2,788 NHP; *Stm P:* 220 lb; 17 kts; By builder. **H** Steel, 3 decks, bridge 246 ft (74.98 m); *Pass:* 229 1st, 523 2nd, 690 3rd.

1913 Laid down as *Munchen* (II) for Norddeutscher Lloyd.
1919 Transferred as part of war reparations to Britain. Still on stocks.
1920 Mar 23: Launched as *Munchen* but under Royal Mail supervision.
1923 Mar 27: Officially transferred to Royal Mail. Renamed *Ohio*.
Apr 4: Maiden voyage Hamburg-Southampton-Cherbourg-New York.
1927 Sold to White Star. Renamed

Albertic.
Apr 22: First voyage Liverpool-Quebec-Montreal.
1928 On the London-St Lawrence berth.
1929 Dec: *Celtic (44)* wrecked. *Albertic* took her place Liverpool-New York.
1933 Mar: Laid up pending disposal.
1934 Sold for £34,000 and broken up at Osaka, Japan.

91 BRITANNIC (III)

Bt 1930 Harland & Wolff, Belfast; *T:* 26,943 g, 16,445 n. **Dim** 683 ft 8 in (208.38 m) × 82 ft 6 in (25.15 m) × 52 ft 11 in (16.13 m). **Eng** Tw scr, 4 stroke dbl acting oil engine; 20 cyls: 33 in (84 cm); *Stroke:* 63 in (160.02 cm); 4,214 NHP; 18 kts; By builder. **H** Steel, 8 decks, dummy forward funnel containing radio room; *Pass:* 479 cabin, 557 tst, 506 3rd.

The last vessel to fly White Star colours.

1929 Aug 6: Launched.
1930 June 28: Maiden voyage Liverpool-Belfast-Glasgow (tail of the Bank)-New York.
1934 Taken over by Cunard-White Star. Liverpool-New York.
1935 London-Havre-Southampton-New York service.
1939 Troopship.
1948 May 22: Resumed Liverpool-New York service of Cunard. White Star colours. *Pass:* 429 1st, 564 tst.

91

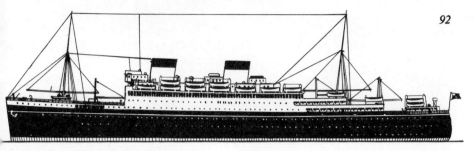

1950 June 1: Collided with the US cargo ship *Pioneer Land* (United States Lines) in Ambrose Channel, New York.
1960 Nov 11: Last voyage Liverpool-New York.
Dec: Sold for scrap to T. H. Ward, Inverkeithing.

92 **GEORGIC** (II)

Details as *Britannic (91)* except: *T:* 27,759 g, 16,839 n. **Dim** Length 682 ft 9 in (208.1 m).

1931 Nov 12: Launched. The last ship to be built for White Star.
1932 June 25: Maiden voyage Liverpool-New York. Captain E. F. Summers.
1933 Replaced *Olympic (64)* during her overhaul. Southampton-New York route.
1935 With *Britannic* on London-New York service.
1940 Apr: converted to troopship; 3,000

troops.
May: Evacuated British troops from Andesfjord and Narvik, Norway.
1941 July 14: Bombed and burnt out at Port Tewfik, Suez Canal.
Oct 27: Raised, taken to Port Sudan.
1942 Mar: Towed to Karachi for further repairs, thence on Dec 11 back to Belfast.
1943-44 Rebuilt, one funnel and one mast.
Dec: Operated by Ministry of War Transport.
1948 Refitted by Palmer & Co at Hebburn for Australian emigrant service.
1950 Chartered back to Cunard but retained White Star colours. Liverpool-New York.
1951 Transferred to Southampton-New York.
1955 Chartered to Australian Government. Nov 19: Final voyage ended at Liverpool.
1956 Feb 1: Arrived Faslane for breaking up by Shipbreaking Industries Ltd.

215